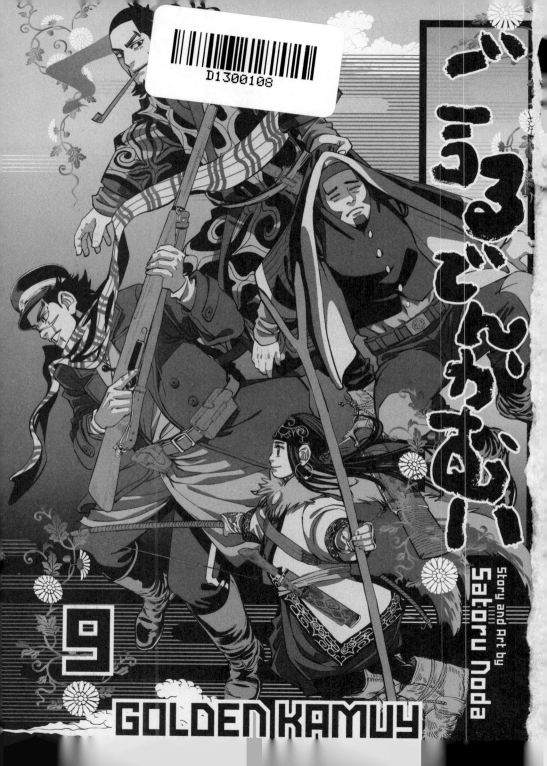

D1300108

Story and Art by Satoru Noda

9

GOLDEN KAMUY

CONTENTS

Story and Art by **Satoru Noda**

The Groups Battling Over the Hidden Gold

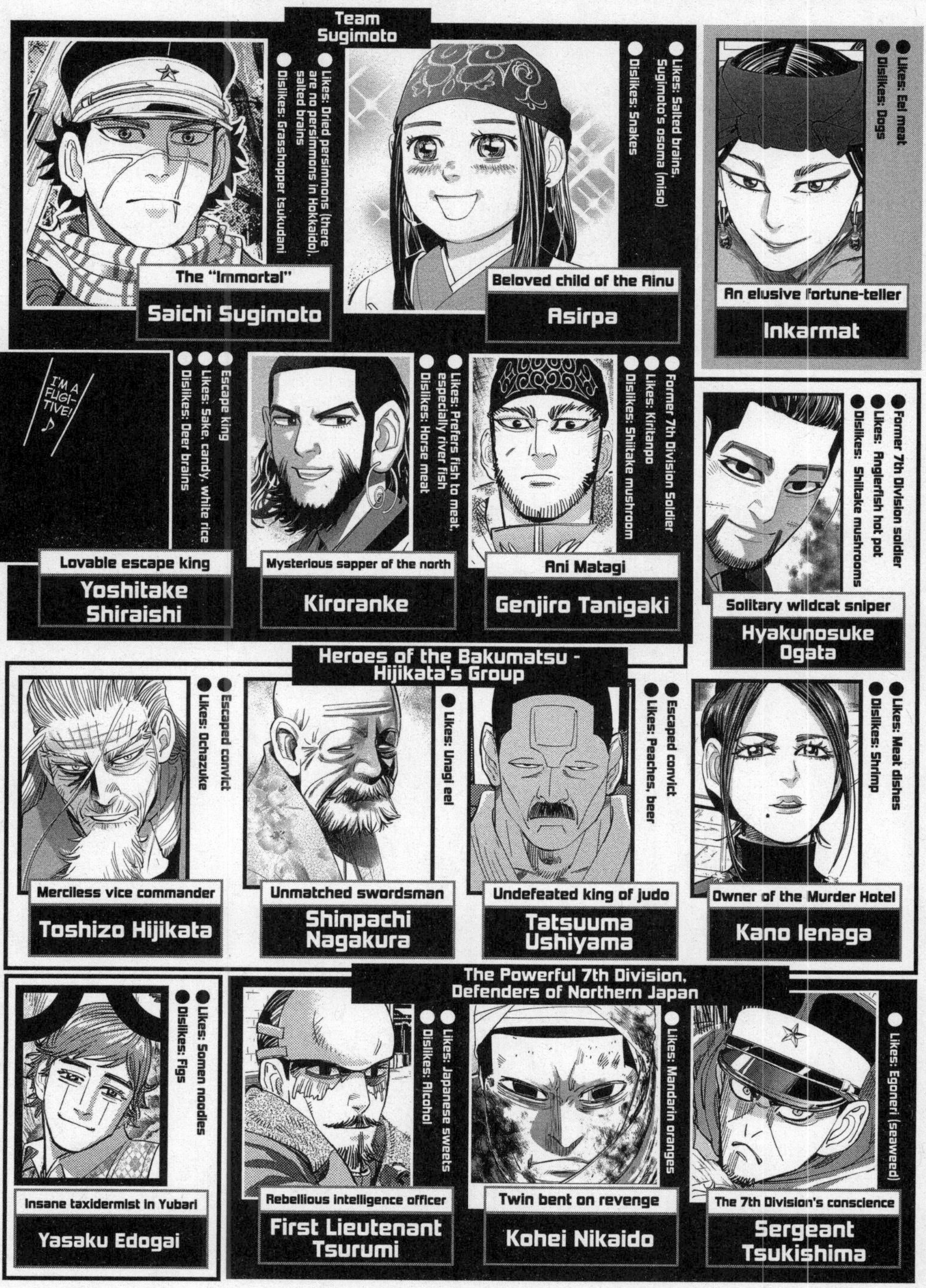

Team Sugimoto
● Likes: Dried persimmons (there are no persimmons in Hokkaido), salted brains
● Dislikes: Grasshopper tsukudani
The "Immortal"
Saichi Sugimoto
● Likes: Salted brains, Sugimoto's osoma (miso)
● Dislikes: Snakes
Beloved child of the Ainu
Asirpa
● Likes: Eel meat
● Dislikes: Dogs
An elusive fortune-teller
Inkarmat
I'M A FUGI-TIVE! ♪
● Escape king
● Likes: Sake, candy, white rice
● Dislikes: Deer brains
Lovable escape king
Yoshitake Shiraishi
● Likes: Prefers fish to meat, especially river fish
● Dislikes: Horse meat
Mysterious sapper of the north
Kiroranke
● Former 7th Division Soldier
● Likes: Kiritanpo
● Dislikes: Shiitake mushroom
Ani Matagi
Genjiro Tanigaki
● Former 7th Division soldier
● Likes: Anglerfish hot pot
● Dislikes: Shiitake mushrooms
Solitary wildcat sniper
Hyakunosuke Ogata
Heroes of the Bakumatsu - Hijikata's Group
● Escaped convict
● Likes: Ochazuke
Merciless vice commander
Toshizo Hijikata
● Likes: Unagi eel
Unmatched swordsman
Shinpachi Nagakura
● Escaped convict
● Likes: Peaches, beer
Undefeated king of judo
Tatsuuma Ushiyama
● Likes: Meat dishes
● Dislikes: Shrimp
Owner of the Murder Hotel
Kano Ienaga
● Likes: Somen noodles
● Dislikes: Figs
Insane taxidermist in Yubari
Yasaku Edogai
The Powerful 7th Division, Defenders of Northern Japan
● Likes: Japanese sweets
● Dislikes: Alcohol
Rebellious intelligence officer
First Lieutenant Tsurumi
● Likes: Mandarin oranges
Twin bent on revenge
Kohei Nikaido
● Likes: Egoneri (seaweed)
The 7th Division's conscience
Sergeant Tsukishima

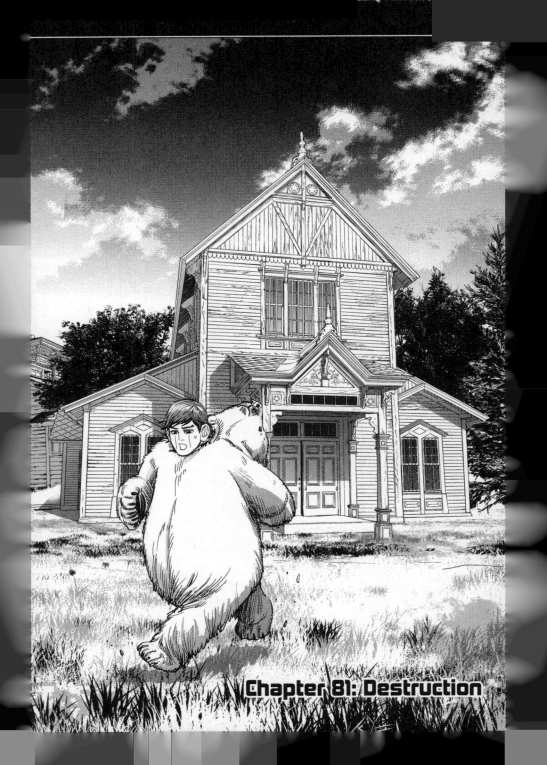

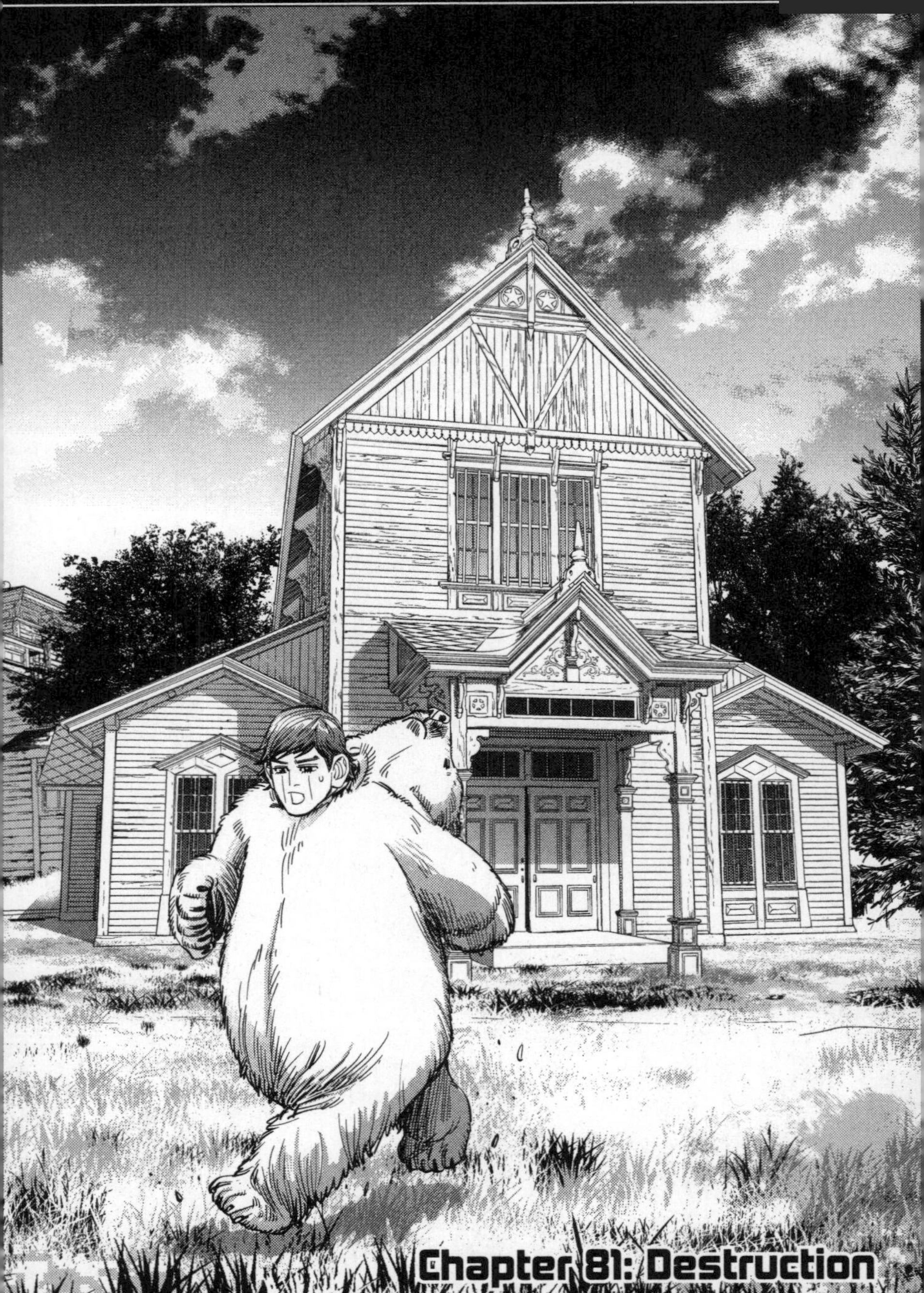
Chapter 81: Destruction

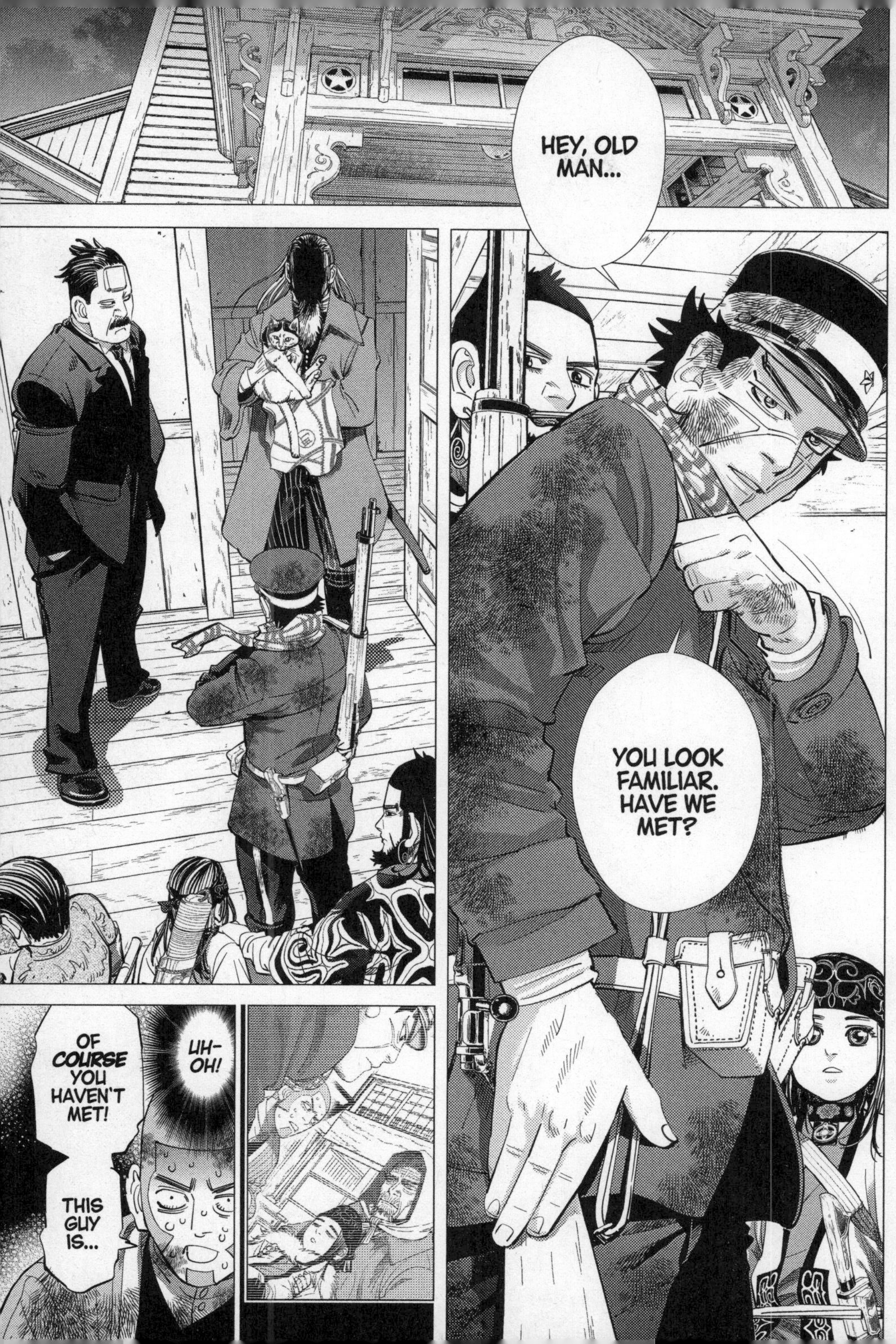
HEY, OLD MAN...
YOU LOOK FAMILIAR. HAVE WE MET?
UH-OH!
OF COURSE YOU HAVEN'T MET!
THIS GUY IS...

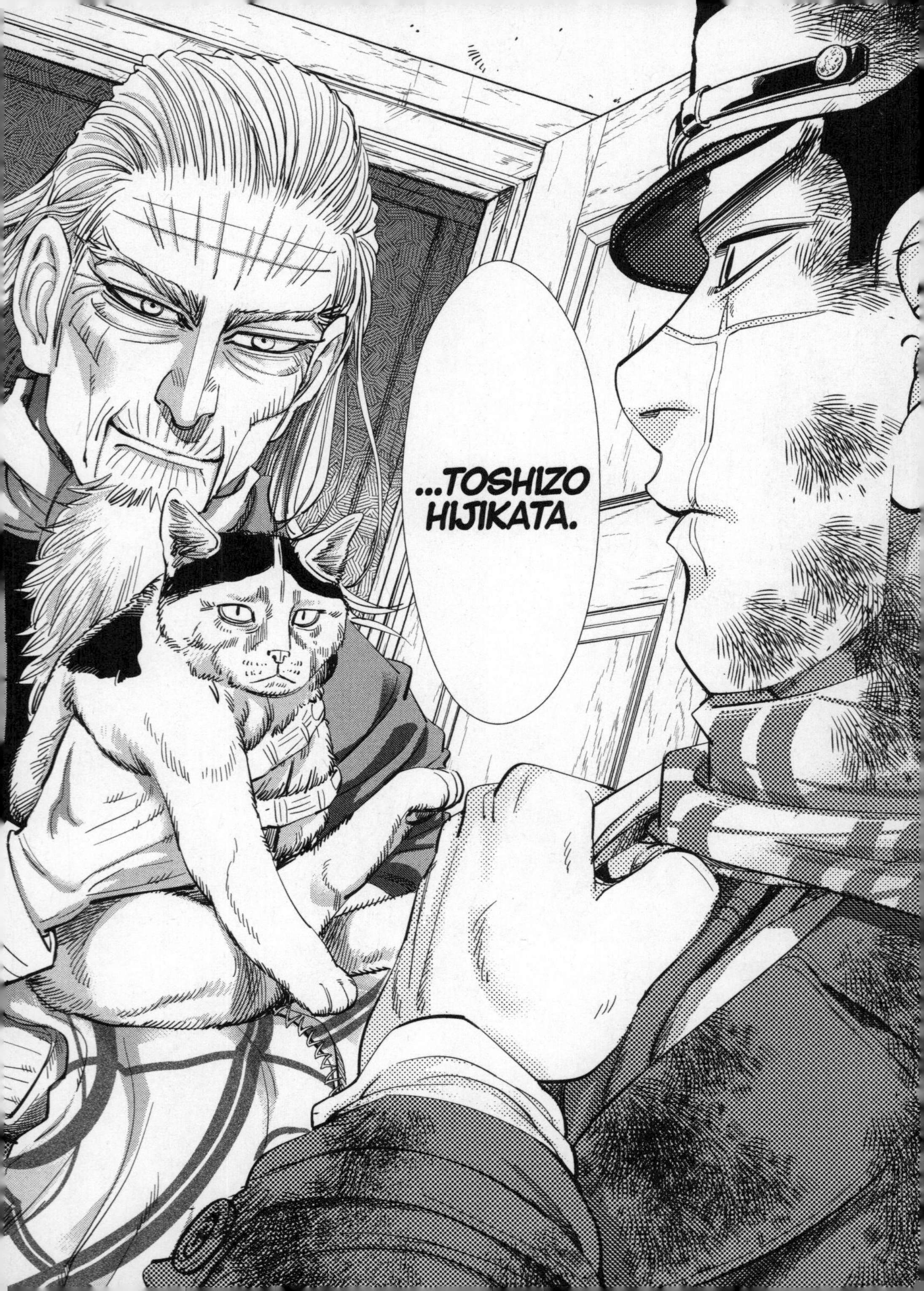
...TOSHIZO HIJIKATA.

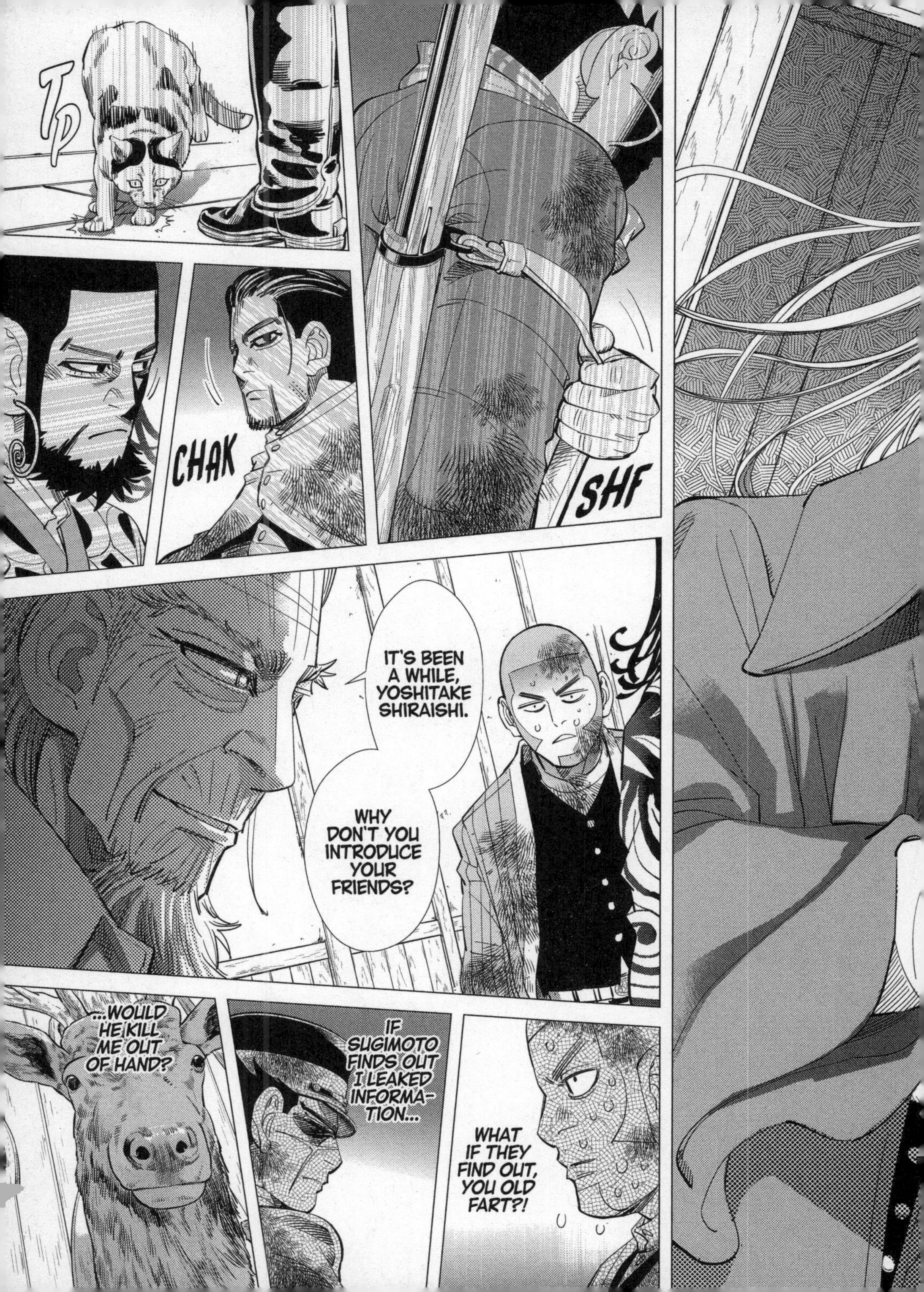
SHF
TP
CHAK
IT'S BEEN A WHILE, YOSHITAKE SHIRAISHI.
WHY DON'T YOU INTRODUCE YOUR FRIENDS?
WHAT IF THEY FIND OUT, YOU OLD FART?!
IF SUGIMOTO FINDS OUT I LEAKED INFORMATION...
...WOULD HE KILL ME OUT OF HAND?

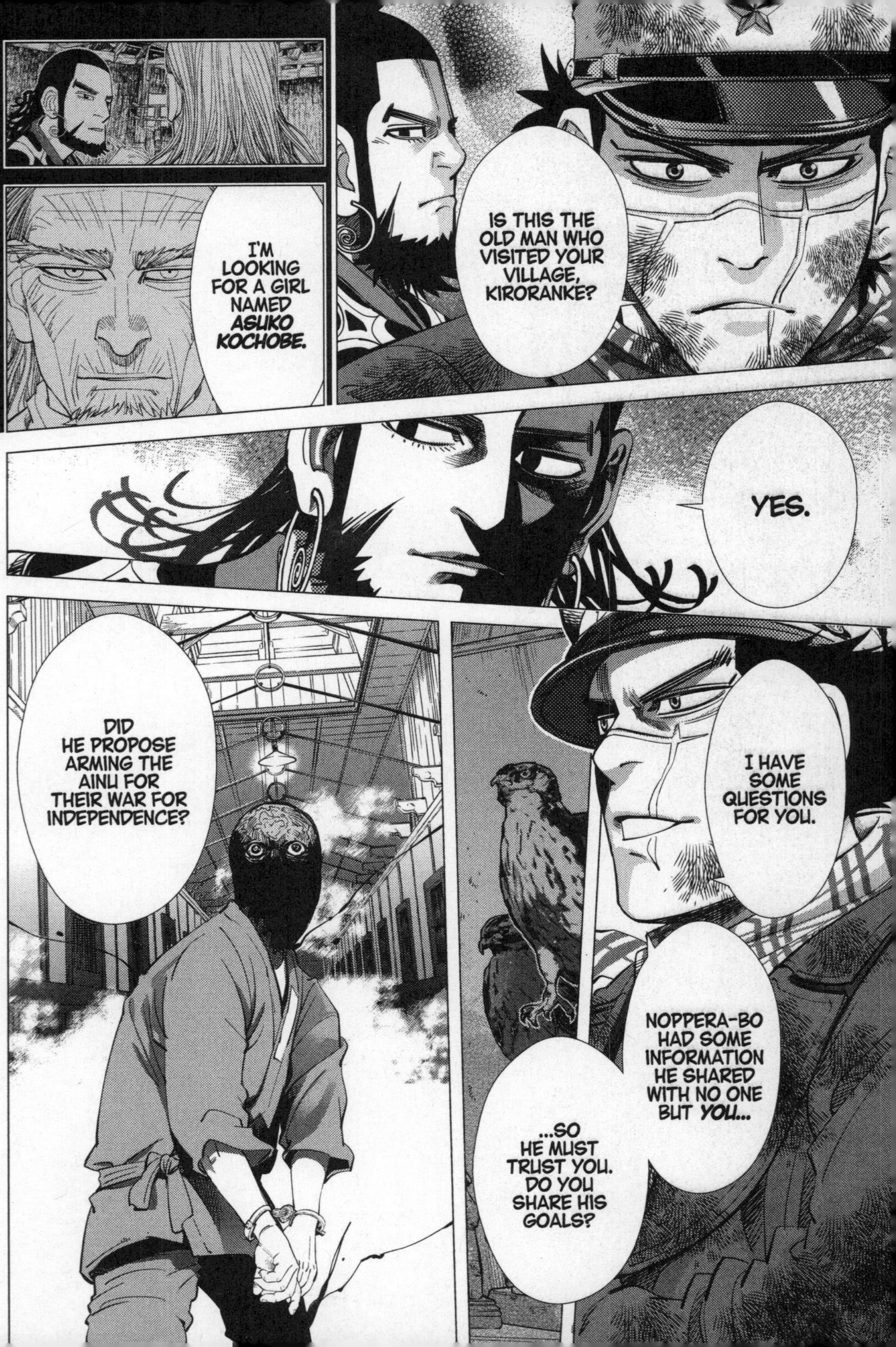
IS THIS THE OLD MAN WHO VISITED YOUR VILLAGE, KIRORANKE?
I'M LOOKING FOR A GIRL NAMED ASUKO KOCHOBE.
YES.
I HAVE SOME QUESTIONS FOR YOU.
NOPPERA-BO HAD SOME INFORMATION HE SHARED WITH NO ONE BUT YOU...
...SO HE MUST TRUST YOU. DO YOU SHARE HIS GOALS?
DID HE PROPOSE ARMING THE AINU FOR THEIR WAR FOR INDEPENDENCE?

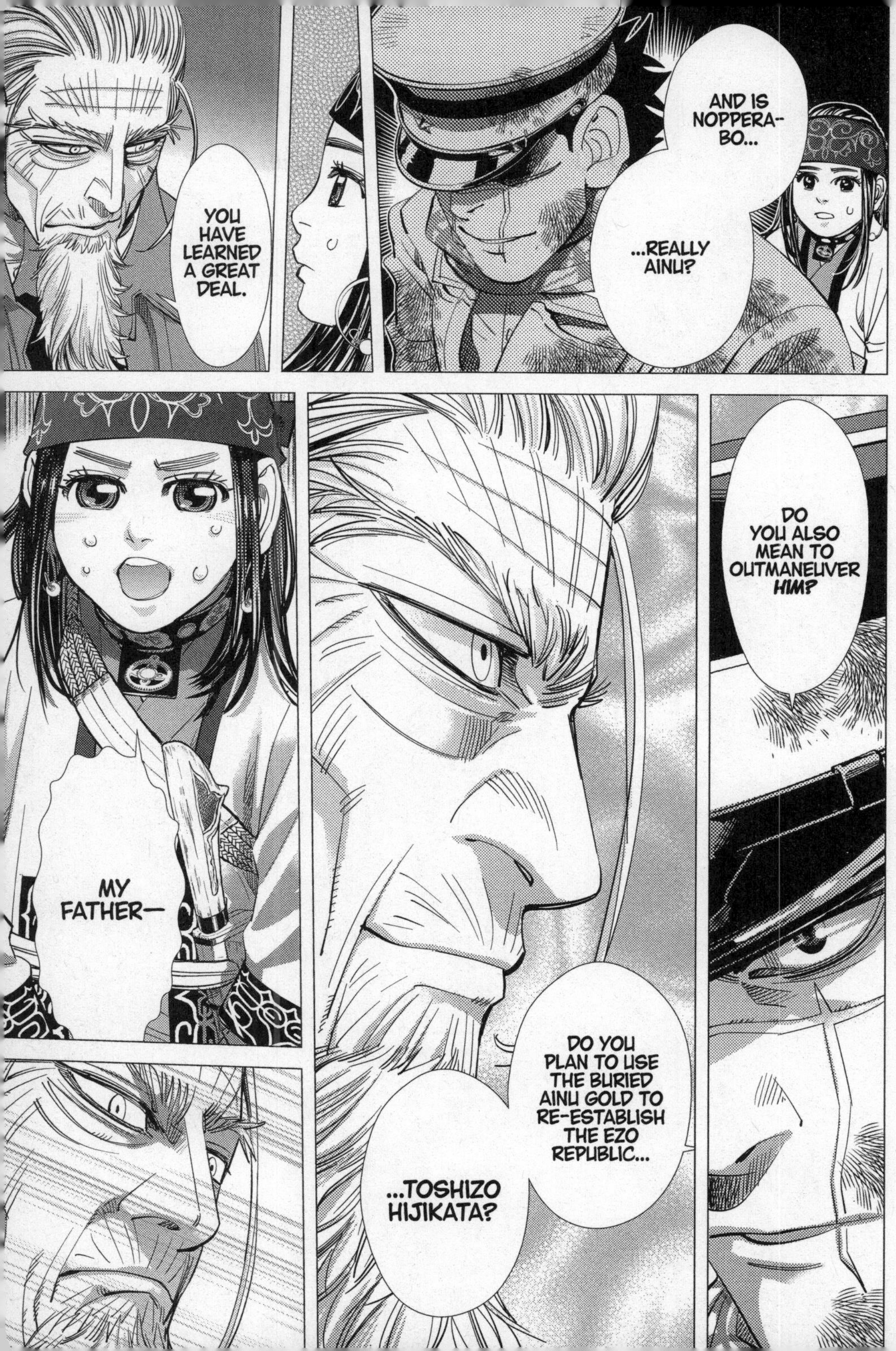
AND IS NOPPERA-BO...
...REALLY AINU?
YOU HAVE LEARNED A GREAT DEAL.
DO YOU ALSO MEAN TO OUTMANEUVER *HIM?*
DO YOU PLAN TO USE THE BURIED AINU GOLD TO RE-ESTABLISH THE EZO REPUBLIC...
...TOSHIZO HIJIKATA?
MY FATHER—

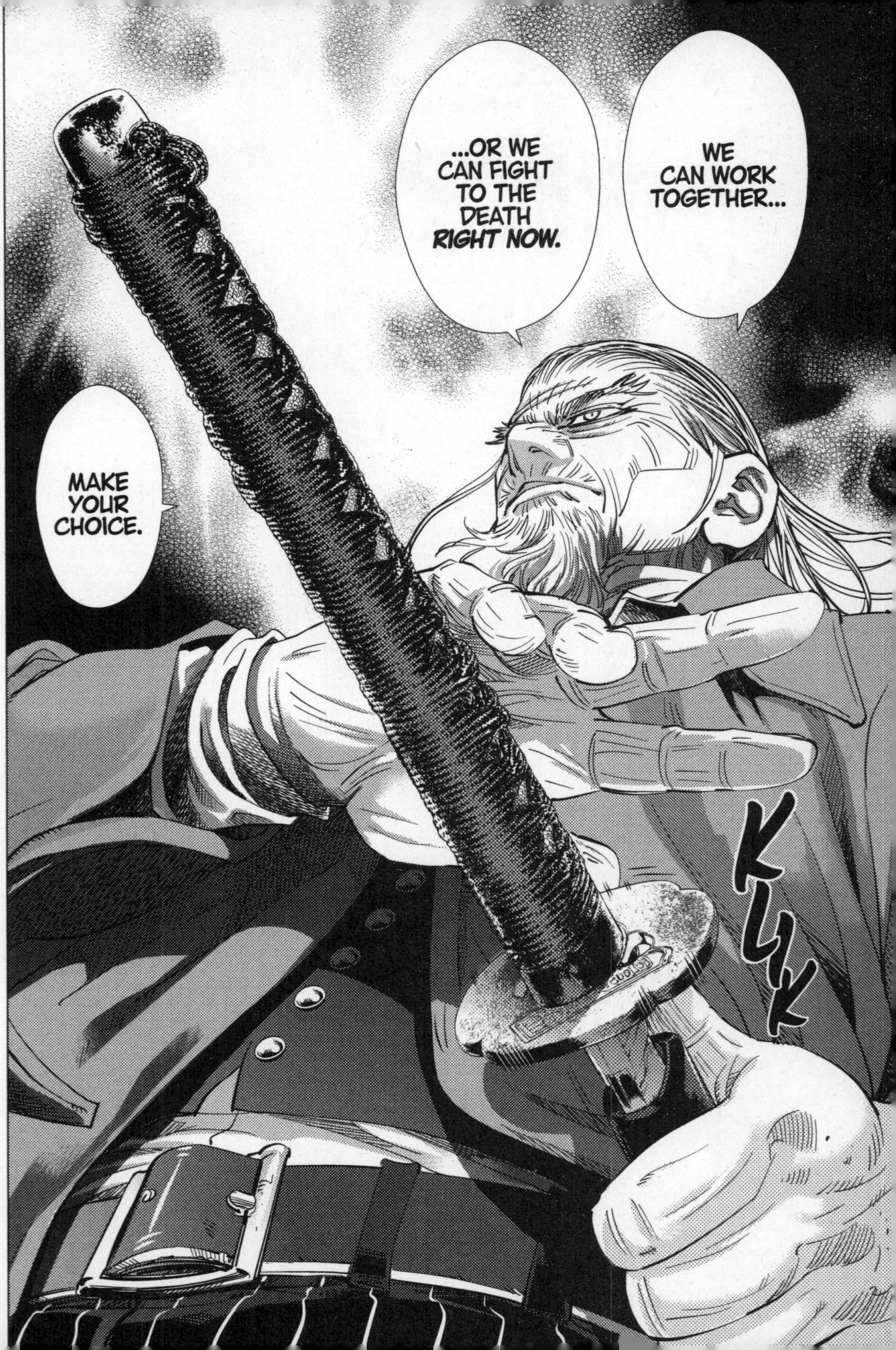
WE CAN WORK TOGETHER...
...OR WE CAN FIGHT TO THE DEATH **RIGHT NOW.**
MAKE YOUR CHOICE.
KLIK

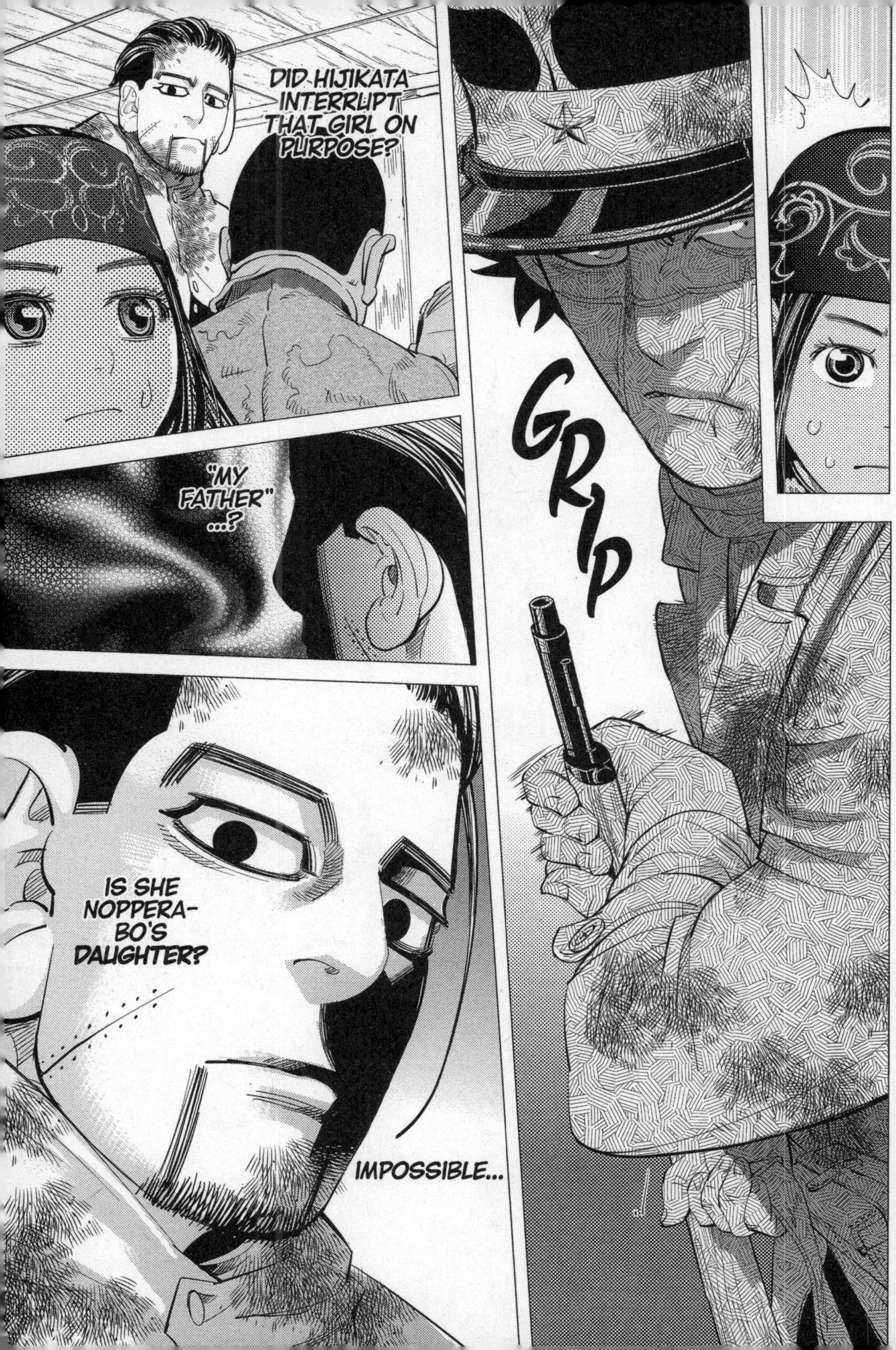
GRIP
DID HIJIKATA INTERRUPT THAT GIRL ON PURPOSE?
"MY FATHER" ...?
IS SHE NOPPERA-BO'S DAUGHTER?
IMPOSSIBLE...

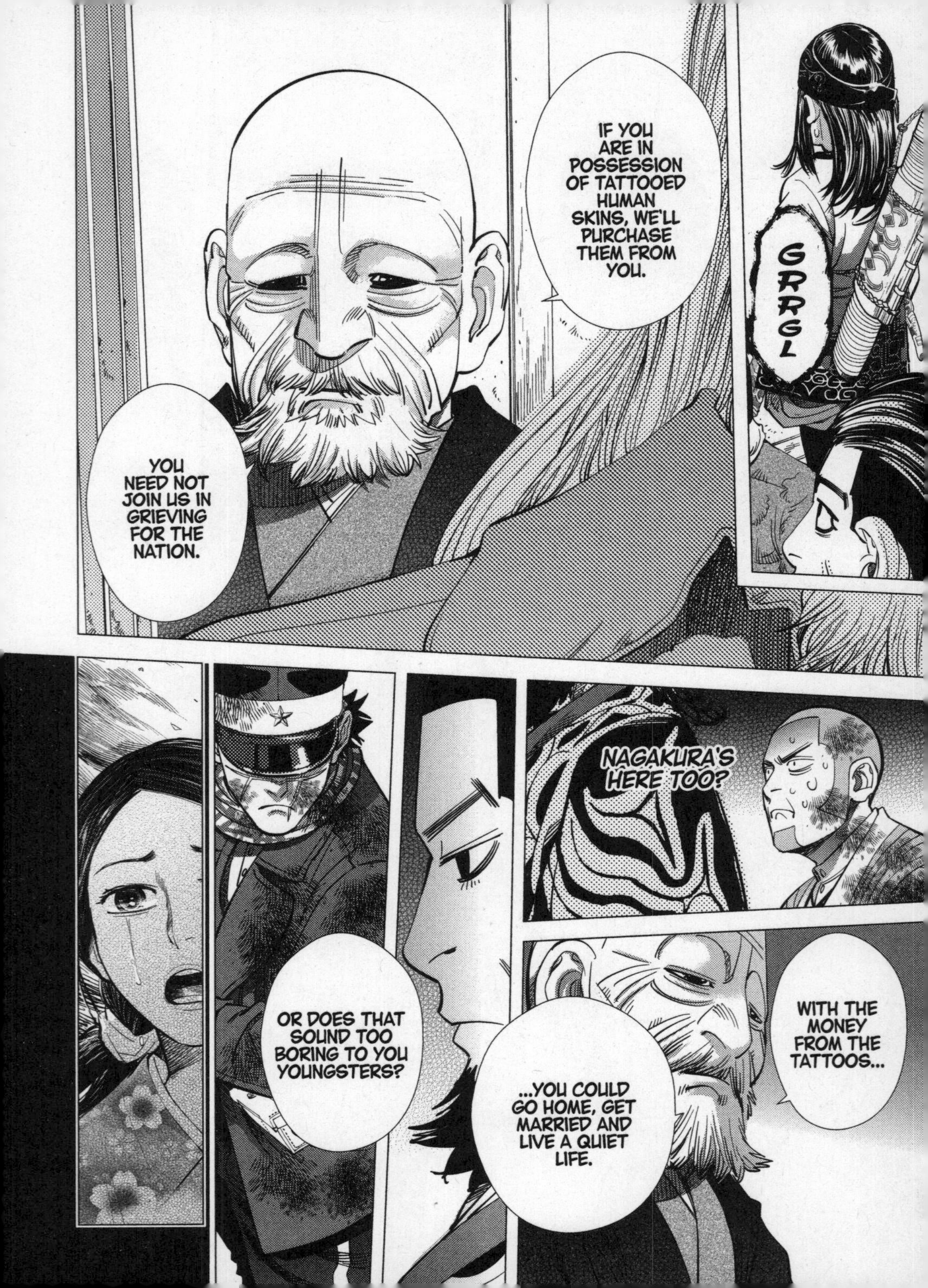
GRRGL
IF YOU ARE IN POSSESSION OF TATTOOED HUMAN SKINS, WE'LL PURCHASE THEM FROM YOU.
YOU NEED NOT JOIN US IN GRIEVING FOR THE NATION.
NAGAKURA'S HERE TOO?
WITH THE MONEY FROM THE TATTOOS...
...YOU COULD GO HOME, GET MARRIED AND LIVE A QUIET LIFE.
OR DOES THAT SOUND TOO BORING TO YOU YOUNGSTERS?

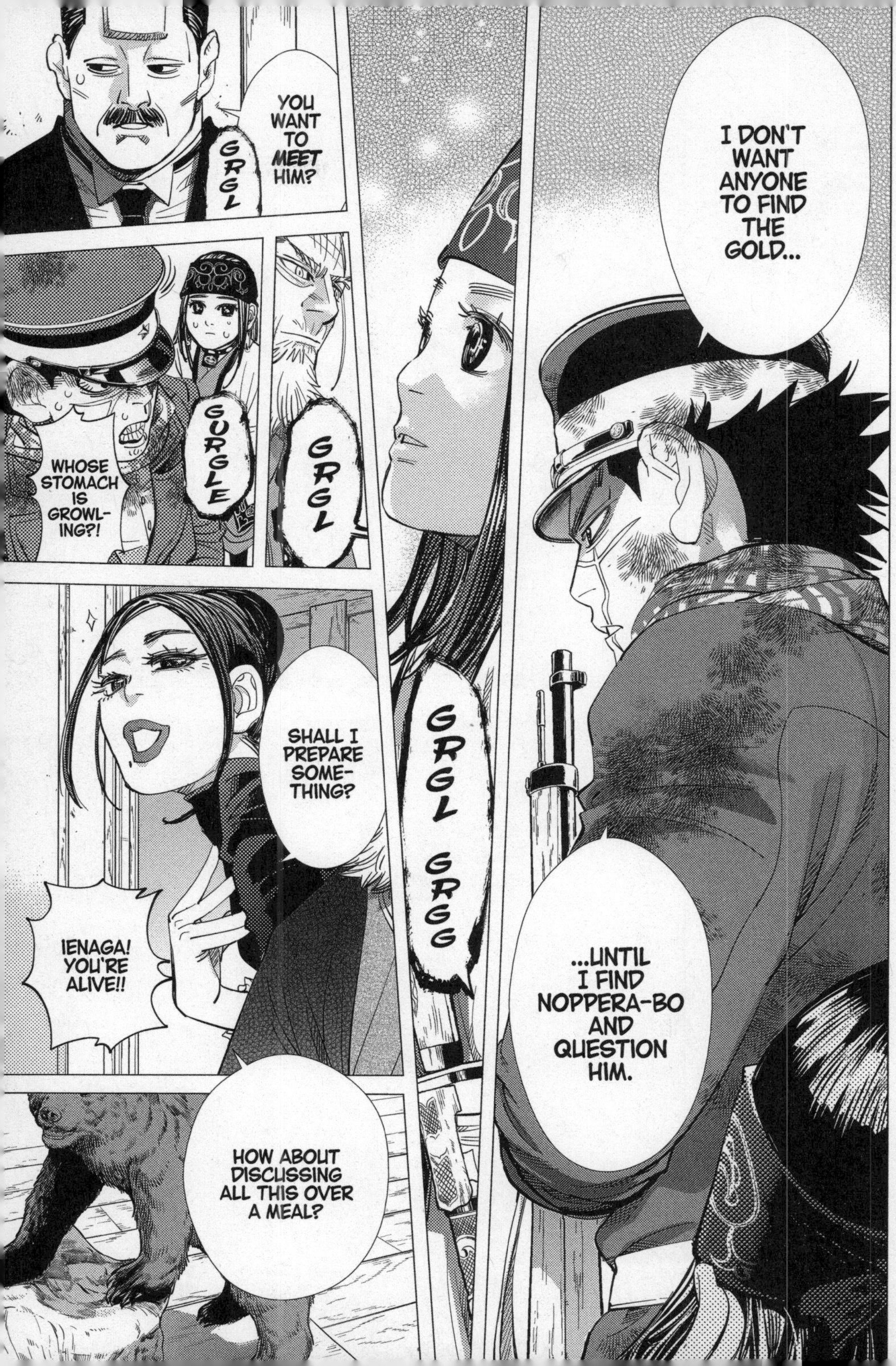
I DON'T WANT ANYONE TO FIND THE GOLD...
...UNTIL I FIND NOPPERA-BO AND QUESTION HIM.
GRGL GRGG
YOU WANT TO MEET HIM?
GRGL
GRGL
GURGLE
WHOSE STOMACH IS GROWLING?!
SHALL I PREPARE SOMETHING?
IENAGA! YOU'RE ALIVE!!
HOW ABOUT DISCUSSING ALL THIS OVER A MEAL?

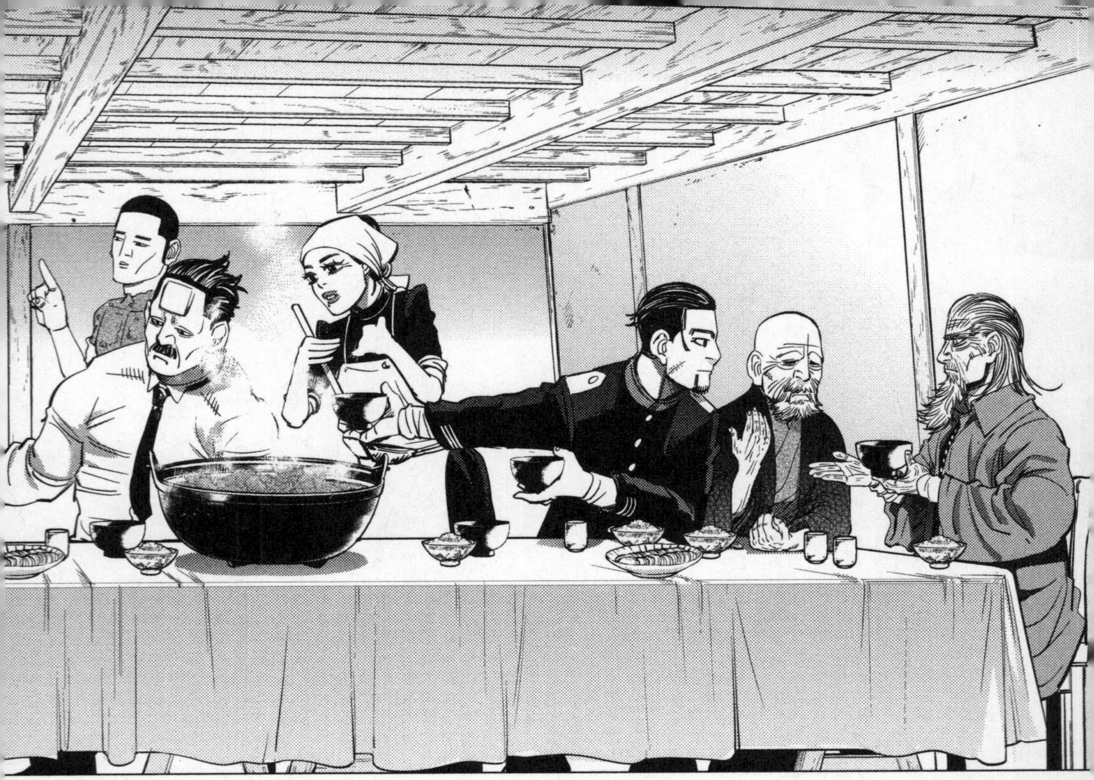

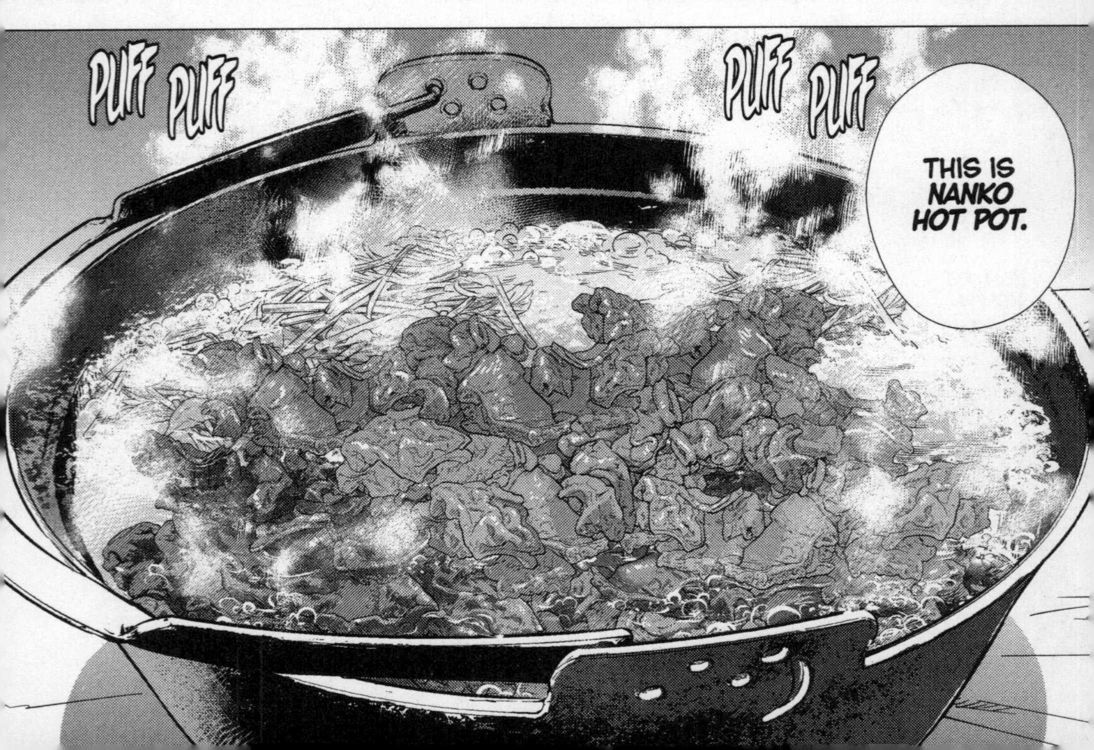
PUFF PUFF
PUFF PUFF
THIS IS NANKO HOT POT.

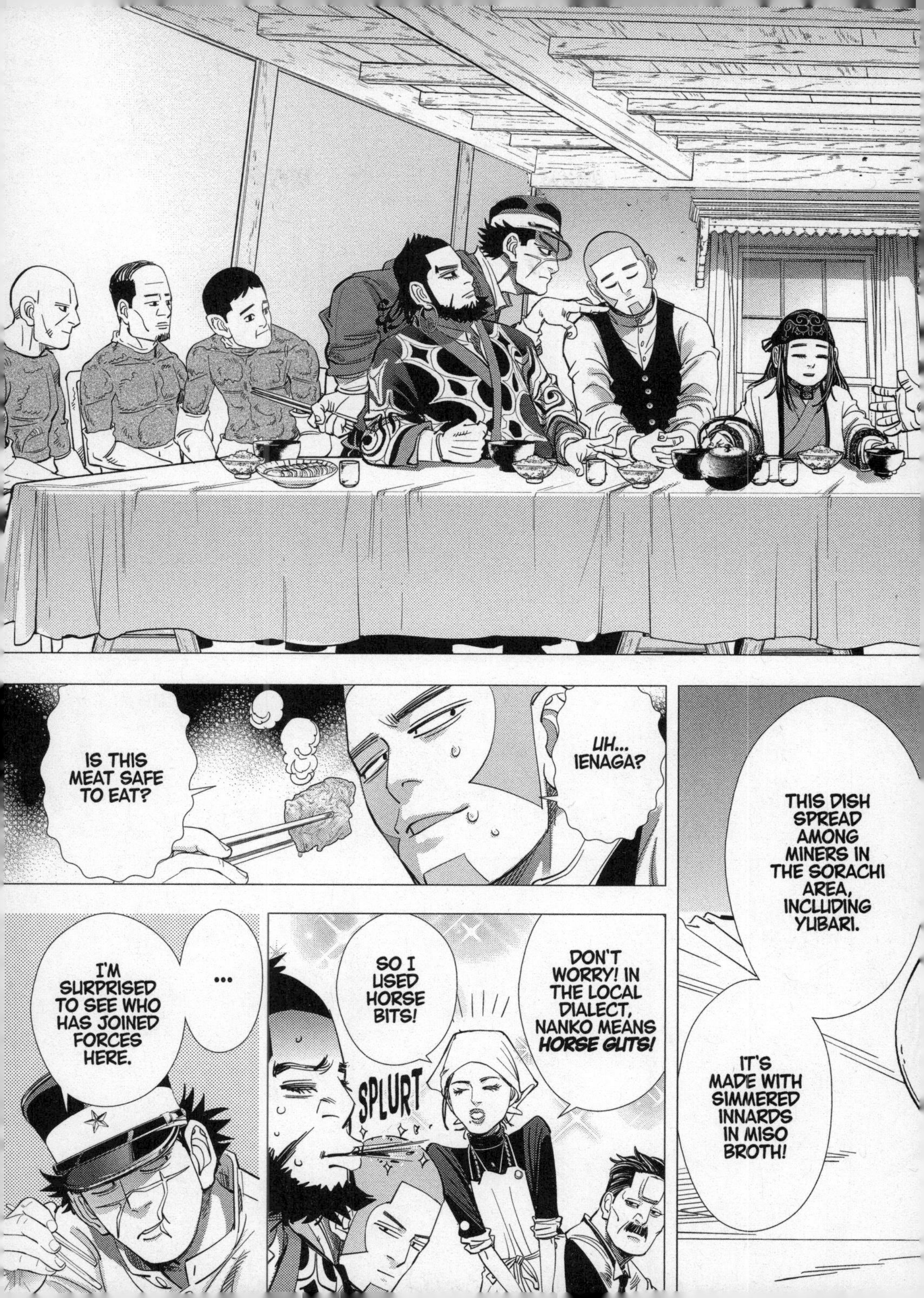
THIS DISH SPREAD AMONG MINERS IN THE SORACHI AREA, INCLUDING YUBARI.
IT'S MADE WITH SIMMERED INNARDS IN MISO BROTH!
UH... IENAGA?
IS THIS MEAT SAFE TO EAT?
DON'T WORRY! IN THE LOCAL DIALECT, NANKO MEANS HORSE GUTS!
SO I USED HORSE BITS!
SPLURT
...
I'M SURPRISED TO SEE WHO HAS JOINED FORCES HERE.

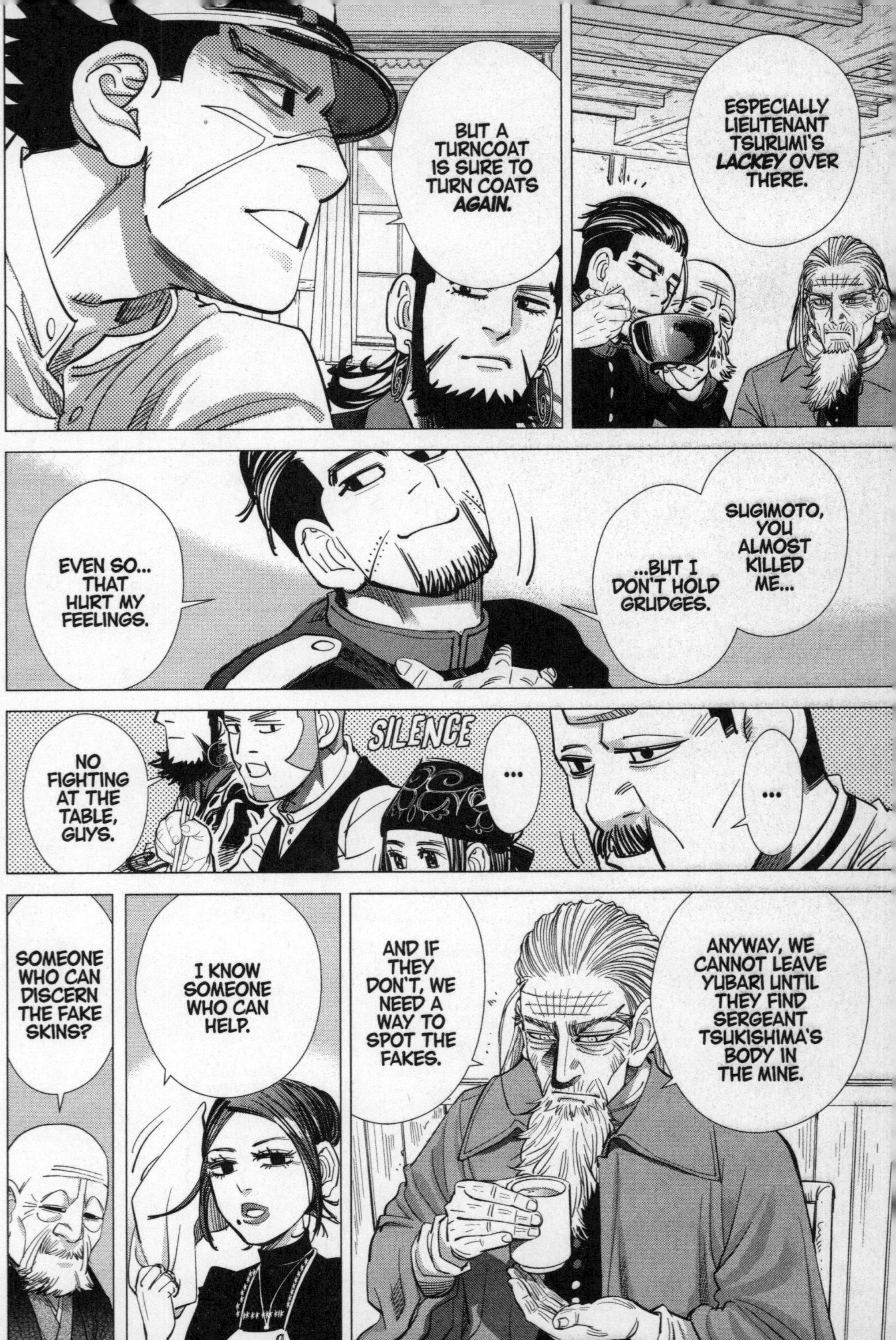
ESPECIALLY LIEUTENANT TSURUMI'S *LACKEY* OVER THERE.
BUT A TURNCOAT IS SURE TO TURN COATS *AGAIN.*
SUGIMOTO, YOU ALMOST KILLED ME...
...BUT I DON'T HOLD GRUDGES.
EVEN SO... THAT HURT MY FEELINGS.
...
SILENCE
...
NO FIGHTING AT THE TABLE, GUYS.
ANYWAY, WE CANNOT LEAVE YUBARI UNTIL THEY FIND SERGEANT TSUKISHIMA'S BODY IN THE MINE.
AND IF THEY DON'T, WE NEED A WAY TO SPOT THE FAKES.
I KNOW SOMEONE WHO CAN HELP.
SOMEONE WHO CAN DISCERN THE FAKE SKINS?

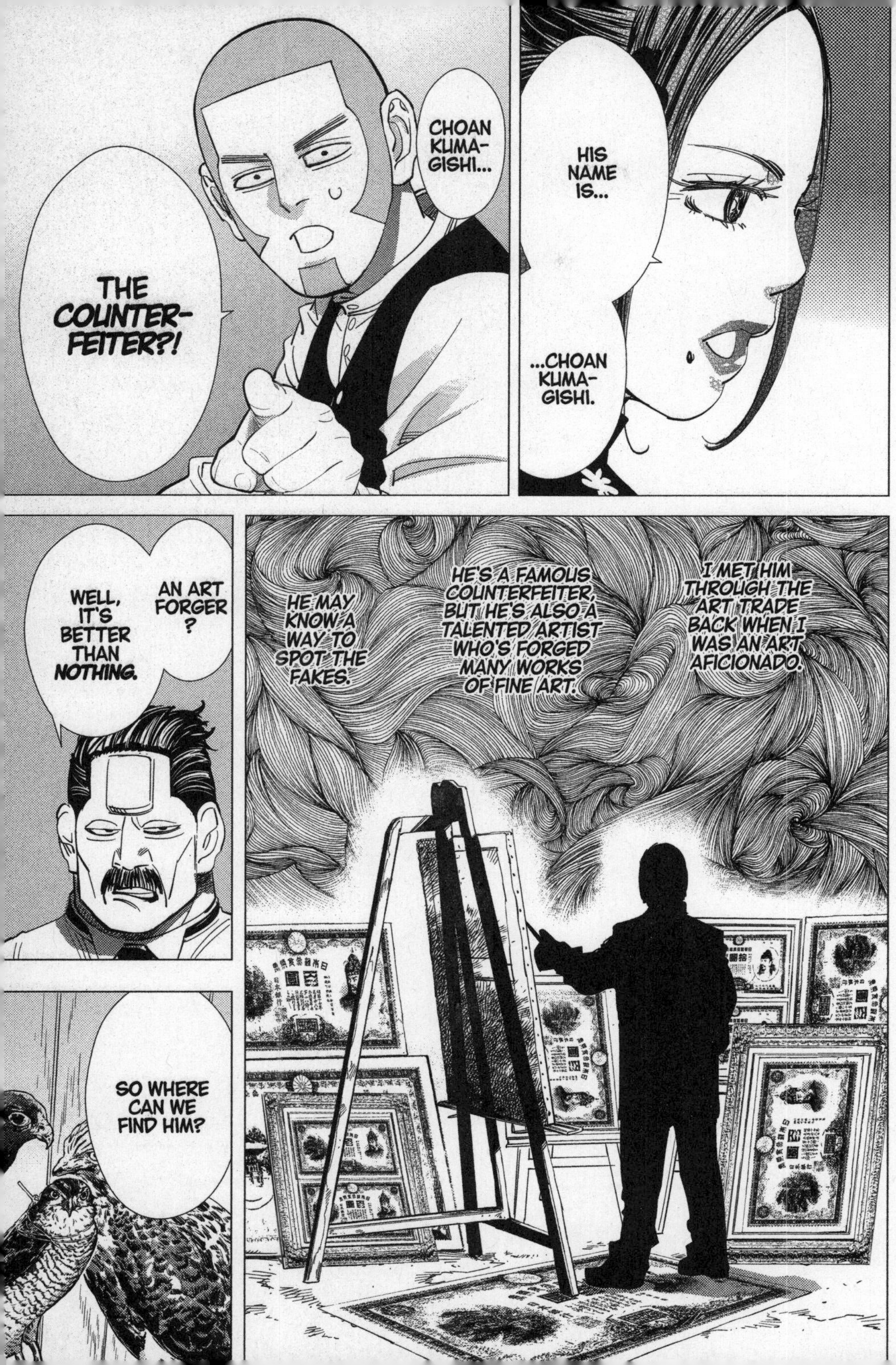
HIS NAME IS...
...CHOAN KUMAGISHI.
CHOAN KUMAGISHI...
THE COUNTERFEITER?!
I MET HIM THROUGH THE ART TRADE BACK WHEN I WAS AN ART AFICIONADO.
HE'S A FAMOUS COUNTERFEITER, BUT HE'S ALSO A TALENTED ARTIST WHO'S FORGED MANY WORKS OF FINE ART.
HE MAY KNOW A WAY TO SPOT THE FAKES.
AN ART FORGER?
WELL, IT'S BETTER THAN NOTHING.
SO WHERE CAN WE FIND HIM?

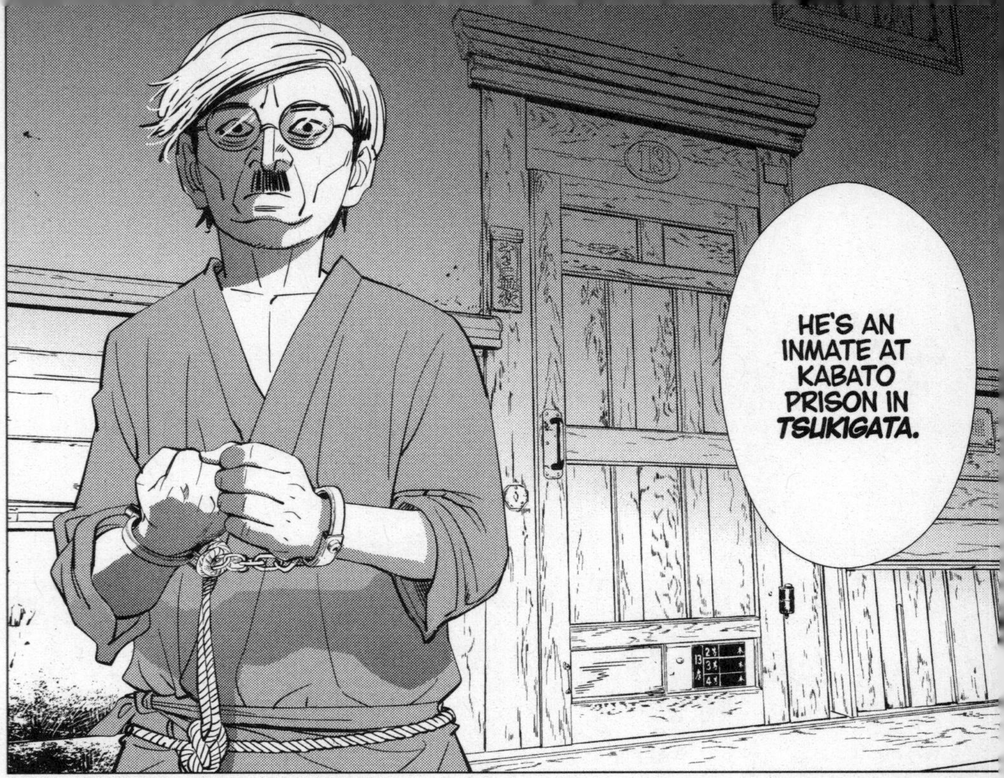
HE'S AN INMATE AT KABATO PRISON IN *TSUKIGATA.*

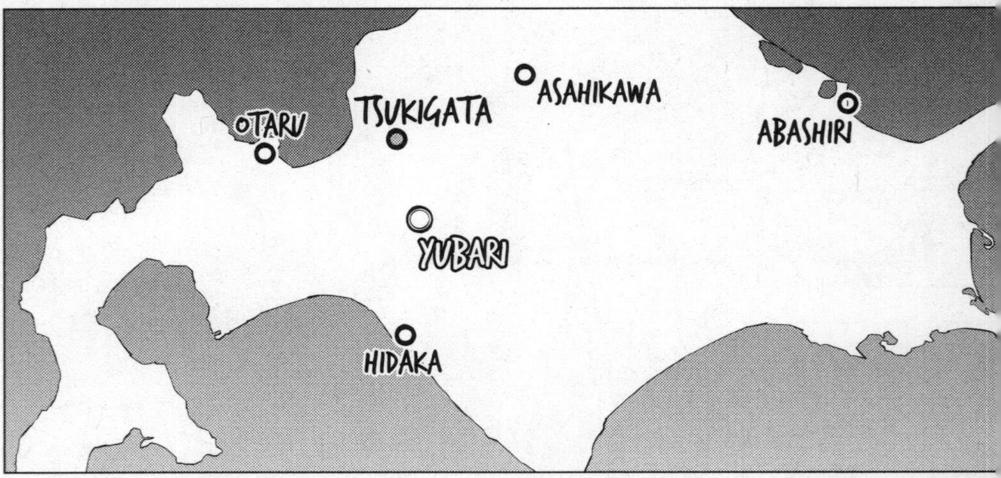
ABASHIRI
ASAHIKAWA
TSUKIGATA
OTARU
YUBARI
HIDAKA

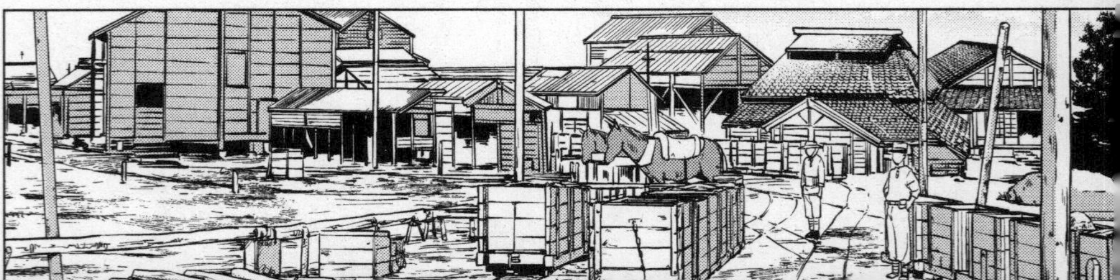

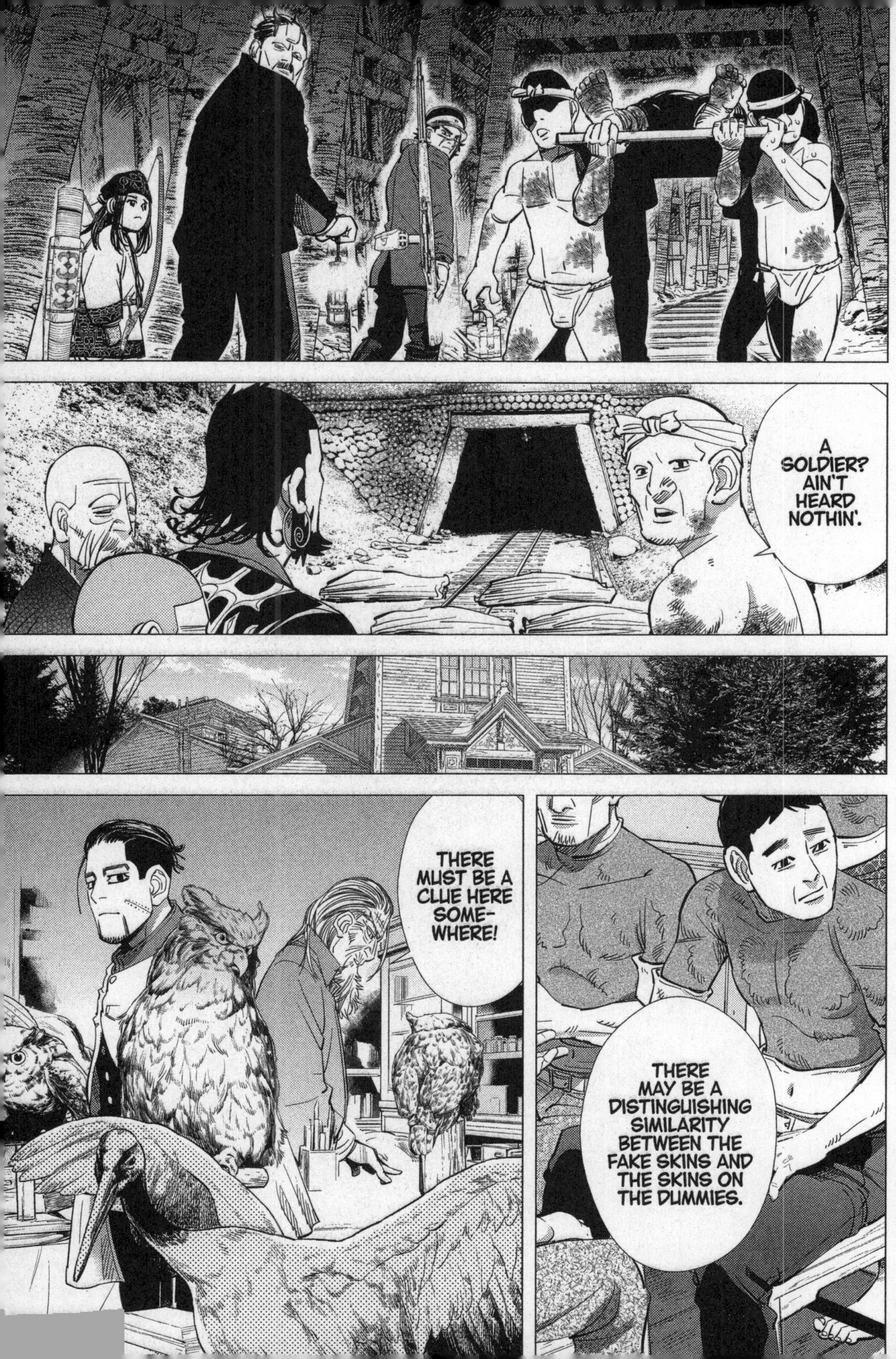
A SOLDIER? AIN'T HEARD NOTHIN'.
THERE MAY BE A DISTINGUISHING SIMILARITY BETWEEN THE FAKE SKINS AND THE SKINS ON THE DUMMIES.
THERE MUST BE A CLUE HERE SOME-WHERE!

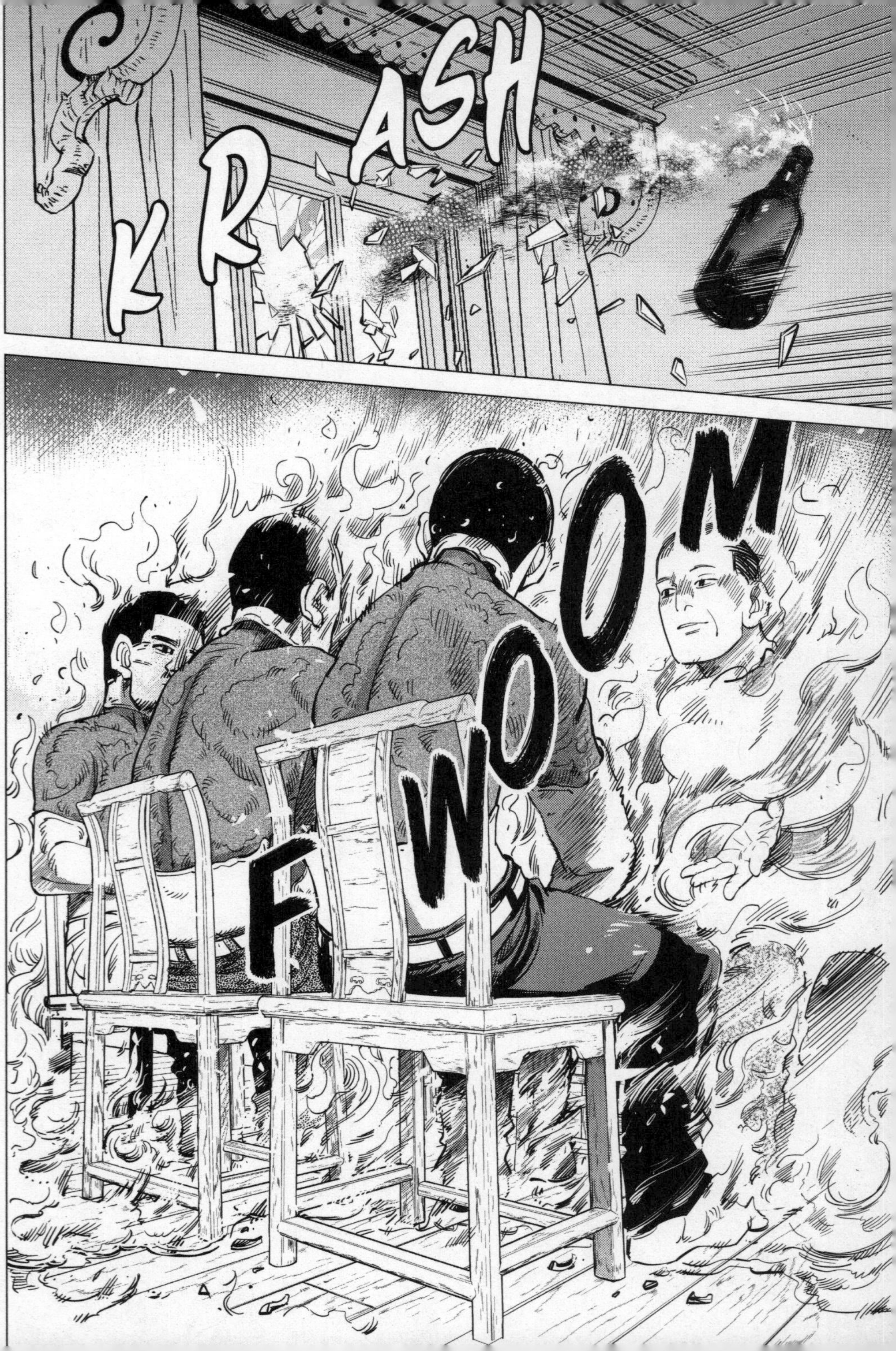
KRASH
FWOOM

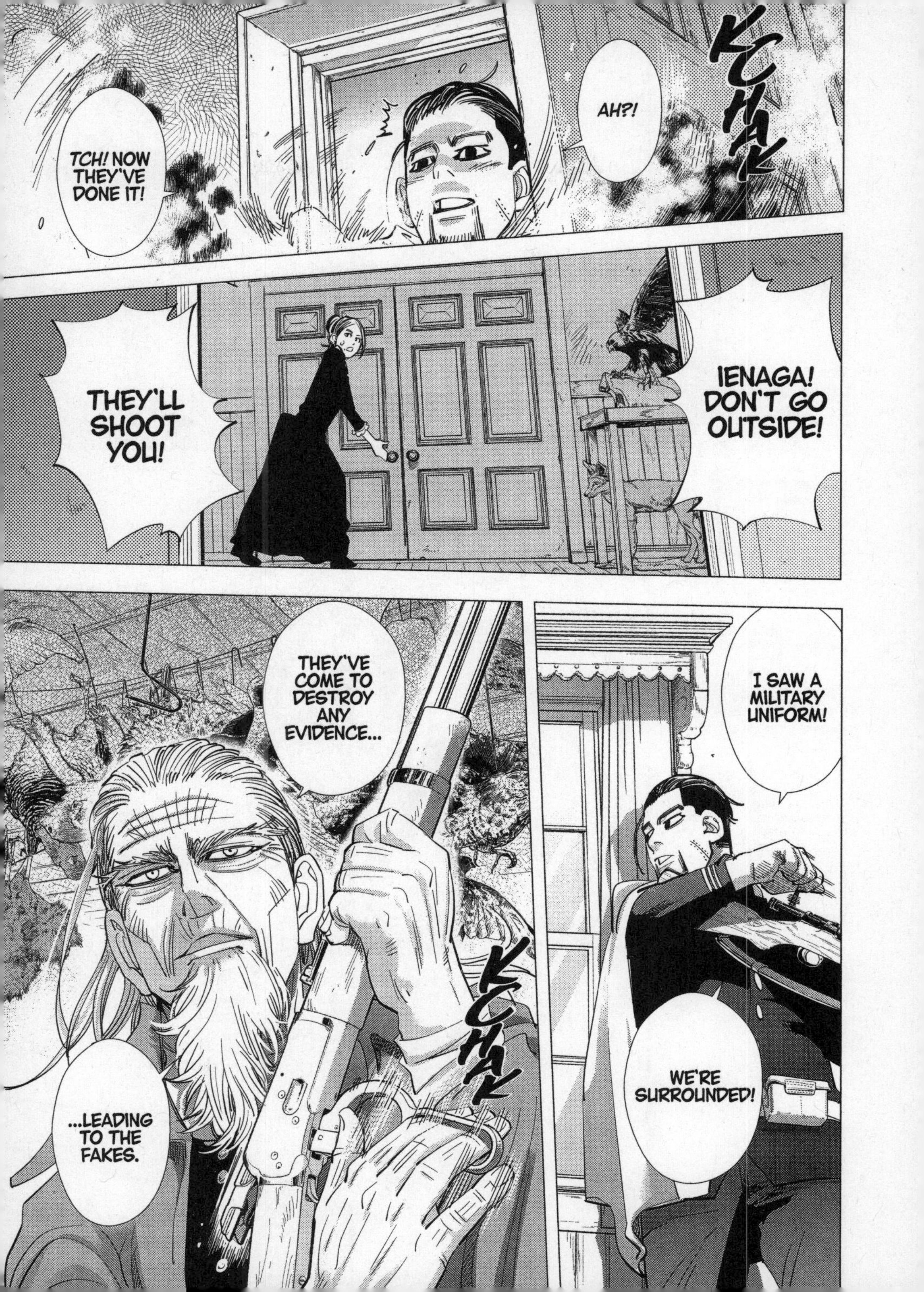
KCHAK
AH?!
TCH! NOW THEY'VE DONE IT!
IENAGA! DON'T GO OUTSIDE!
THEY'LL SHOOT YOU!
I SAW A MILITARY UNIFORM!
WE'RE SURROUNDED!
THEY'VE COME TO DESTROY ANY EVIDENCE...
KCHAK
...LEADING TO THE FAKES.

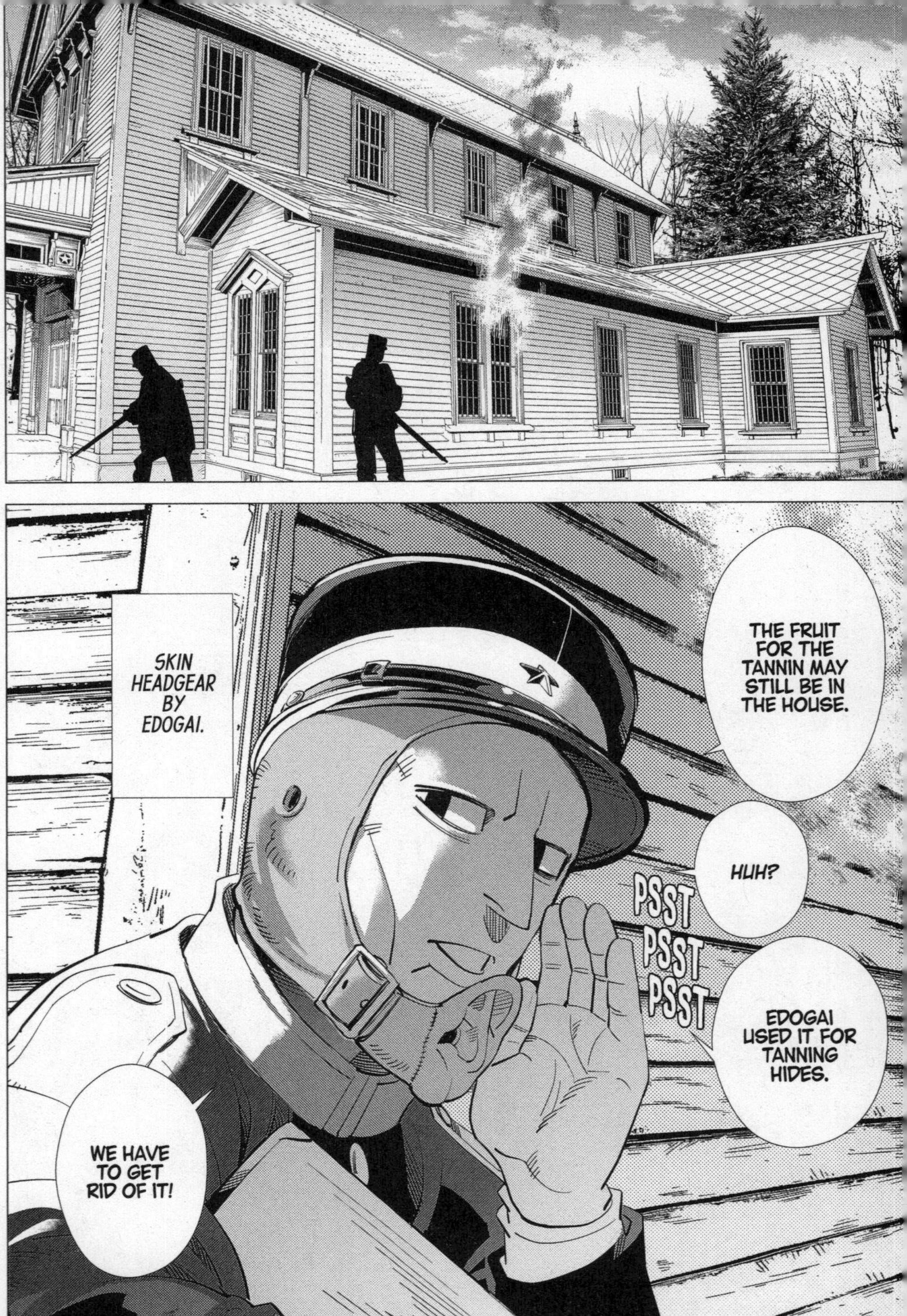
THE FRUIT FOR THE TANNIN MAY STILL BE IN THE HOUSE.
SKIN HEADGEAR BY EDOGAI.
HUH?
PSST PSST PSST
EDOGAI USED IT FOR TANNING HIDES.
WE HAVE TO GET RID OF IT!

Chapter 82: Nikaido

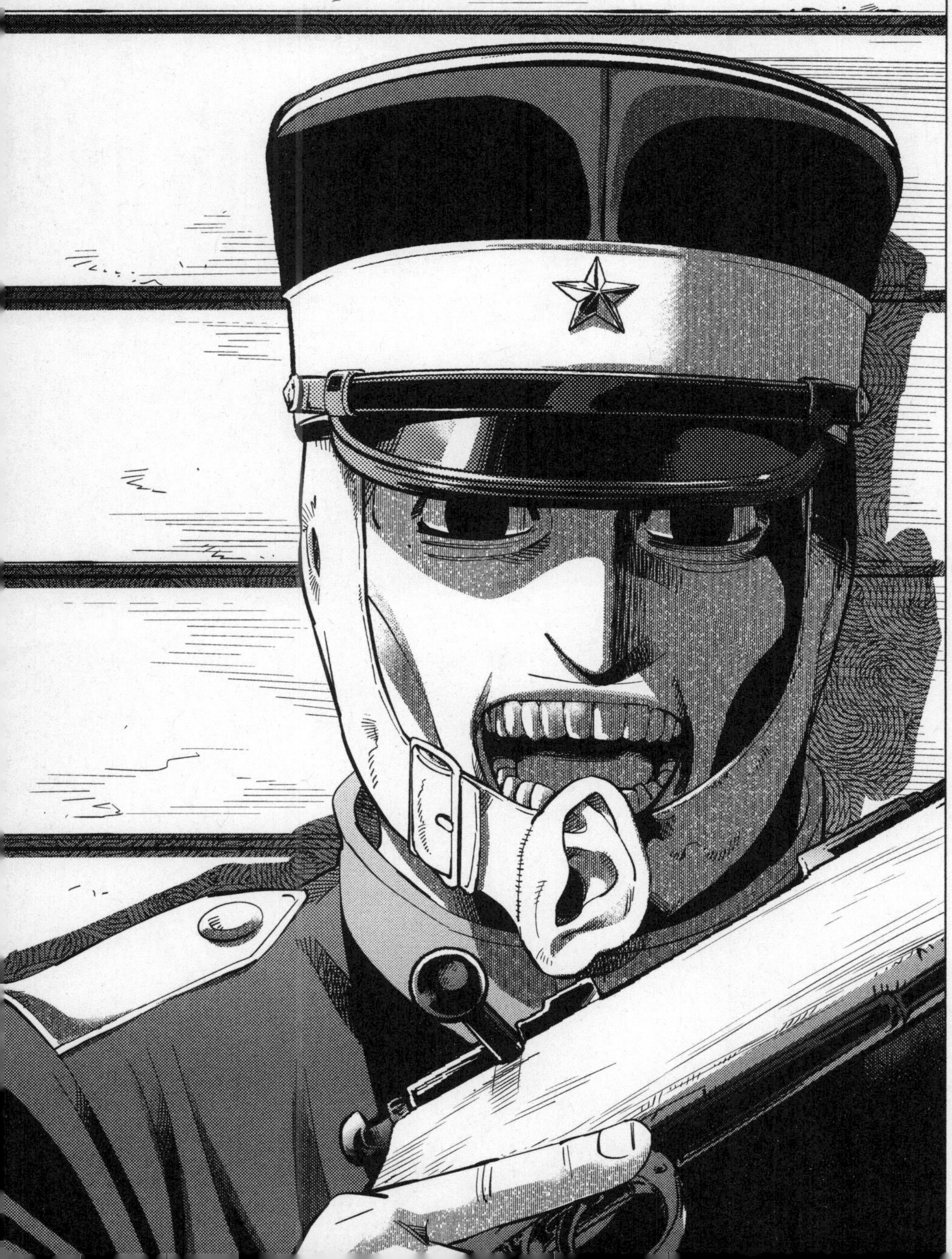

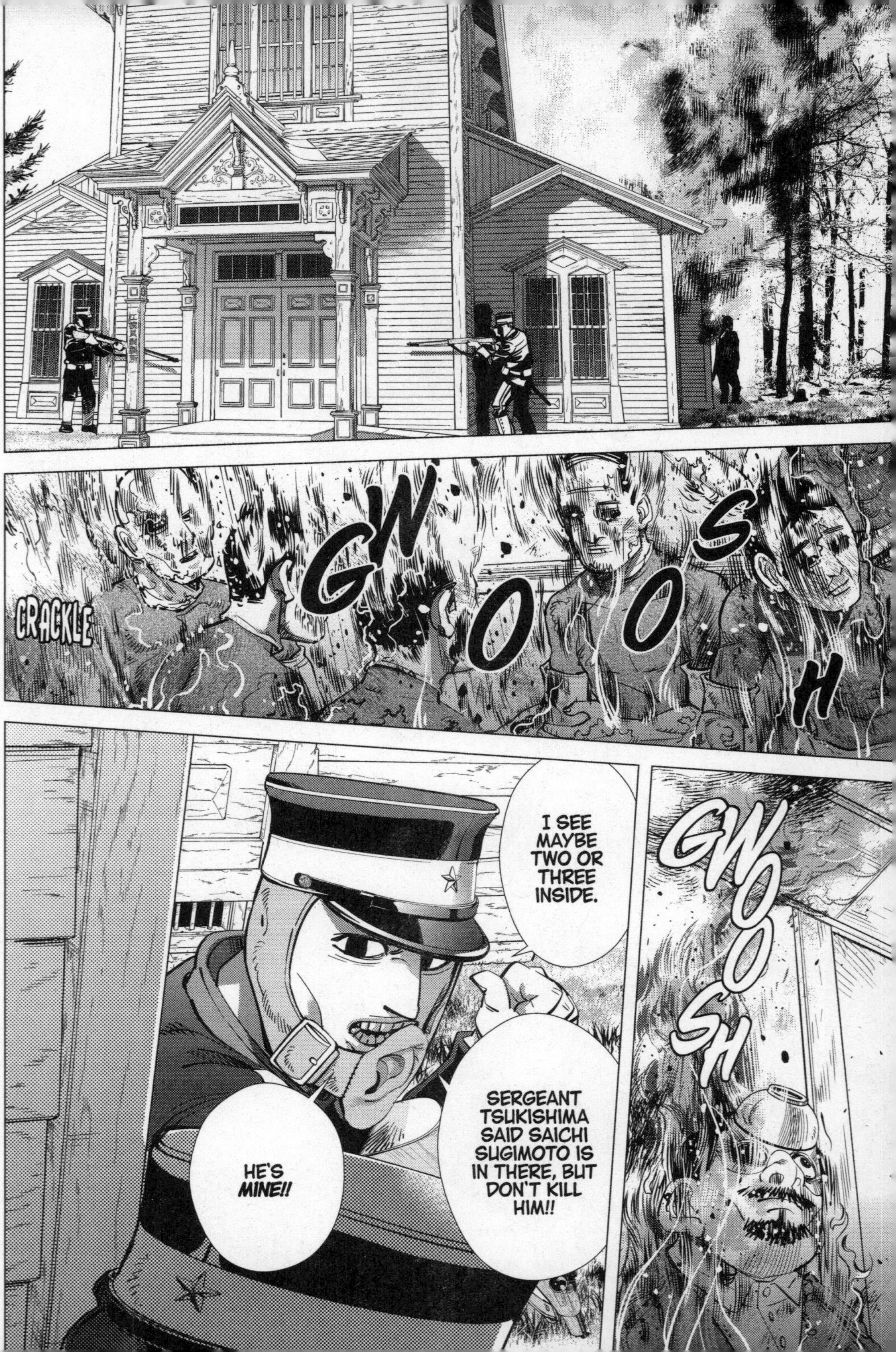
GWOOSH
CRACKLE
GWOOSH
I SEE MAYBE TWO OR THREE INSIDE.
SERGEANT TSUKISHIMA SAID SAICHI SUGIMOTO IS IN THERE, BUT DON'T KILL HIM!!
HE'S *MINE!!*

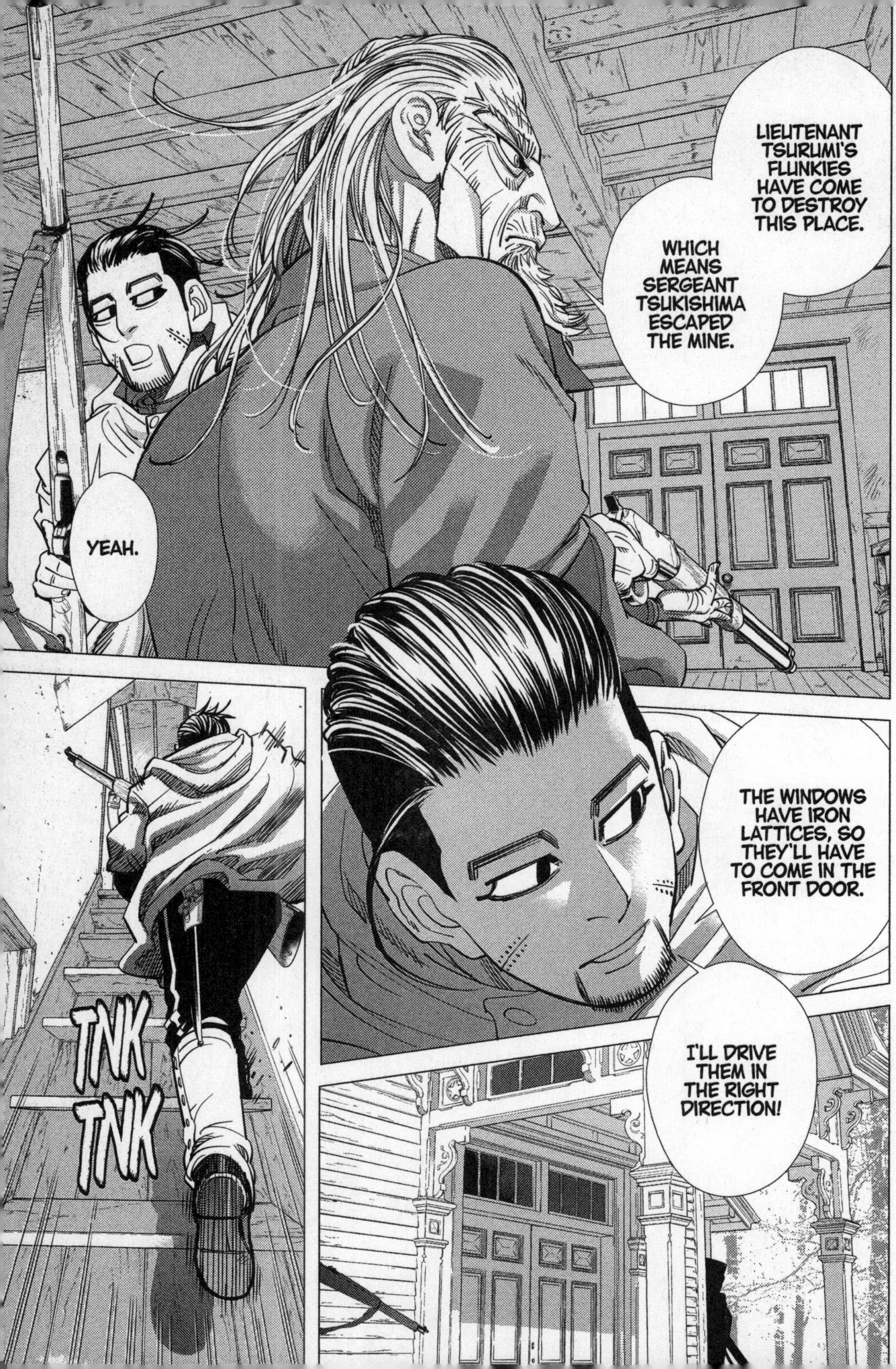
LIEUTENANT TSURUMI'S FLUNKIES HAVE COME TO DESTROY THIS PLACE.
WHICH MEANS SERGEANT TSUKISHIMA ESCAPED THE MINE.
YEAH.
THE WINDOWS HAVE IRON LATTICES, SO THEY'LL HAVE TO COME IN THE FRONT DOOR.
I'LL DRIVE THEM IN THE RIGHT DIRECTION!
TNK TNK

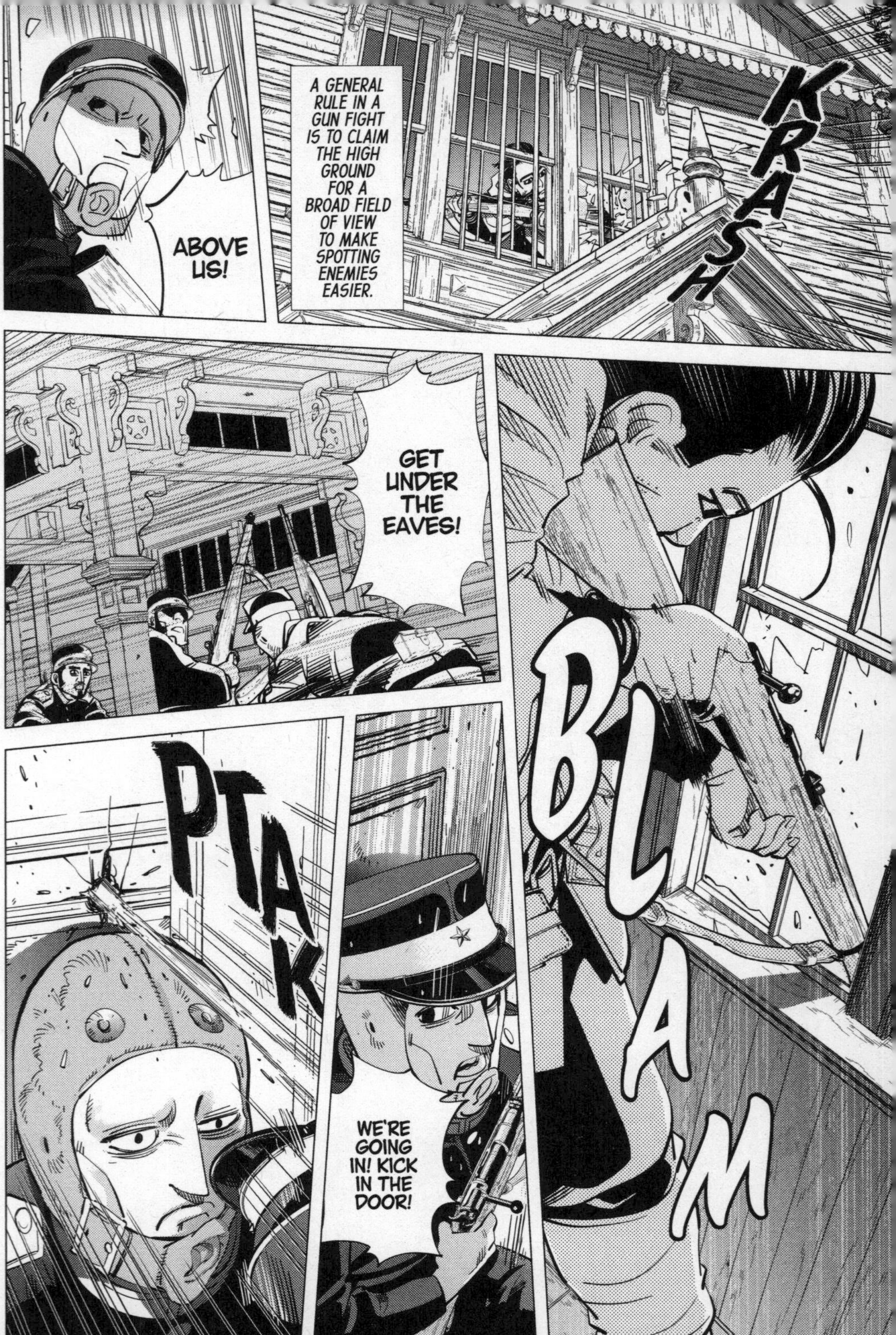
A GENERAL RULE IN A GUN FIGHT IS TO CLAIM THE HIGH GROUND FOR A BROAD FIELD OF VIEW TO MAKE SPOTTING ENEMIES EASIER.
KRASH
ABOVE US!
BLAM
GET UNDER THE EAVES!
WE'RE GOING IN! KICK IN THE DOOR!
PTAK

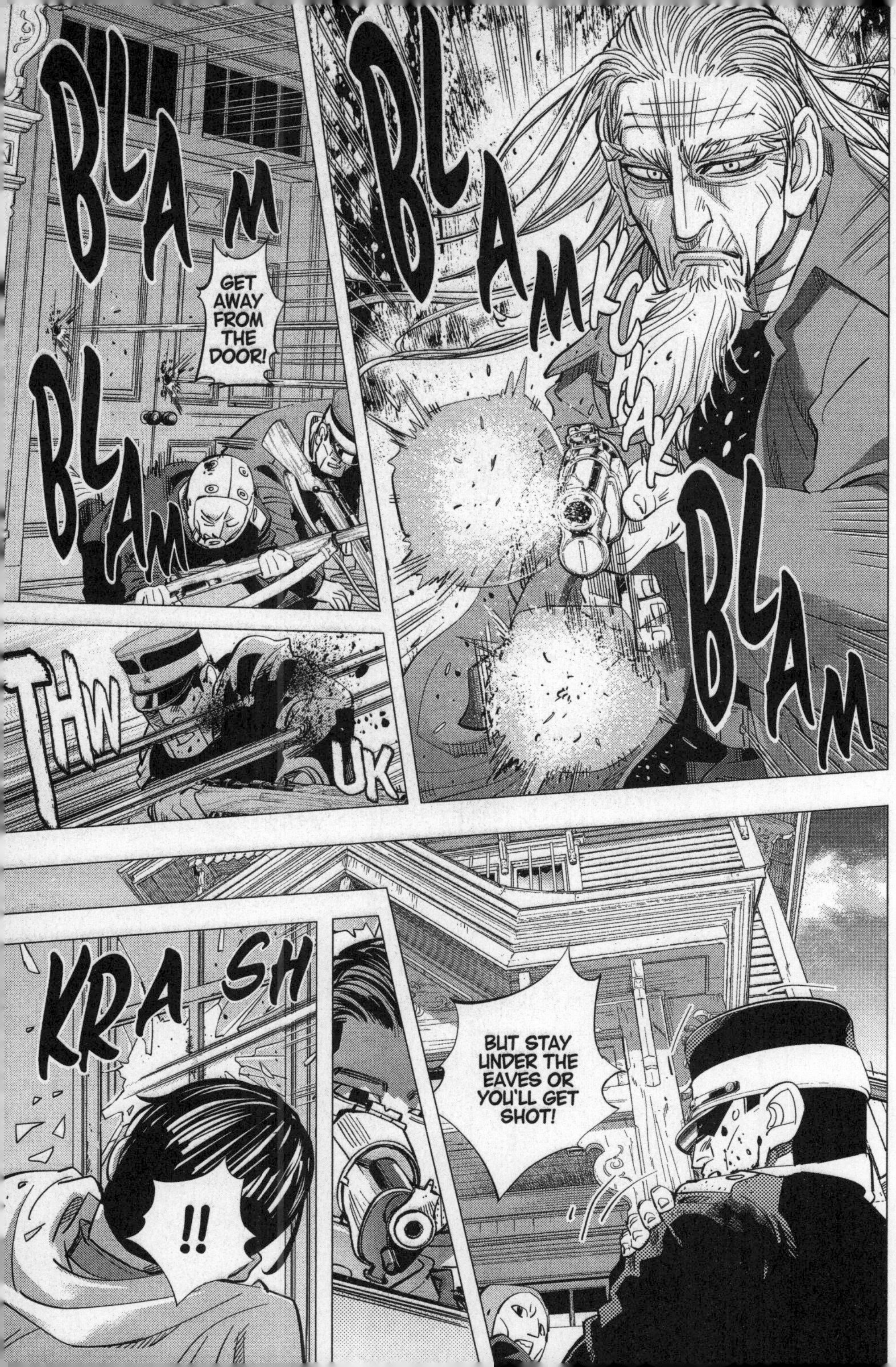
BLAM
KCHAK
BLAM
BLAM
GET AWAY FROM THE DOOR!
BLAM
THWUK
BUT STAY UNDER THE EAVES OR YOU'LL GET SHOT!
KRASH
!!

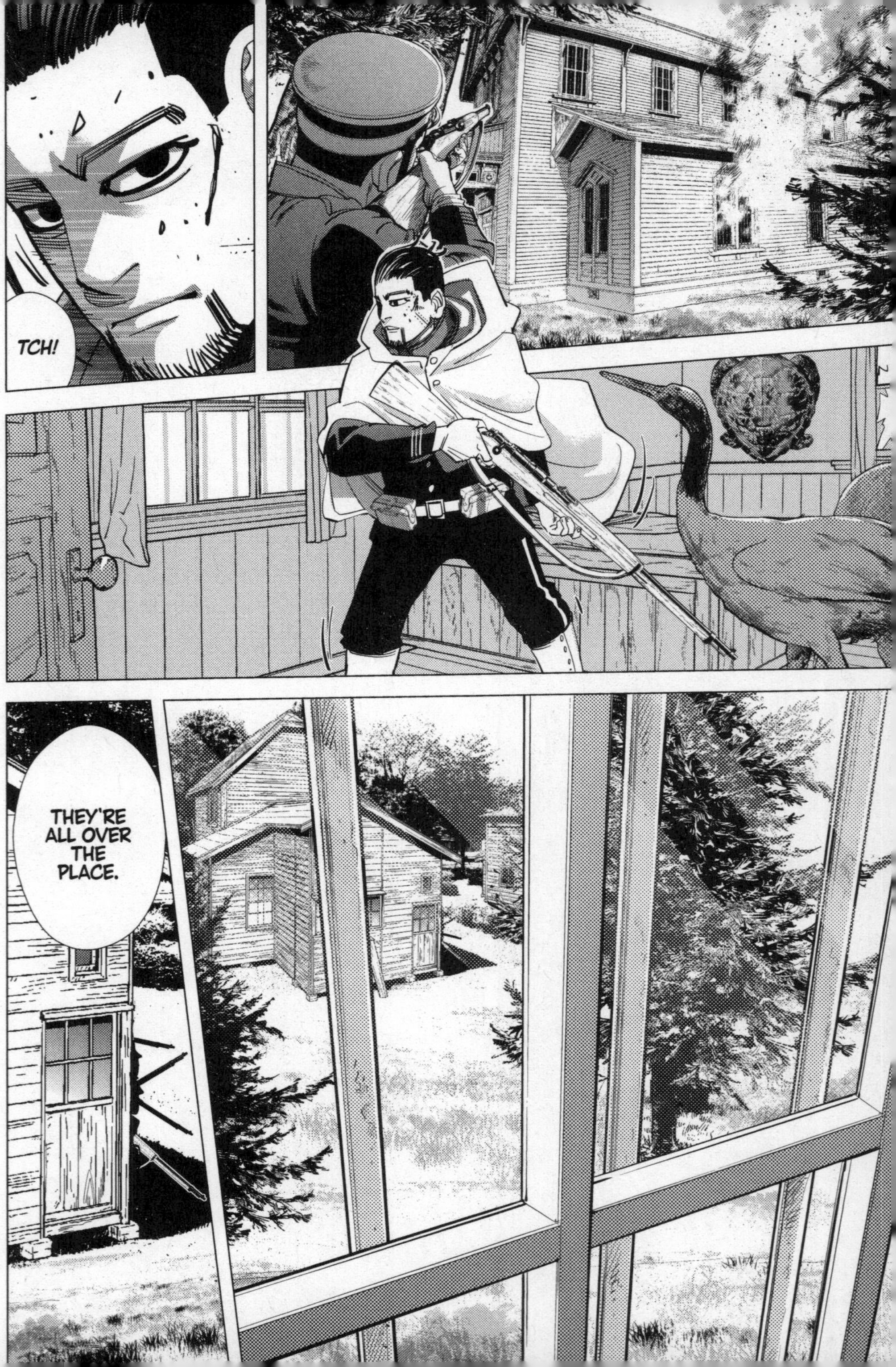
TCH!
THEY'RE ALL OVER THE PLACE.

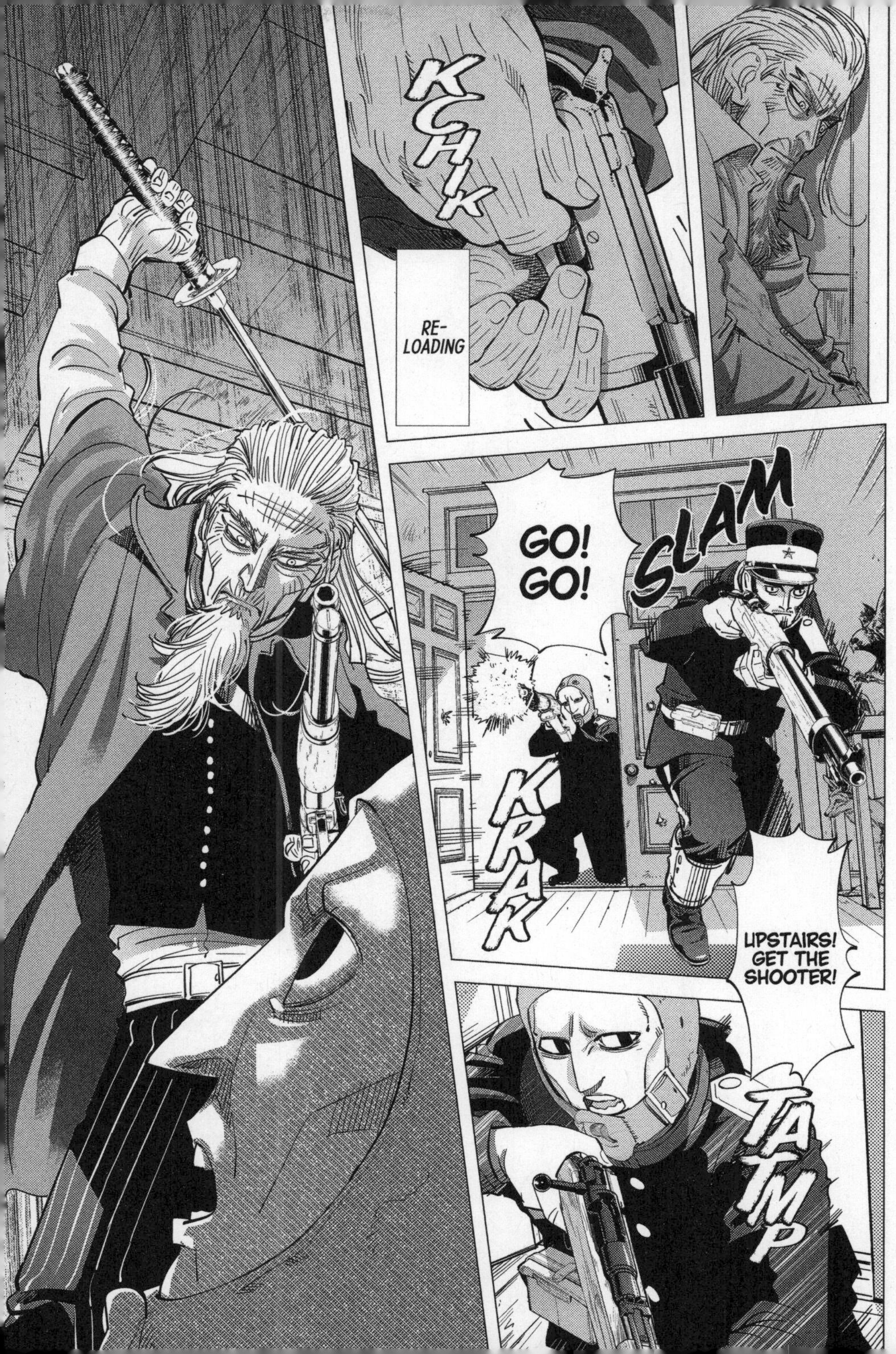
KCHIK
RE-LOADING
SLAM
GO! GO!
KRAK
UPSTAIRS! GET THE SHOOTER!
TATMP

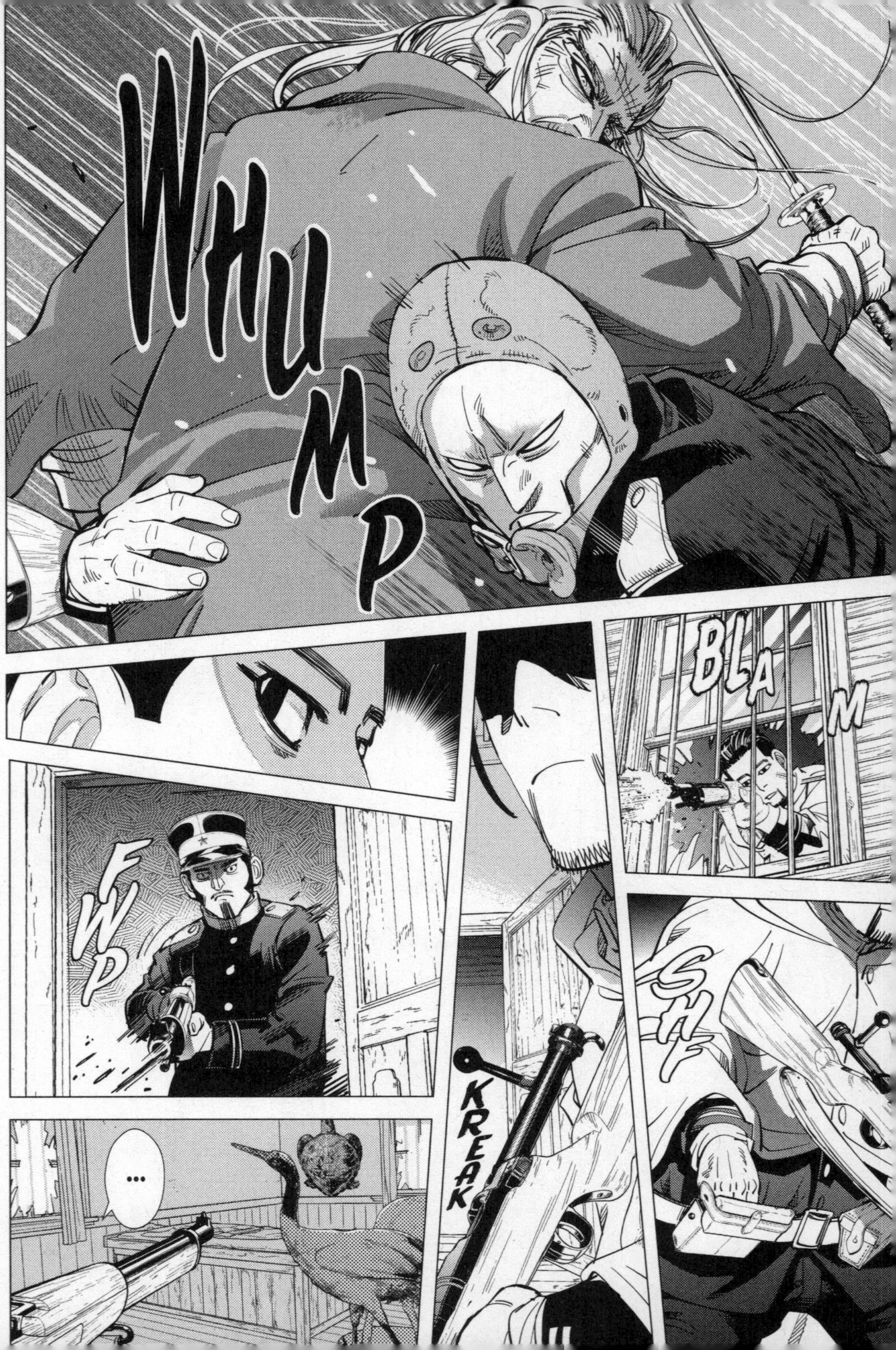
WHUMP
BLAM
FWP
SHF
KREAK
...

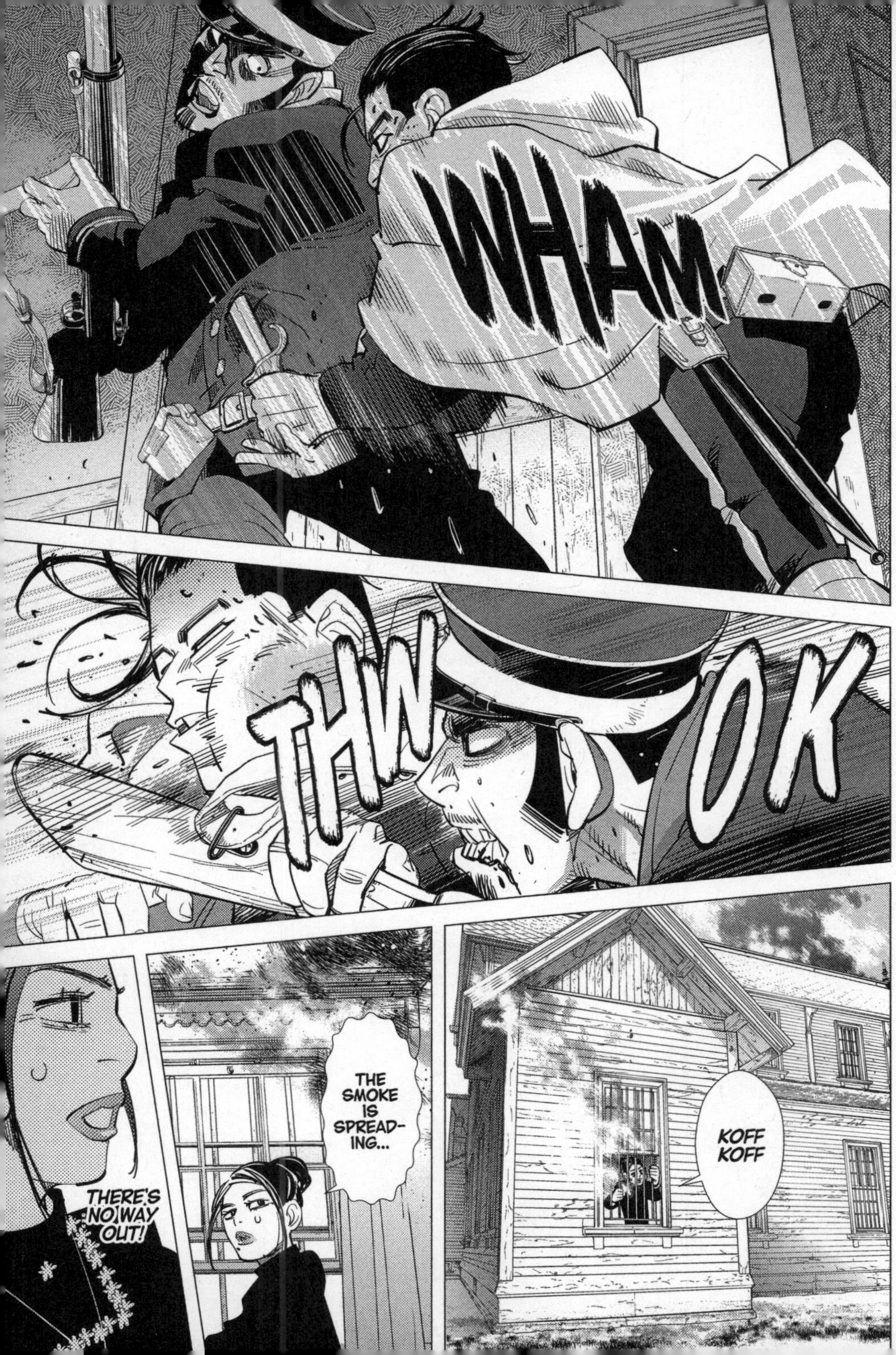
WHAM
THWOK
KOFF KOFF
THE SMOKE IS SPREAD-ING...
THERE'S NO WAY OUT!

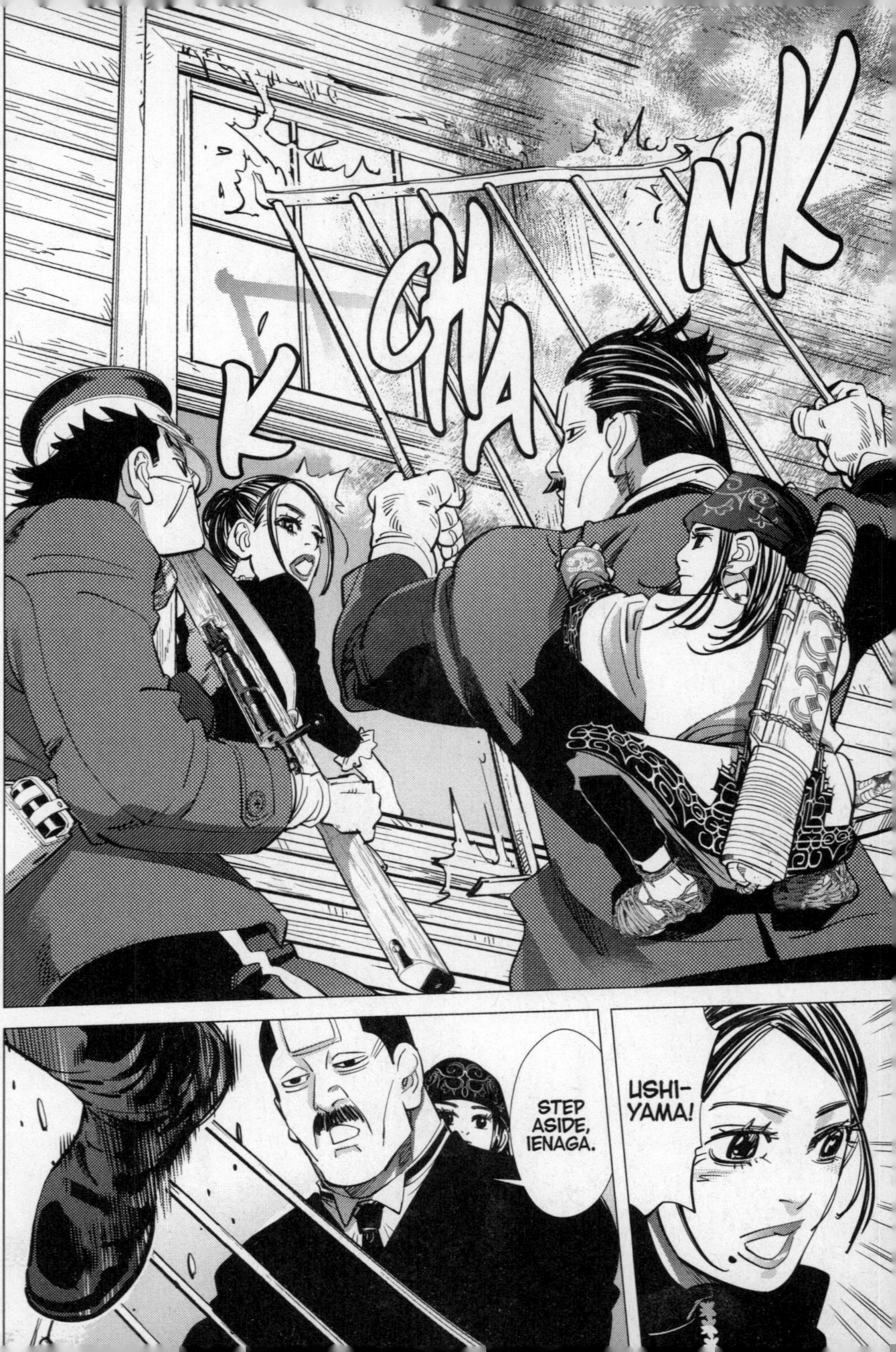
K CHA NK
USHI-YAMA!
STEP ASIDE, IENAGA.

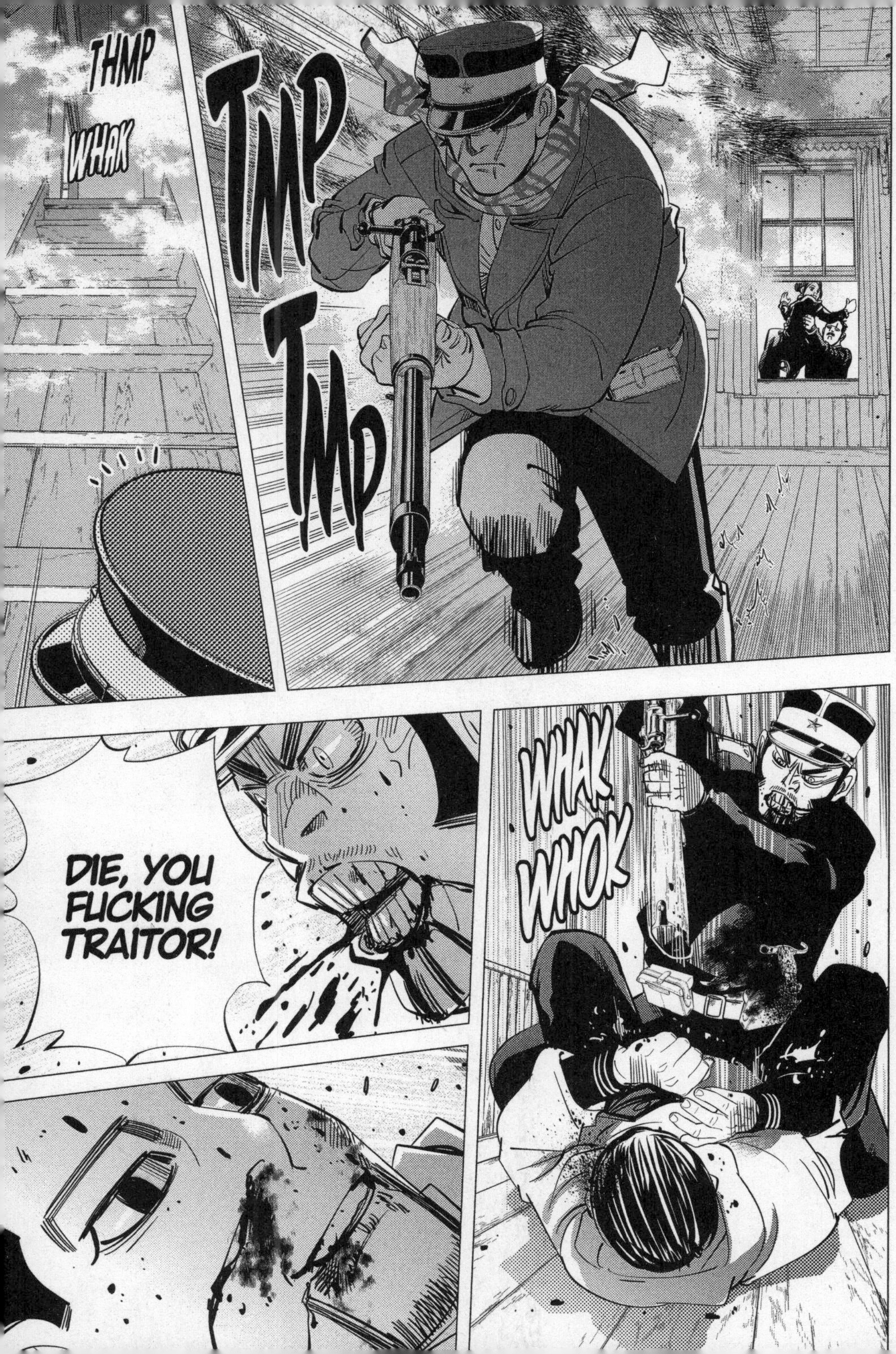
THMP
WHAK
TMP TMP
WHAK WHOK
DIE, YOU FUCKING TRAITOR!

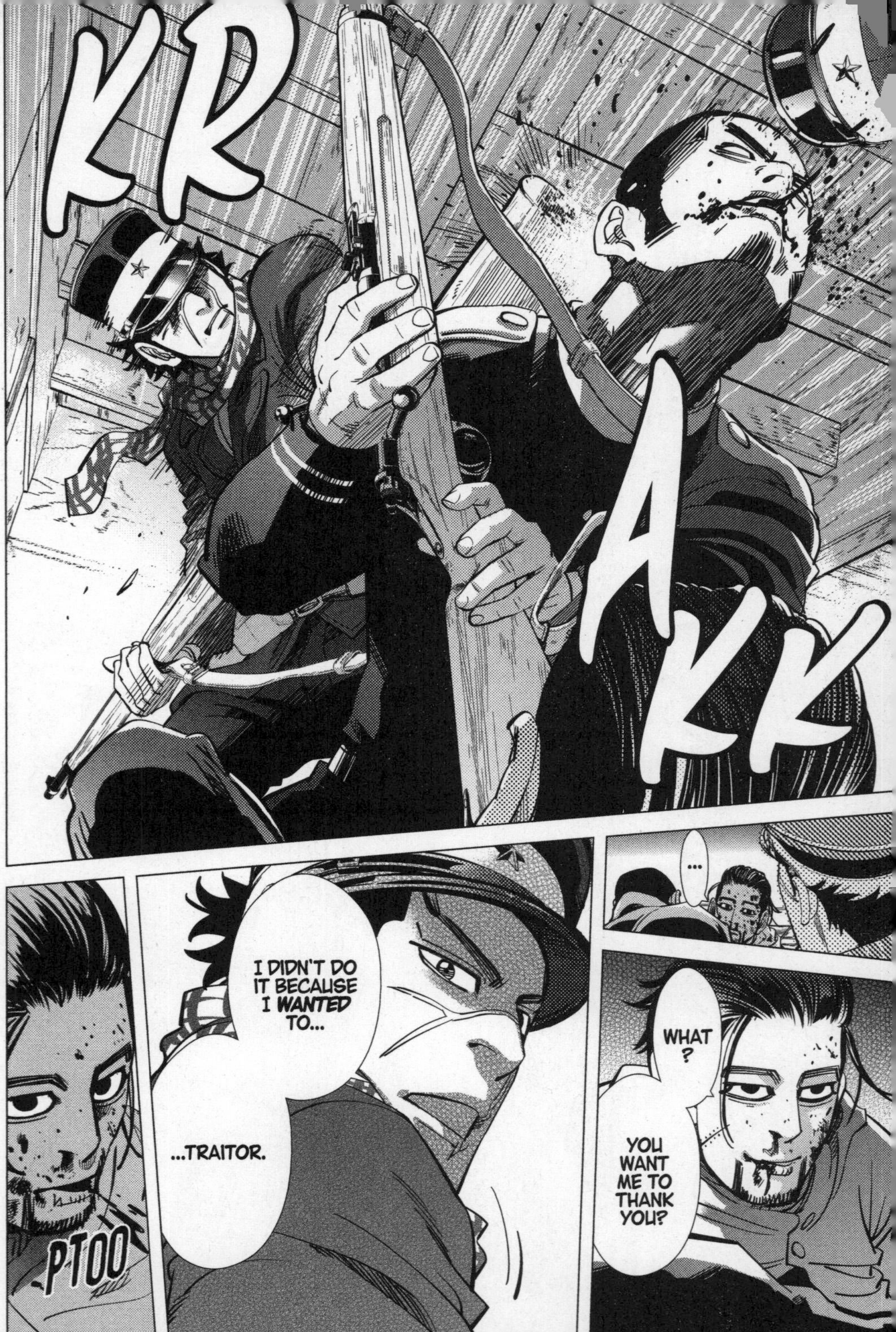
KR
AKK
...
WHAT?
YOU WANT ME TO THANK YOU?
I DIDN'T DO IT BECAUSE I WANTED TO...
...TRAITOR.
PTOO

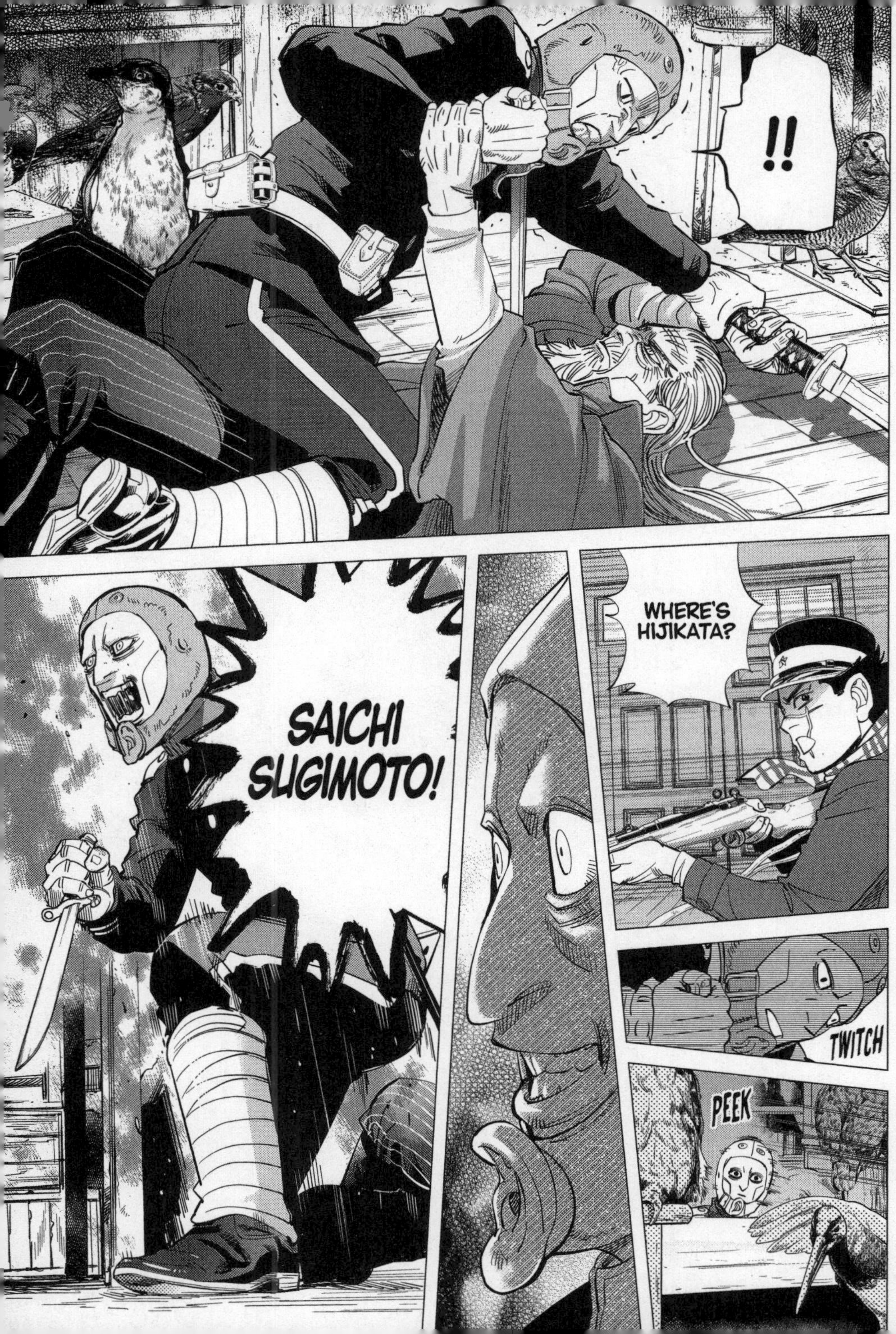
!!
WHERE'S HIJIKATA?
TWITCH
PEEK
SAICHI SUGIMOTO!

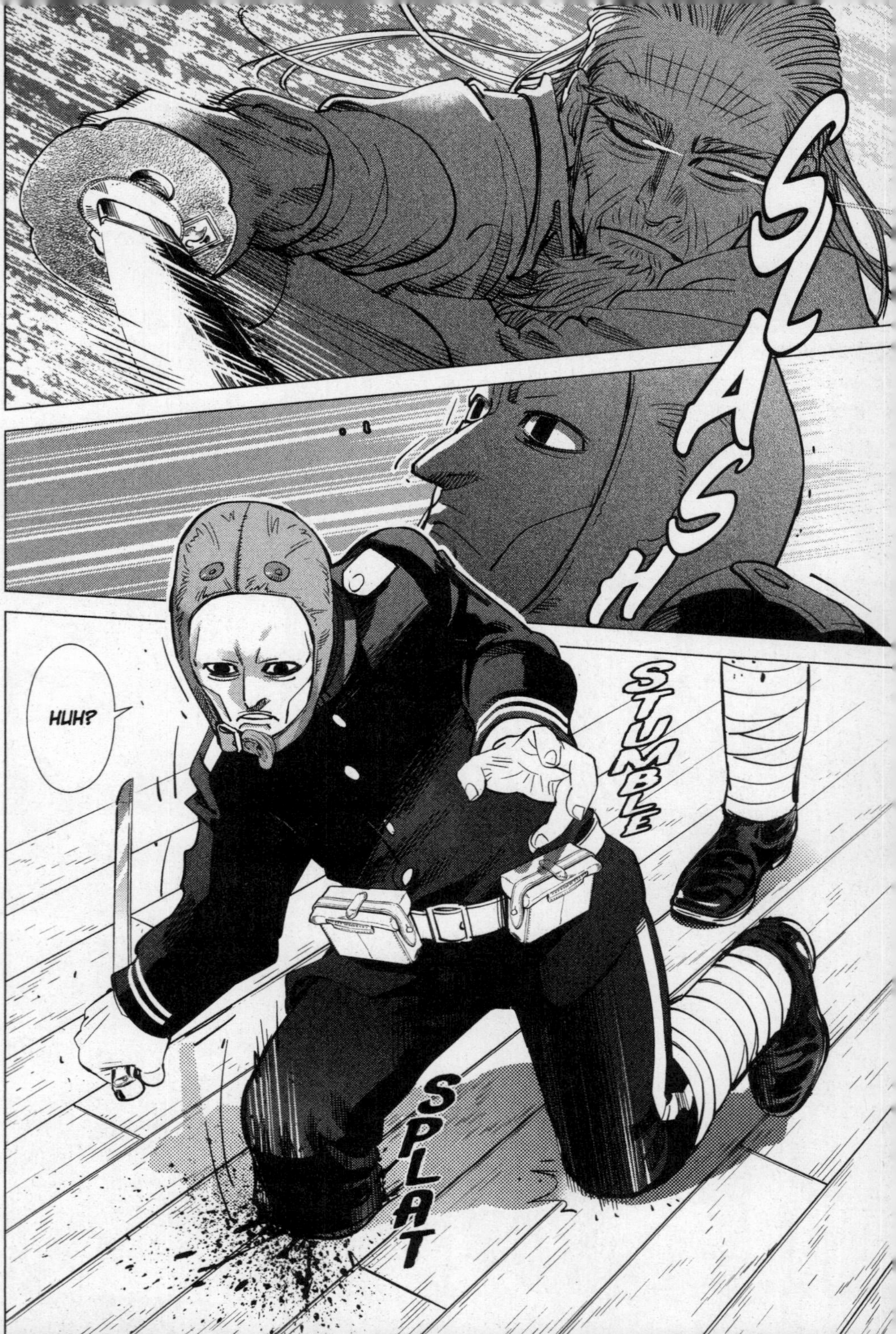
SLASH
STUMBLE
HUH?
SPLAT

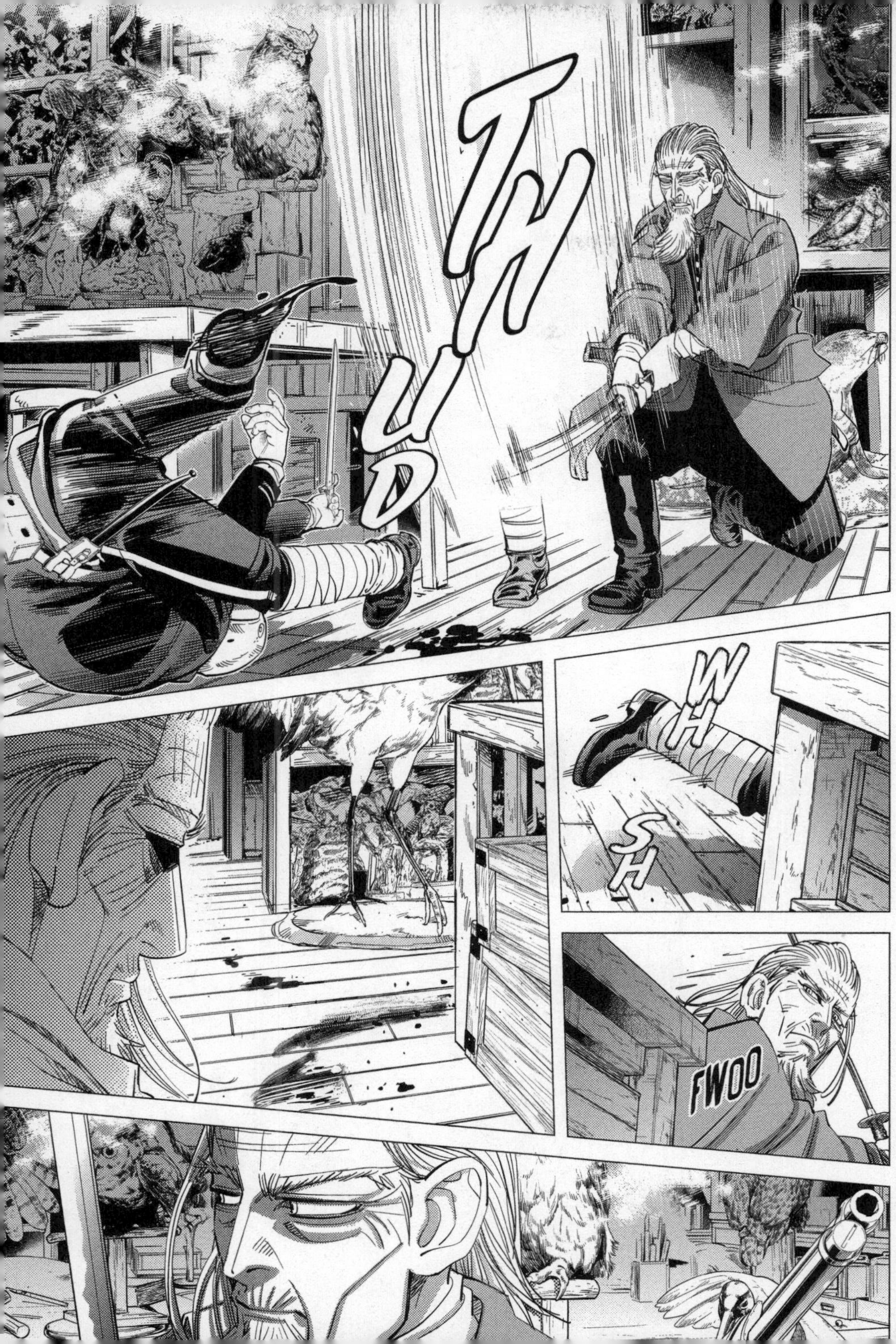
THUD
WHSH
FWOO

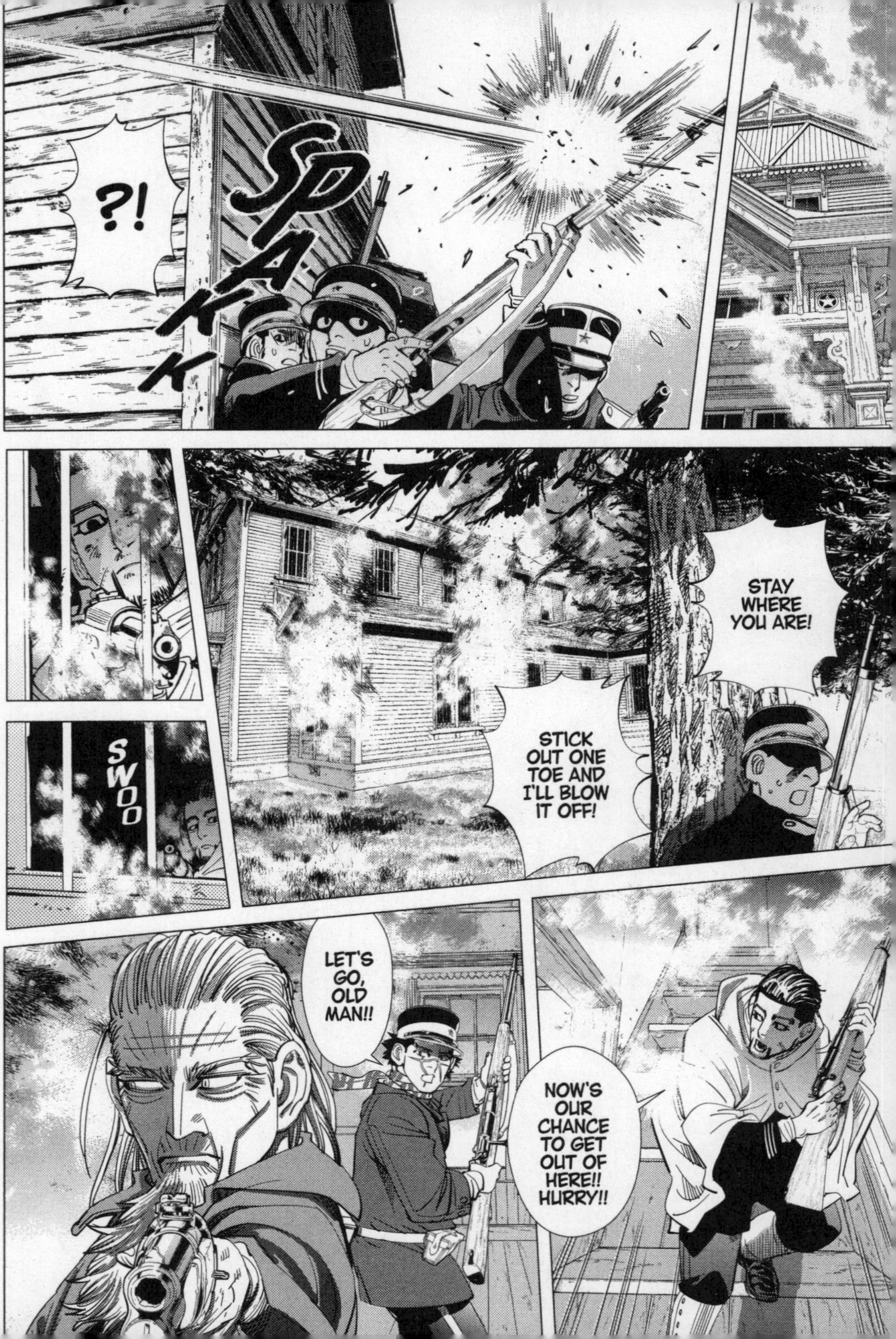
?!
SPAKK
STAY WHERE YOU ARE!
STICK OUT ONE TOE AND I'LL BLOW IT OFF!
SWOO
NOW'S OUR CHANCE TO GET OUT OF HERE!! HURRY!!
LET'S GO, OLD MAN!!

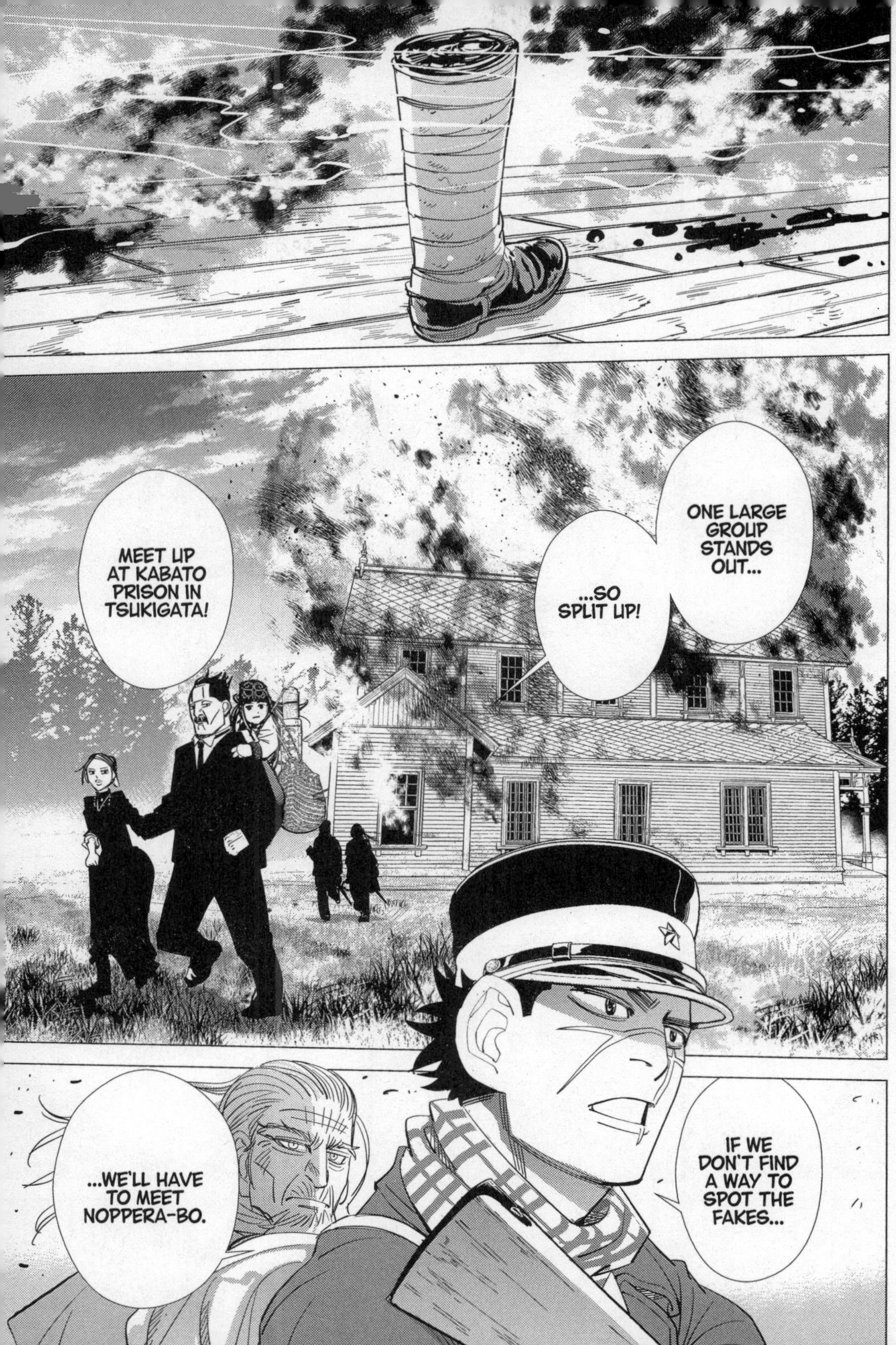
ONE LARGE GROUP STANDS OUT...
...SO SPLIT UP!
MEET UP AT KABATO PRISON IN TSUKIGATA!
IF WE DON'T FIND A WAY TO SPOT THE FAKES...
...WE'LL HAVE TO MEET NOPPERA-BO.

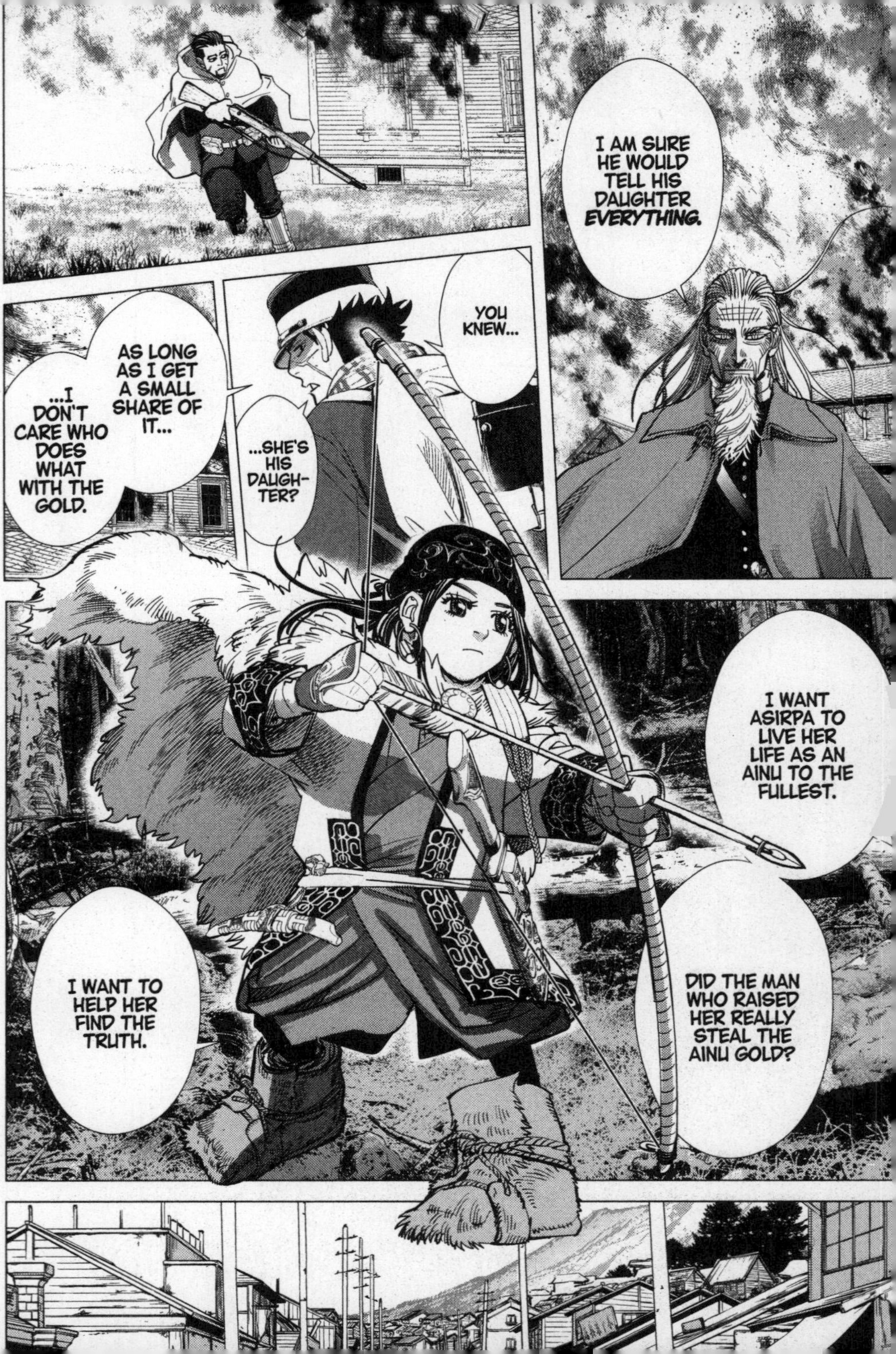
I AM SURE HE WOULD TELL HIS DAUGHTER *EVERYTHING.*
YOU KNEW...
...SHE'S HIS DAUGHTER?
AS LONG AS I GET A SMALL SHARE OF IT...
...I DON'T CARE WHO DOES WHAT WITH THE GOLD.
I WANT ASIRPA TO LIVE HER LIFE AS AN AINU TO THE FULLEST.
DID THE MAN WHO RAISED HER REALLY STEAL THE AINU GOLD?
I WANT TO HELP HER FIND THE TRUTH.

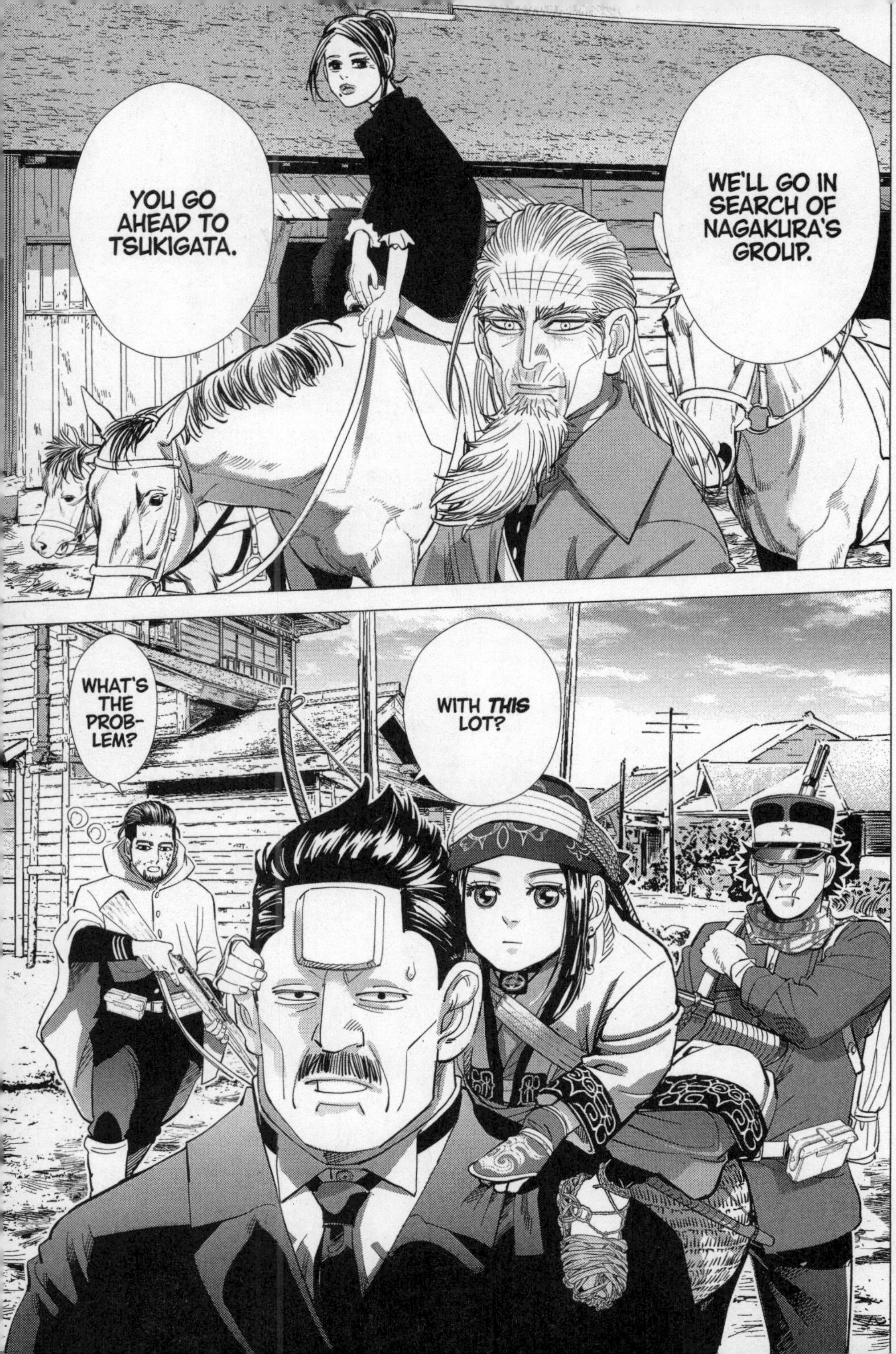
WE'LL GO IN SEARCH OF NAGAKURA'S GROUP.
YOU GO AHEAD TO TSUKIGATA.
WITH *THIS* LOT?
WHAT'S THE PROB-LEM?

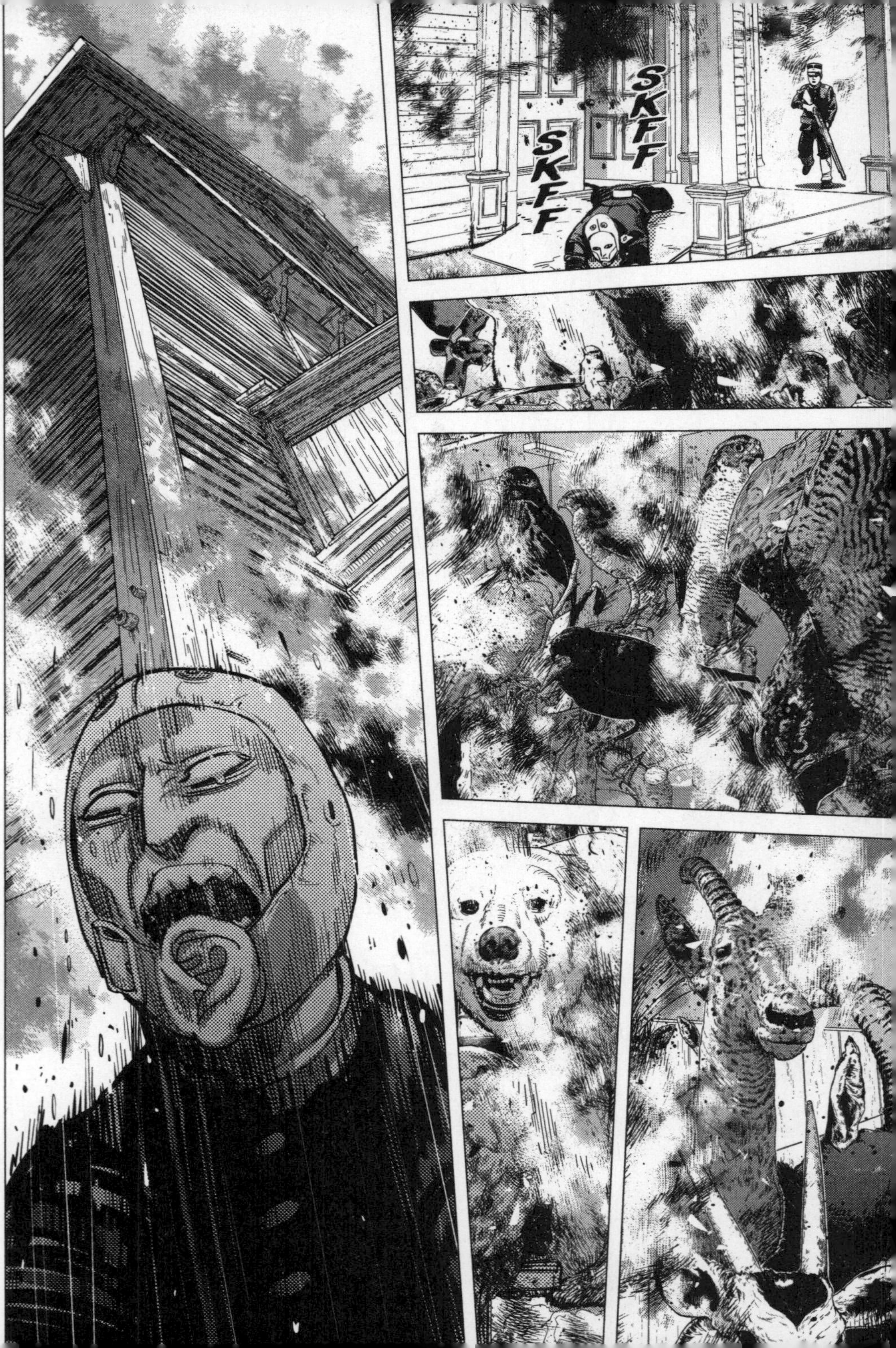
SKFF
SKFF

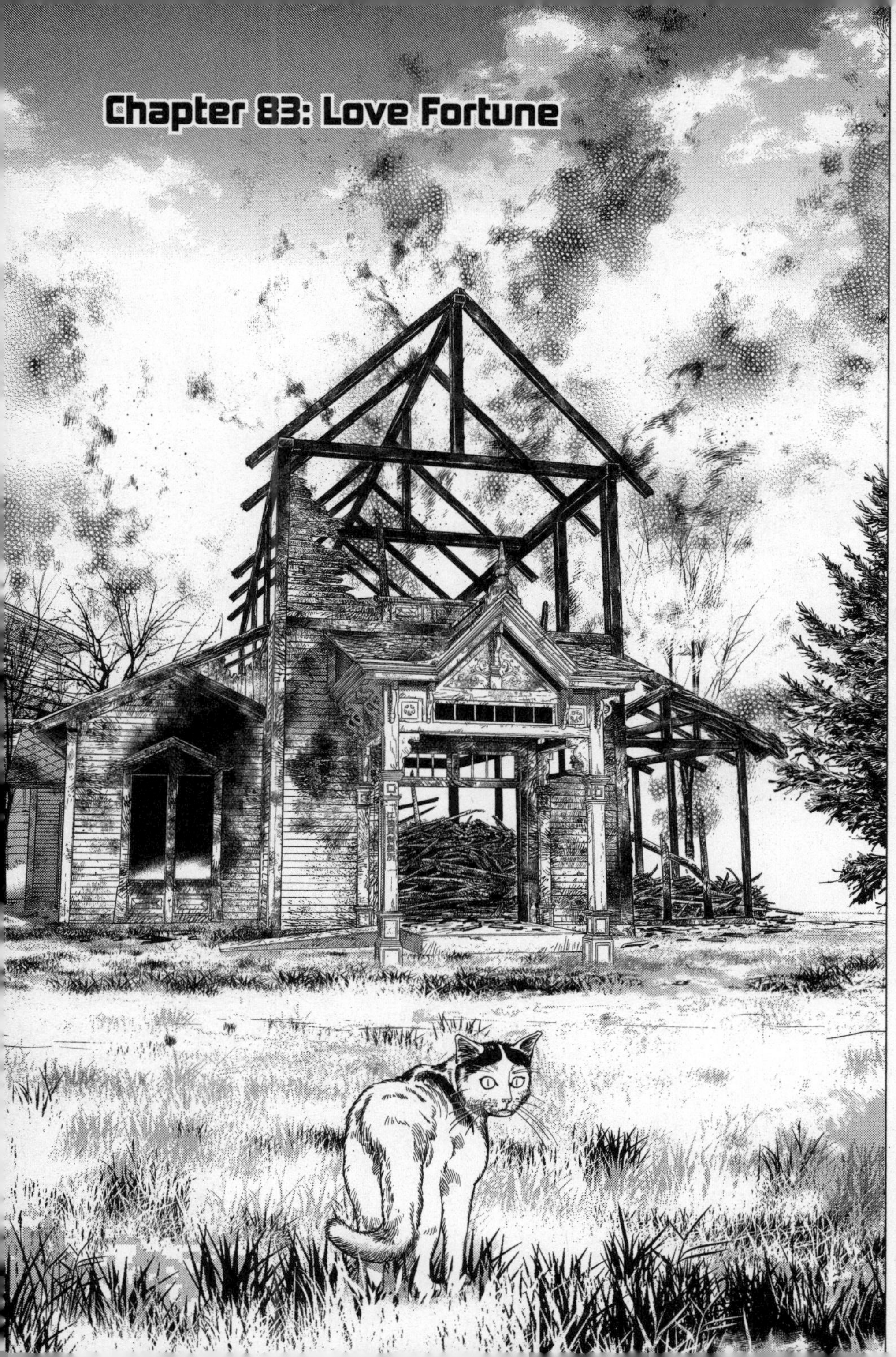
Chapter 83: Love Fortune

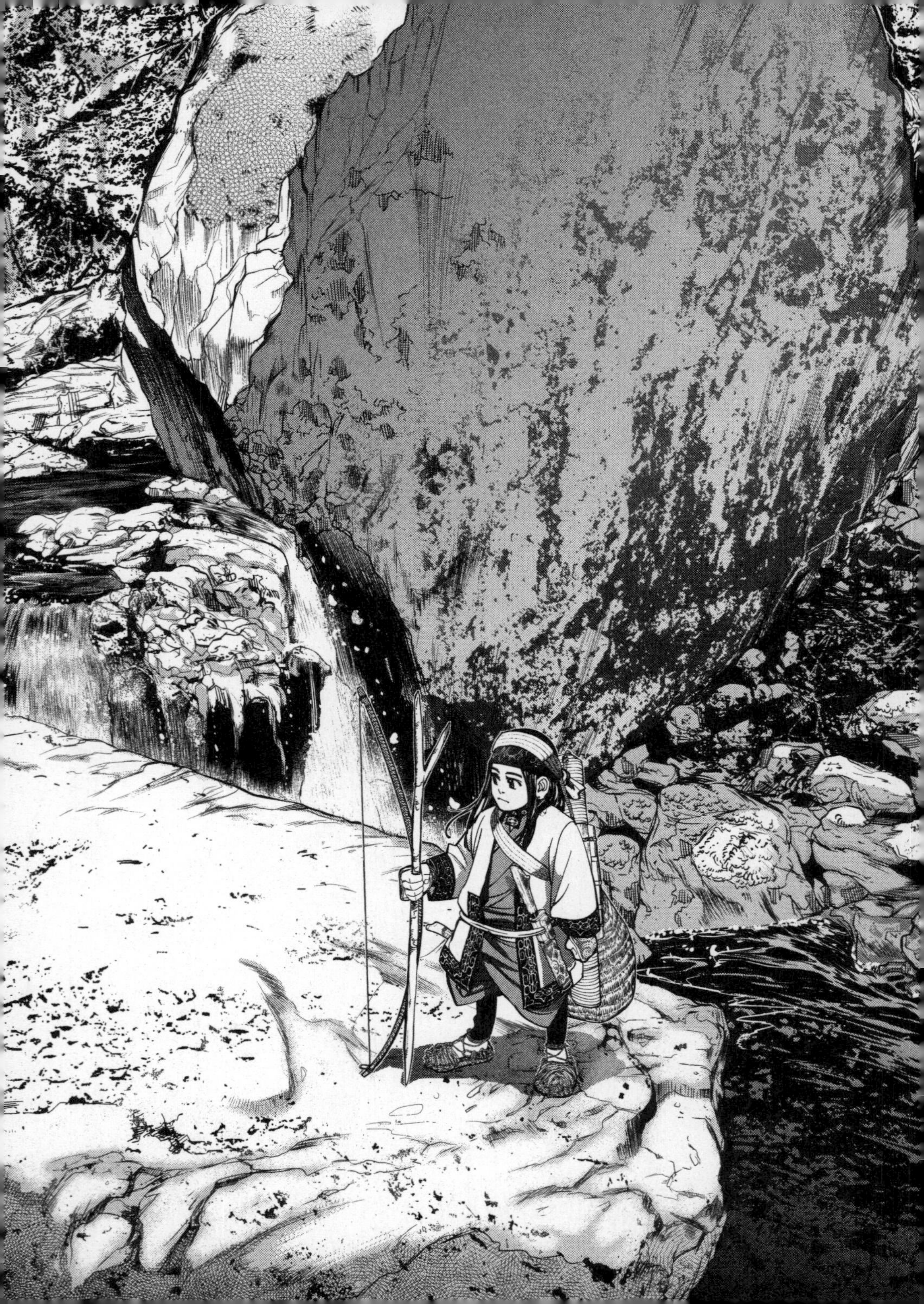

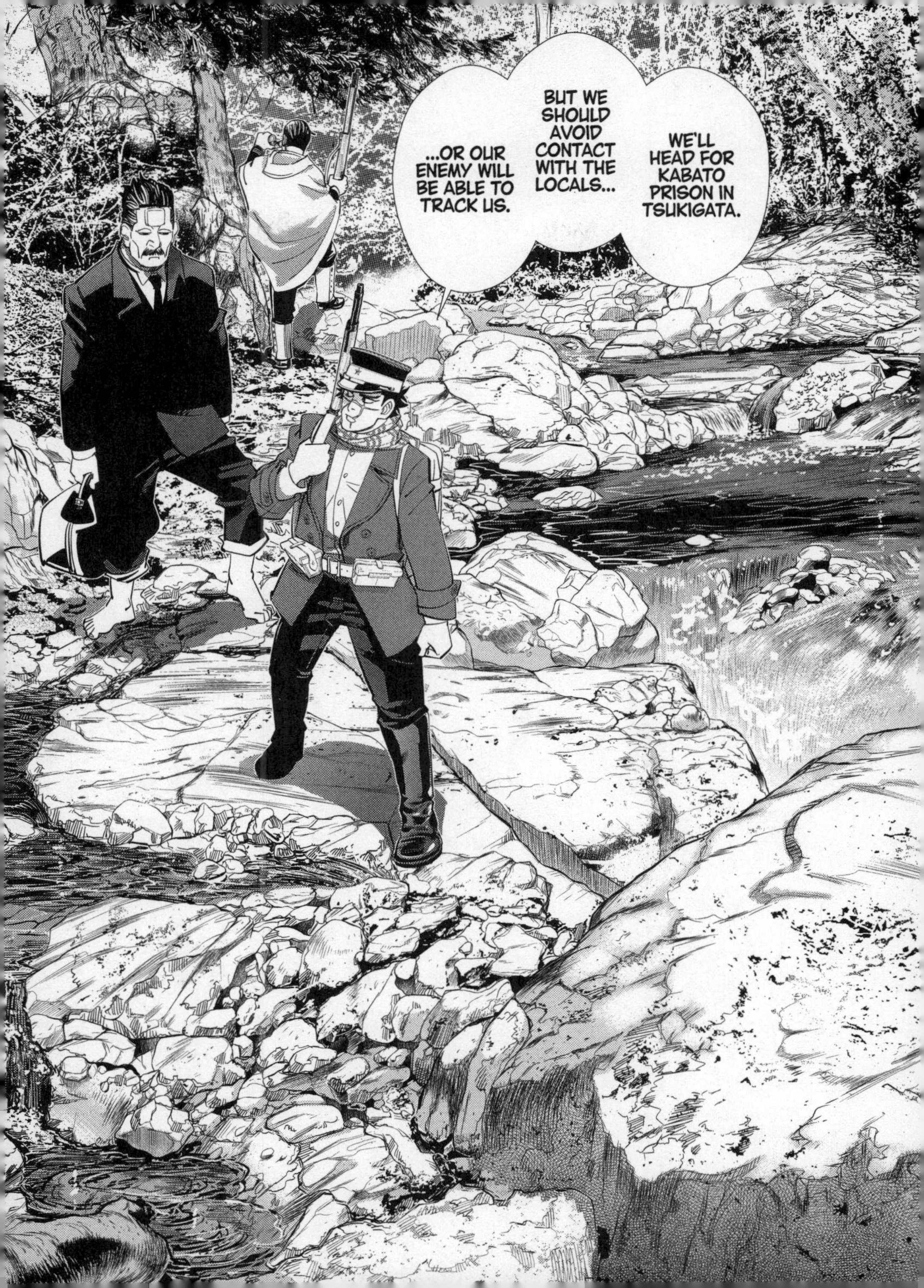
WE'LL HEAD FOR KABATO PRISON IN TSUKIGATA.
BUT WE SHOULD AVOID CONTACT WITH THE LOCALS...
...OR OUR ENEMY WILL BE ABLE TO TRACK US.

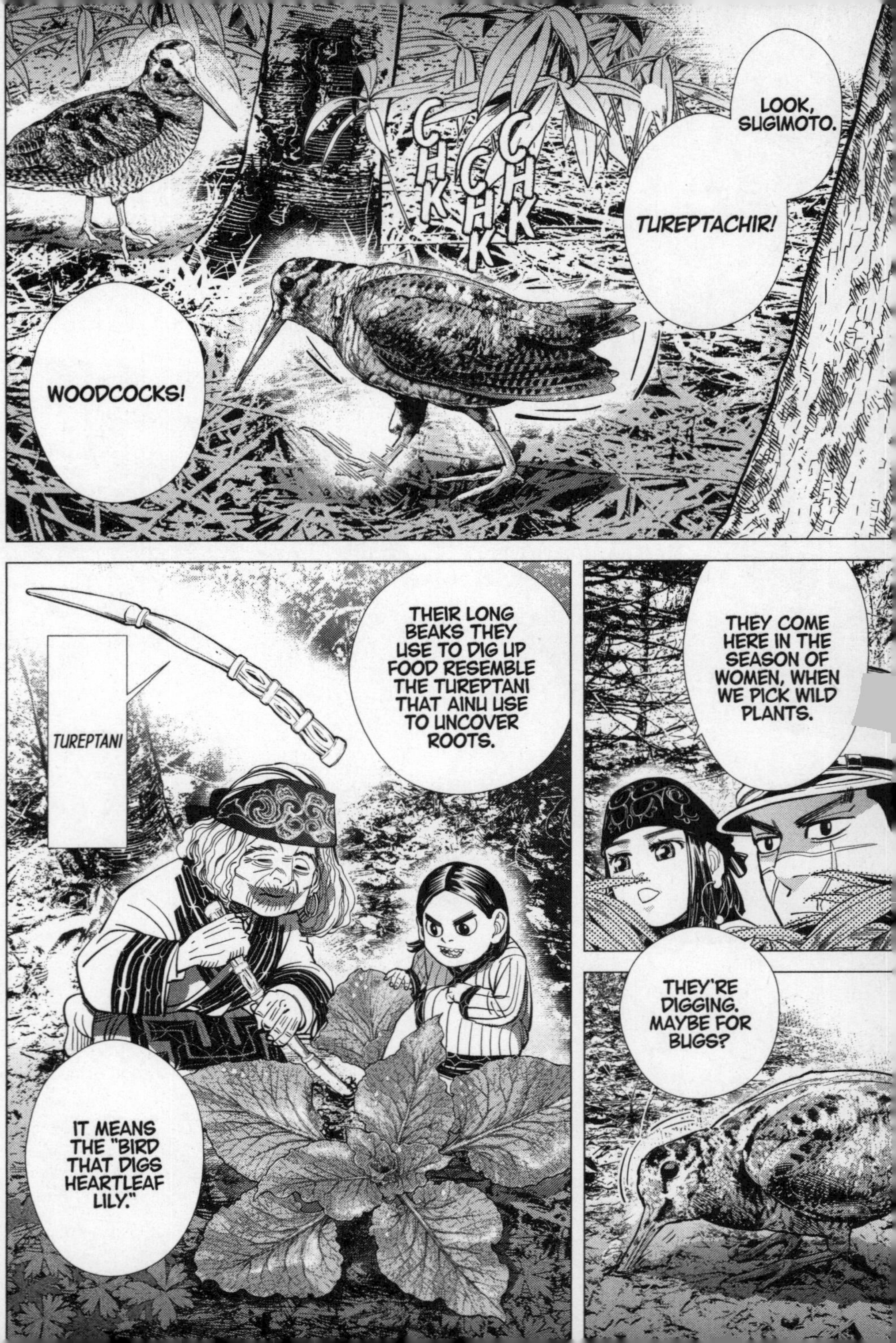
LOOK, SUGIMOTO.
TUREPTACHIR!
CHK CHK CHK
WOODCOCKS!
THEY COME HERE IN THE SEASON OF WOMEN, WHEN WE PICK WILD PLANTS.
THEY'RE DIGGING. MAYBE FOR BUGS?
THEIR LONG BEAKS THEY USE TO DIG UP FOOD RESEMBLE THE TUREPTANI THAT AINU USE TO UNCOVER ROOTS.
TUREPTANI
IT MEANS THE "BIRD THAT DIGS HEARTLEAF LILY."

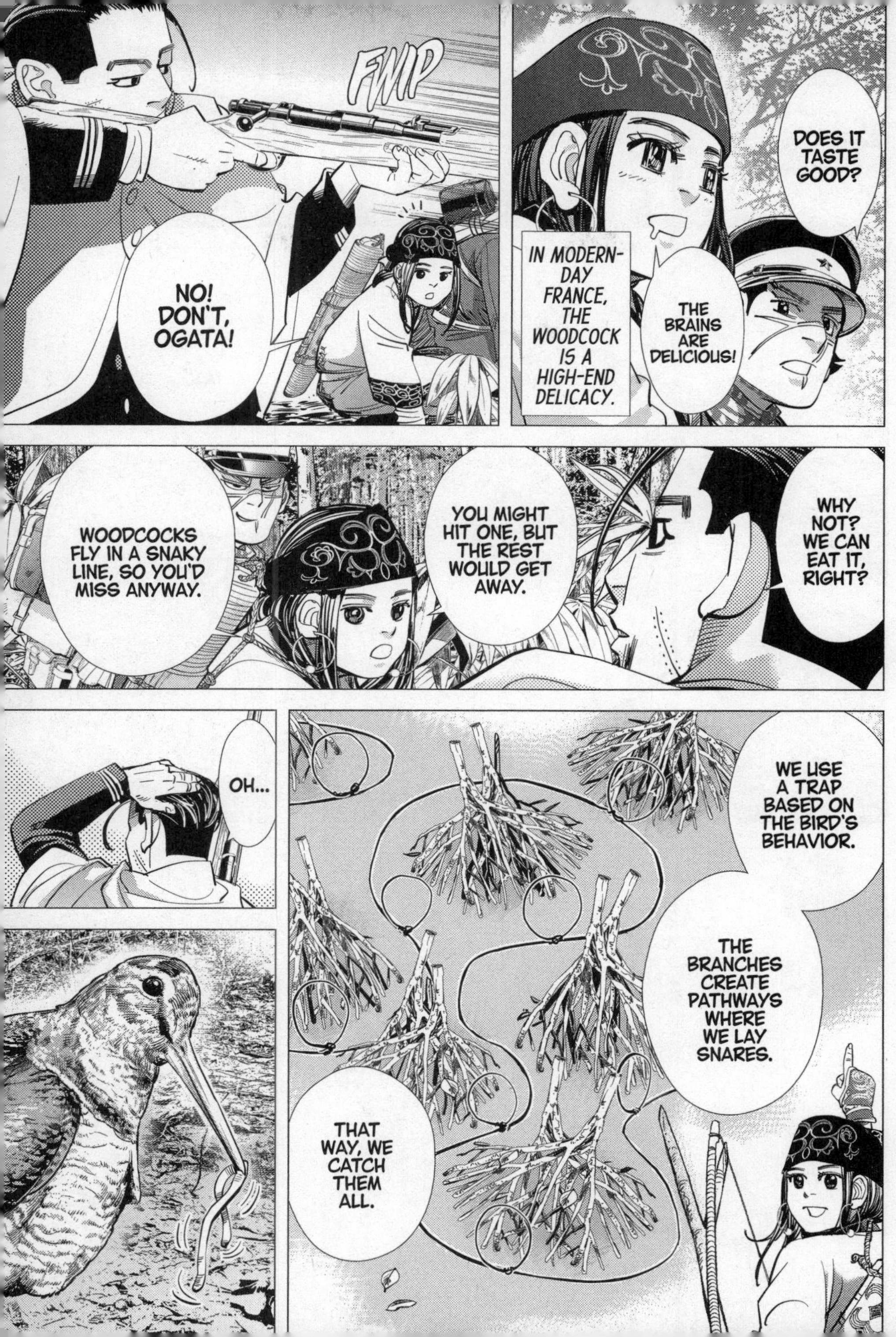
DOES IT TASTE GOOD?
THE BRAINS ARE DELICIOUS!
IN MODERN-DAY FRANCE, THE WOODCOCK IS A HIGH-END DELICACY.
FWIP
NO! DON'T, OGATA!
WHY NOT? WE CAN EAT IT, RIGHT?
YOU MIGHT HIT ONE, BUT THE REST WOULD GET AWAY.
WOODCOCKS FLY IN A SNAKY LINE, SO YOU'D MISS ANYWAY.
WE USE A TRAP BASED ON THE BIRD'S BEHAVIOR.
THE BRANCHES CREATE PATHWAYS WHERE WE LAY SNARES.
THAT WAY, WE CATCH THEM ALL.
OH...

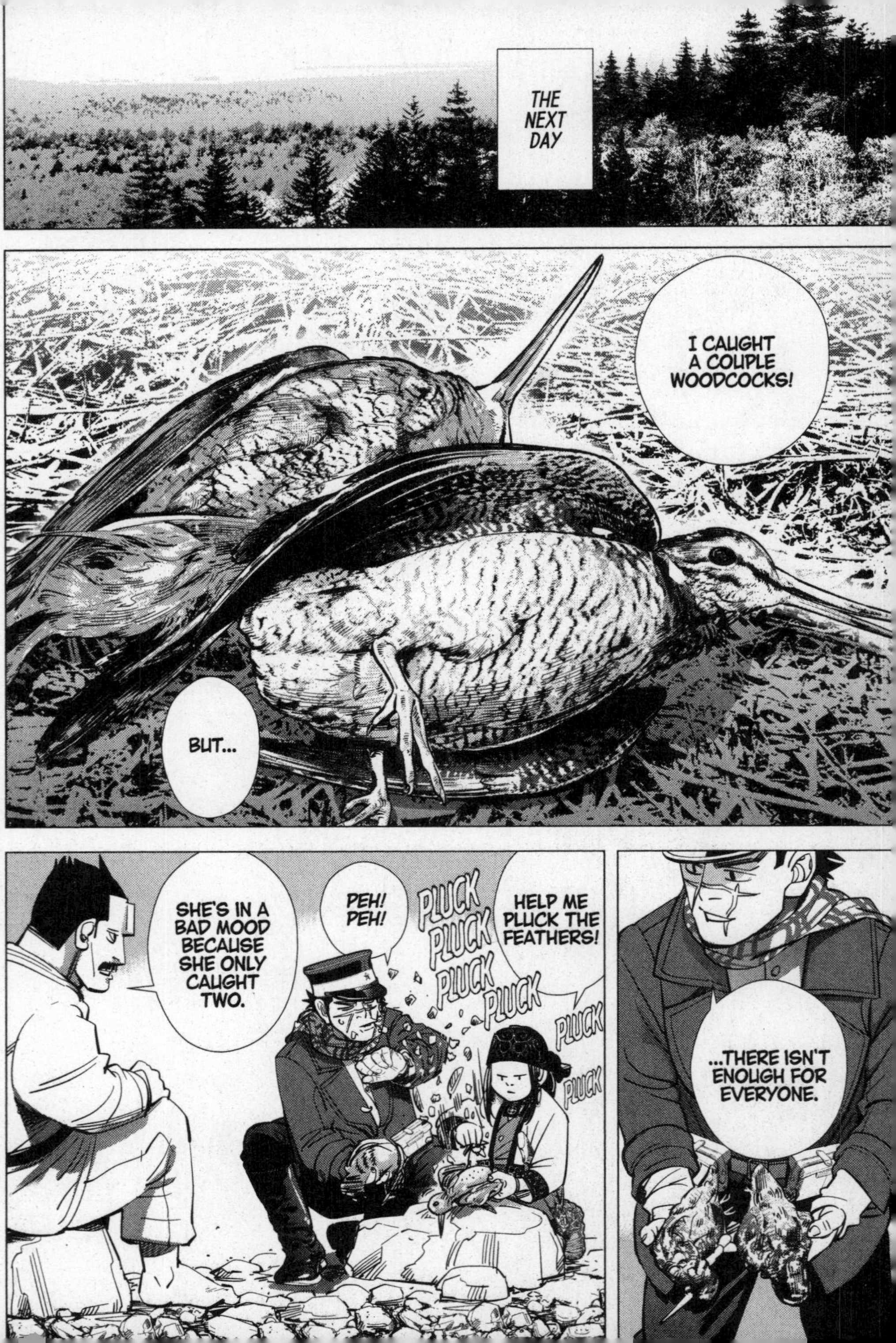
THE NEXT DAY
I CAUGHT A COUPLE WOODCOCKS!
BUT...
...THERE ISN'T ENOUGH FOR EVERYONE.
HELP ME PLUCK THE FEATHERS!
PLUCK PLUCK PLUCK PLUCK PLUCK PLUCK
PEH! PEH!
SHE'S IN A BAD MOOD BECAUSE SHE ONLY CAUGHT TWO.

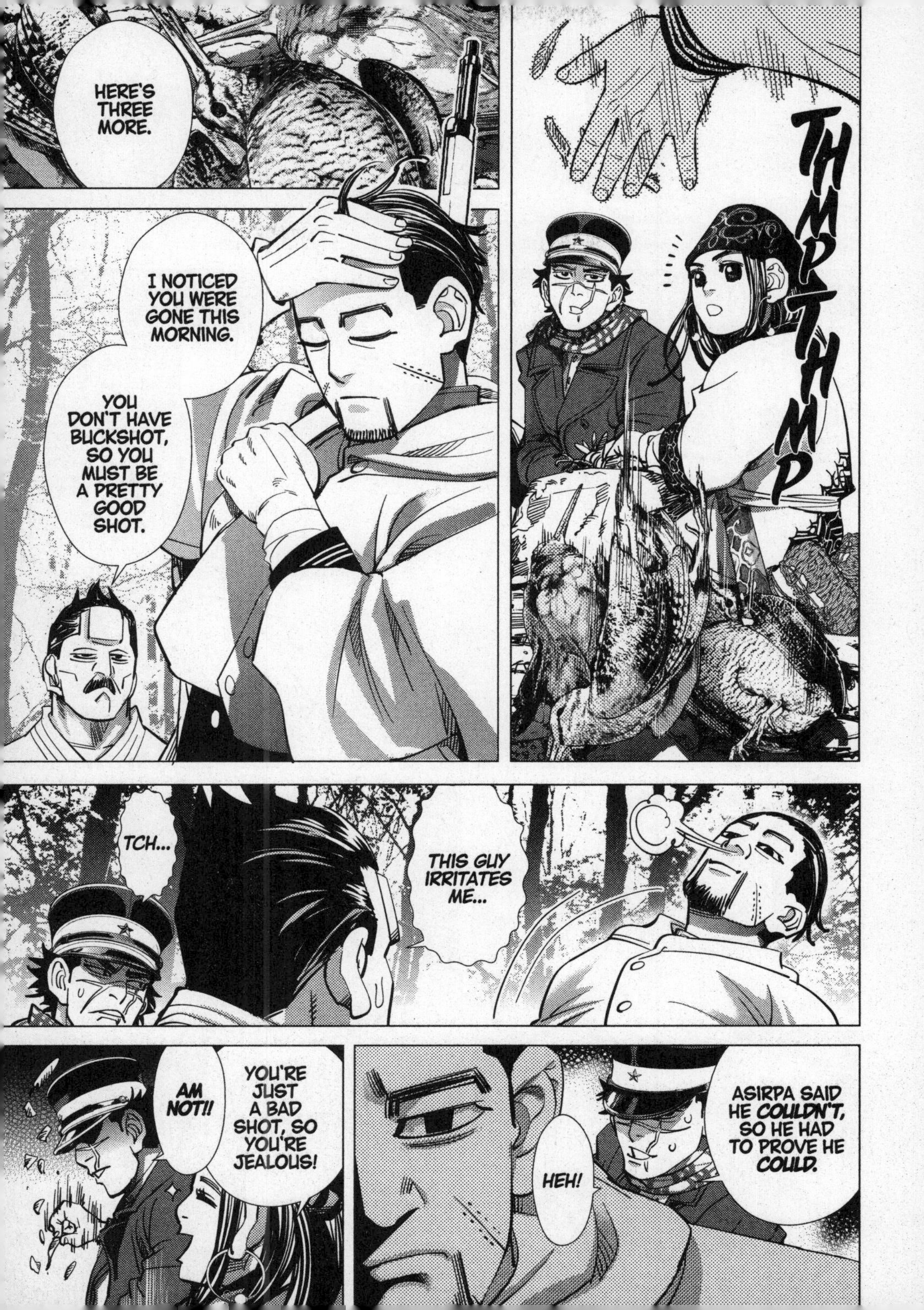
THMP THMP THMP
HERE'S THREE MORE.
I NOTICED YOU WERE GONE THIS MORNING.
YOU DON'T HAVE BUCKSHOT, SO YOU MUST BE A PRETTY GOOD SHOT.
THIS GUY IRRITATES ME...
TCH...
ASIRPA SAID HE *COULDN'T*, SO HE HAD TO PROVE HE *COULD*.
HEH!
YOU'RE JUST A BAD SHOT, SO YOU'RE JEALOUS!
AM NOT!!

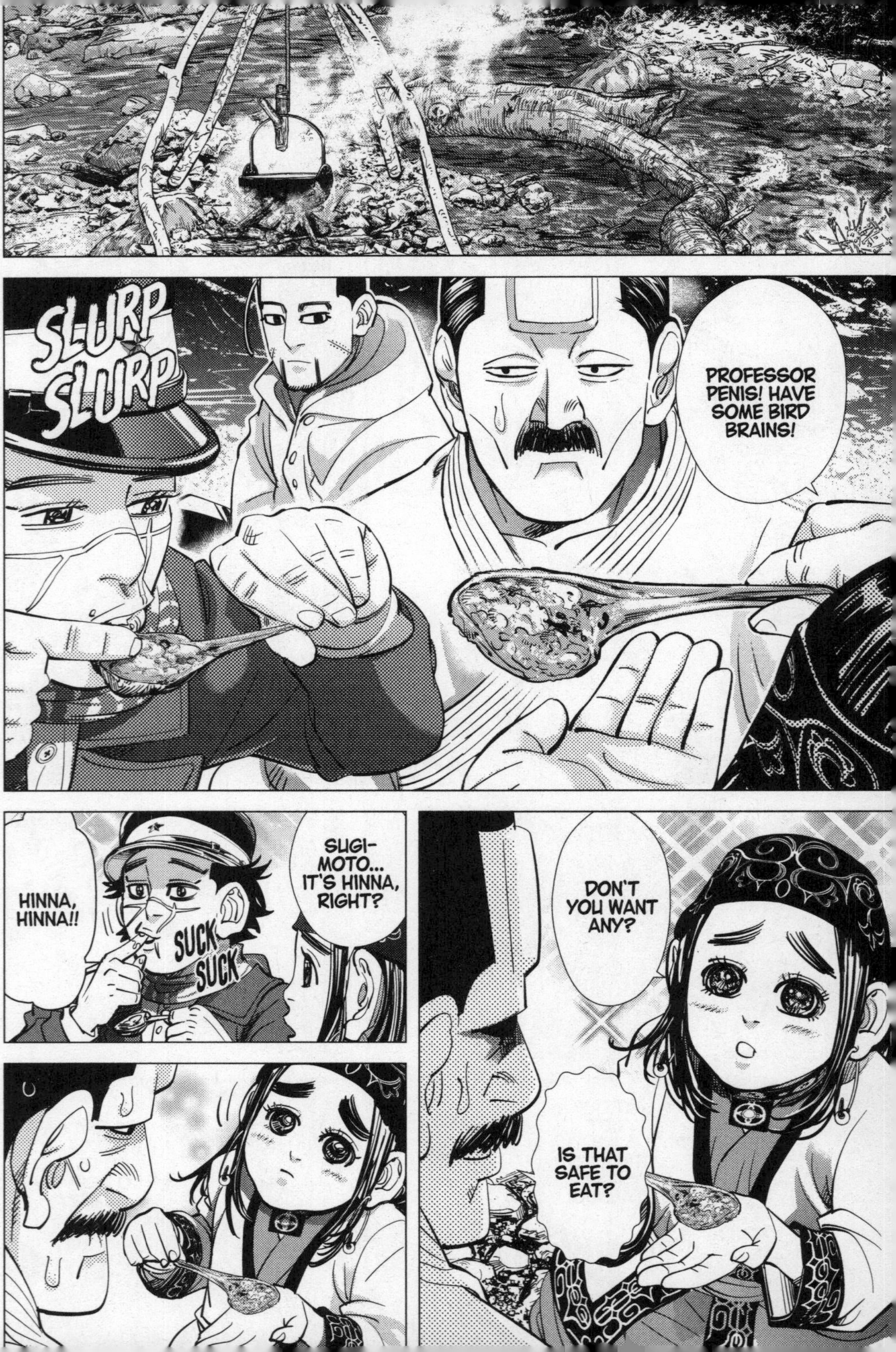
PROFESSOR PENIS! HAVE SOME BIRD BRAINS!
SLURP SLURP
DON'T YOU WANT ANY?
IS THAT SAFE TO EAT?
SUGI-MOTO... IT'S HINNA, RIGHT?
HINNA, HINNA!!
SUCK SUCK

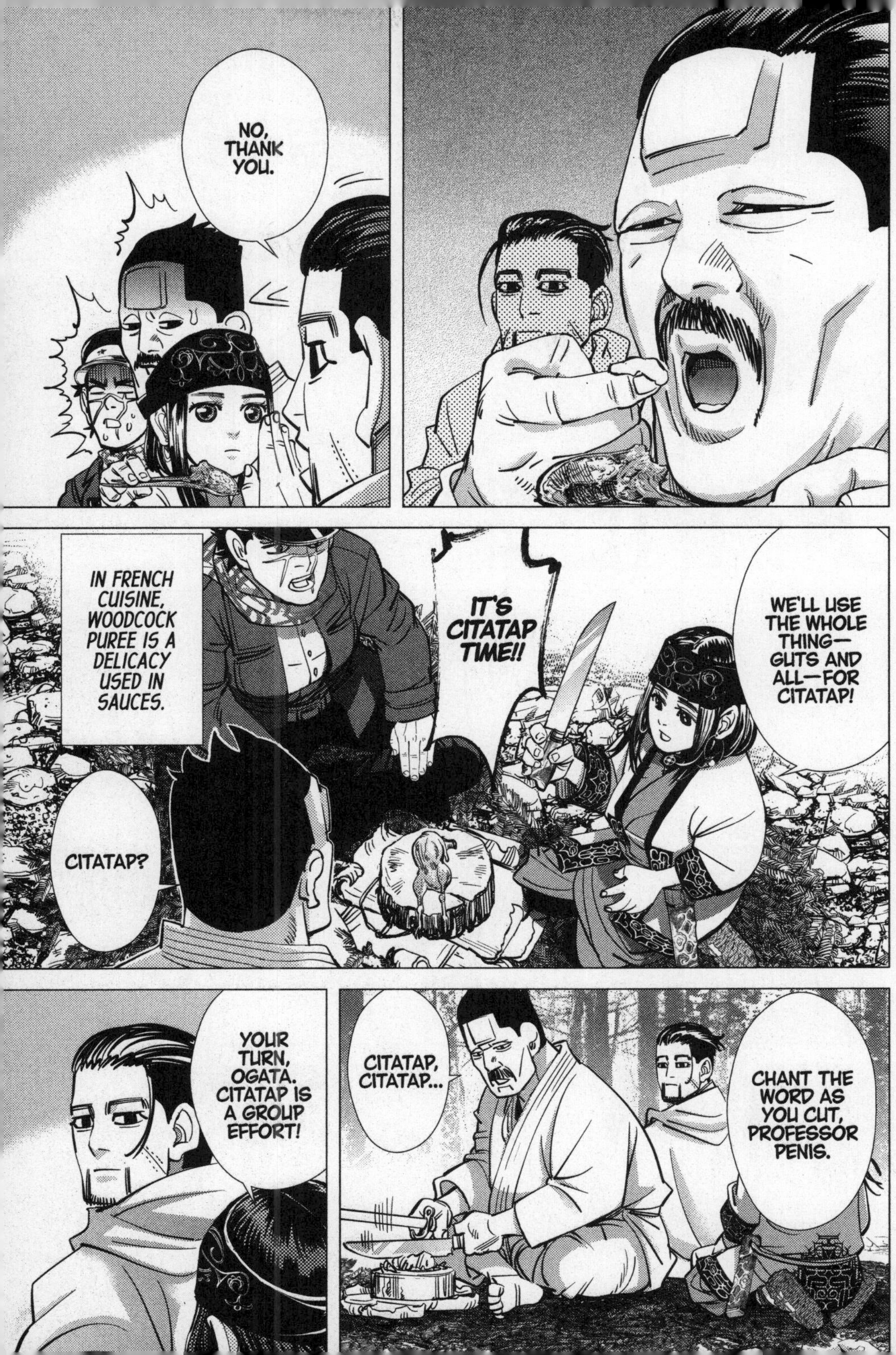
NO, THANK YOU.
WE'LL USE THE WHOLE THING— GUTS AND ALL—FOR CITATAP!
IT'S CITATAP TIME!!
IN FRENCH CUISINE, WOODCOCK PUREE IS A DELICACY USED IN SAUCES.
CITATAP?
CHANT THE WORD AS YOU CUT, PROFESSOR PENIS.
CITATAP, CITATAP...
YOUR TURN, OGATA. CITATAP IS A GROUP EFFORT!

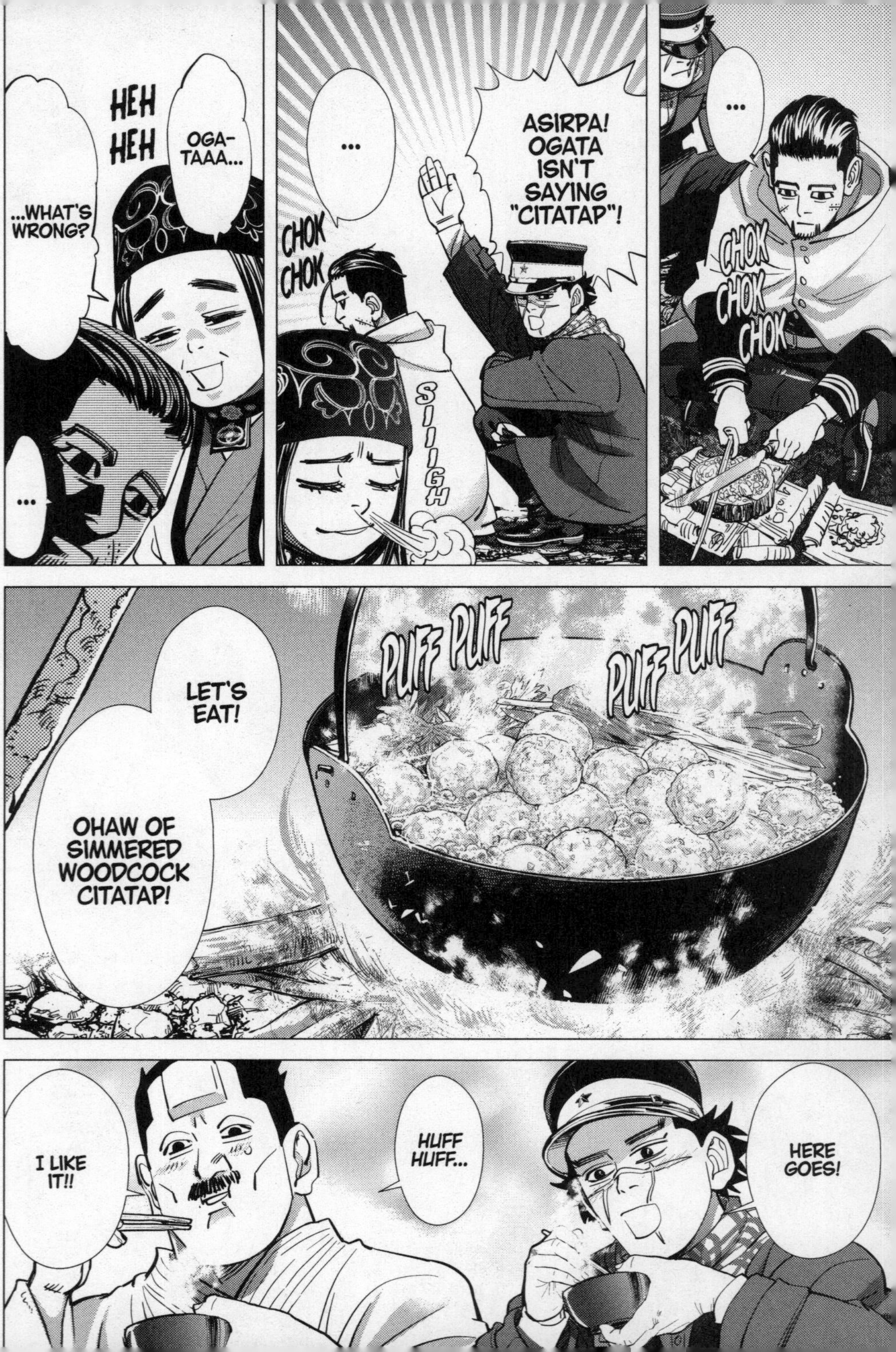
...
CHOK
CHOK
CHOK
ASIRPA! OGATA ISN'T SAYING "CITATAP"!
...
CHOK CHOK
SIIIGH
OGA-TAAA...
HEH HEH
...WHAT'S WRONG?
...
PUFF PUFF
PUFF PUFF
LET'S EAT!
OHAW OF SIMMERED WOODCOCK CITATAP!
HERE GOES!
HUFF HUFF...
I LIKE IT!!

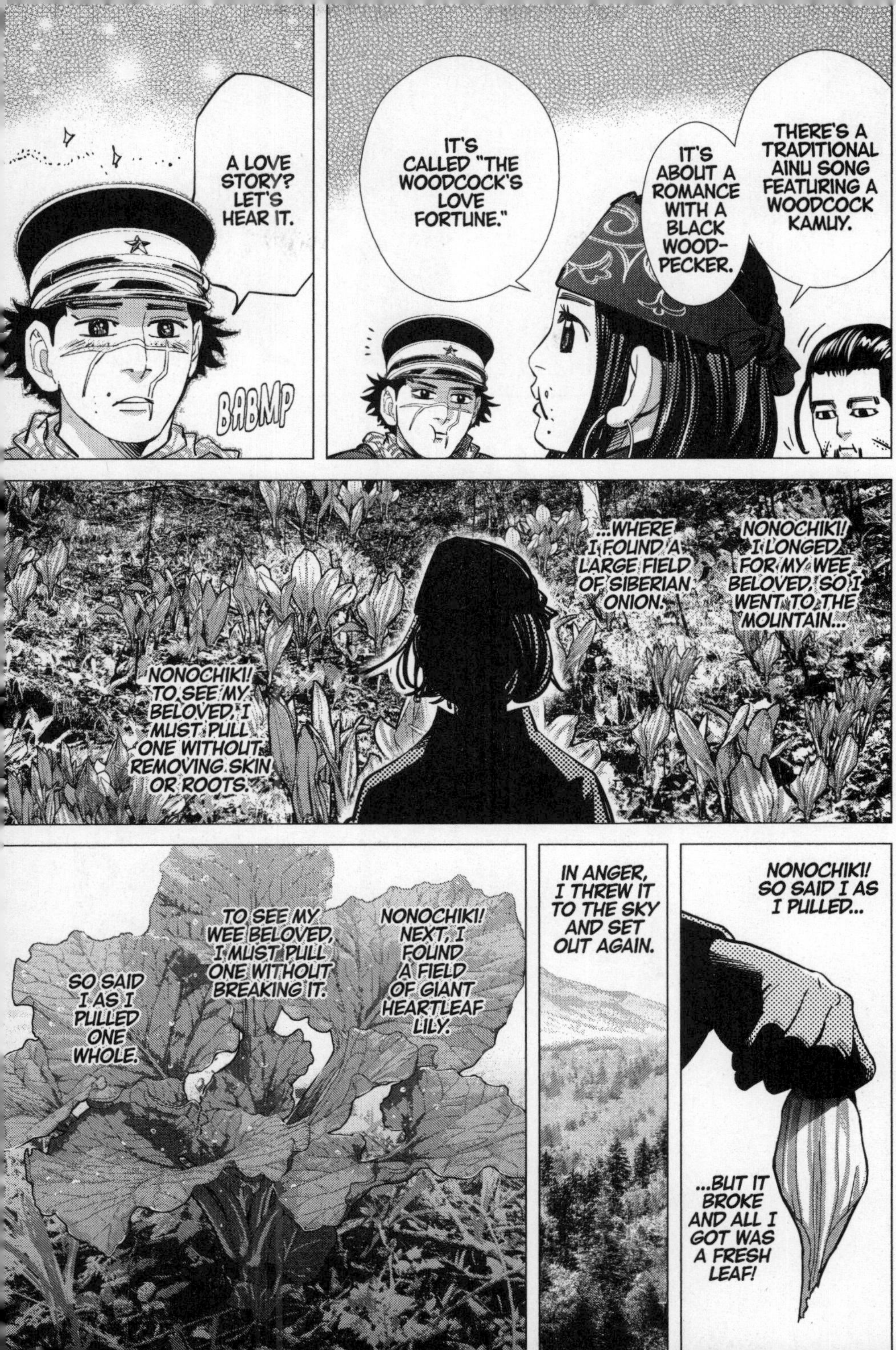
THERE'S A TRADITIONAL AINU SONG FEATURING A WOODCOCK KAMUY.
IT'S ABOUT A ROMANCE WITH A BLACK WOOD-PECKER.
IT'S CALLED "THE WOODCOCK'S LOVE FORTUNE."
A LOVE STORY? LET'S HEAR IT.
BABMP
NONOCHIKI! I LONGED FOR MY WEE BELOVED, SO I WENT TO THE MOUNTAIN...
...WHERE I FOUND A LARGE FIELD OF SIBERIAN ONION.
NONOCHIKI! TO SEE MY BELOVED, I MUST PULL ONE WITHOUT REMOVING SKIN OR ROOTS.
NONOCHIKI! SO SAID I AS I PULLED...
...BUT IT BROKE AND ALL I GOT WAS A FRESH LEAF!
IN ANGER, I THREW IT TO THE SKY AND SET OUT AGAIN.
NONOCHIKI! NEXT, I FOUND A FIELD OF GIANT HEARTLEAF LILY.
TO SEE MY WEE BELOVED, I MUST PULL ONE WITHOUT BREAKING IT.
SO SAID I AS I PULLED ONE WHOLE.

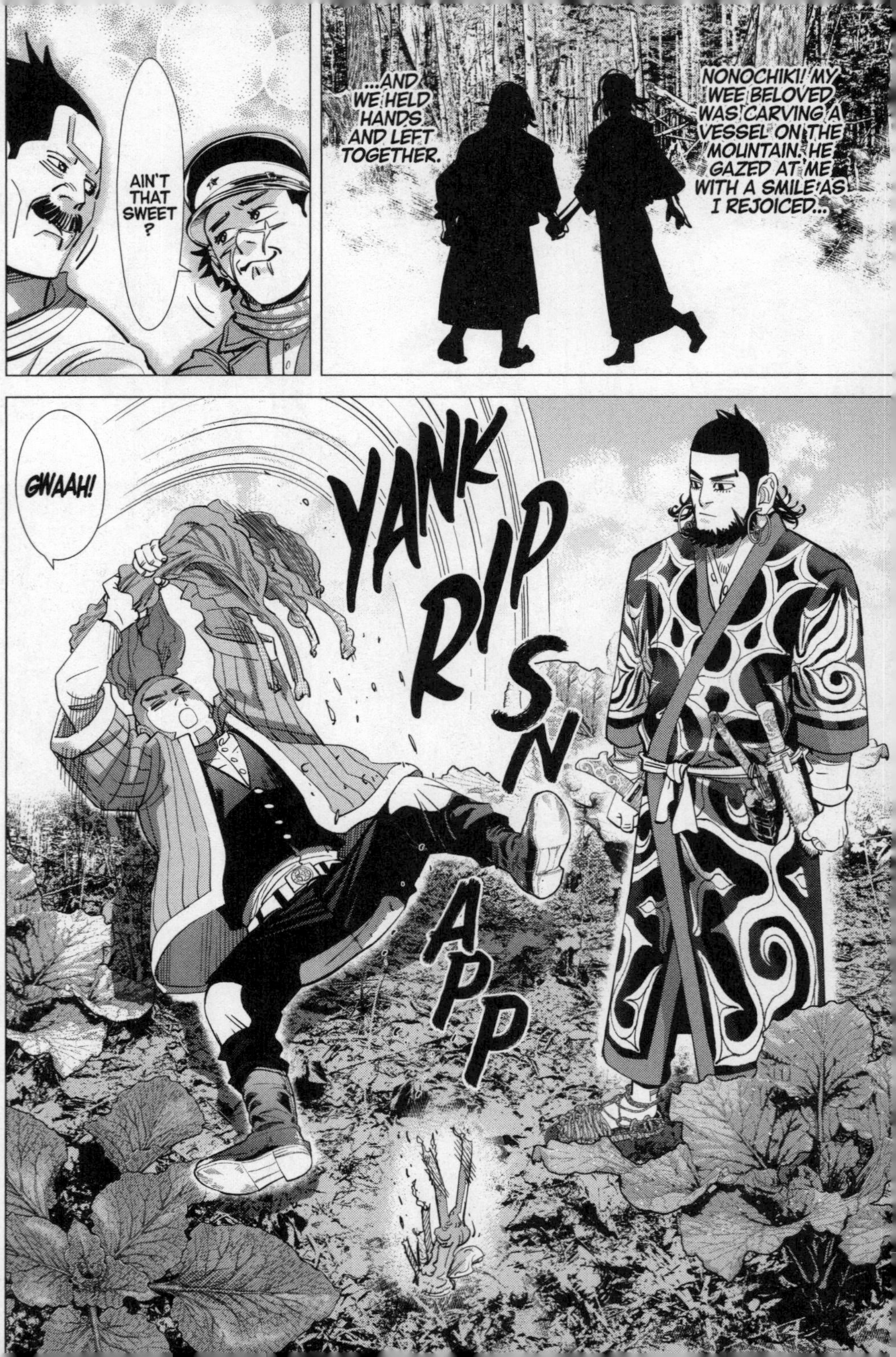
NONOCHIKI! MY WEE BELOVED WAS CARVING A VESSEL ON THE MOUNTAIN. HE GAZED AT ME WITH A SMILE AS I REJOICED...
...AND WE HELD HANDS AND LEFT TOGETHER.
AIN'T THAT SWEET?
YANK
RIP
SNAPP
GWAAH!

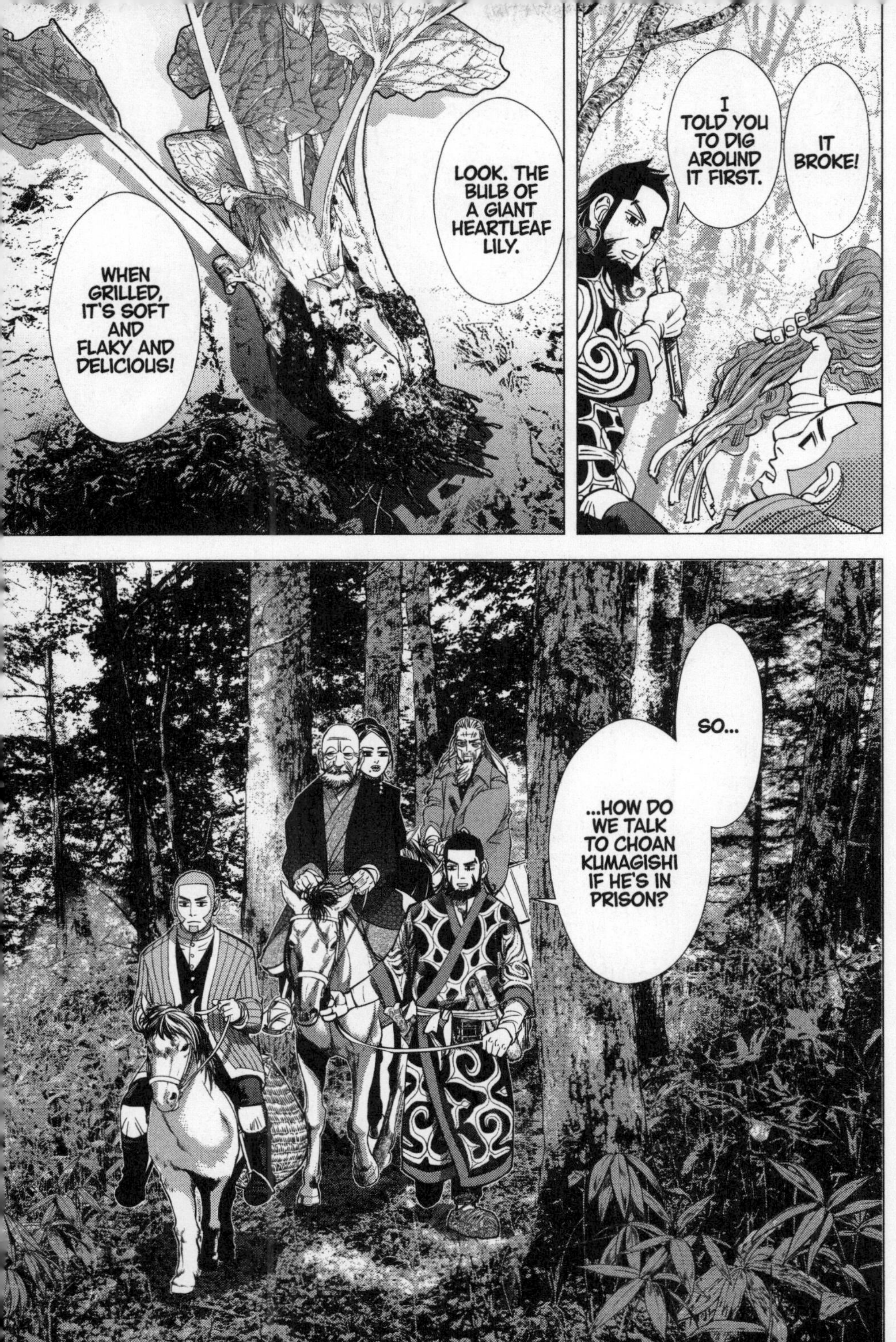
IT BROKE!
I TOLD YOU TO DIG AROUND IT FIRST.
LOOK. THE BULB OF A GIANT HEARTLEAF LILY.
WHEN GRILLED, IT'S SOFT AND FLAKY AND DELICIOUS!
SO...
...HOW DO WE TALK TO CHOAN KUMAGISHI IF HE'S IN PRISON?

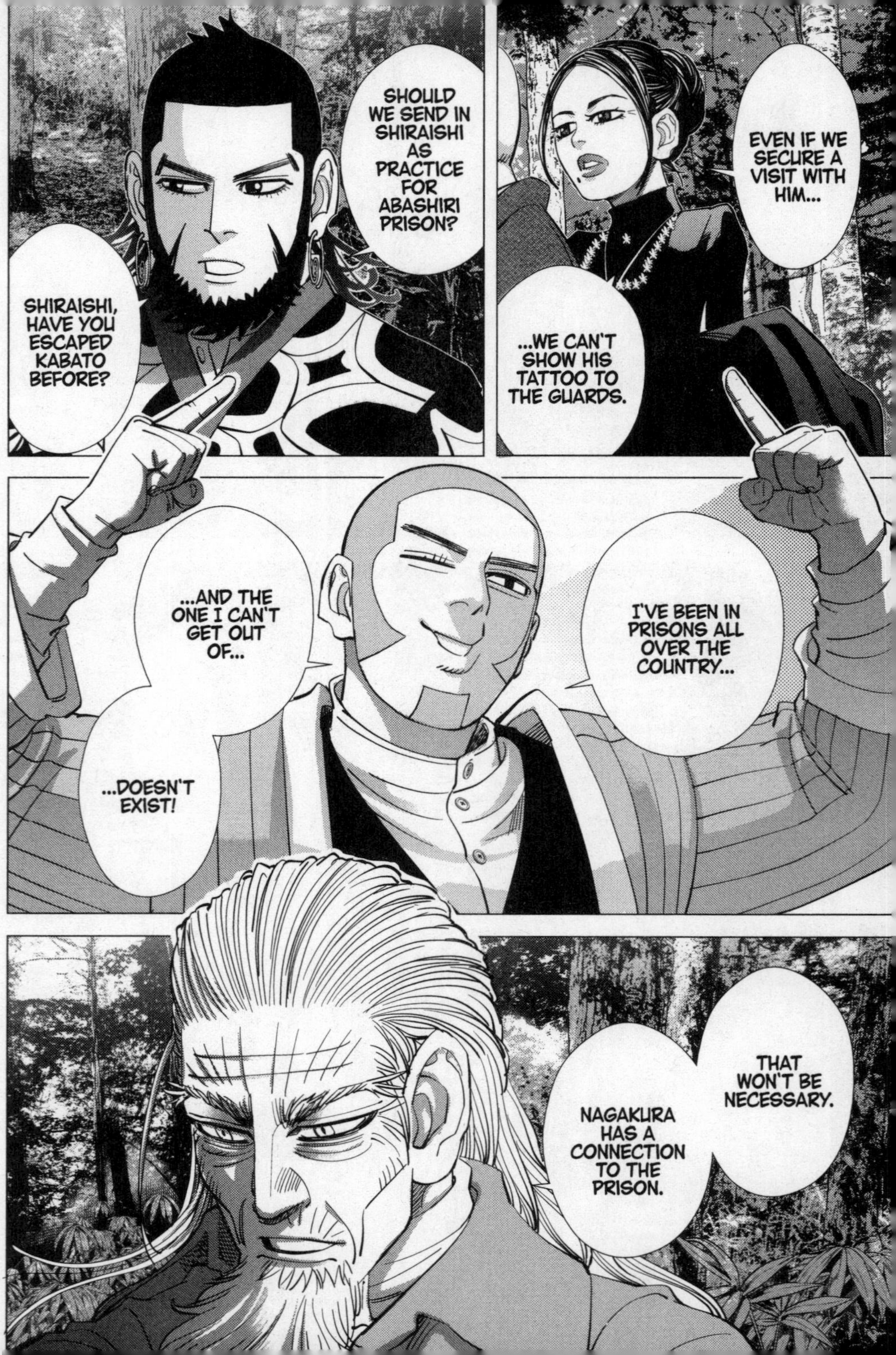
EVEN IF WE SECURE A VISIT WITH HIM...
...WE CAN'T SHOW HIS TATTOO TO THE GUARDS.
SHOULD WE SEND IN SHIRAISHI AS PRACTICE FOR ABASHIRI PRISON?
SHIRAISHI, HAVE YOU ESCAPED KABATO BEFORE?
I'VE BEEN IN PRISONS ALL OVER THE COUNTRY...
...AND THE ONE I CAN'T GET OUT OF...
...DOESN'T EXIST!
THAT WON'T BE NECESSARY.
NAGAKURA HAS A CONNECTION TO THE PRISON.

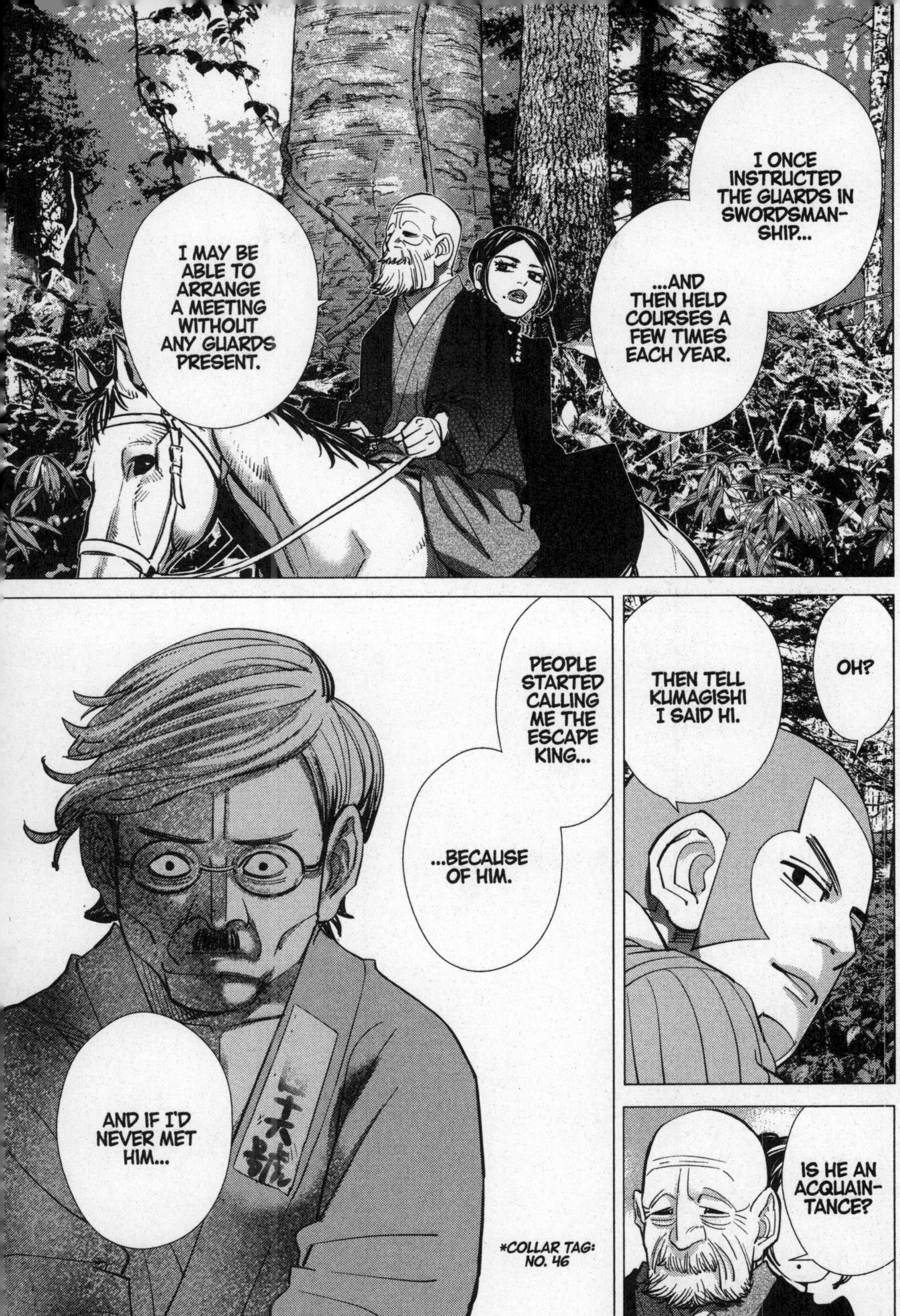
I ONCE INSTRUCTED THE GUARDS IN SWORDSMAN-SHIP...
...AND THEN HELD COURSES A FEW TIMES EACH YEAR.
I MAY BE ABLE TO ARRANGE A MEETING WITHOUT ANY GUARDS PRESENT.
OH?
THEN TELL KUMAGISHI I SAID HI.
IS HE AN ACQUAIN-TANCE?
PEOPLE STARTED CALLING ME THE ESCAPE KING...
...BECAUSE OF HIM.
AND IF I'D NEVER MET HIM...
*COLLAR TAG: NO. 46

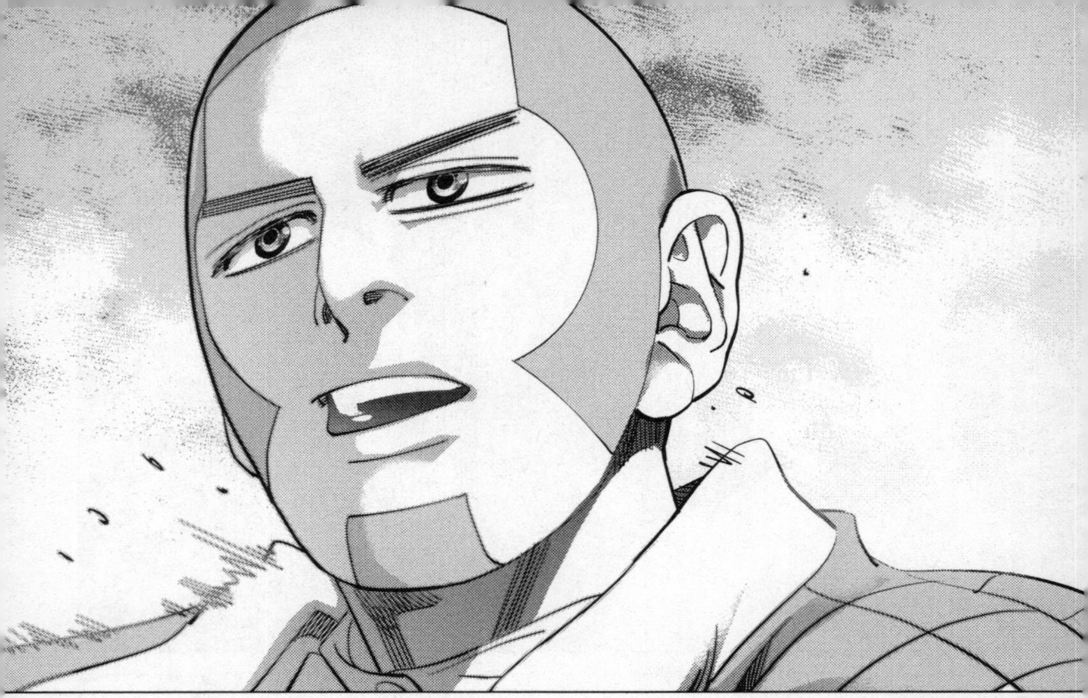
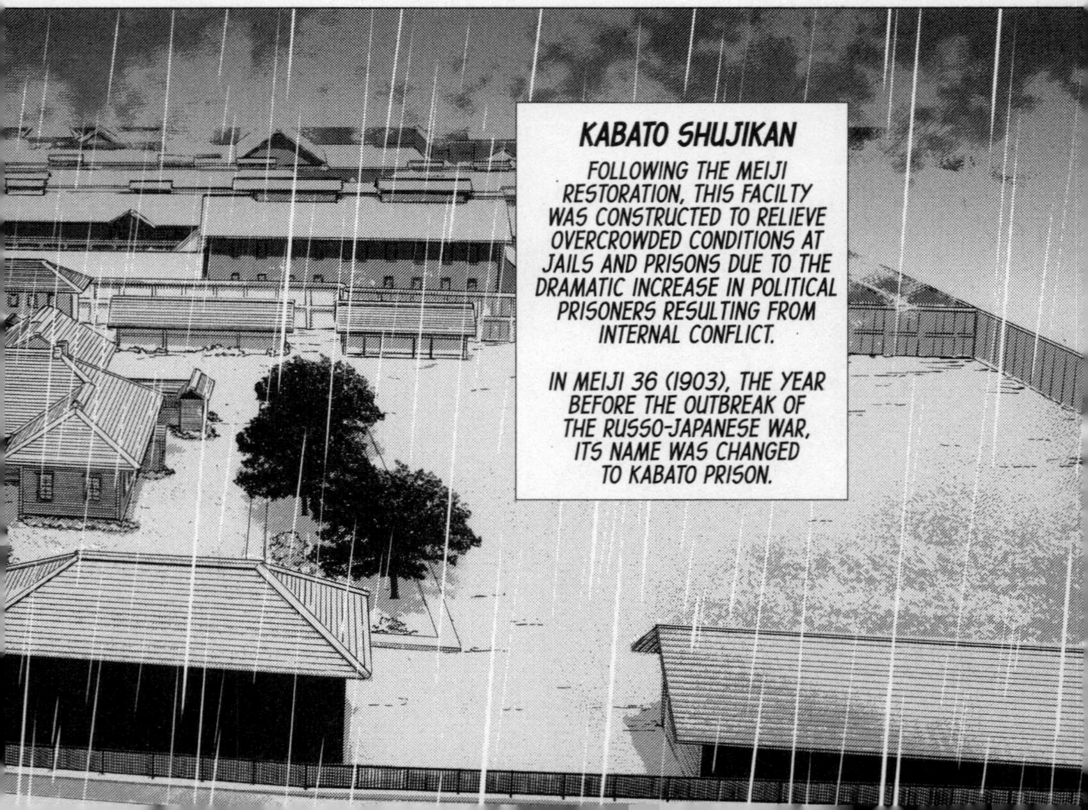
KABATO SHUJIKAN
FOLLOWING THE MEIJI RESTORATION, THIS FACILTY WAS CONSTRUCTED TO RELIEVE OVERCROWDED CONDITIONS AT JAILS AND PRISONS DUE TO THE DRAMATIC INCREASE IN POLITICAL PRISONERS RESULTING FROM INTERNAL CONFLICT.
IN MEIJI 36 (1903), THE YEAR BEFORE THE OUTBREAK OF THE RUSSO-JAPANESE WAR, ITS NAME WAS CHANGED TO KABATO PRISON.

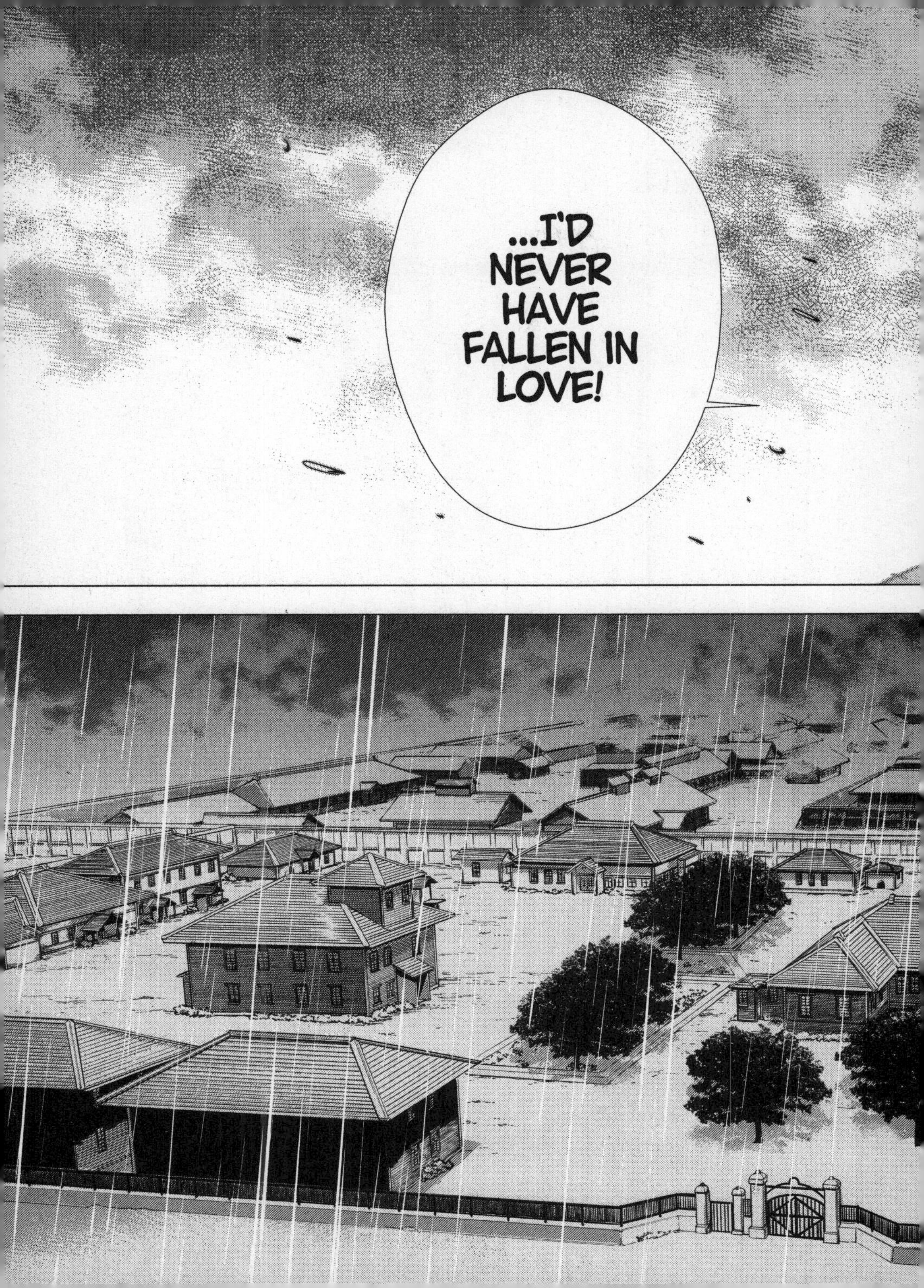
...I'D NEVER HAVE FALLEN IN LOVE!

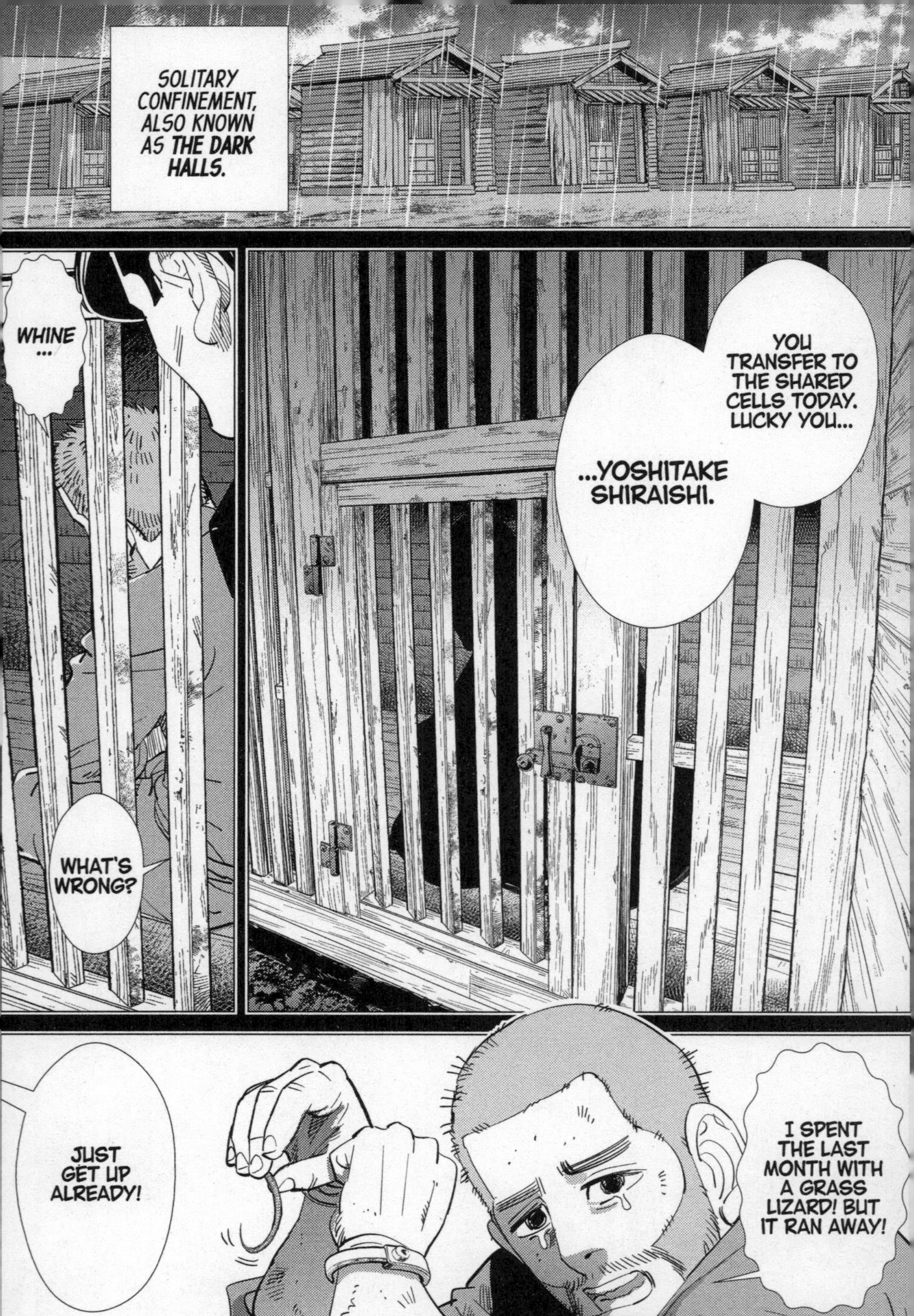

SOLITARY CONFINEMENT, ALSO KNOWN AS THE DARK HALLS.
YOU TRANSFER TO THE SHARED CELLS TODAY. LUCKY YOU...
...YOSHITAKE SHIRAISHI.
WHINE ...
WHAT'S WRONG?
I SPENT THE LAST MONTH WITH A GRASS LIZARD! BUT IT RAN AWAY!
JUST GET UP ALREADY!

Chapter 84: Imprisoned

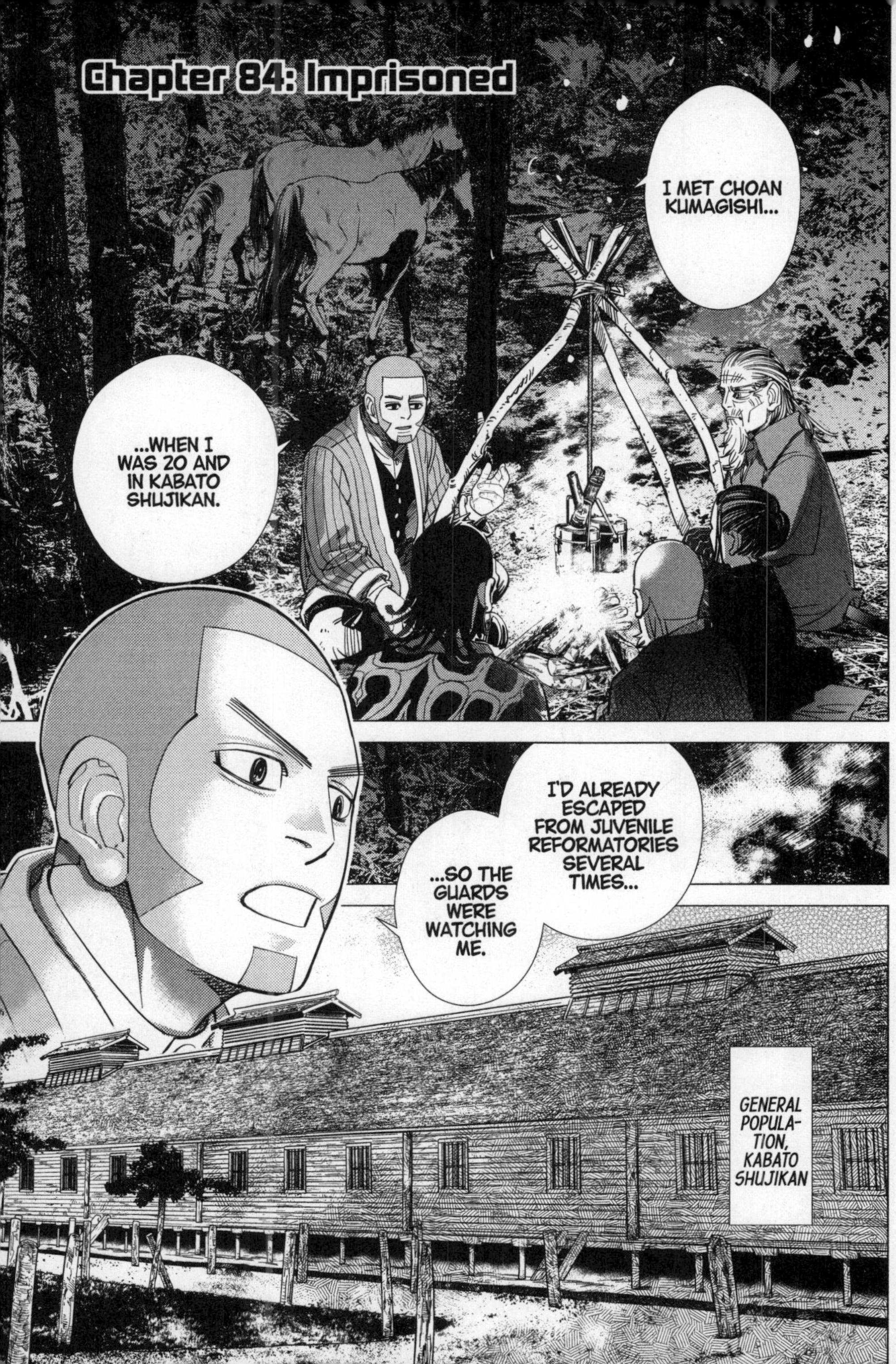
I MET CHOAN KUMAGISHI...
...WHEN I WAS 20 AND IN KABATO SHUJIKAN.
I'D ALREADY ESCAPED FROM JUVENILE REFORMATORIES SEVERAL TIMES...
...SO THE GUARDS WERE WATCHING ME.
GENERAL POPULA-TION, KABATO SHUJIKAN

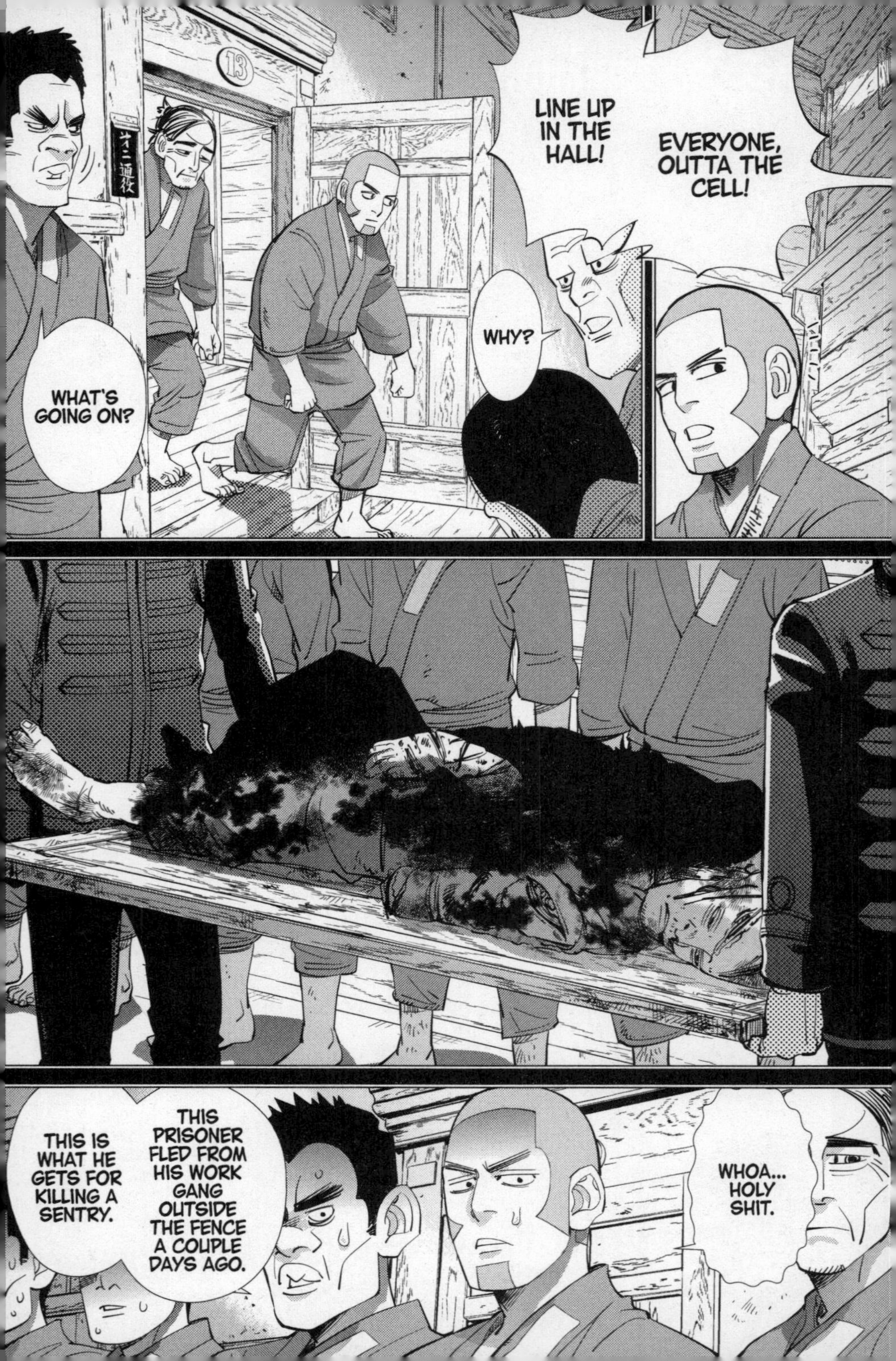
EVERYONE, OUTTA THE CELL!
LINE UP IN THE HALL!
WHY?
WHAT'S GOING ON?
WHOA... HOLY SHIT.
THIS PRISONER FLED FROM HIS WORK GANG OUTSIDE THE FENCE A COUPLE DAYS AGO.
THIS IS WHAT HE GETS FOR KILLING A SENTRY.

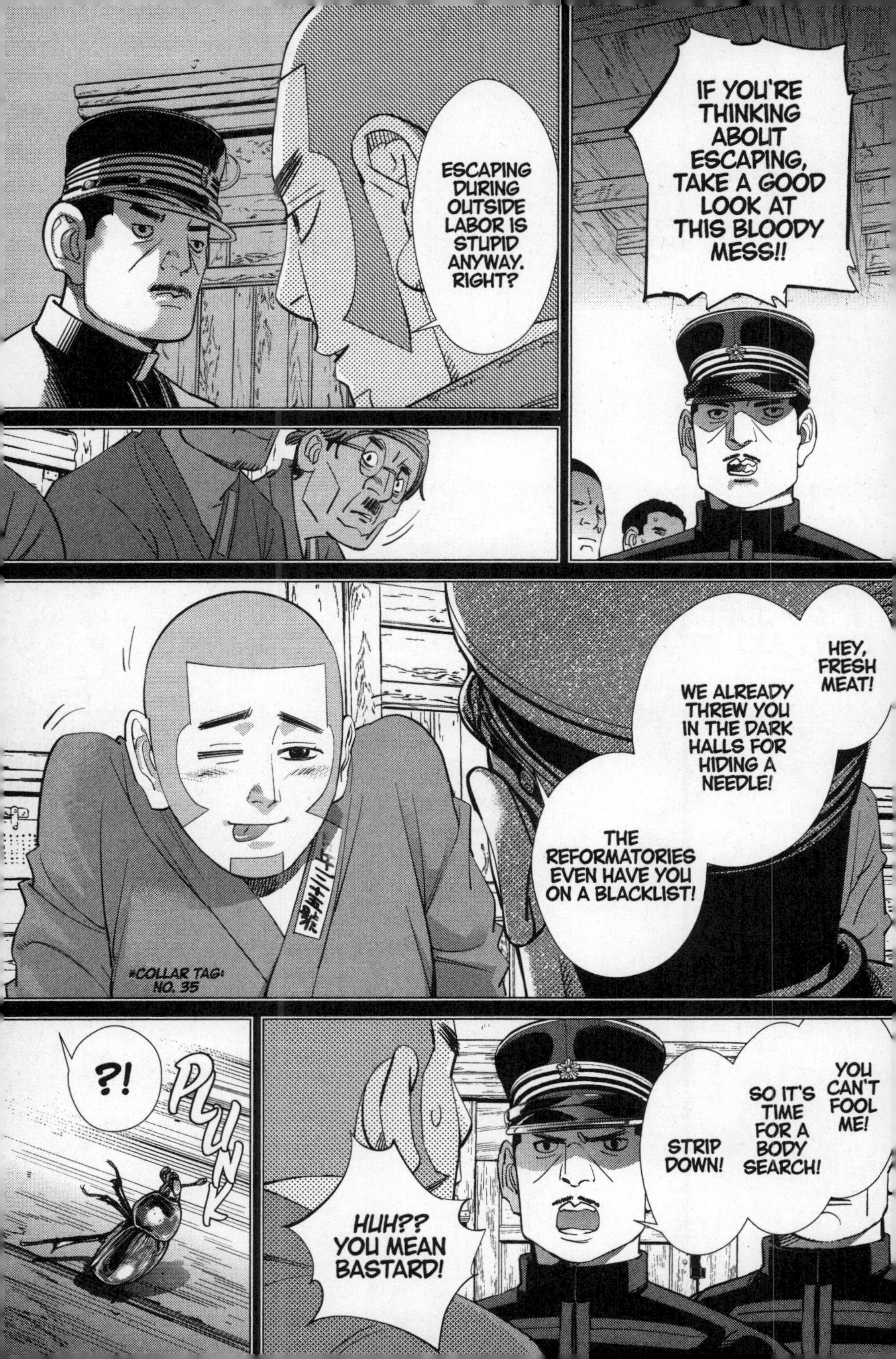
IF YOU'RE THINKING ABOUT ESCAPING, TAKE A GOOD LOOK AT THIS BLOODY MESS!!
ESCAPING DURING OUTSIDE LABOR IS STUPID ANYWAY. RIGHT?
HEY, FRESH MEAT!
WE ALREADY THREW YOU IN THE DARK HALLS FOR HIDING A NEEDLE!
THE REFORMATORIES EVEN HAVE YOU ON A BLACKLIST!
*COLLAR TAG: NO. 35
YOU CAN'T FOOL ME!
SO IT'S TIME FOR A BODY SEARCH!
STRIP DOWN!
HUH?? YOU MEAN BASTARD!
?!
PLUNK

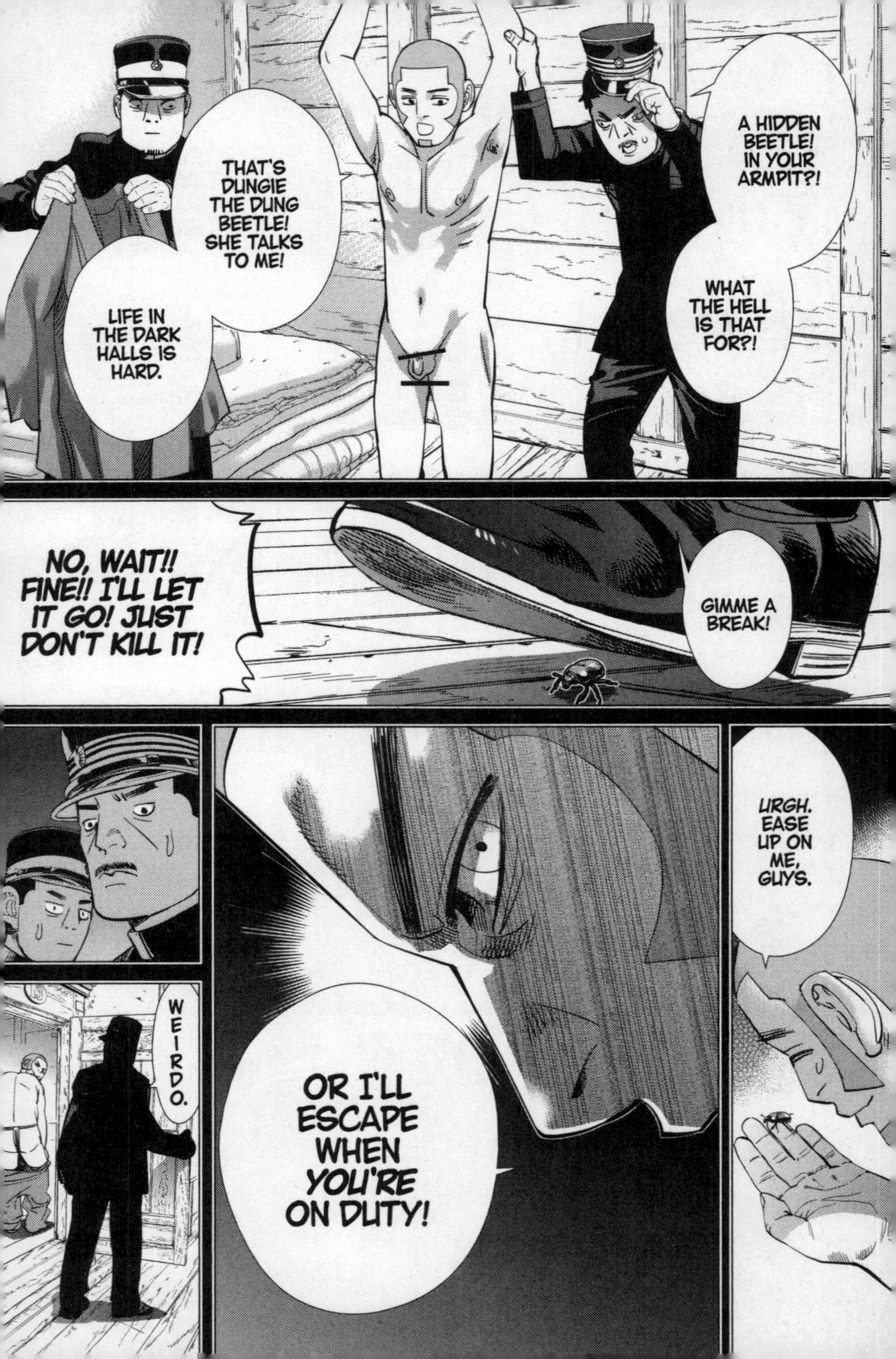
A HIDDEN BEETLE! IN YOUR ARMPIT?!
WHAT THE HELL IS THAT FOR?!
THAT'S DUNGIE THE DUNG BEETLE! SHE TALKS TO ME!
LIFE IN THE DARK HALLS IS HARD.
GIMME A BREAK!
NO, WAIT!! FINE!! I'LL LET IT GO! JUST DON'T KILL IT!
URGH. EASE UP ON ME, GUYS.
OR I'LL ESCAPE WHEN YOU'RE ON DUTY!
WEIRDO.

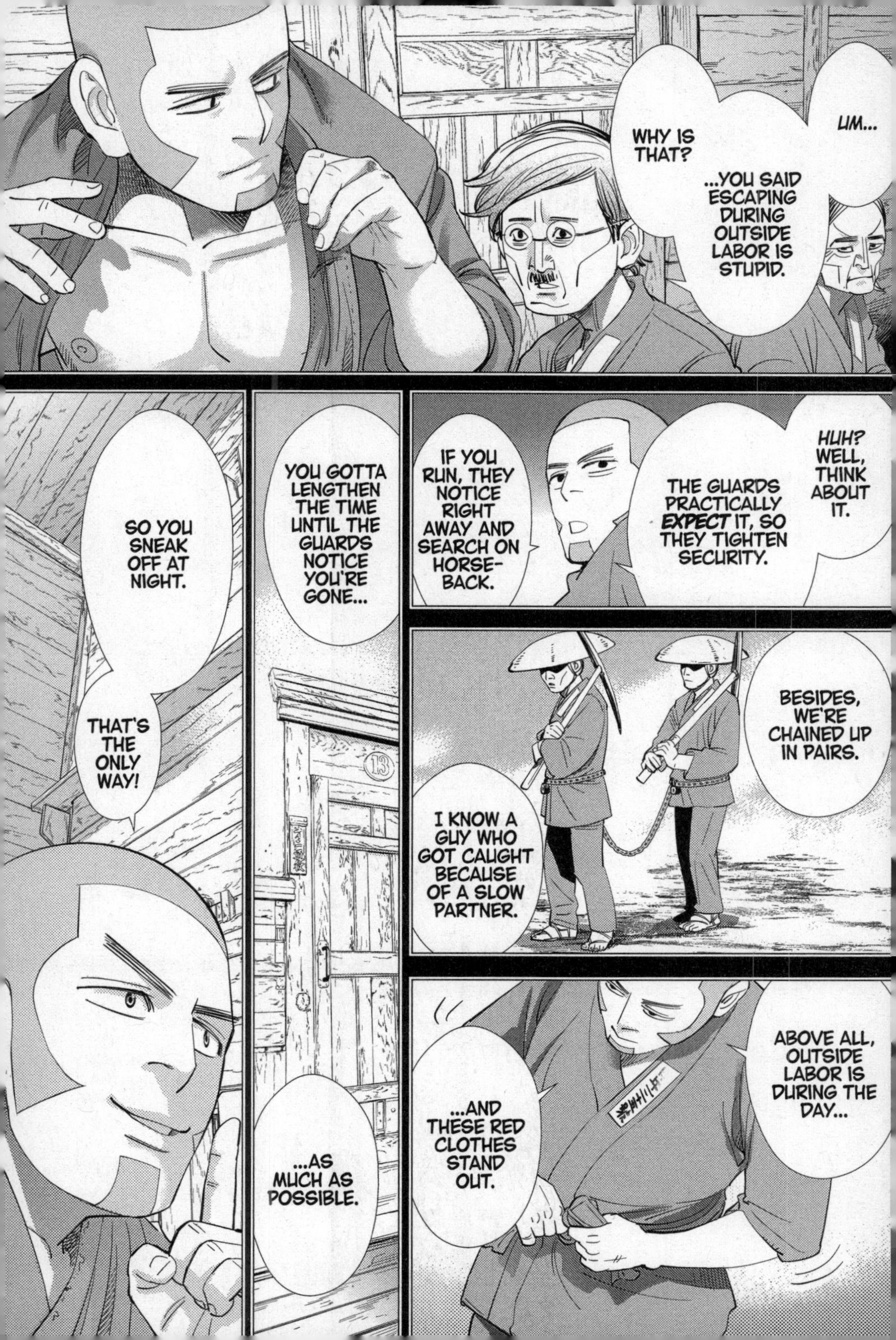

UM...
...YOU SAID ESCAPING DURING OUTSIDE LABOR IS STUPID.
WHY IS THAT?
HUH? WELL, THINK ABOUT IT.
THE GUARDS PRACTICALLY *EXPECT* IT, SO THEY TIGHTEN SECURITY.
IF YOU RUN, THEY NOTICE RIGHT AWAY AND SEARCH ON HORSE-BACK.
BESIDES, WE'RE CHAINED UP IN PAIRS.
I KNOW A GUY WHO GOT CAUGHT BECAUSE OF A SLOW PARTNER.
ABOVE ALL, OUTSIDE LABOR IS DURING THE DAY...
...AND THESE RED CLOTHES STAND OUT.
YOU GOTTA LENGTHEN THE TIME UNTIL THE GUARDS NOTICE YOU'RE GONE...
...AS MUCH AS POSSIBLE.
SO YOU SNEAK OFF AT NIGHT.
THAT'S THE ONLY WAY!

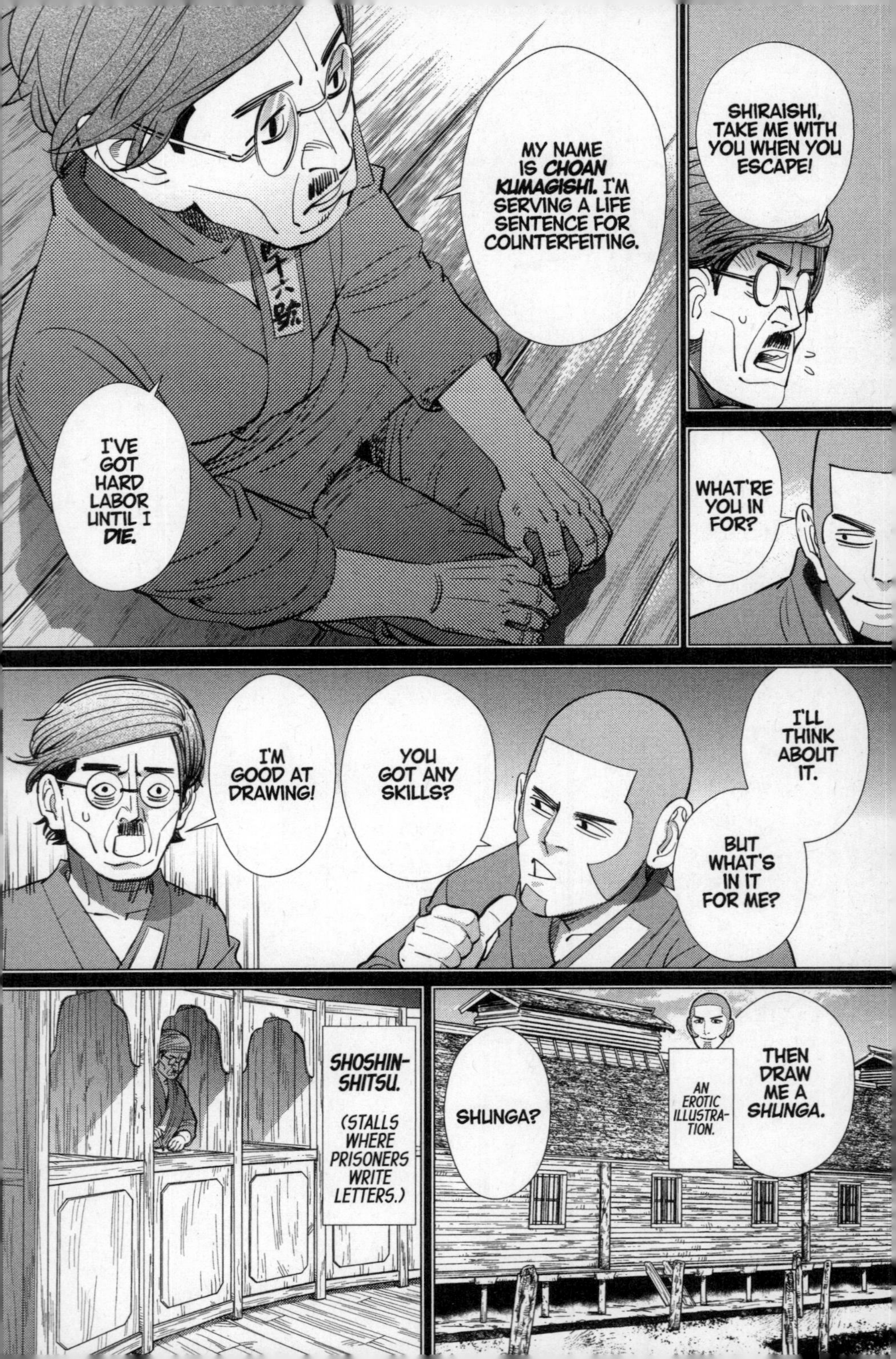
SHIRAISHI, TAKE ME WITH YOU WHEN YOU ESCAPE!
WHAT'RE YOU IN FOR?
MY NAME IS CHOAN KUMAGISHI. I'M SERVING A LIFE SENTENCE FOR COUNTERFEITING.
I'VE GOT HARD LABOR UNTIL I DIE.
I'LL THINK ABOUT IT.
BUT WHAT'S IN IT FOR ME?
YOU GOT ANY SKILLS?
I'M GOOD AT DRAWING!
THEN DRAW ME A SHUNGA.
AN EROTIC ILLUSTRATION.
SHUNGA?
SHOSHIN-SHITSU.
(STALLS WHERE PRISONERS WRITE LETTERS.)

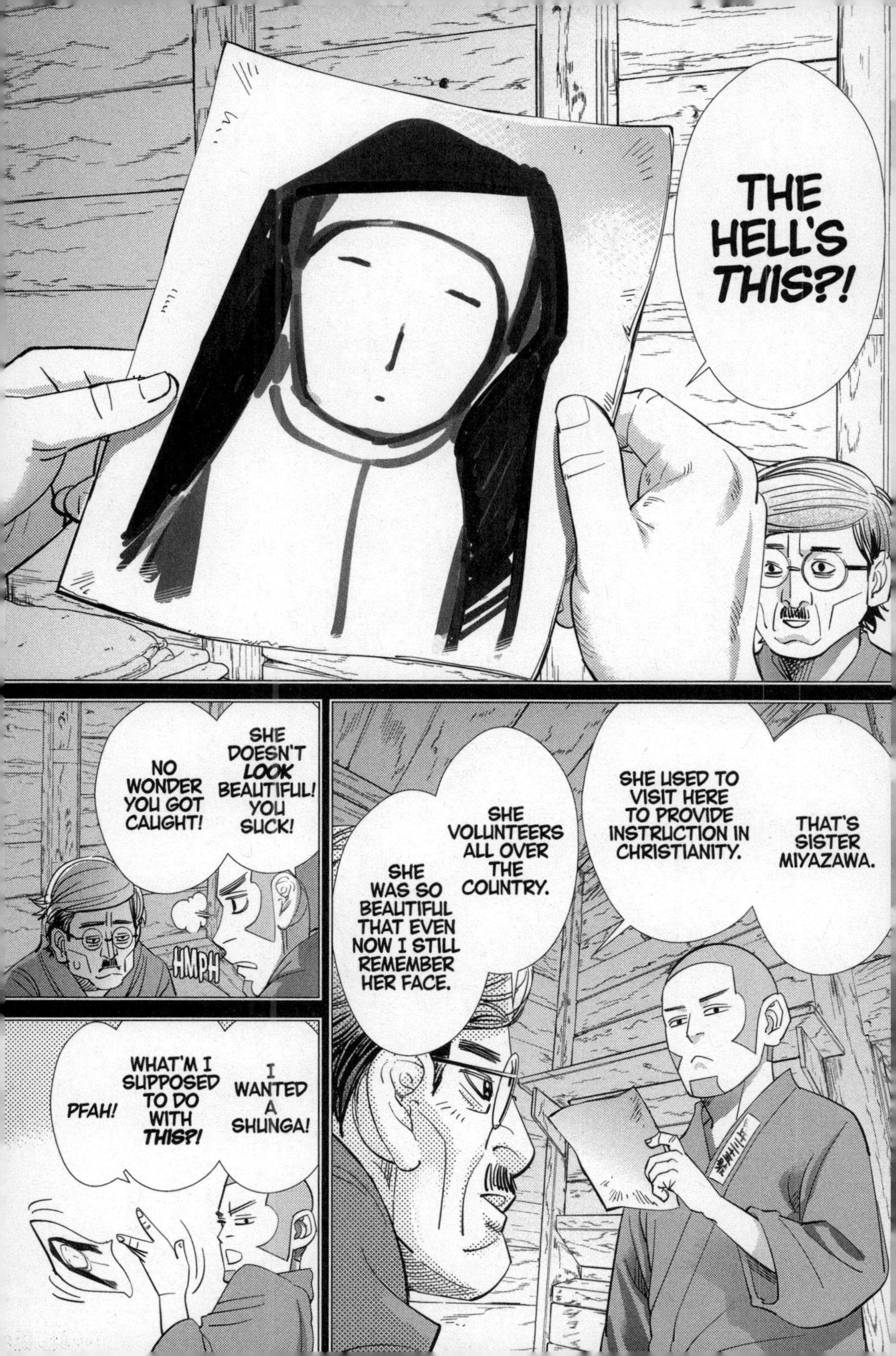
THE HELL'S THIS?!
THAT'S SISTER MIYAZAWA.
SHE USED TO VISIT HERE TO PROVIDE INSTRUCTION IN CHRISTIANITY.
SHE VOLUNTEERS ALL OVER THE COUNTRY.
SHE WAS SO BEAUTIFUL THAT EVEN NOW I STILL REMEMBER HER FACE.
SHE DOESN'T LOOK BEAUTIFUL! YOU SUCK!
NO WONDER YOU GOT CAUGHT!
HMPH
I WANTED A SHUNGA!
WHAT'M I SUPPOSED TO DO WITH THIS?!
PFAH!

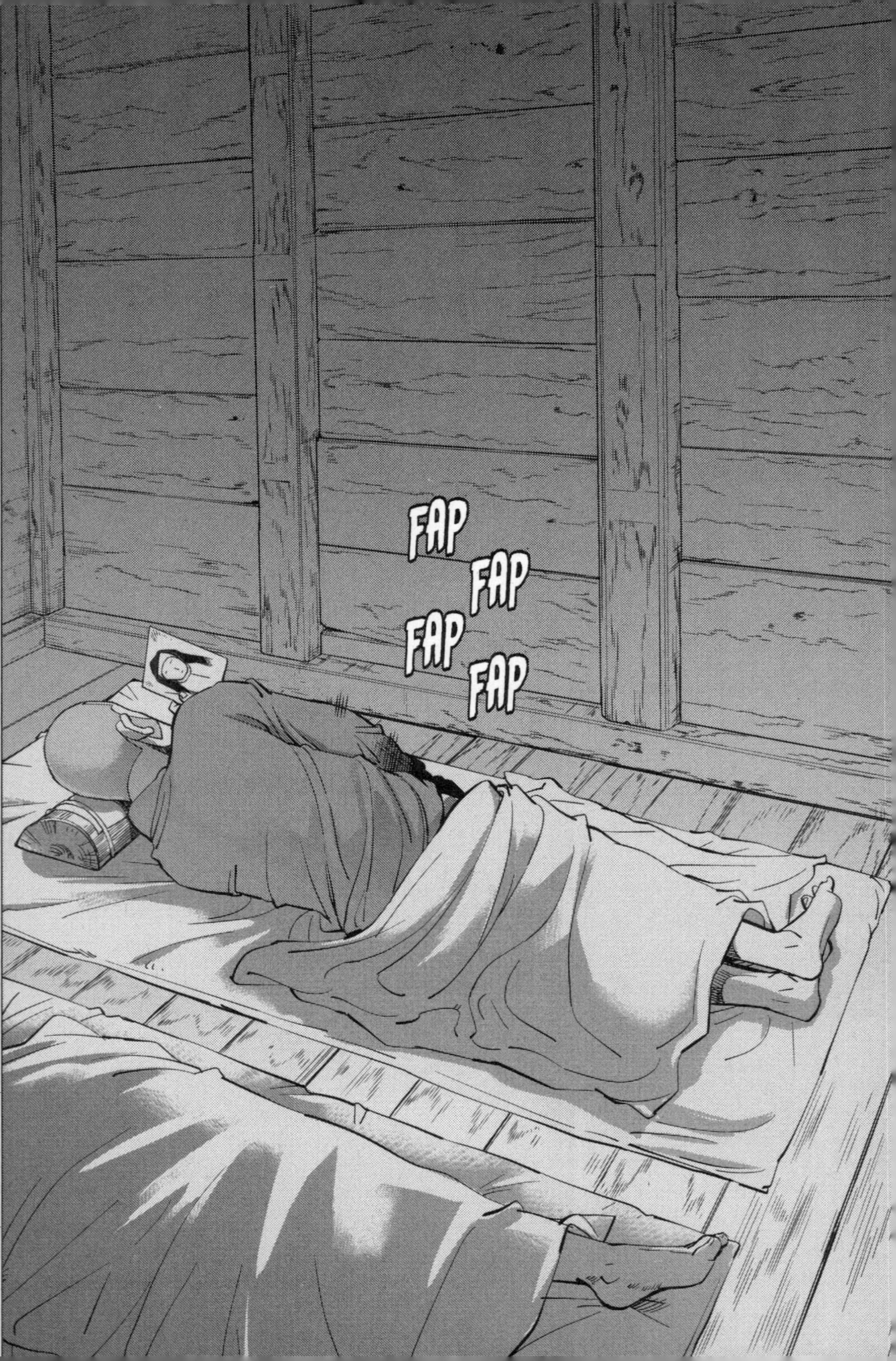
FAP
FAP
FAP
FAP

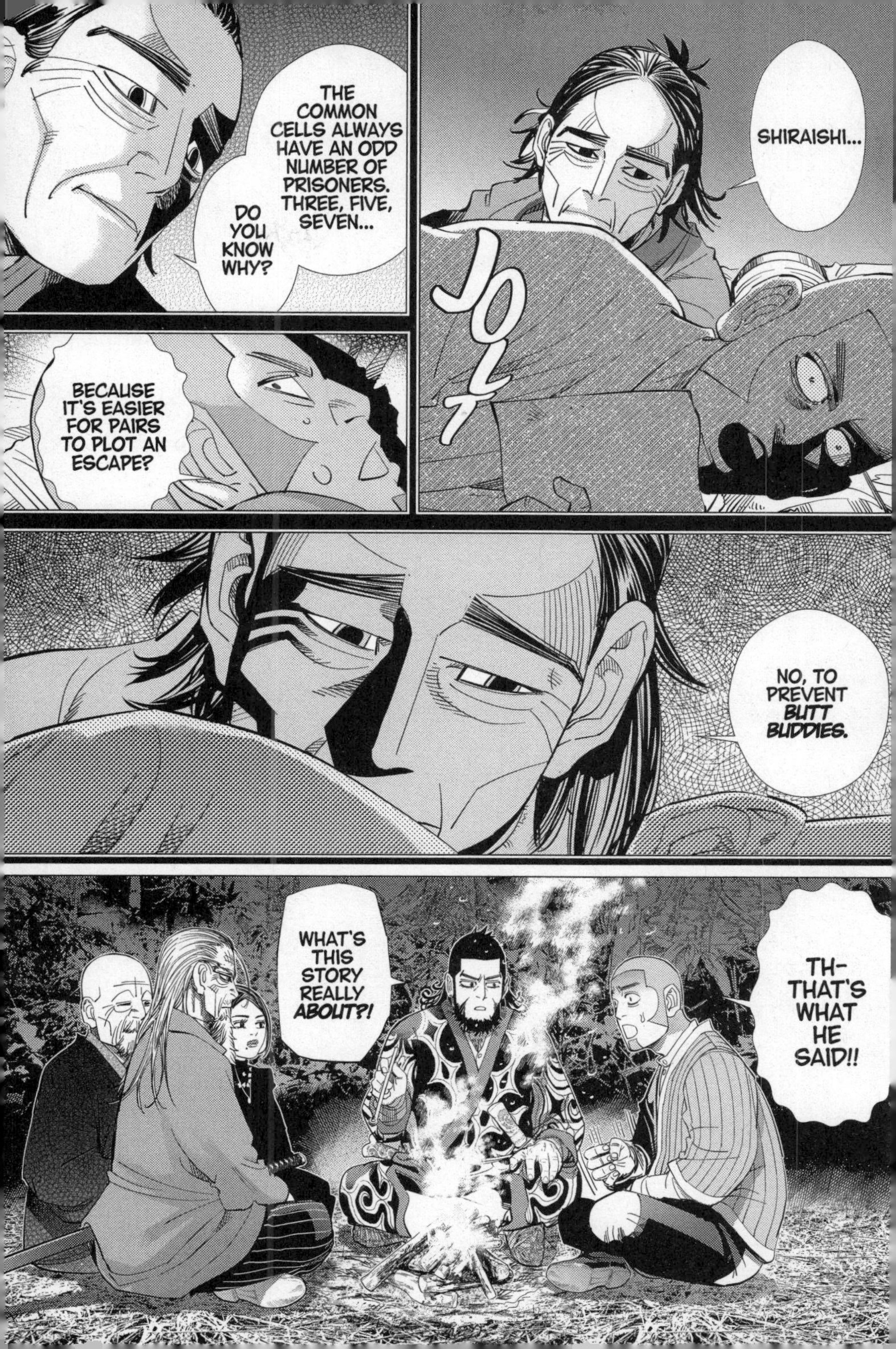
SHIRAISHI...
JOLT
THE COMMON CELLS ALWAYS HAVE AN ODD NUMBER OF PRISONERS. THREE, FIVE, SEVEN...
DO YOU KNOW WHY?
BECAUSE IT'S EASIER FOR PAIRS TO PLOT AN ESCAPE?
NO, TO PREVENT *BUTT BUDDIES.*
TH-THAT'S WHAT HE SAID!!
WHAT'S THIS STORY REALLY *ABOUT?!*

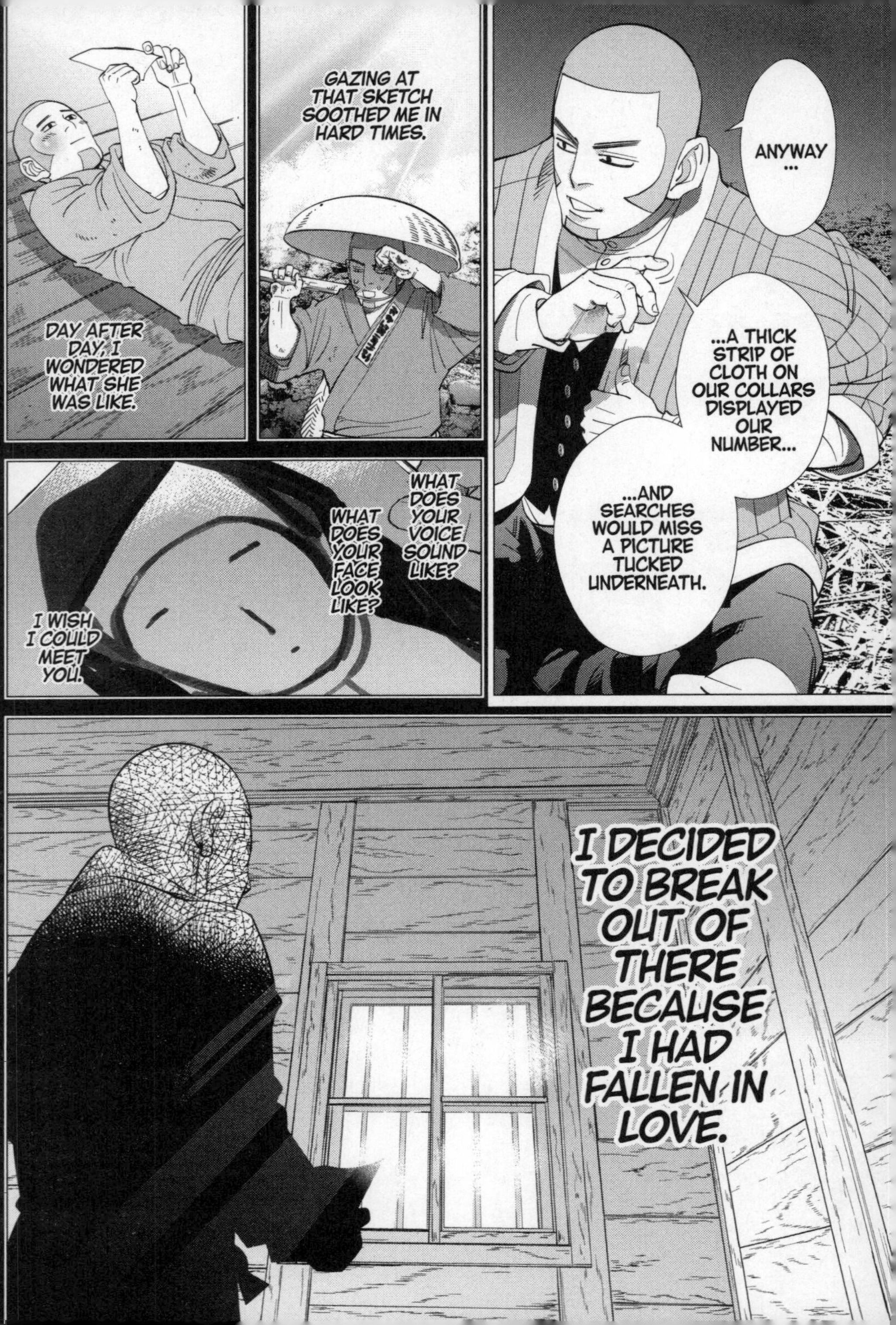

ANYWAY ...
...A THICK STRIP OF CLOTH ON OUR COLLARS DISPLAYED OUR NUMBER...
...AND SEARCHES WOULD MISS A PICTURE TUCKED UNDERNEATH.
GAZING AT THAT SKETCH SOOTHED ME IN HARD TIMES.
DAY AFTER DAY, I WONDERED WHAT SHE WAS LIKE.
WHAT DOES YOUR VOICE SOUND LIKE?
WHAT DOES YOUR FACE LOOK LIKE?
I WISH I COULD MEET YOU.
I DECIDED TO BREAK OUT OF THERE BECAUSE I HAD FALLEN IN LOVE.

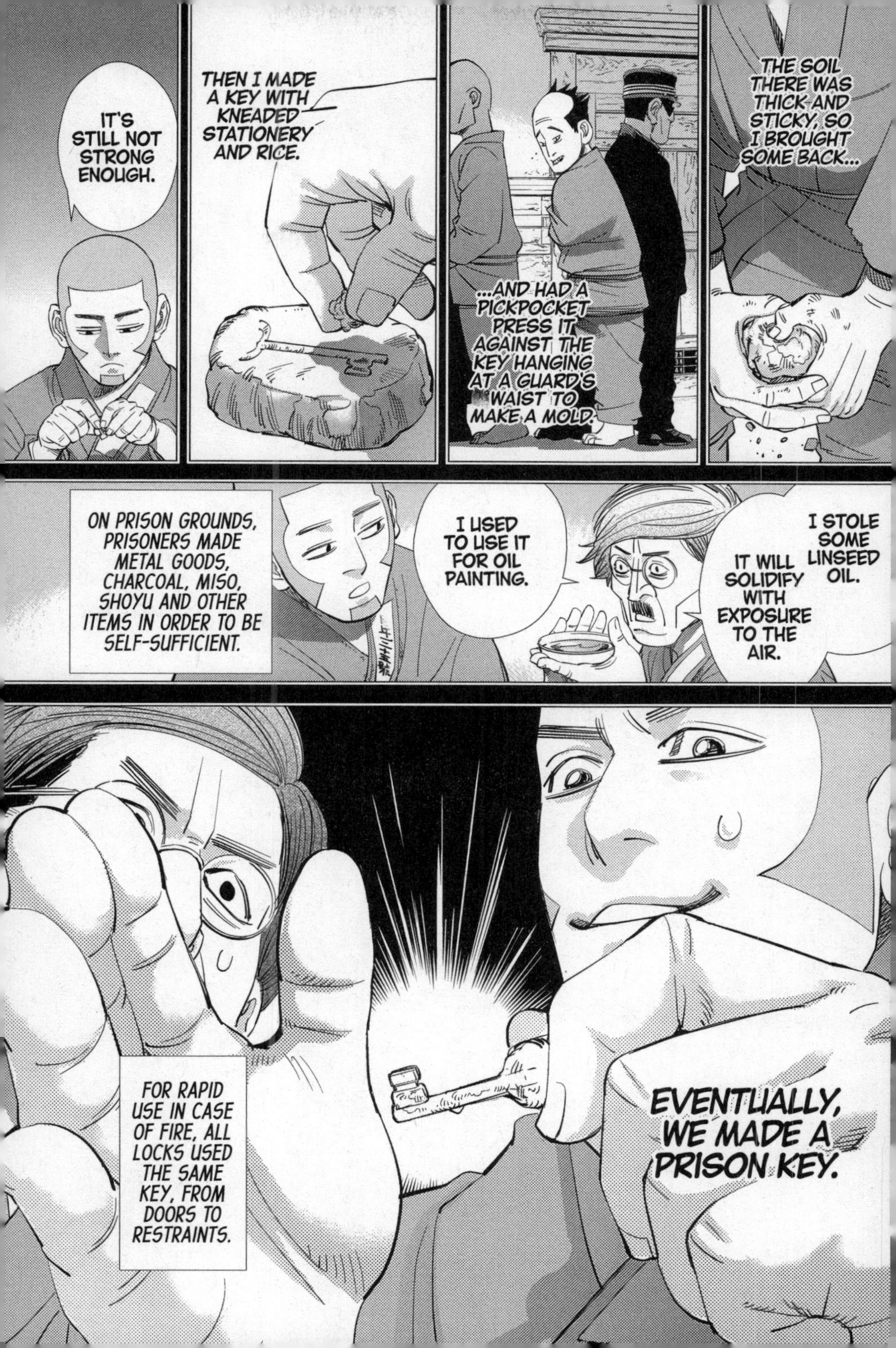
THE SOIL THERE WAS THICK AND STICKY, SO I BROUGHT SOME BACK...
...AND HAD A PICKPOCKET PRESS IT AGAINST THE KEY HANGING AT A GUARD'S WAIST TO MAKE A MOLD.
THEN I MADE A KEY WITH KNEADED STATIONERY AND RICE.
IT'S STILL NOT STRONG ENOUGH.
I STOLE SOME LINSEED OIL.
IT WILL SOLIDIFY WITH EXPOSURE TO THE AIR.
I USED TO USE IT FOR OIL PAINTING.
ON PRISON GROUNDS, PRISONERS MADE METAL GOODS, CHARCOAL, MISO, SHOYU AND OTHER ITEMS IN ORDER TO BE SELF-SUFFICIENT.
EVENTUALLY, WE MADE A PRISON KEY.
FOR RAPID USE IN CASE OF FIRE, ALL LOCKS USED THE SAME KEY, FROM DOORS TO RESTRAINTS.

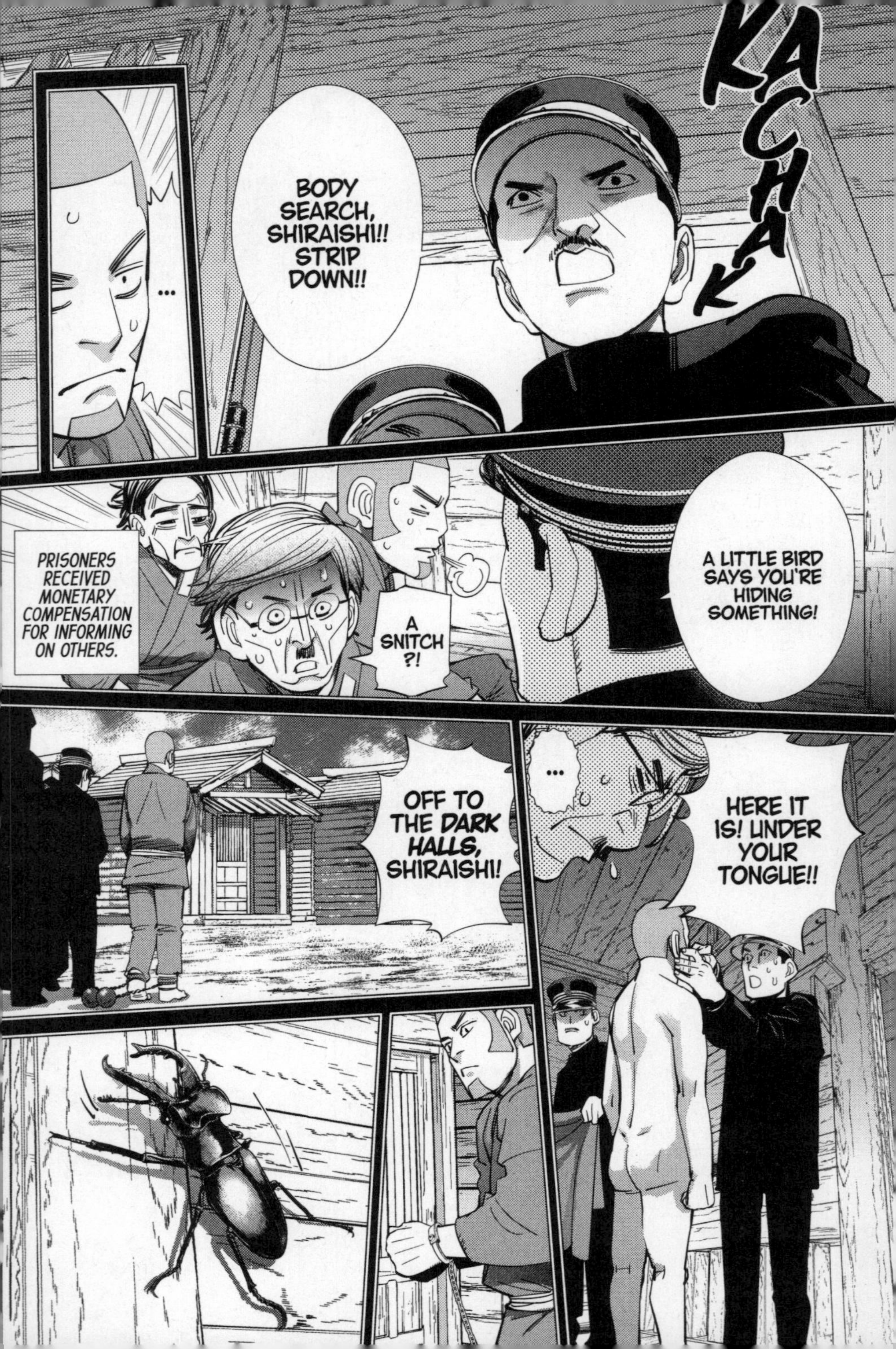
KACHAK
BODY SEARCH, SHIRAISHI!! STRIP DOWN!!
...
A LITTLE BIRD SAYS YOU'RE HIDING SOMETHING!
A SNITCH?!
PRISONERS RECEIVED MONETARY COMPENSATION FOR INFORMING ON OTHERS.
HERE IT IS! UNDER YOUR TONGUE!!
...
OFF TO THE DARK HALLS, SHIRAISHI!

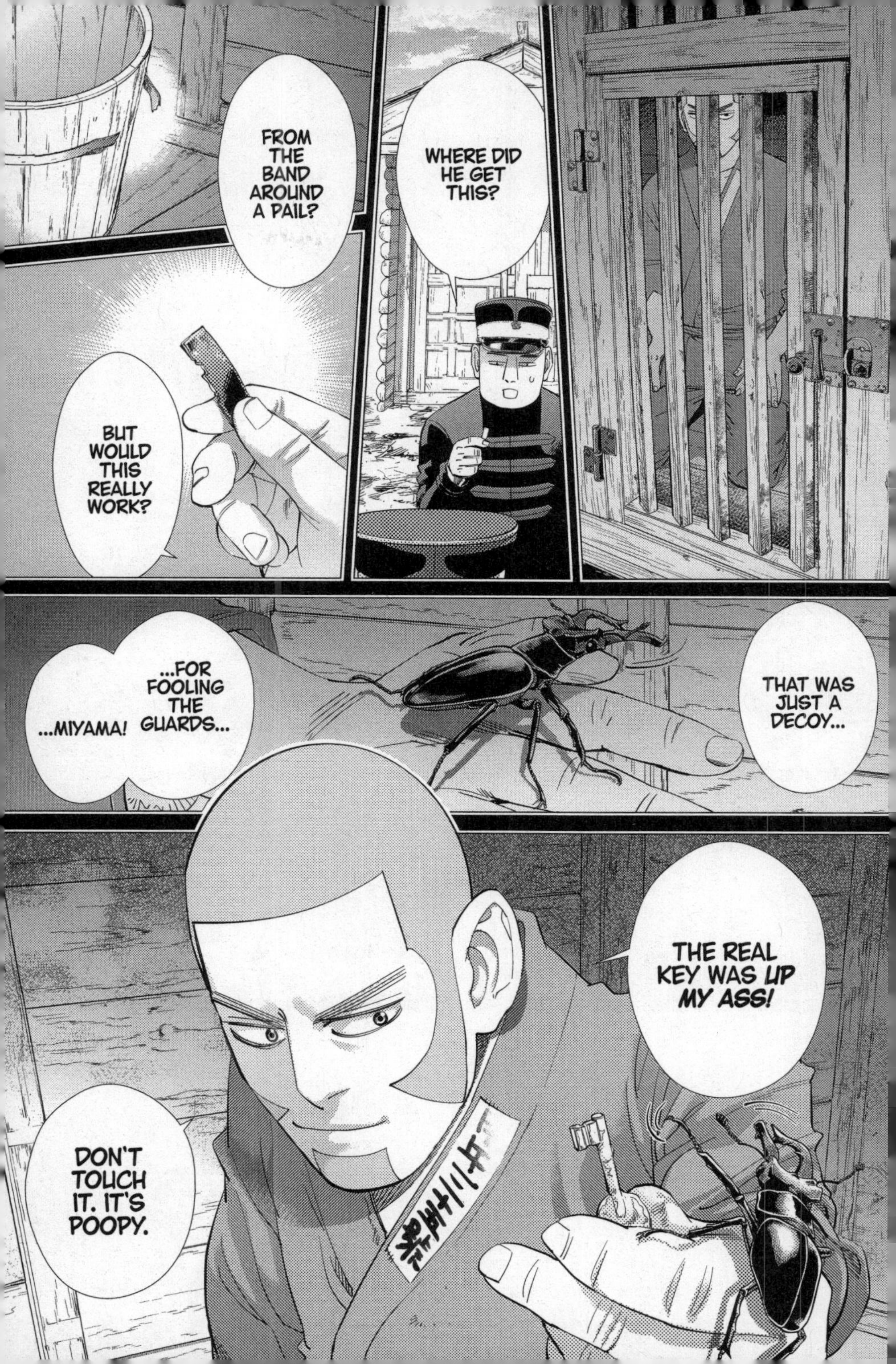
WHERE DID HE GET THIS?
FROM THE BAND AROUND A PAIL?
BUT WOULD THIS REALLY WORK?
THAT WAS JUST A DECOY...
...FOR FOOLING THE GUARDS...
...MIYAMA!
THE REAL KEY WAS *UP MY ASS!*
DON'T TOUCH IT. IT'S POOPY.

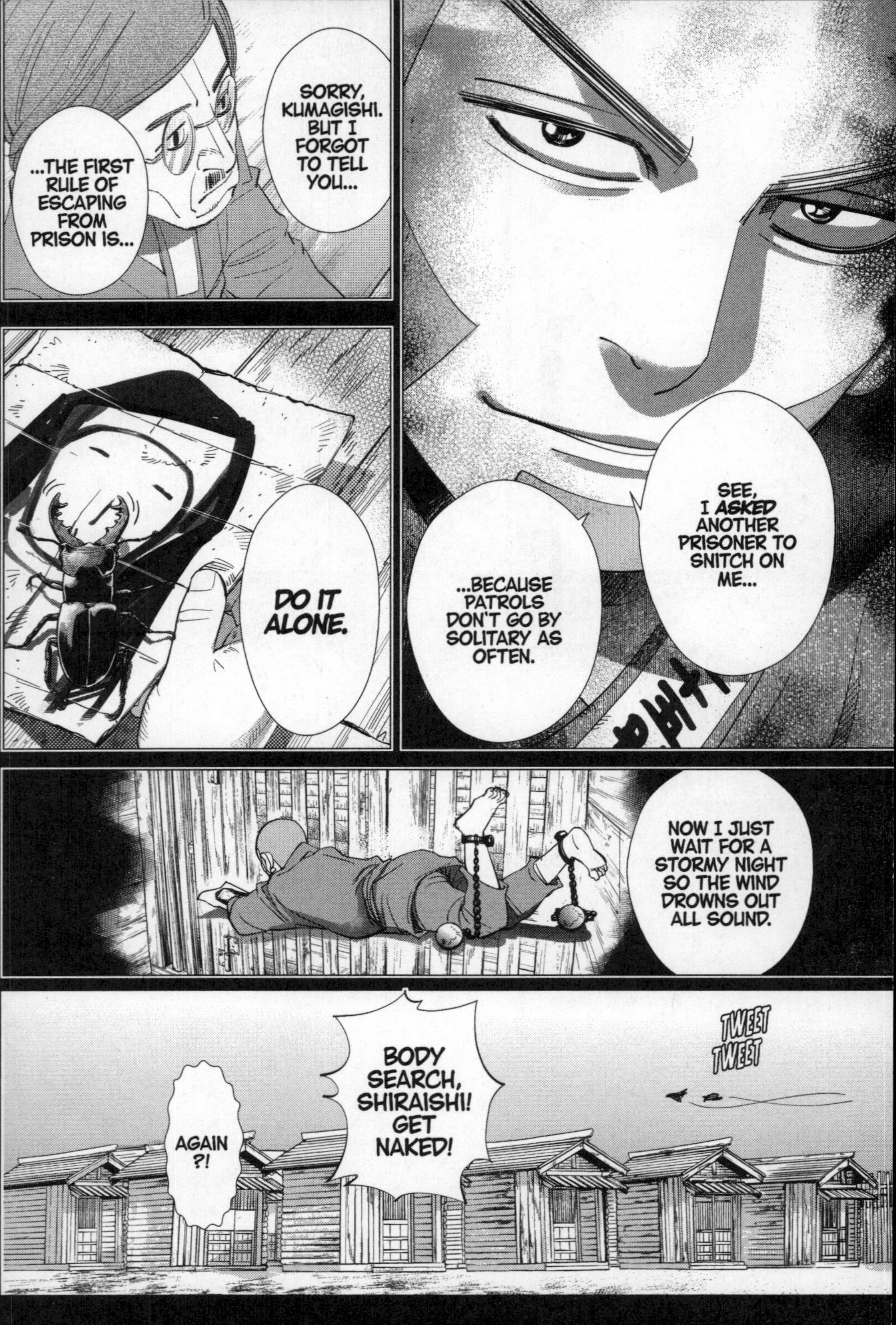
SEE, I ASKED ANOTHER PRISONER TO SNITCH ON ME...
...BECAUSE PATROLS DON'T GO BY SOLITARY AS OFTEN.
SORRY, KUMAGISHI. BUT I FORGOT TO TELL YOU...
...THE FIRST RULE OF ESCAPING FROM PRISON IS...
DO IT ALONE.
NOW I JUST WAIT FOR A STORMY NIGHT SO THE WIND DROWNS OUT ALL SOUND.
TWEET TWEET
BODY SEARCH, SHIRAISHI! GET NAKED!
AGAIN ?!

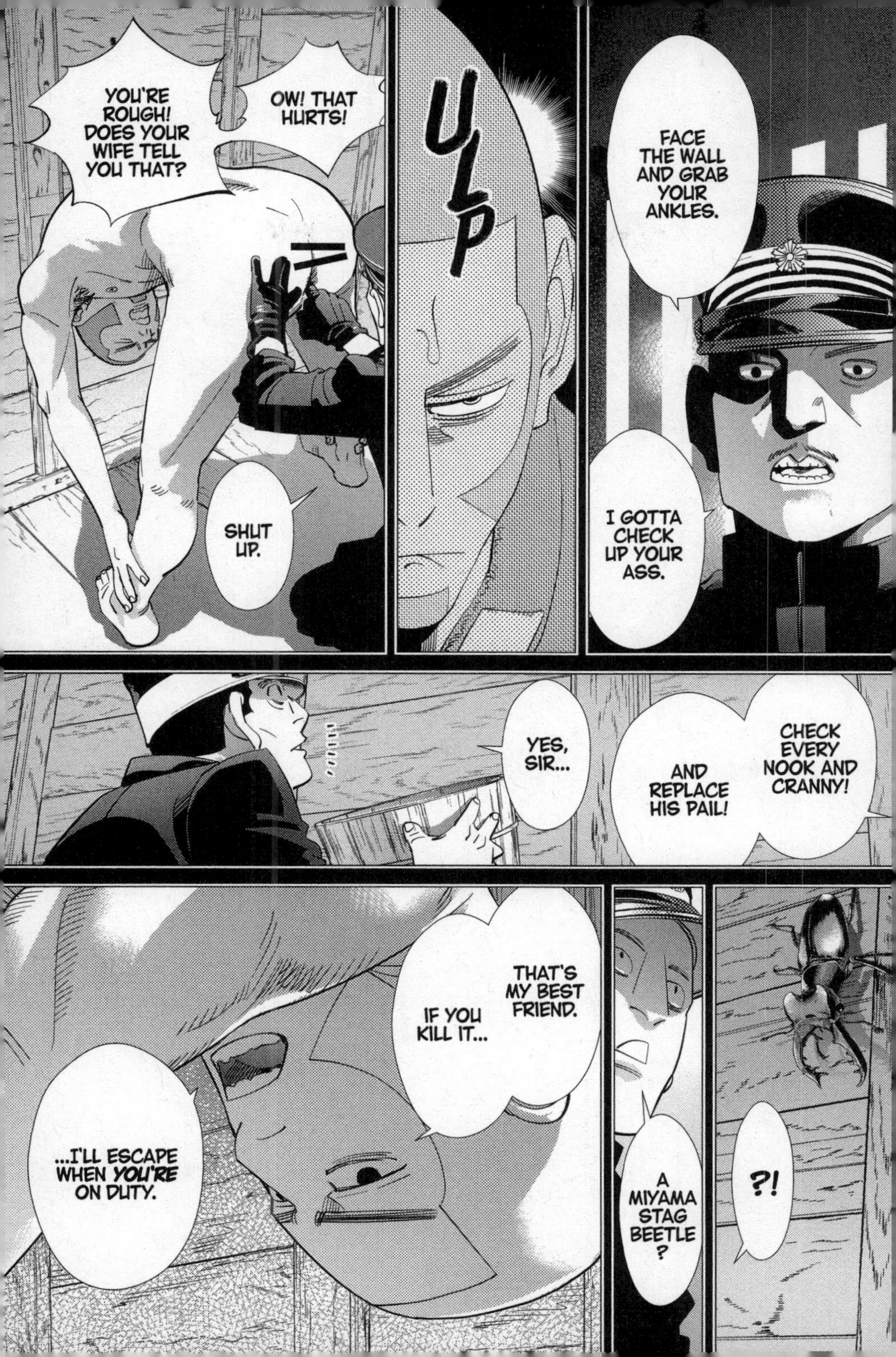
FACE THE WALL AND GRAB YOUR ANKLES.
I GOTTA CHECK UP YOUR ASS.
ULP
OW! THAT HURTS!
YOU'RE ROUGH! DOES YOUR WIFE TELL YOU THAT?
SHUT UP.
CHECK EVERY NOOK AND CRANNY!
AND REPLACE HIS PAIL!
YES, SIR...
?!
A MIYAMA STAG BEETLE?
THAT'S MY BEST FRIEND.
IF YOU KILL IT...
...I'LL ESCAPE WHEN *YOU'RE* ON DUTY.

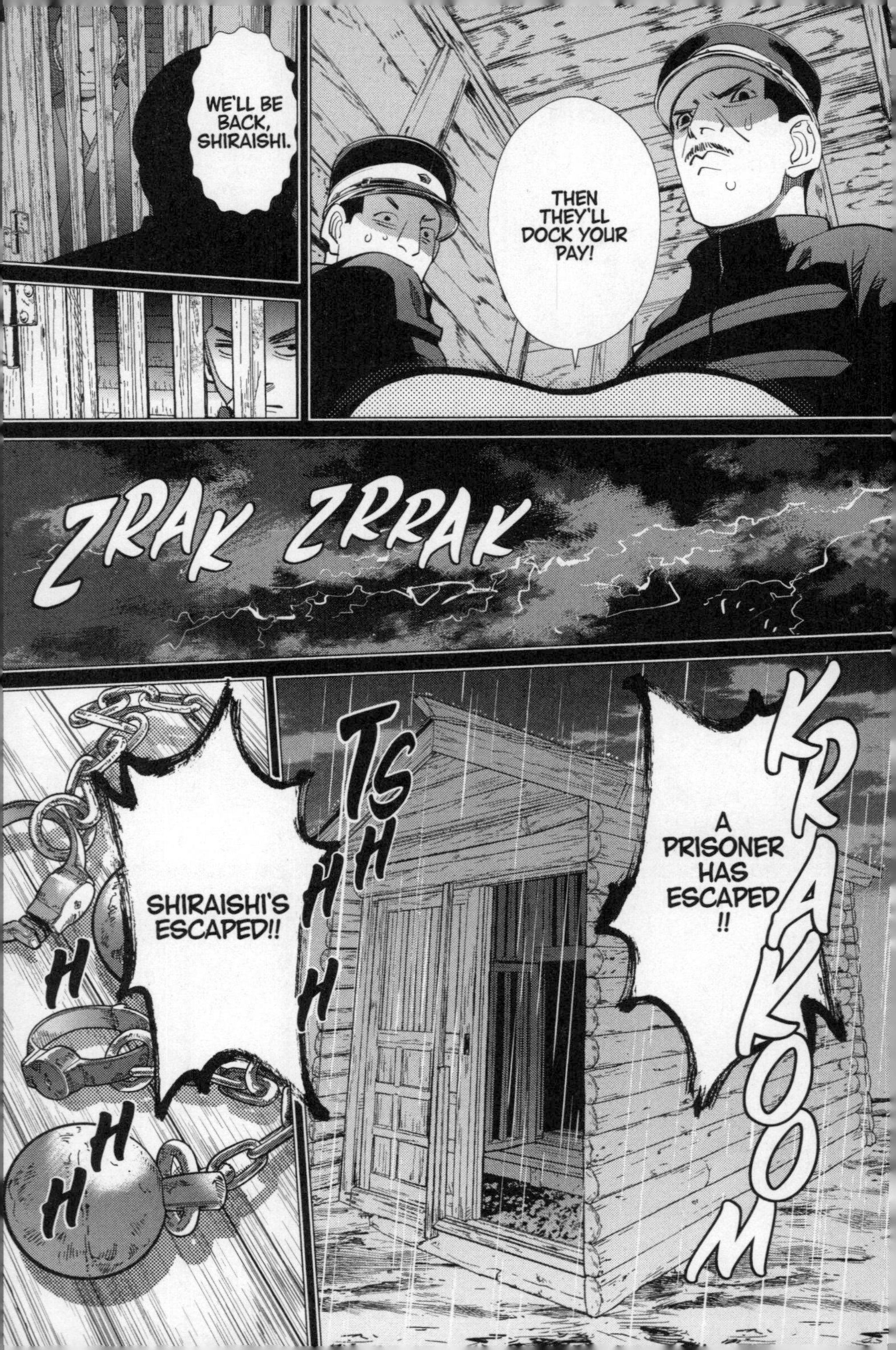
THEN THEY'LL DOCK YOUR PAY!
WE'LL BE BACK, SHIRAISHI.
ZRAK ZRRAK
KRAKOOM
A PRISONER HAS ESCAPED!!
TSHHHH
SHIRAISHI'S ESCAPED!!
HHHH

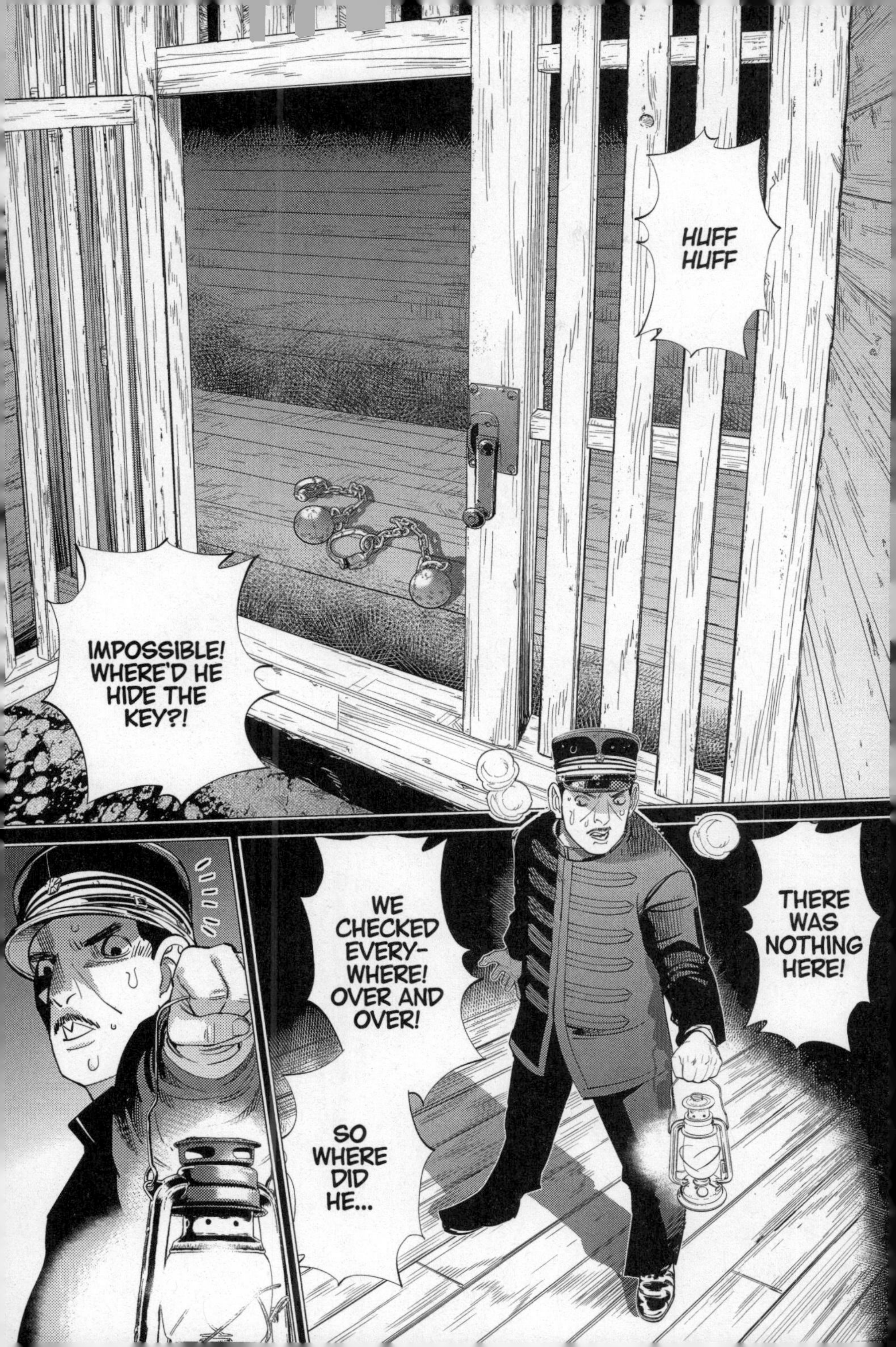
HUFF HUFF
IMPOSSIBLE! WHERE'D HE HIDE THE KEY?!
THERE WAS NOTHING HERE!
WE CHECKED EVERY-WHERE! OVER AND OVER!
SO WHERE DID HE...

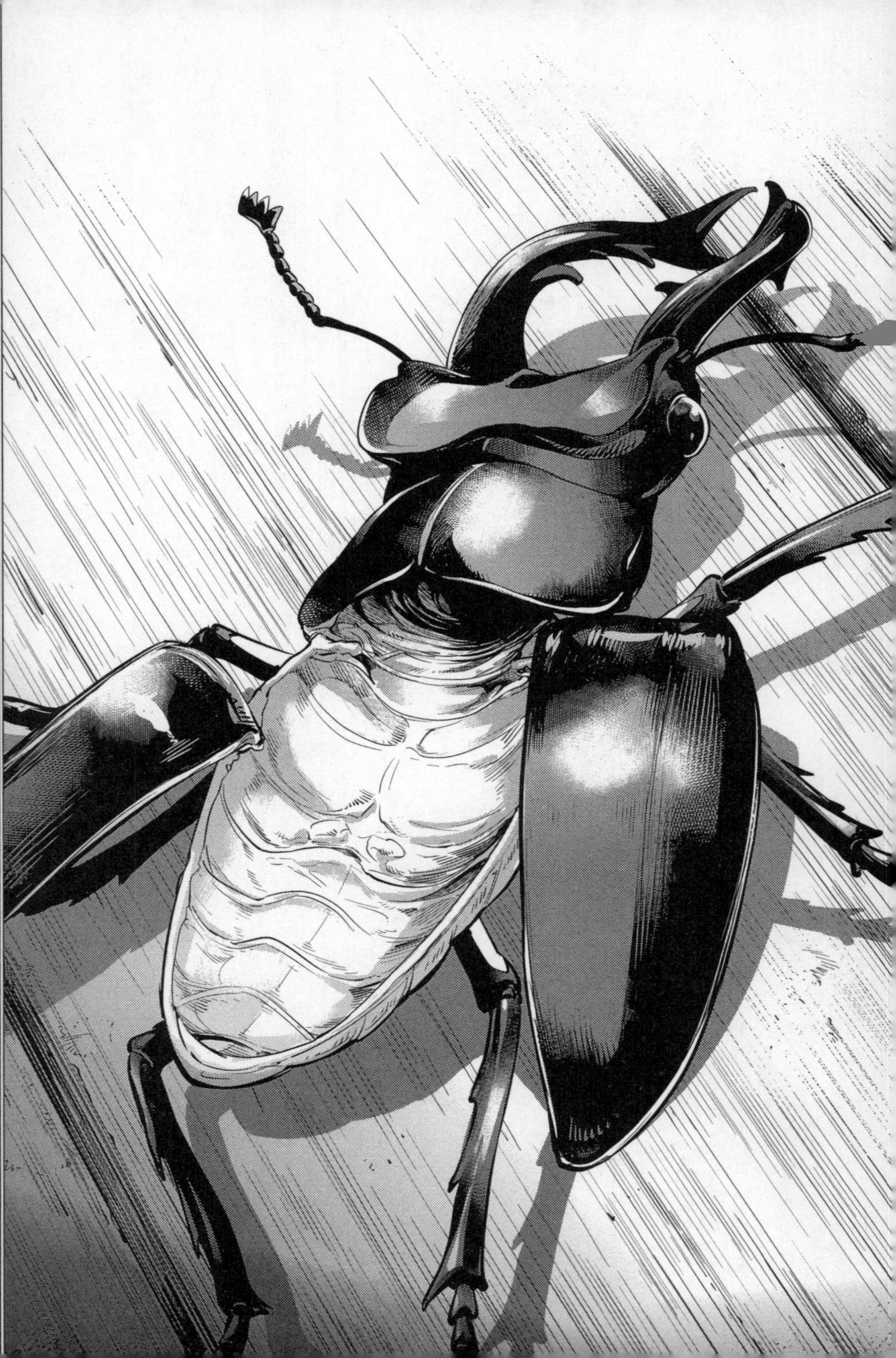

GOLDEN KAMUY

PRISON BREAK ROMANCE

Chapter 85: The Long Road of Love

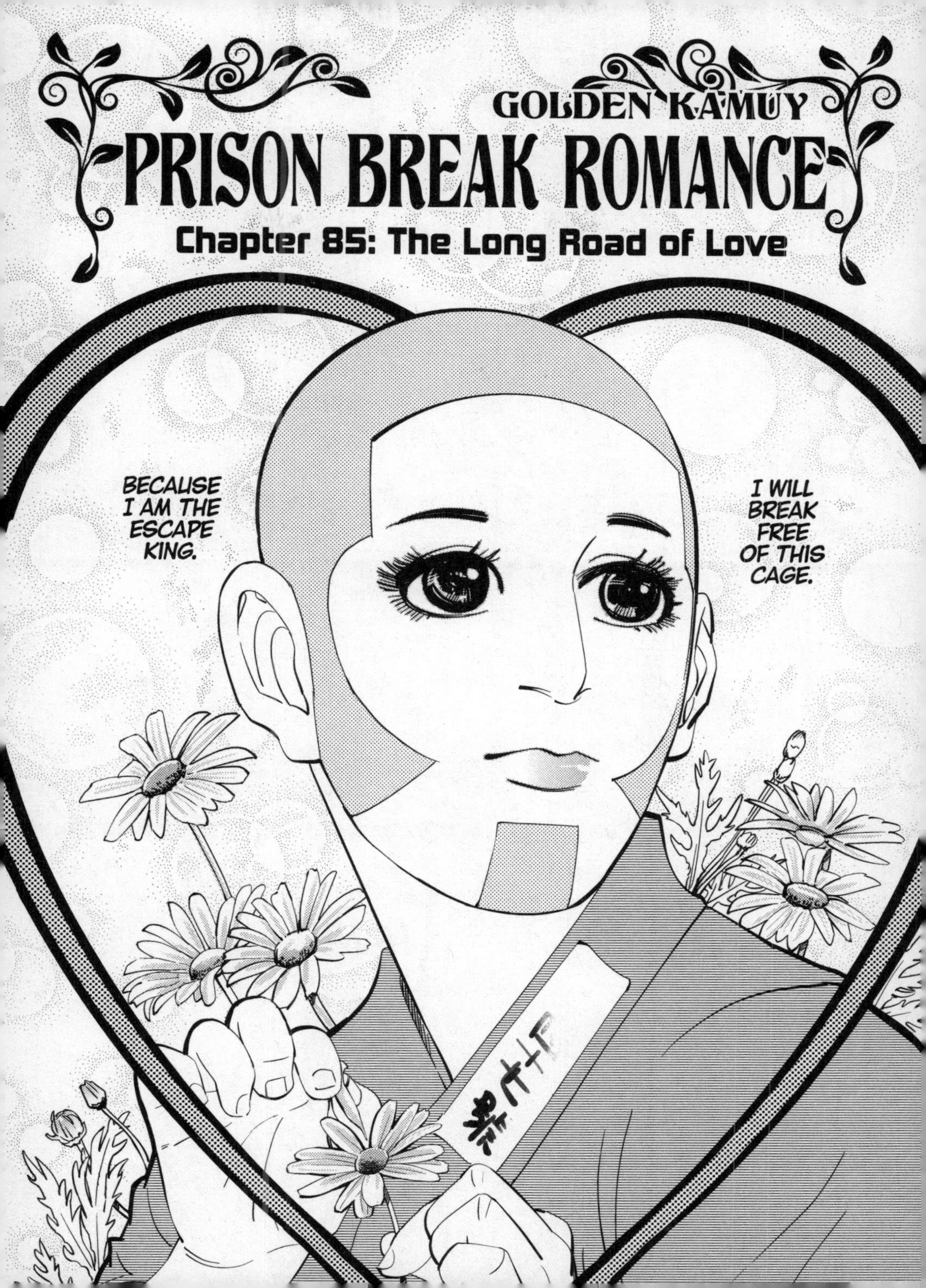
I WILL BREAK FREE OF THIS CAGE.
BECAUSE I AM THE ESCAPE KING.

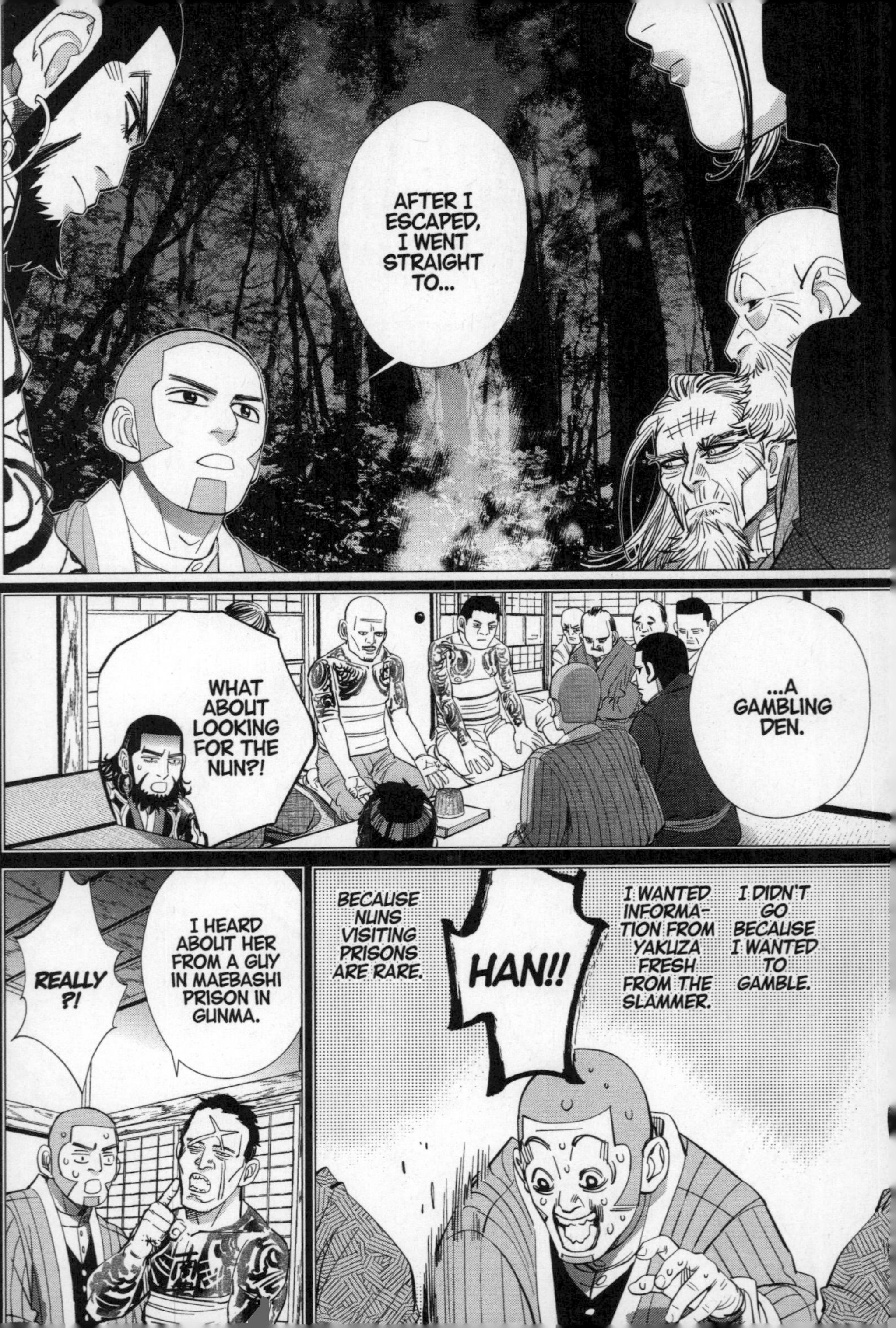
AFTER I ESCAPED, I WENT STRAIGHT TO...
...A GAMBLING DEN.
WHAT ABOUT LOOKING FOR THE NUN?!
I DIDN'T GO BECAUSE I WANTED TO GAMBLE.
I WANTED INFORMATION FROM YAKUZA FRESH FROM THE SLAMMER.
HAN!!
BECAUSE NUNS VISITING PRISONS ARE RARE.
I HEARD ABOUT HER FROM A GUY IN MAEBASHI PRISON IN GUNMA.
REALLY?!

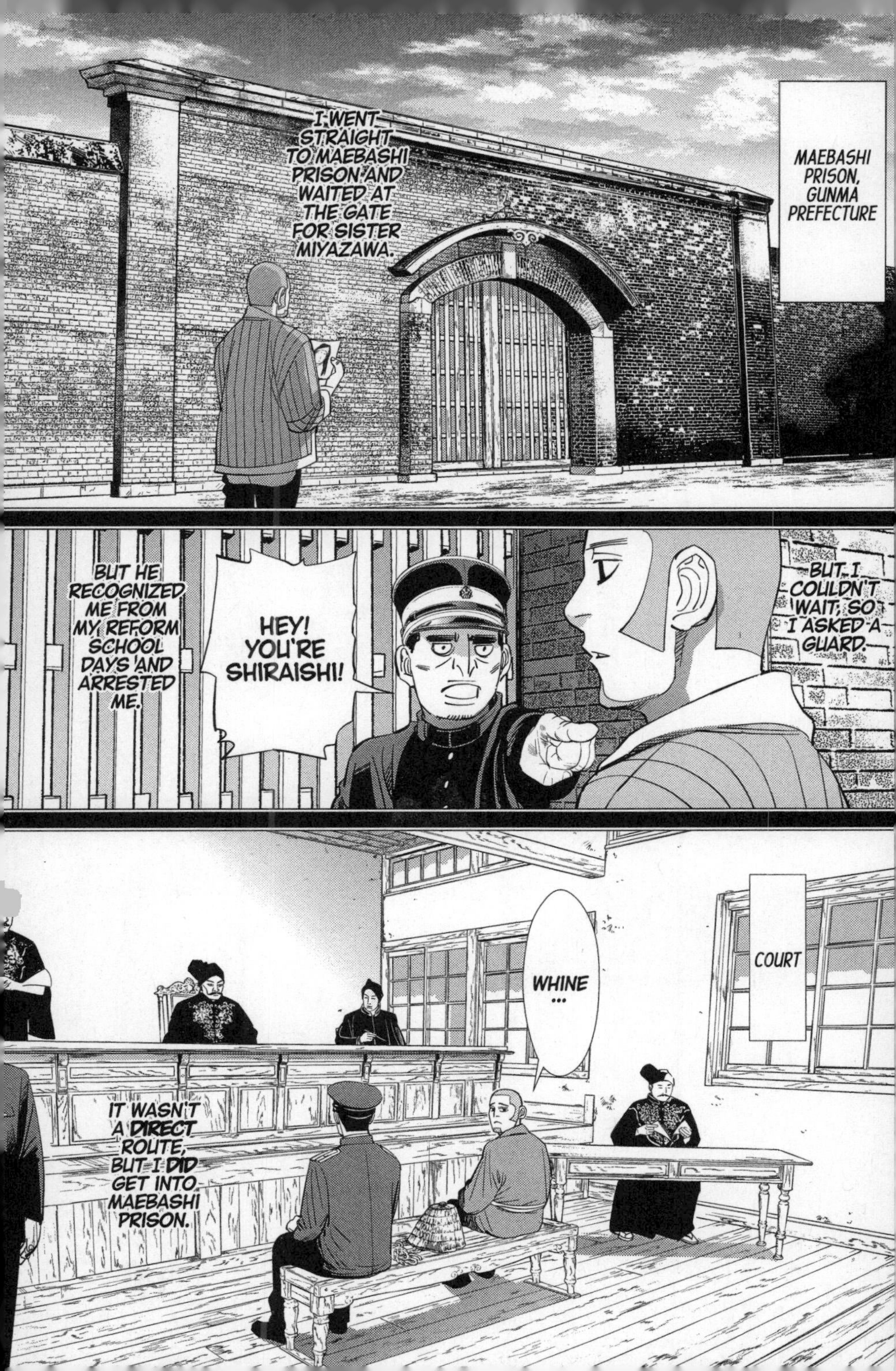
MAEBASHI PRISON, GUNMA PREFECTURE
I WENT STRAIGHT TO MAEBASHI PRISON AND WAITED AT THE GATE FOR SISTER MIYAZAWA.
BUT I COULDN'T WAIT, SO I ASKED A GUARD.
HEY! YOU'RE SHIRAISHI!
BUT HE RECOGNIZED ME FROM MY REFORM SCHOOL DAYS AND ARRESTED ME.
COURT
WHINE ...
IT WASN'T A DIRECT ROUTE, BUT I DID GET INTO MAEBASHI PRISON.

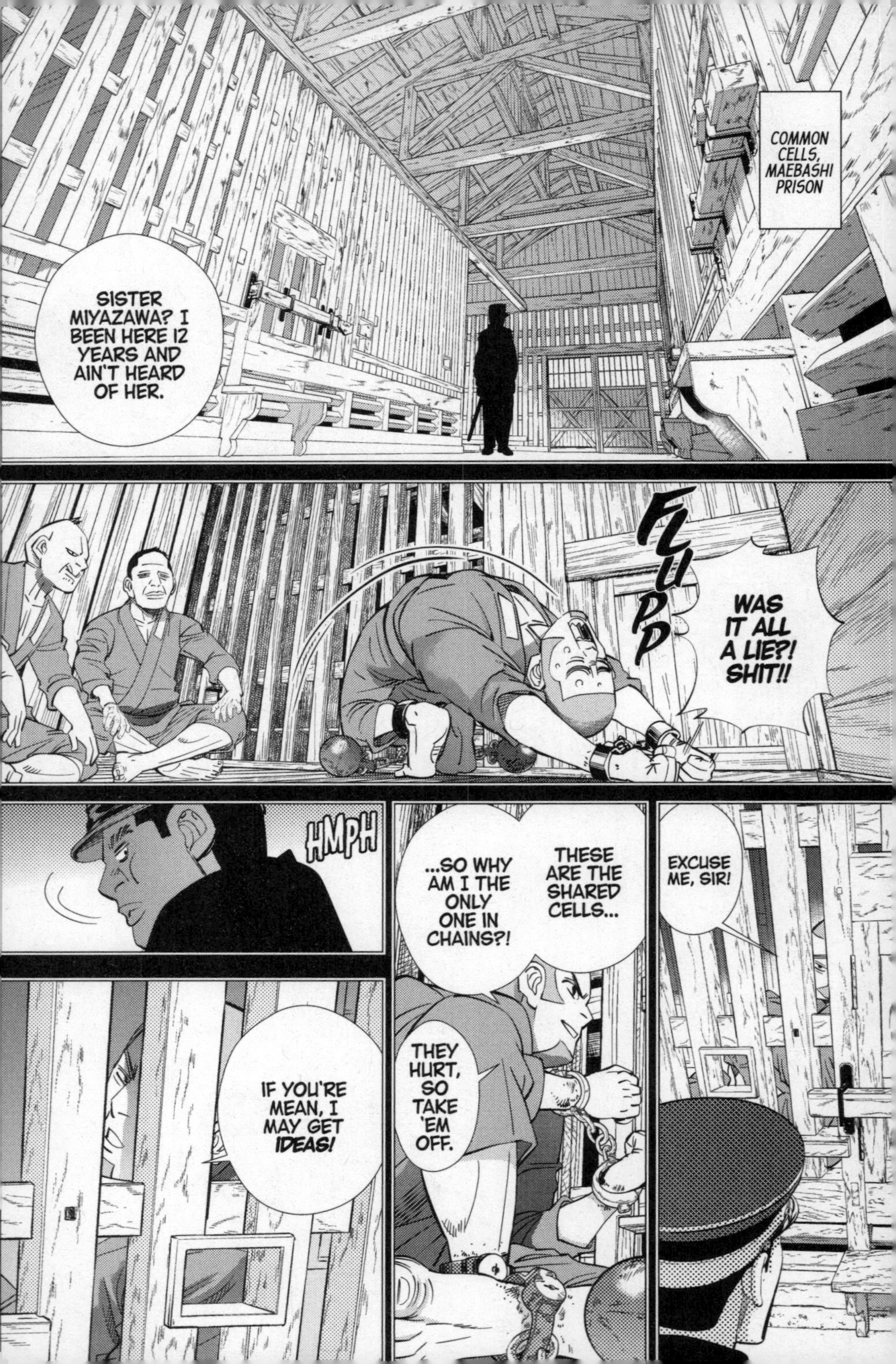
COMMON CELLS, MAEBASHI PRISON
SISTER MIYAZAWA? I BEEN HERE 12 YEARS AND AIN'T HEARD OF HER.
FLUPP
WAS IT ALL A LIE?! SHIT!!
EXCUSE ME, SIR!
THESE ARE THE SHARED CELLS...
...SO WHY AM I THE ONLY ONE IN CHAINS?!
THEY HURT, SO TAKE 'EM OFF.
HMPH
IF YOU'RE MEAN, I MAY GET IDEAS!

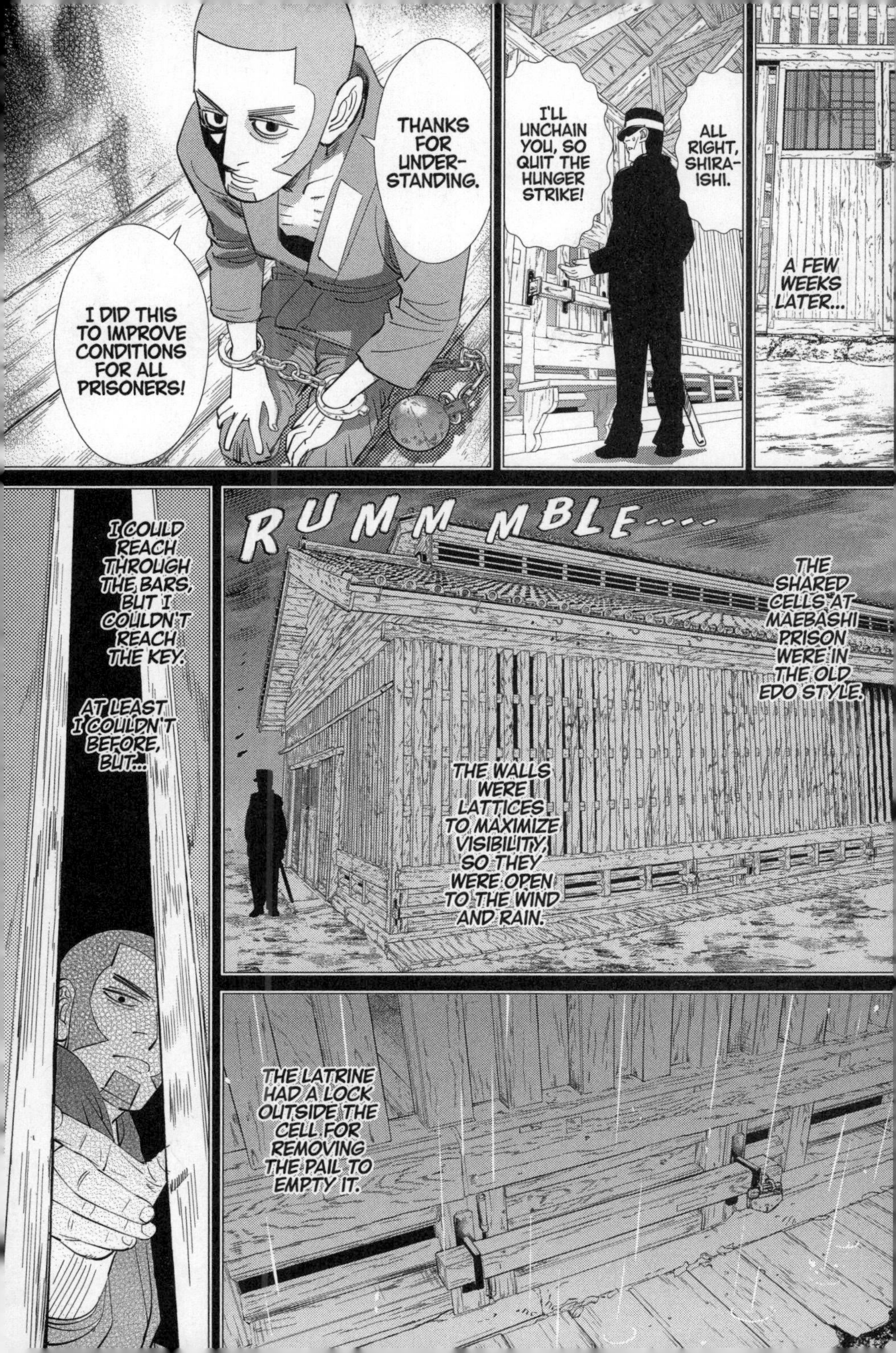
A FEW WEEKS LATER...
ALL RIGHT, SHIRA-ISHI.
I'LL UNCHAIN YOU, SO QUIT THE HUNGER STRIKE!
THANKS FOR UNDER-STANDING.
I DID THIS TO IMPROVE CONDITIONS FOR ALL PRISONERS!
RUMMMBLE....
THE SHARED CELLS AT MAEBASHI PRISON WERE IN THE OLD EDO STYLE.
THE WALLS WERE LATTICES TO MAXIMIZE VISIBILITY, SO THEY WERE OPEN TO THE WIND AND RAIN.
THE LATRINE HAD A LOCK OUTSIDE THE CELL FOR REMOVING THE PAIL TO EMPTY IT.
I COULD REACH THROUGH THE BARS, BUT I COULDN'T REACH THE KEY.
AT LEAST I COULDN'T BEFORE, BUT...

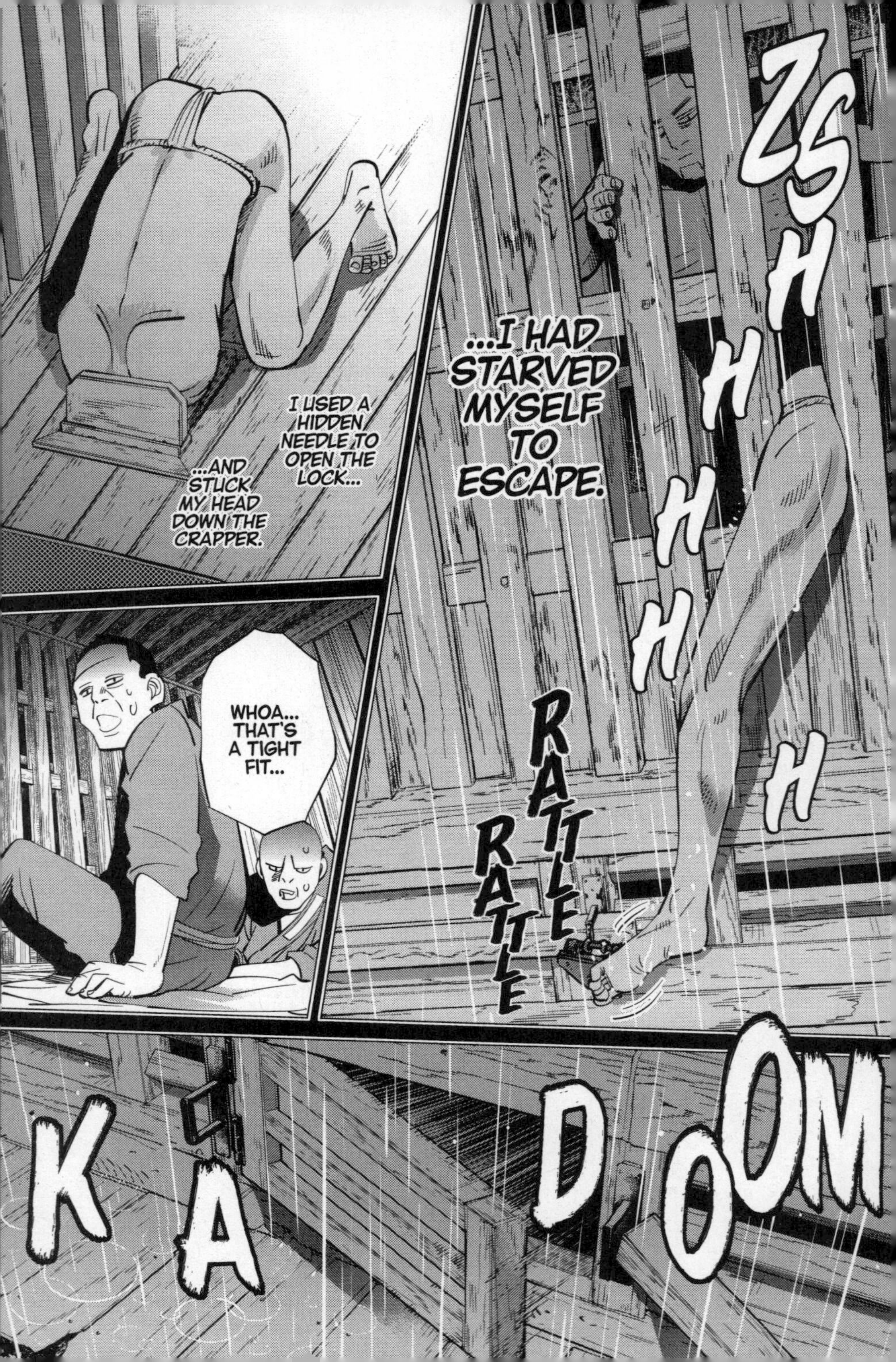
ZSHHHHHHH
...I HAD STARVED MYSELF TO ESCAPE.
RATTLE RATTLE
I USED A HIDDEN NEEDLE TO OPEN THE LOCK...
...AND STUCK MY HEAD DOWN THE CRAPPER.
WHOA... THAT'S A TIGHT FIT...
KADOOOM

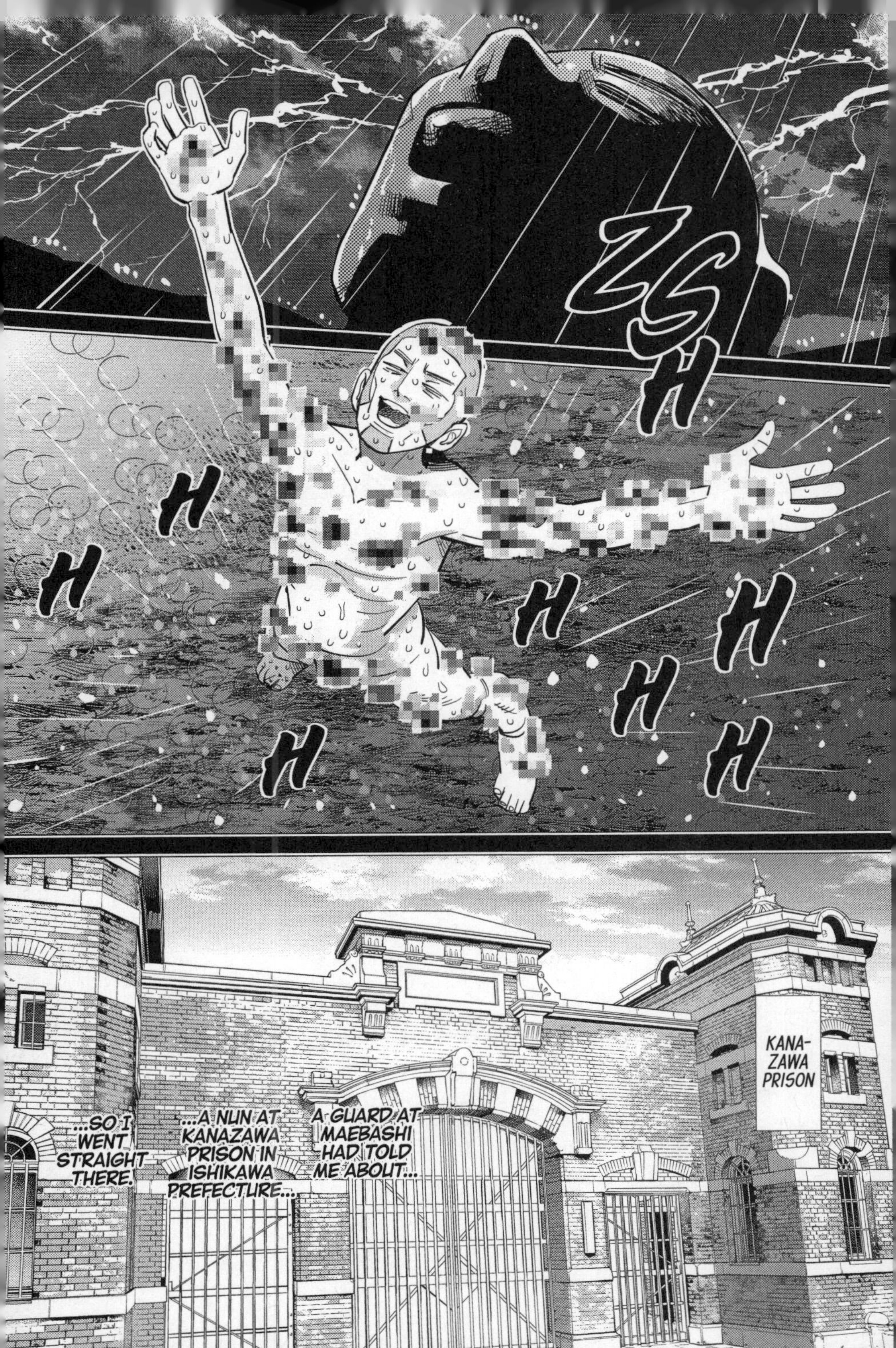
ZSH
H H H H H H H H H
KANA-ZAWA PRISON
A GUARD AT MAEBASHI HAD TOLD ME ABOUT...
...A NUN AT KANAZAWA PRISON IN ISHIKAWA PREFECTURE...
...SO I WENT STRAIGHT THERE.

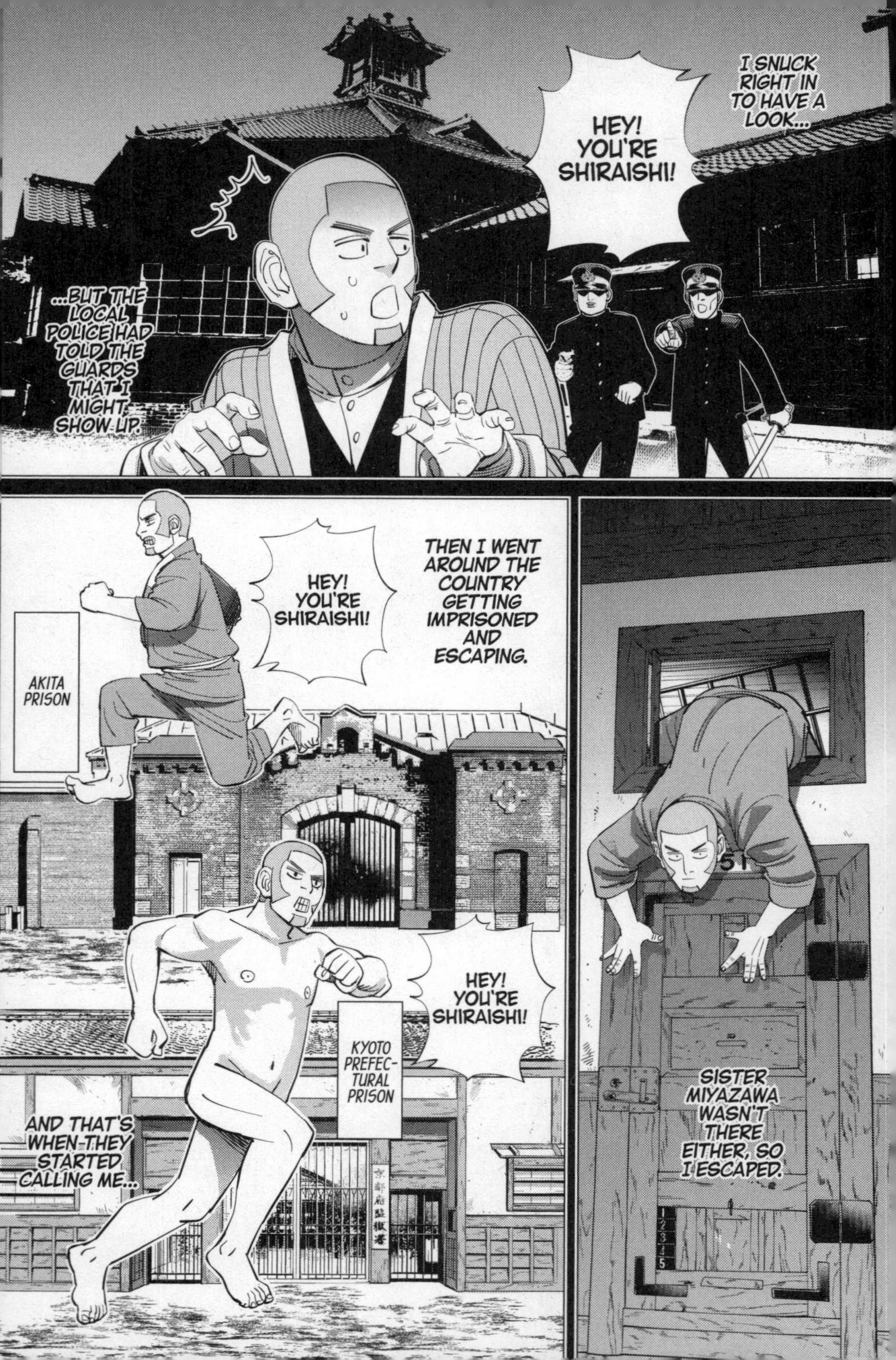
I SNUCK RIGHT IN TO HAVE A LOOK...
HEY! YOU'RE SHIRAISHI!
...BUT THE LOCAL POLICE HAD TOLD THE GUARDS THAT I MIGHT SHOW UP.
SISTER MIYAZAWA WASN'T THERE EITHER, SO I ESCAPED.
THEN I WENT AROUND THE COUNTRY GETTING IMPRISONED AND ESCAPING.
HEY! YOU'RE SHIRAISHI!
AKITA PRISON
HEY! YOU'RE SHIRAISHI!
KYOTO PREFEC-TURAL PRISON
AND THAT'S WHEN THEY STARTED CALLING ME...

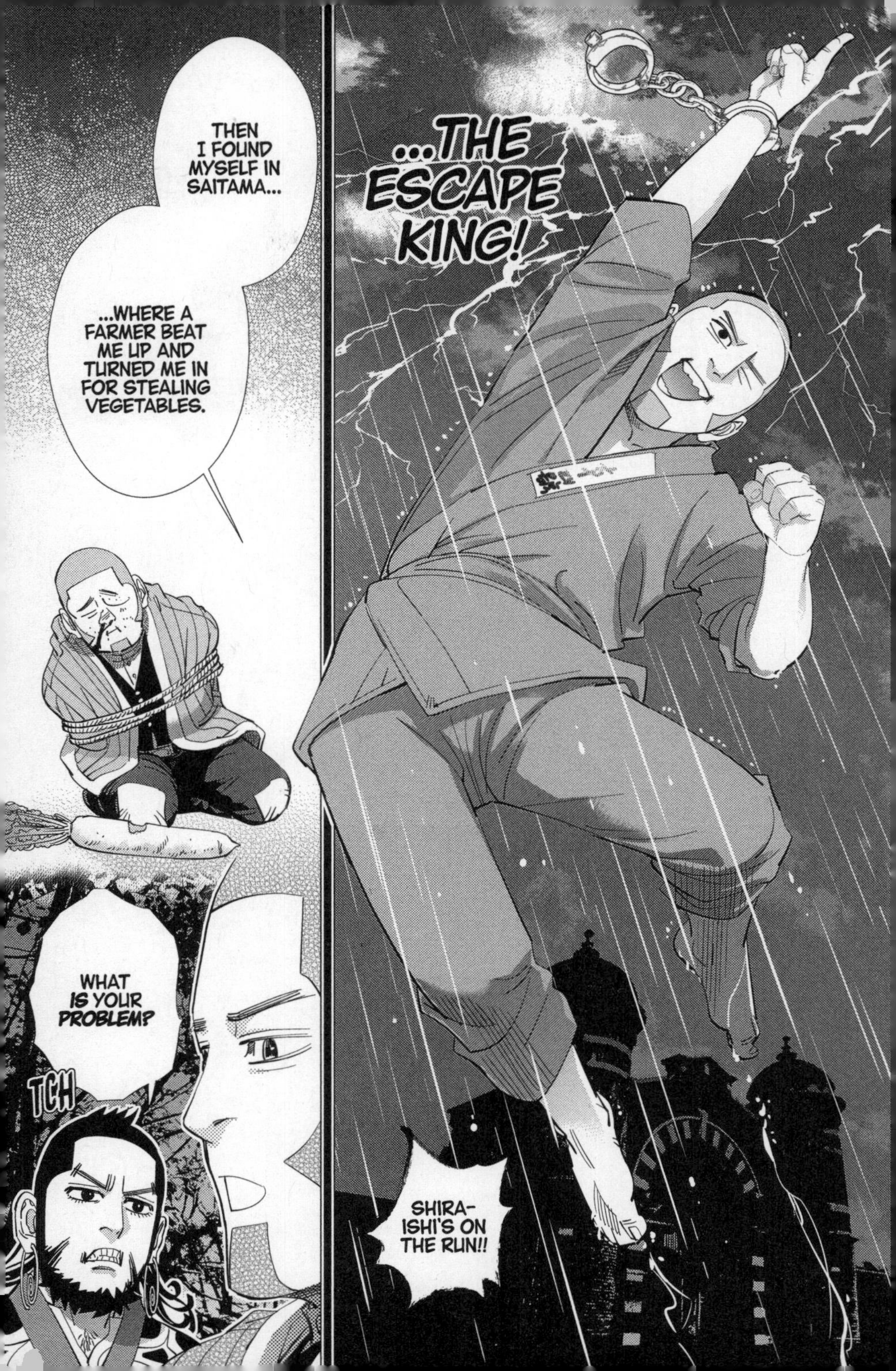
...THE ESCAPE KING!
SHIRA-ISHI'S ON THE RUN!!
THEN I FOUND MYSELF IN SAITAMA...
...WHERE A FARMER BEAT ME UP AND TURNED ME IN FOR STEALING VEGETABLES.
WHAT IS YOUR PROBLEM?
TCH

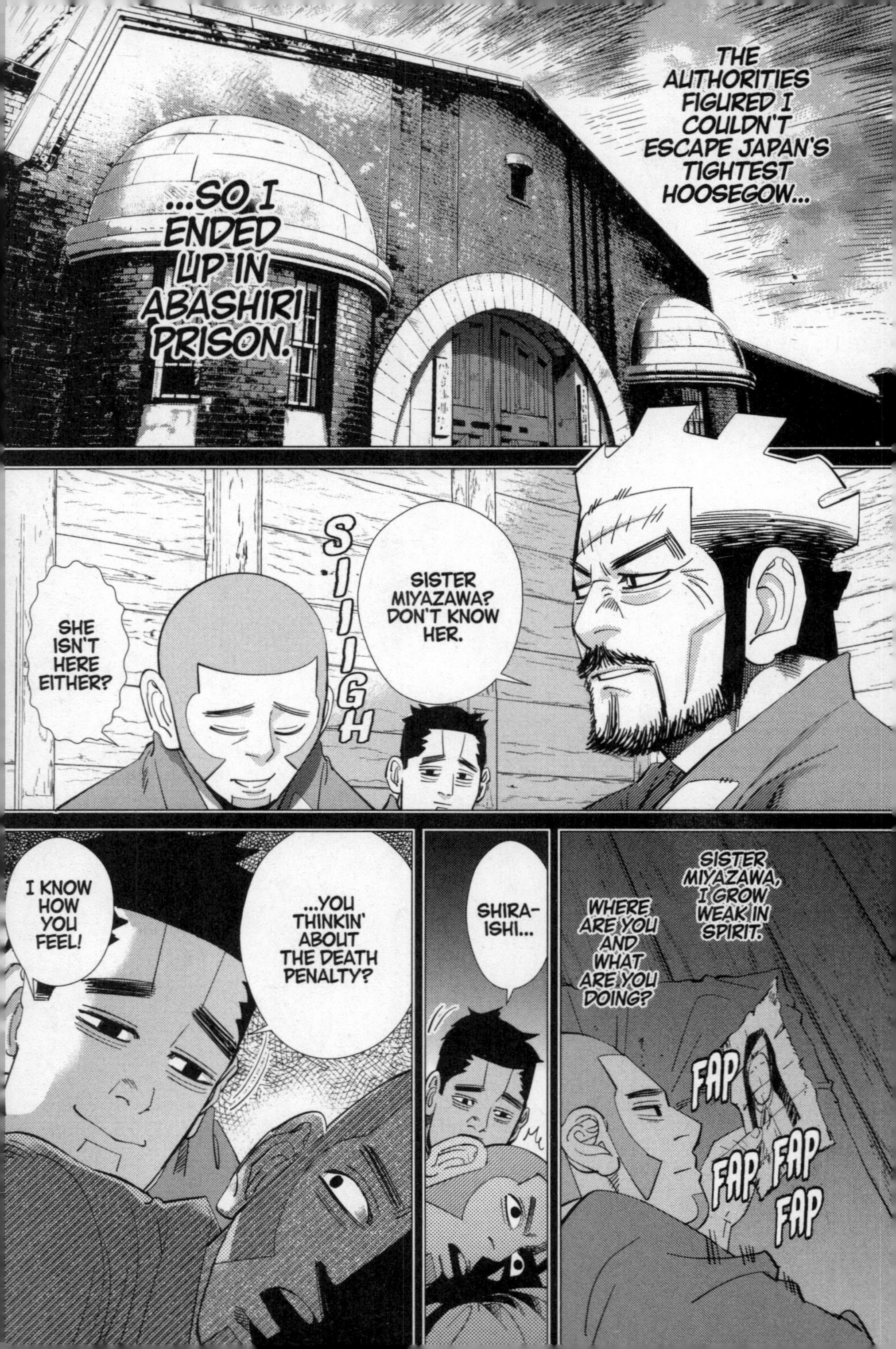
THE AUTHORITIES FIGURED I COULDN'T ESCAPE JAPAN'S TIGHTEST HOOSEGOW...
...SO I ENDED UP IN ABASHIRI PRISON.
SISTER MIYAZAWA? DON'T KNOW HER.
SIIIGH
SHE ISN'T HERE EITHER?
SISTER MIYAZAWA, I GROW WEAK IN SPIRIT.
WHERE ARE YOU AND WHAT ARE YOU DOING?
FAP
FAP FAP
FAP
SHIRA-ISHI...
...YOU THINKIN' ABOUT THE DEATH PENALTY?
I KNOW HOW YOU FEEL!

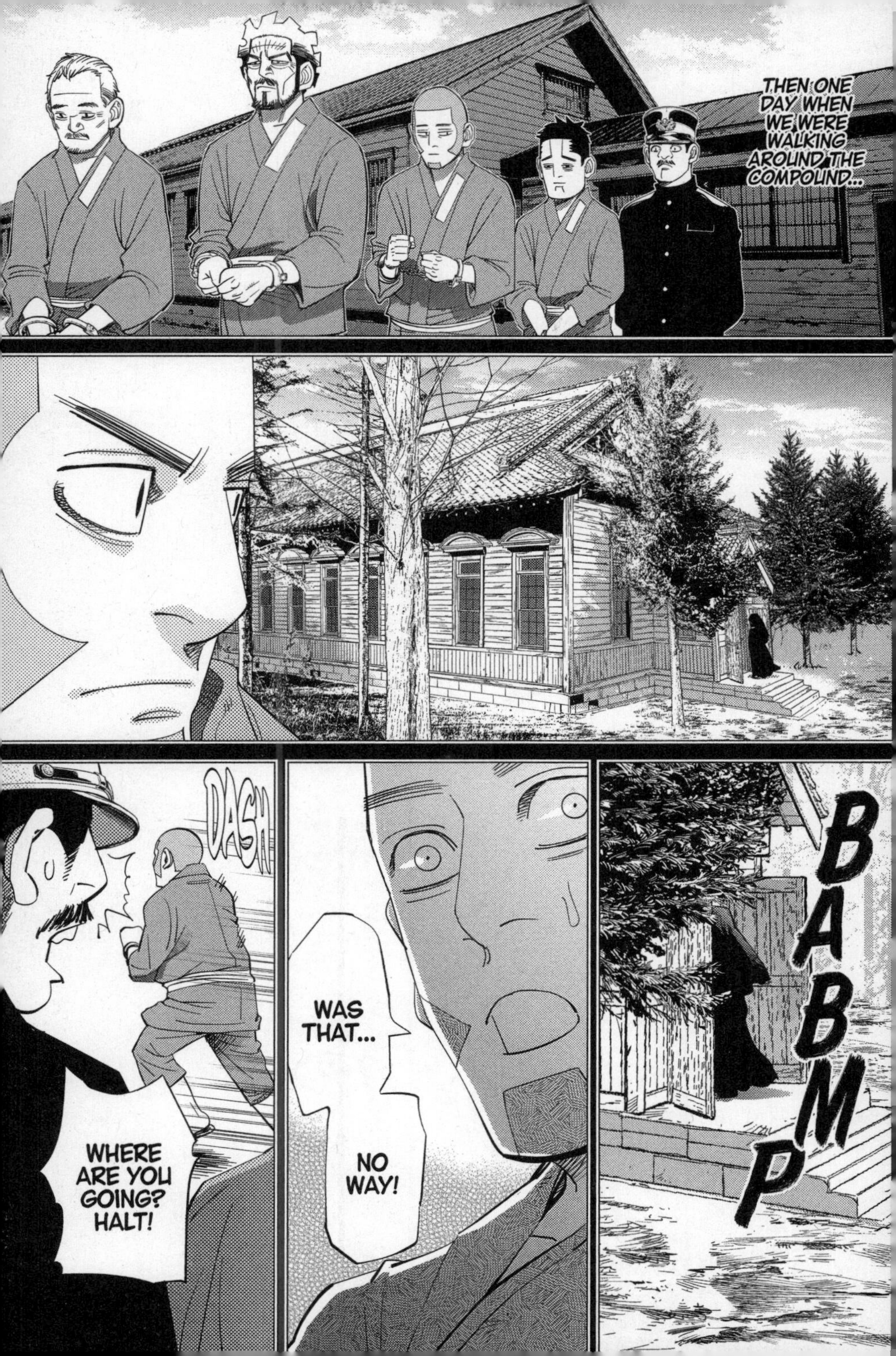
THEN ONE DAY WHEN WE WERE WALKING AROUND THE COMPOUND...
BABMP
WAS THAT...
NO WAY!
DASH
WHERE ARE YOU GOING? HALT!

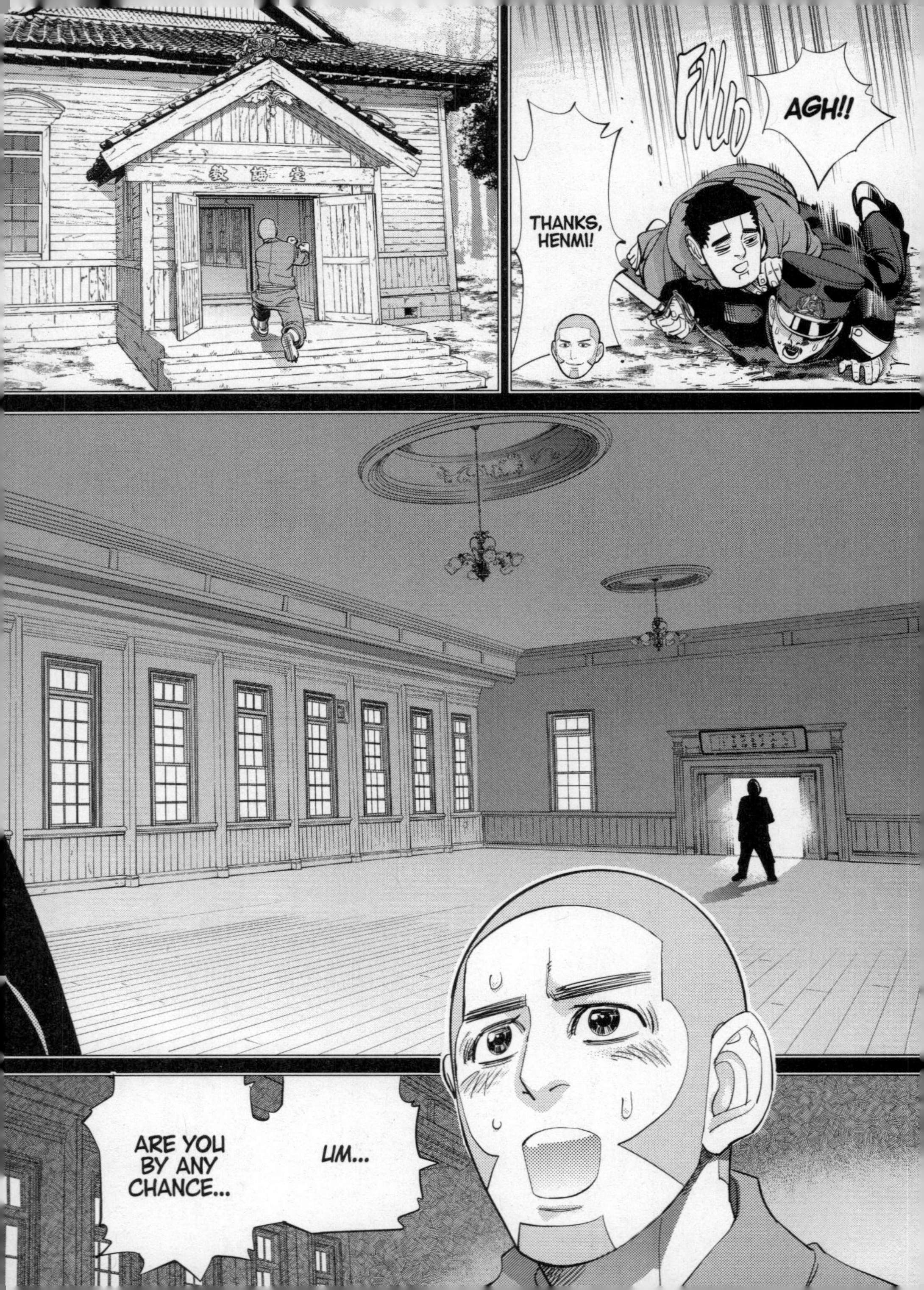
AGH!!
FWUD
THANKS, HENMI!
UM...
ARE YOU BY ANY CHANCE...

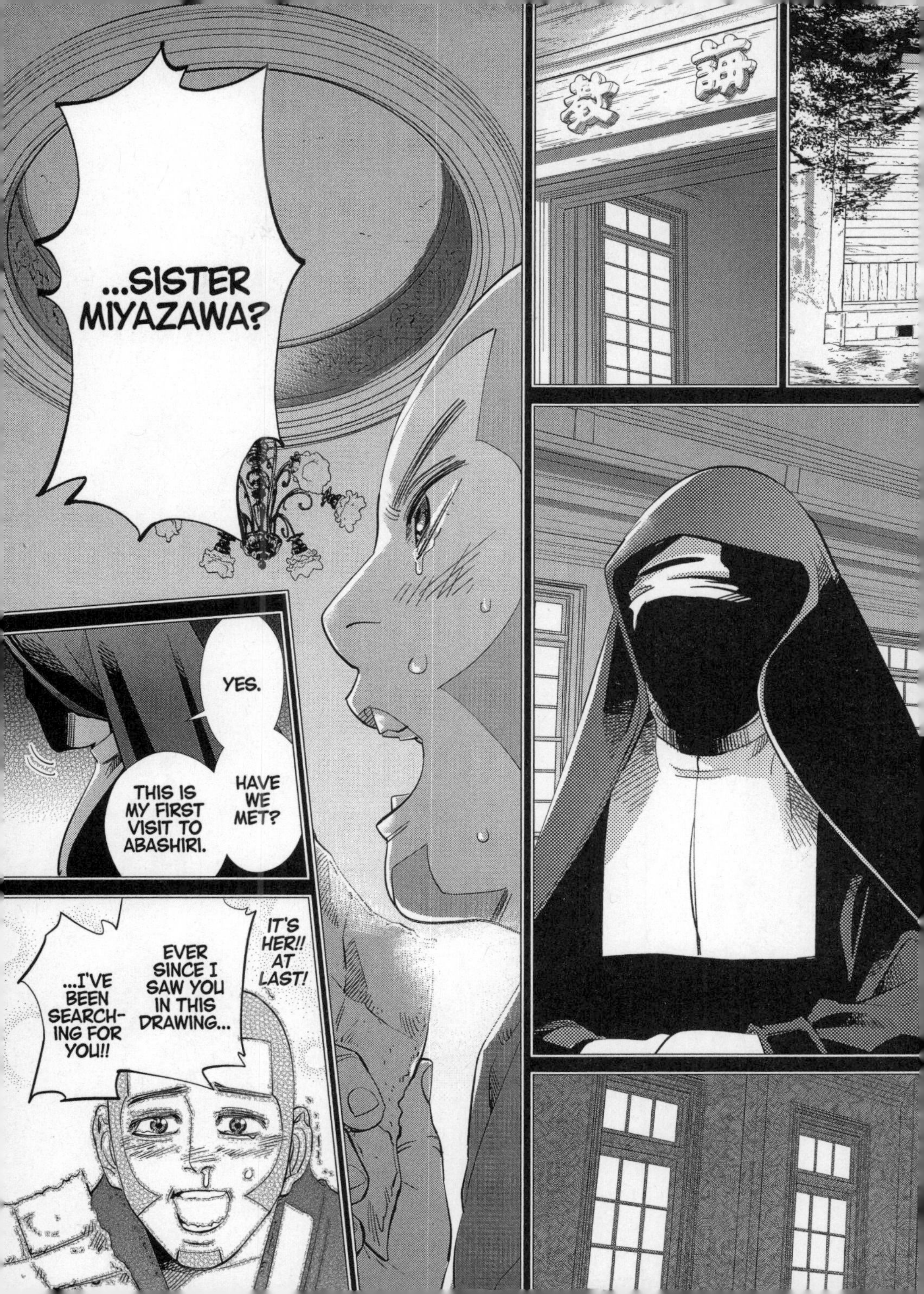
教誨
...SISTER MIYAZAWA?
YES.
HAVE WE MET?
THIS IS MY FIRST VISIT TO ABASHIRI.
IT'S HER!! AT LAST!
EVER SINCE I SAW YOU IN THIS DRAWING...
...I'VE BEEN SEARCHING FOR YOU!!

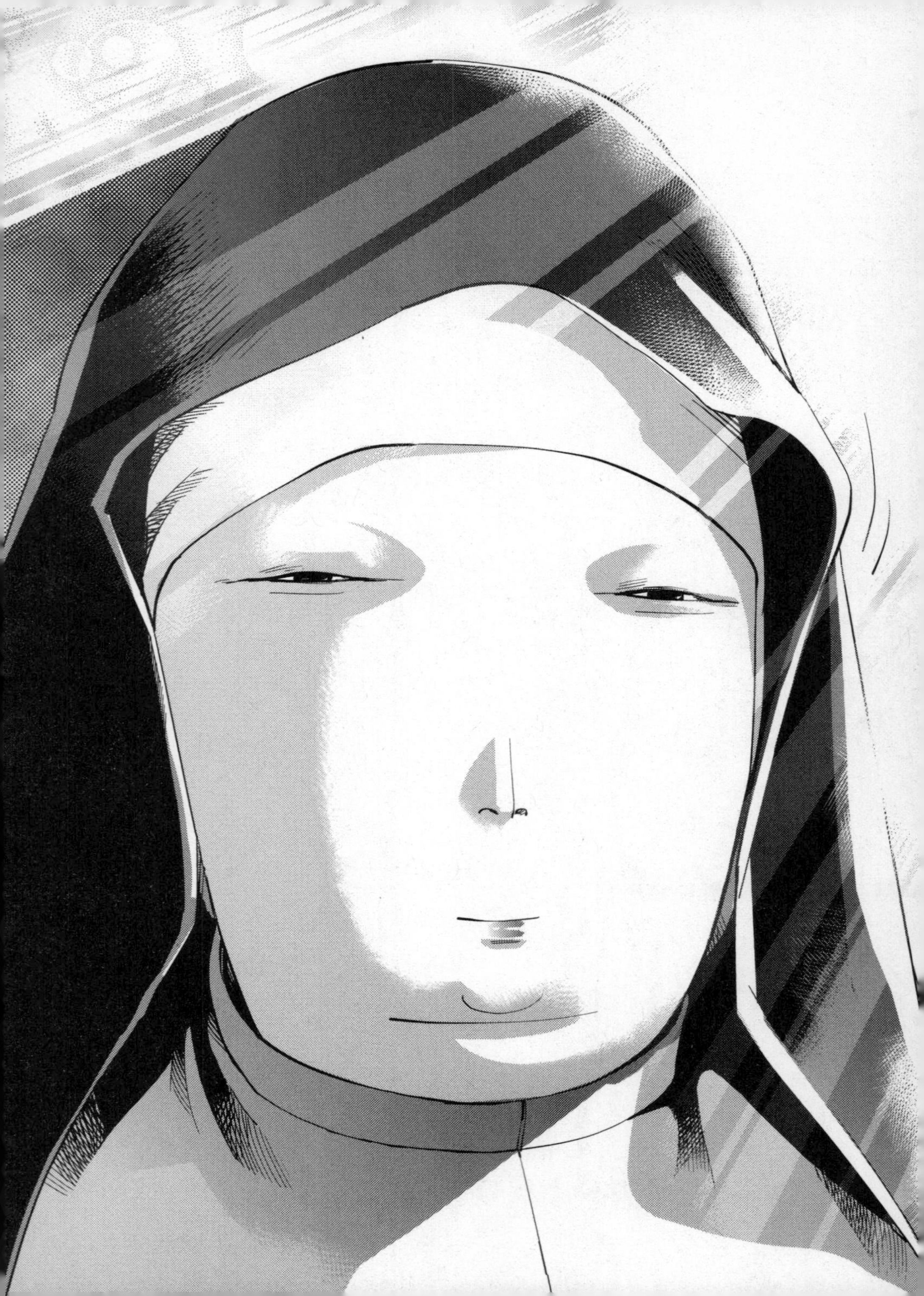

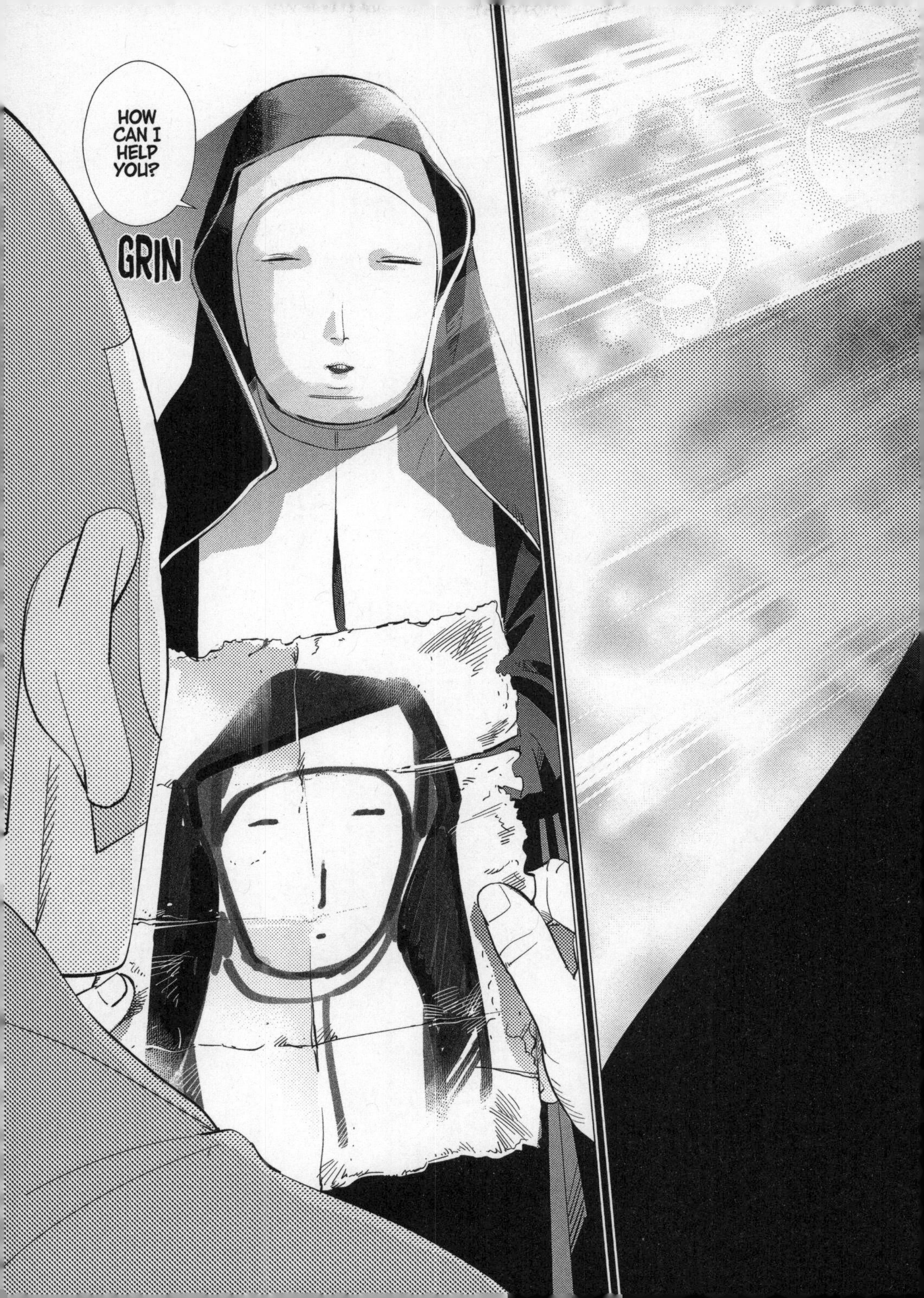
HOW CAN I HELP YOU?
GRIN

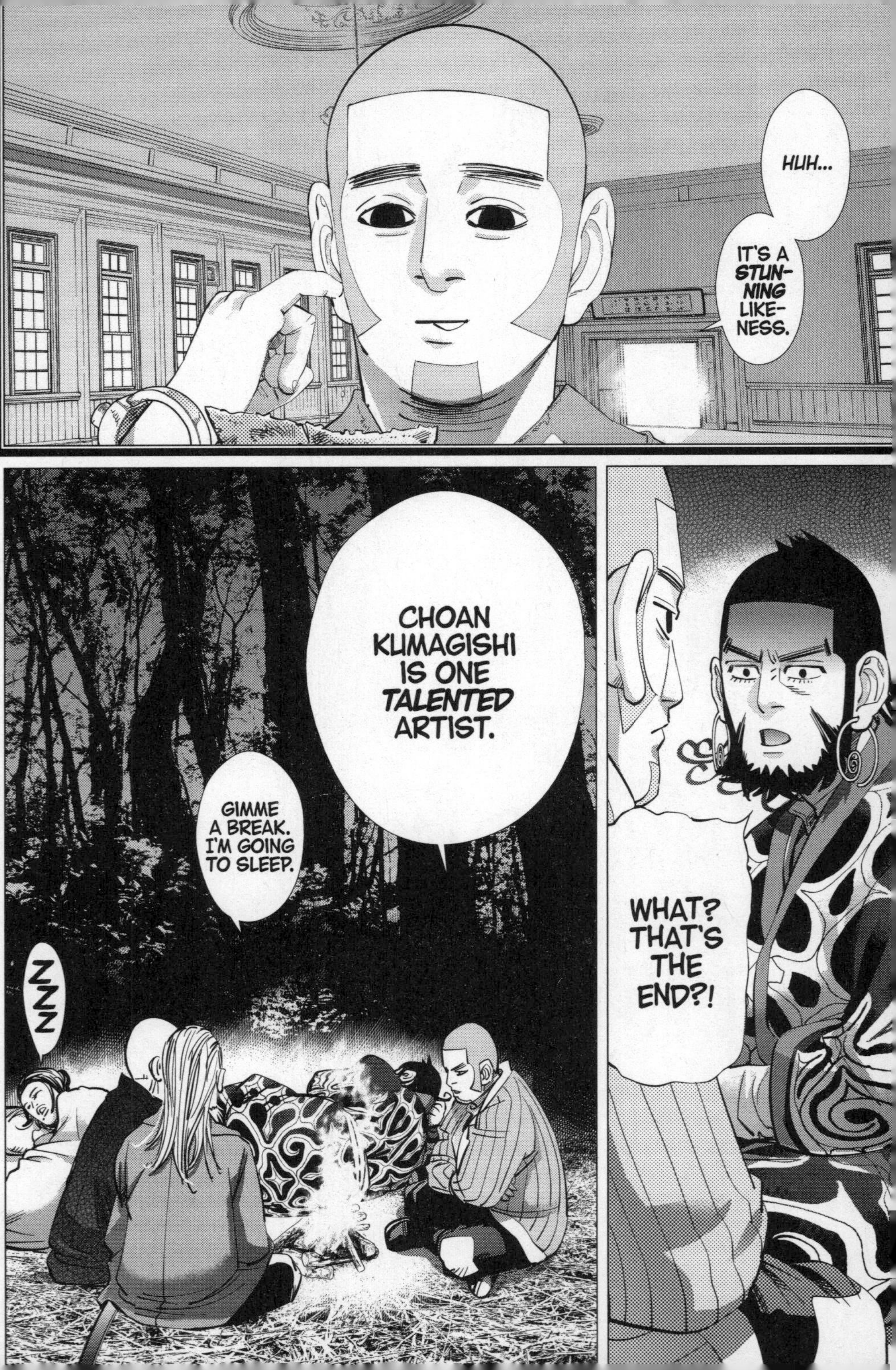
HUH...
IT'S A STUNNING LIKENESS.
WHAT? THAT'S THE END?!
CHOAN KUMAGISHI IS ONE TALENTED ARTIST.
GIMME A BREAK. I'M GOING TO SLEEP.
ZZZ

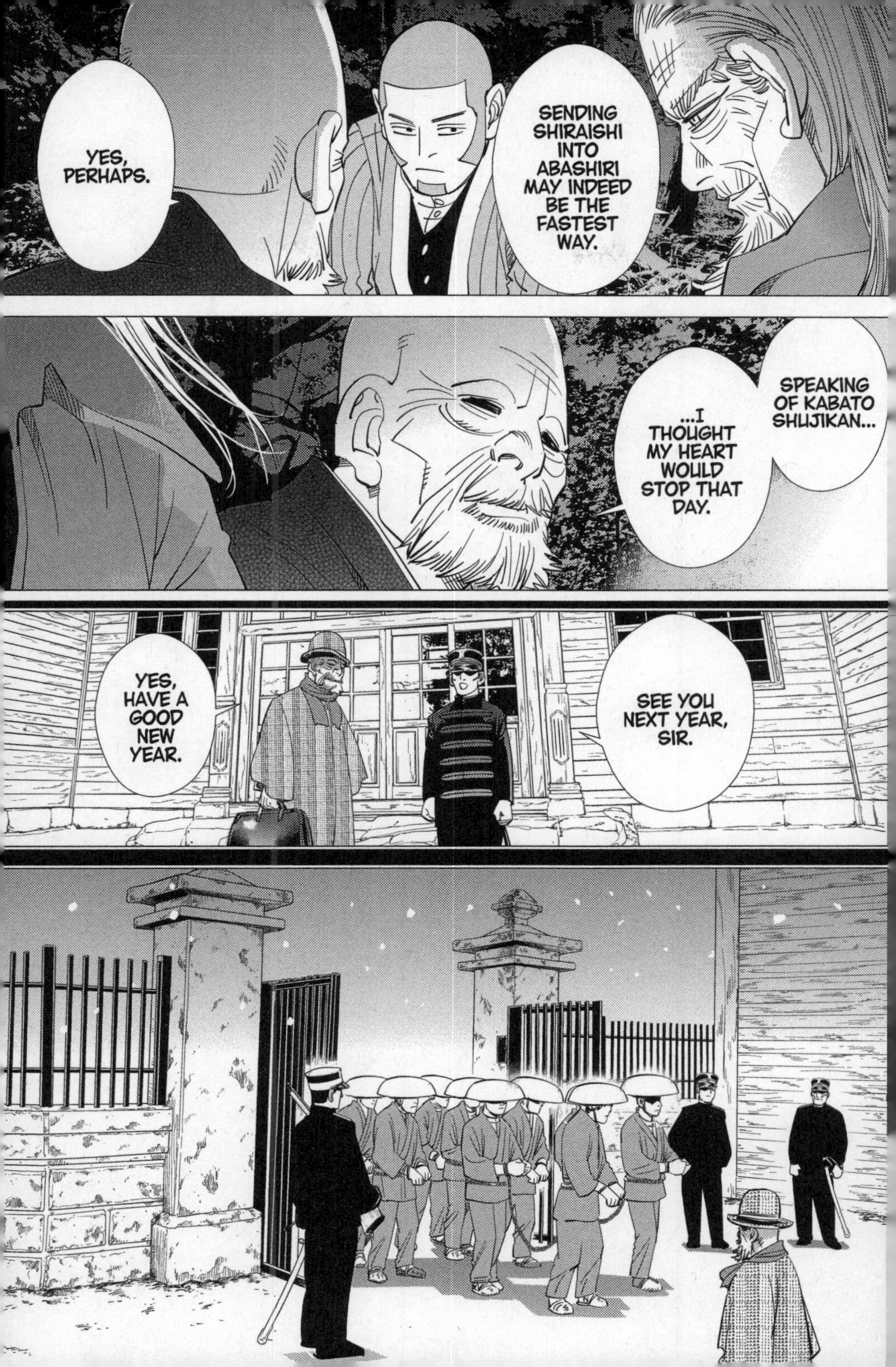
SENDING SHIRAISHI INTO ABASHIRI MAY INDEED BE THE FASTEST WAY.
YES, PERHAPS.
SPEAKING OF KABATO SHUJIKAN...
...I THOUGHT MY HEART WOULD STOP THAT DAY.
SEE YOU NEXT YEAR, SIR.
YES, HAVE A GOOD NEW YEAR.

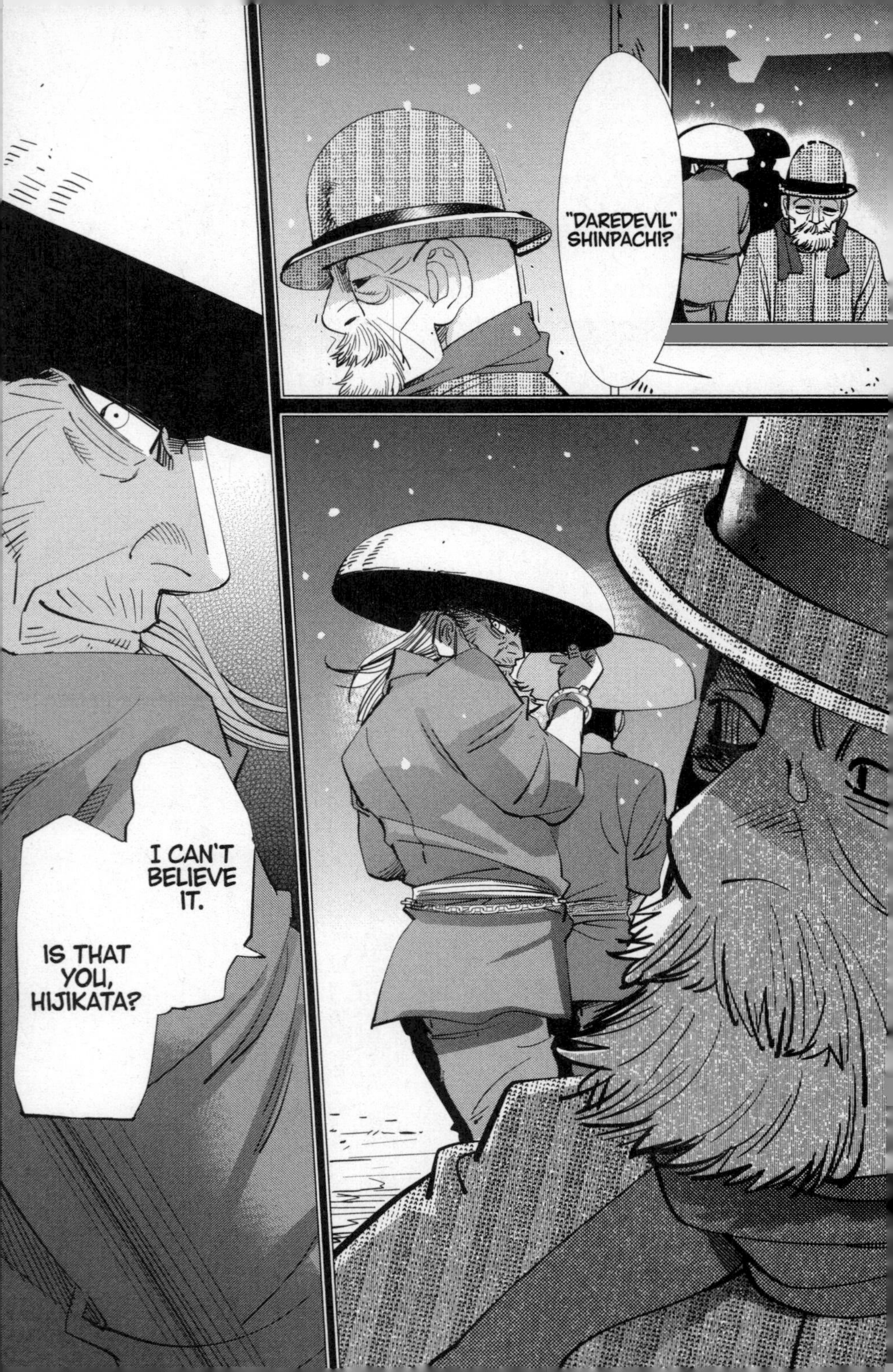
"DAREDEVIL" SHINPACHI?
I CAN'T BELIEVE IT.
IS THAT YOU, HIJIKATA?

Chapter 86: Let's Talk About the Past

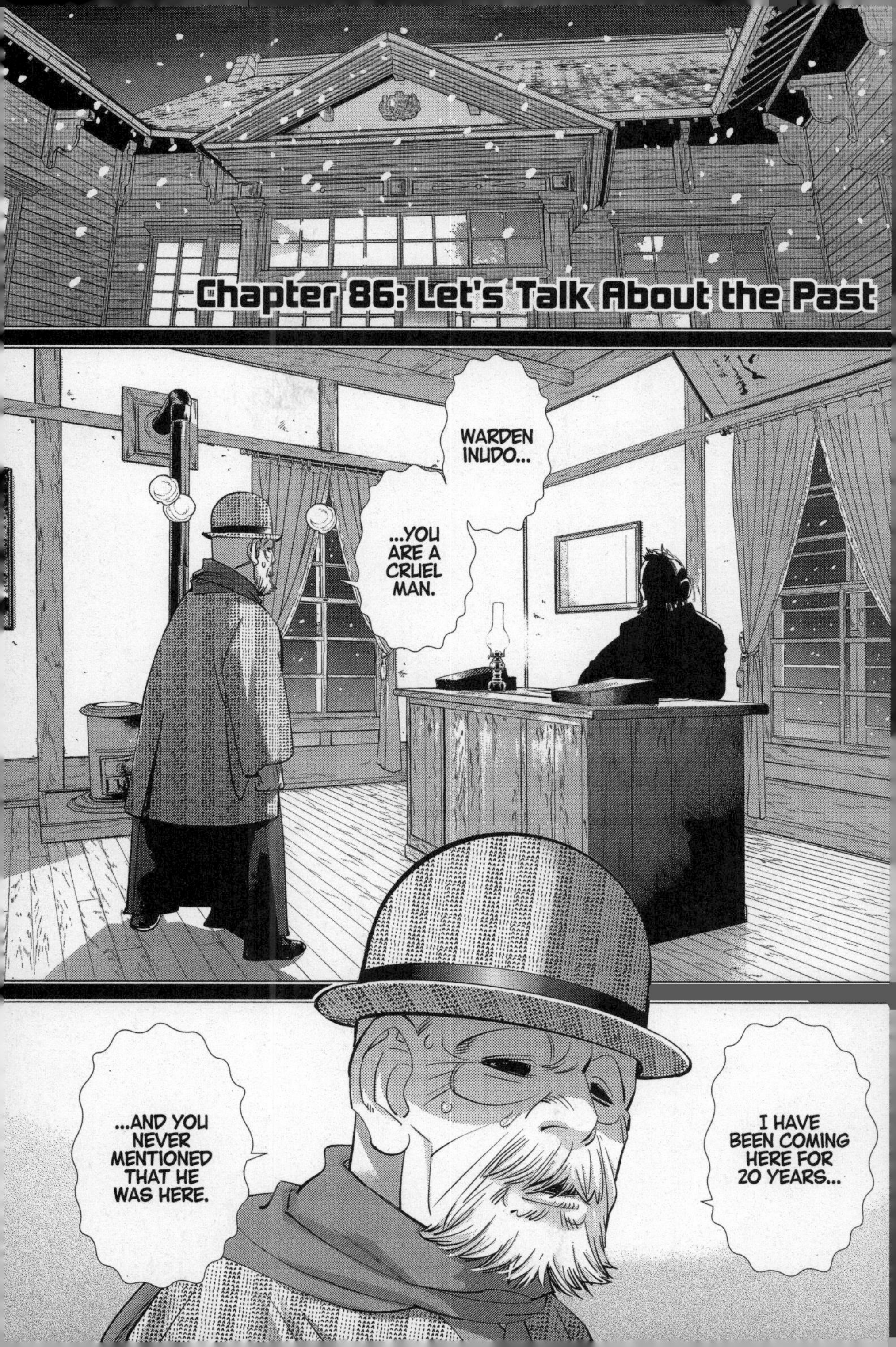
WARDEN INUDO...
...YOU ARE A CRUEL MAN.
I HAVE BEEN COMING HERE FOR 20 YEARS...
...AND YOU NEVER MENTIONED THAT HE WAS HERE.

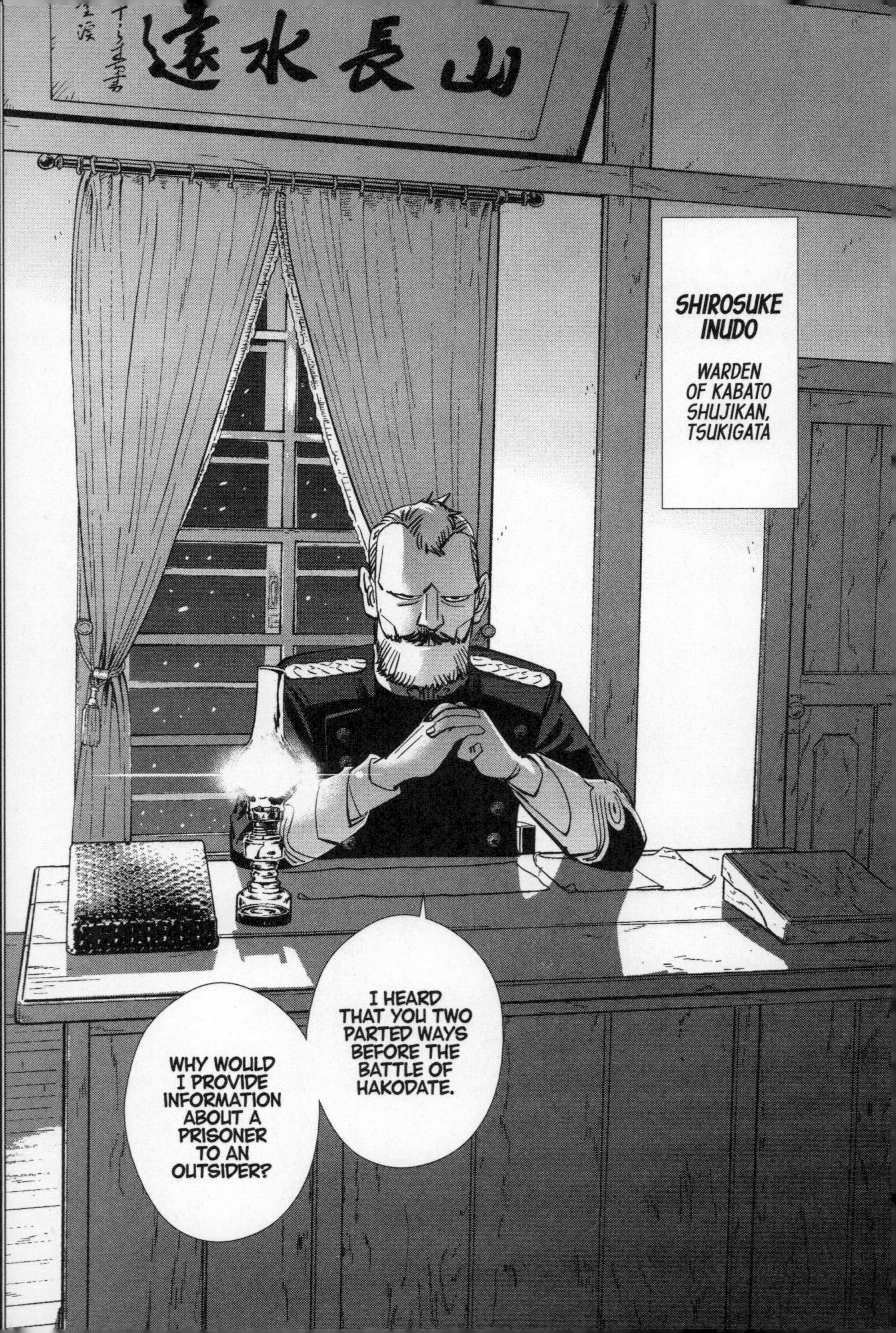
山長水遠
SHIROSUKE INUDO
WARDEN OF KABATO SHUJIKAN, TSUKIGATA
I HEARD THAT YOU TWO PARTED WAYS BEFORE THE BATTLE OF HAKODATE.
WHY WOULD I PROVIDE INFORMATION ABOUT A PRISONER TO AN OUTSIDER?

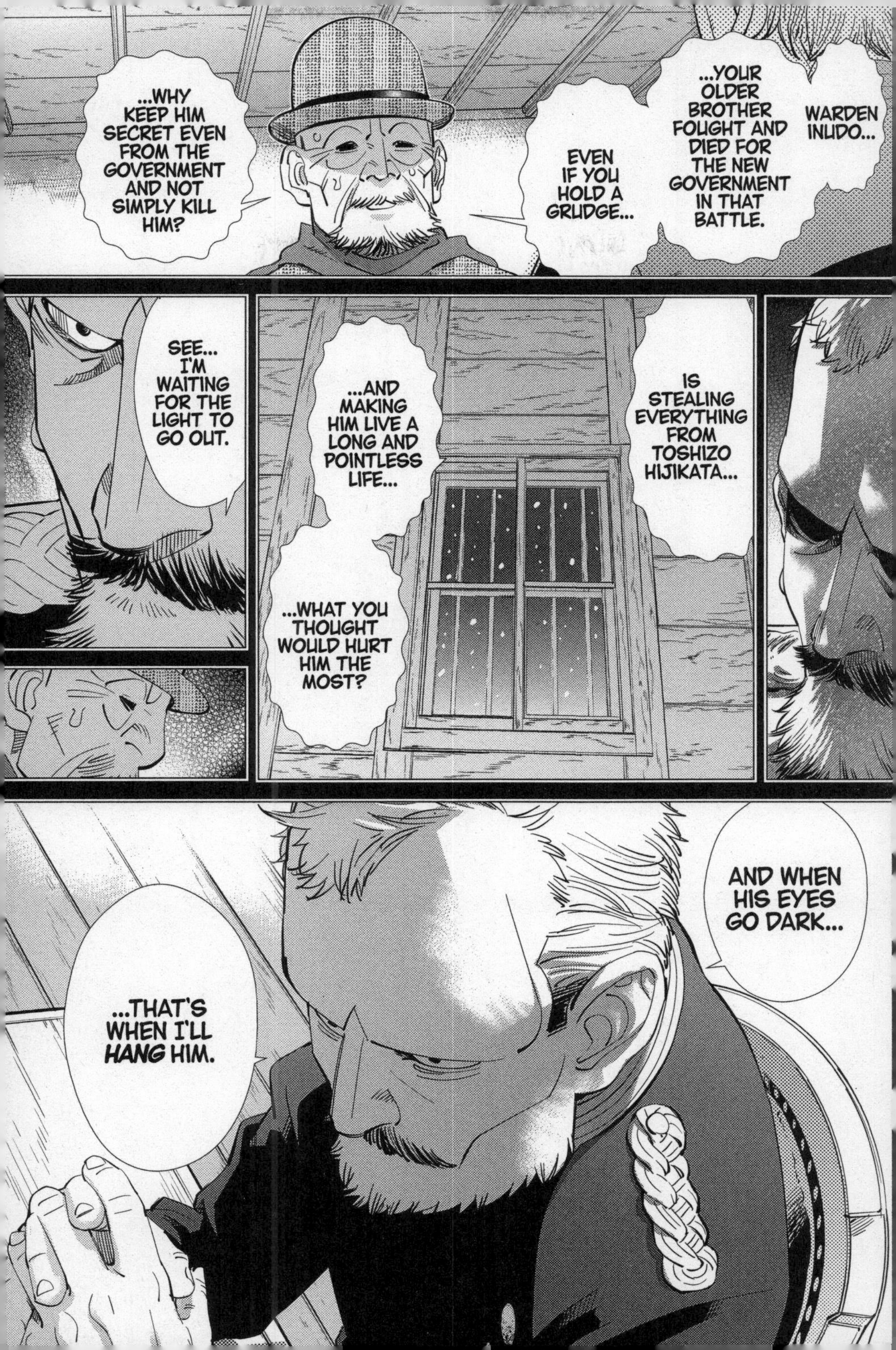
WARDEN INUDO...
...YOUR OLDER BROTHER FOUGHT AND DIED FOR THE NEW GOVERNMENT IN THAT BATTLE.
EVEN IF YOU HOLD A GRUDGE...
...WHY KEEP HIM SECRET EVEN FROM THE GOVERNMENT AND NOT SIMPLY KILL HIM?
IS STEALING EVERYTHING FROM TOSHIZO HIJIKATA...
...AND MAKING HIM LIVE A LONG AND POINTLESS LIFE...
...WHAT YOU THOUGHT WOULD HURT HIM THE MOST?
SEE... I'M WAITING FOR THE LIGHT TO GO OUT.
AND WHEN HIS EYES GO DARK...
...THAT'S WHEN I'LL *HANG* HIM.

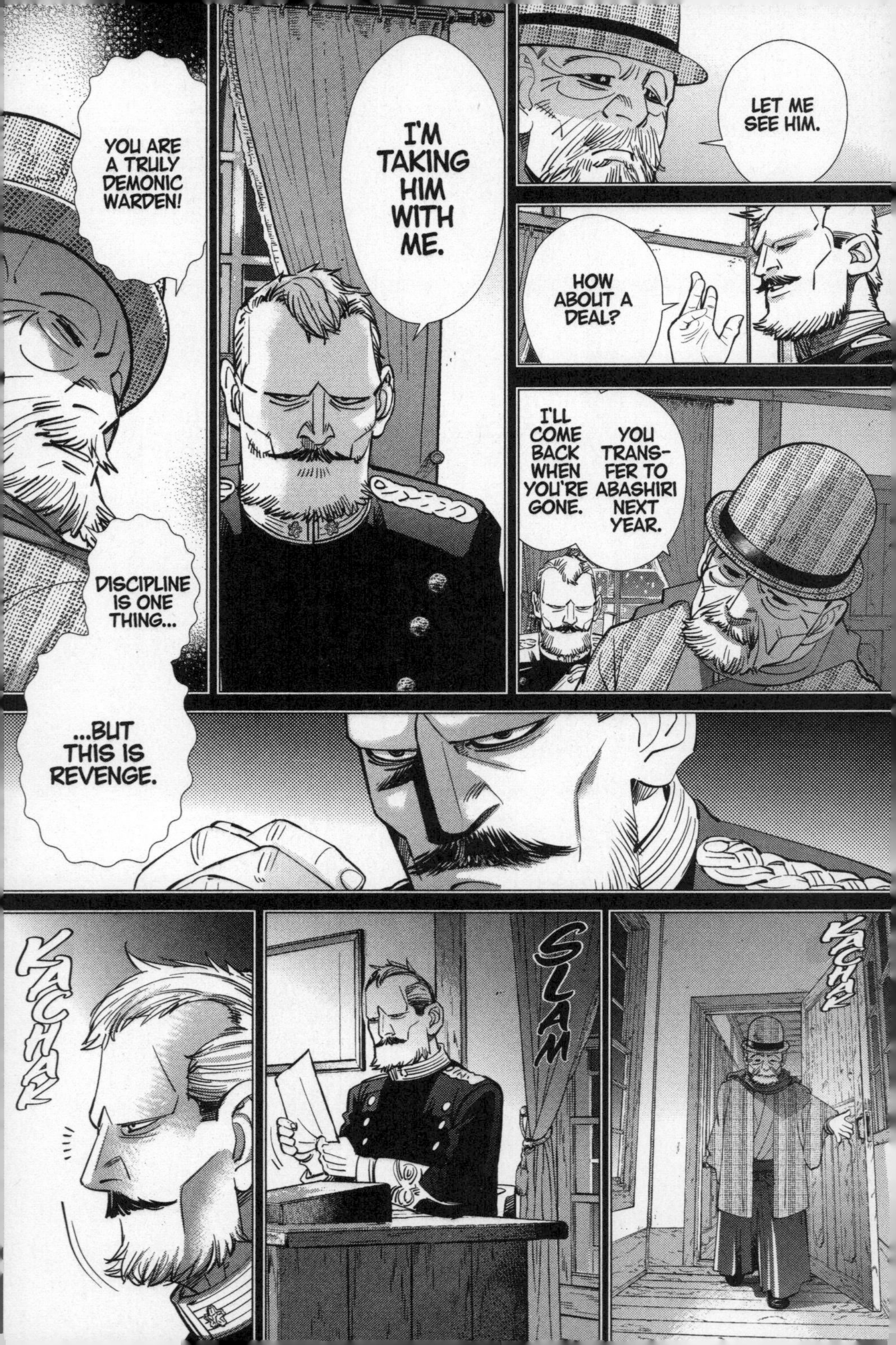
LET ME SEE HIM.
HOW ABOUT A DEAL?
YOU TRANSFER TO ABASHIRI NEXT YEAR.
I'LL COME BACK WHEN YOU'RE GONE.
I'M TAKING HIM WITH ME.
YOU ARE A TRULY DEMONIC WARDEN!
DISCIPLINE IS ONE THING...
...BUT THIS IS REVENGE.
KACHA
SLAM
KACHA

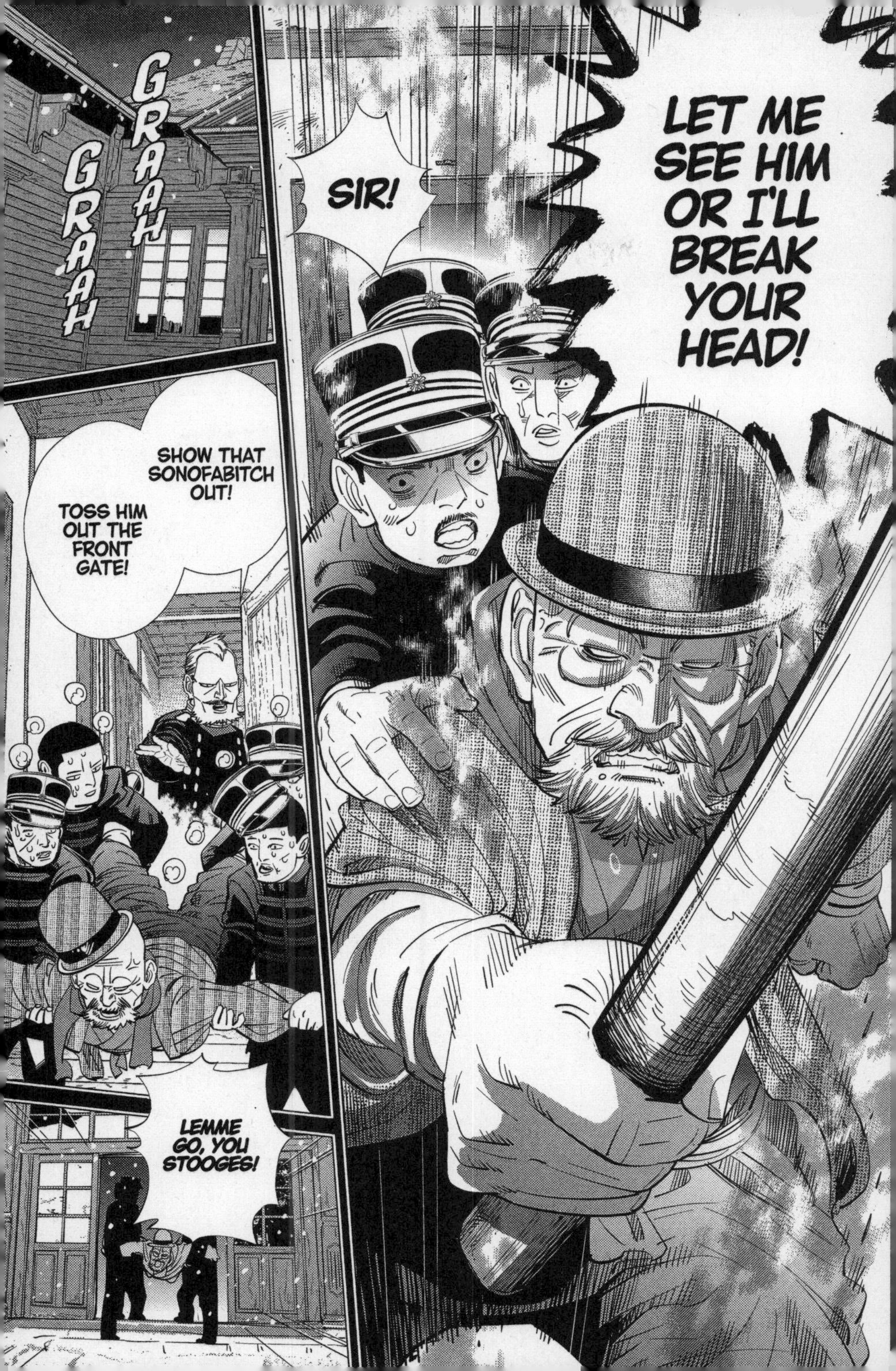
LET ME SEE HIM OR I'LL BREAK YOUR HEAD!
SIR!
GRAAH
GRAAH
SHOW THAT SONOFABITCH OUT!
TOSS HIM OUT THE FRONT GATE!
LEMME GO, YOU STOOGES!

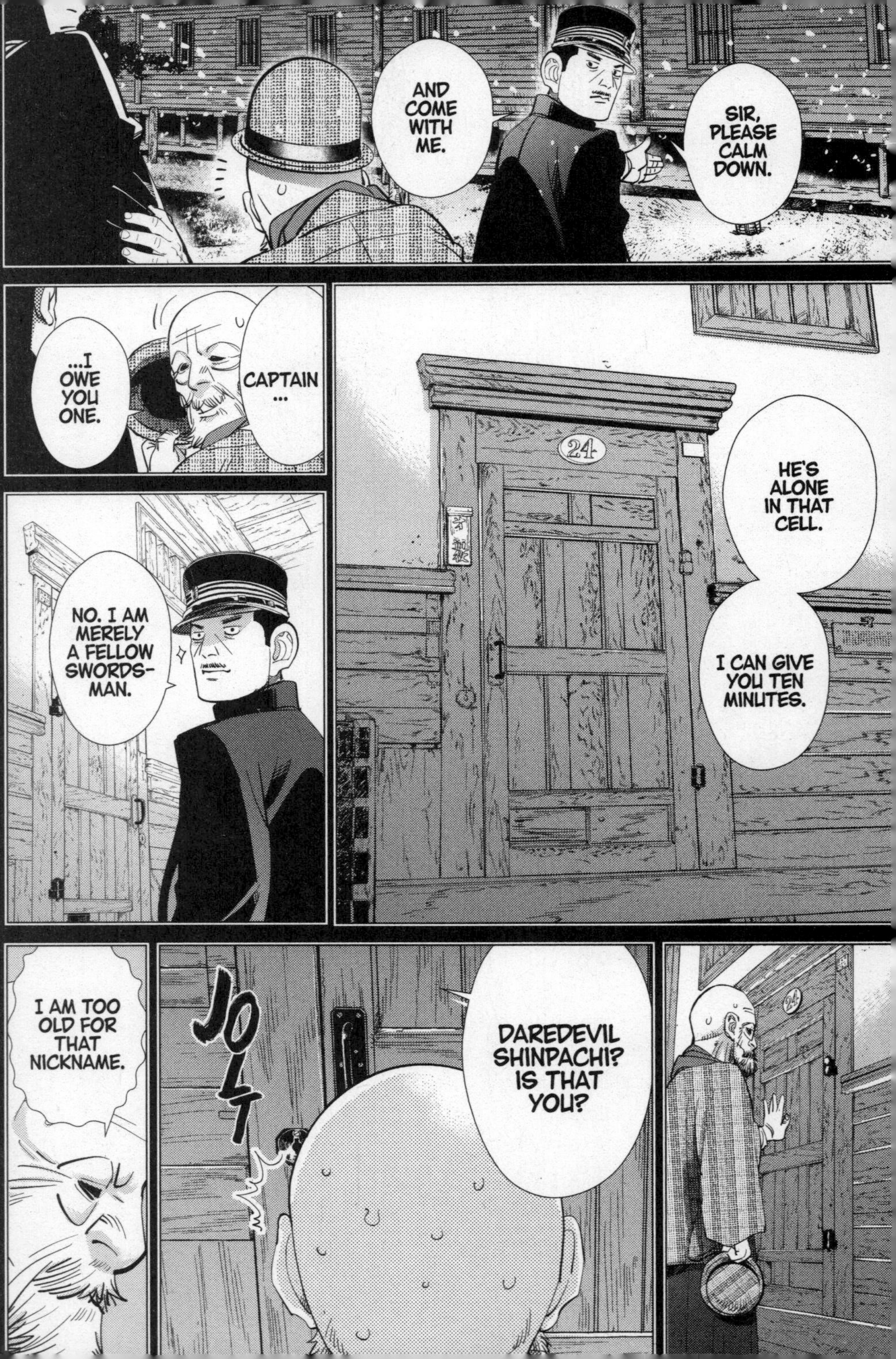
SIR, PLEASE CALM DOWN.
AND COME WITH ME.
HE'S ALONE IN THAT CELL.
I CAN GIVE YOU TEN MINUTES.
CAPTAIN...
...I OWE YOU ONE.
NO. I AM MERELY A FELLOW SWORDS-MAN.
DAREDEVIL SHINPACHI? IS THAT YOU?
JOLT
I AM TOO OLD FOR THAT NICKNAME.

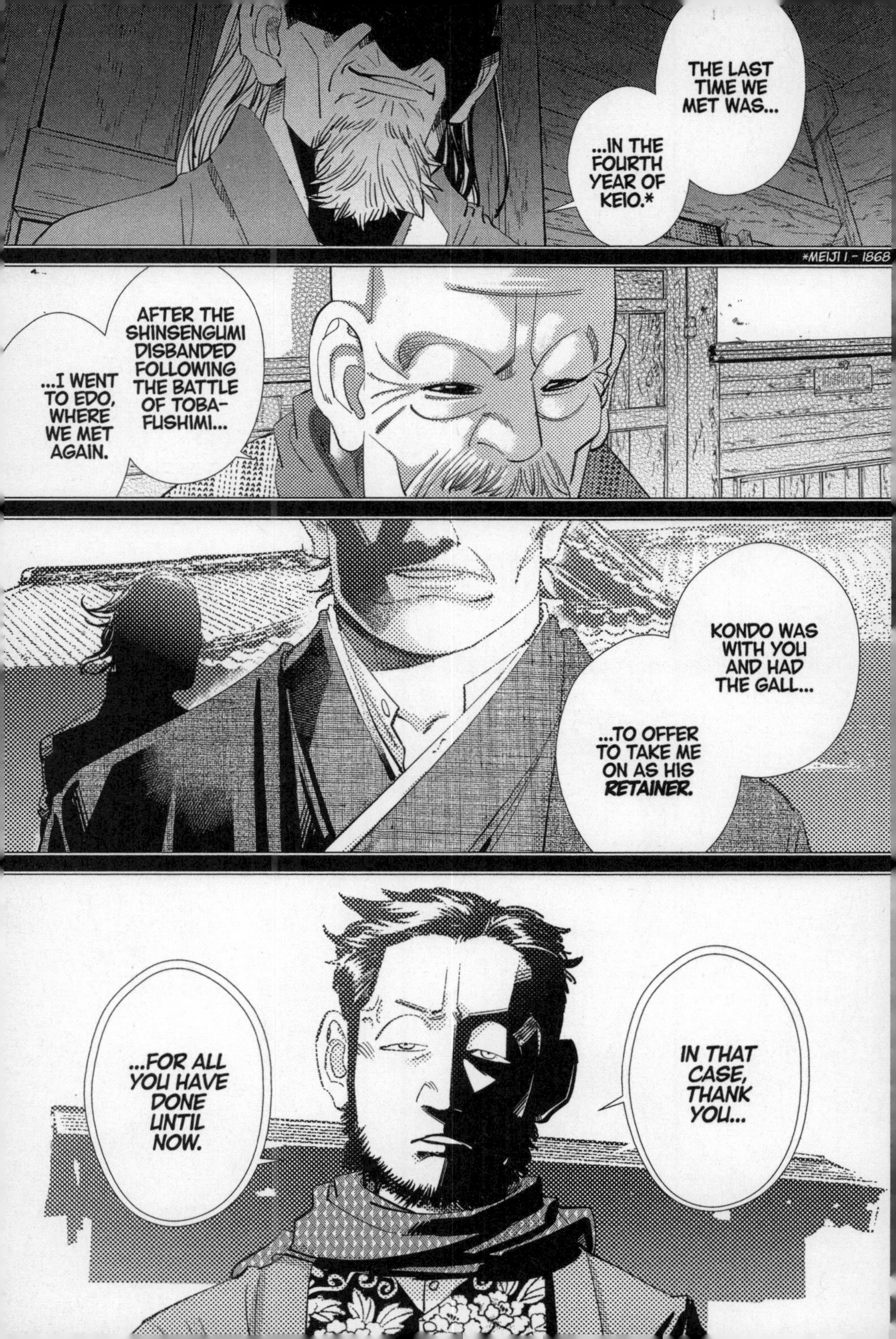
THE LAST TIME WE MET WAS...
...IN THE FOURTH YEAR OF KEIO.*
*MEIJI 1 - 1868
AFTER THE SHINSENGUMI DISBANDED FOLLOWING THE BATTLE OF TOBA-FUSHIMI...
...I WENT TO EDO, WHERE WE MET AGAIN.
KONDO WAS WITH YOU AND HAD THE GALL...
...TO OFFER TO TAKE ME ON AS HIS ***RETAINER.***
IN THAT CASE, THANK YOU...
...FOR ALL YOU HAVE DONE UNTIL NOW.

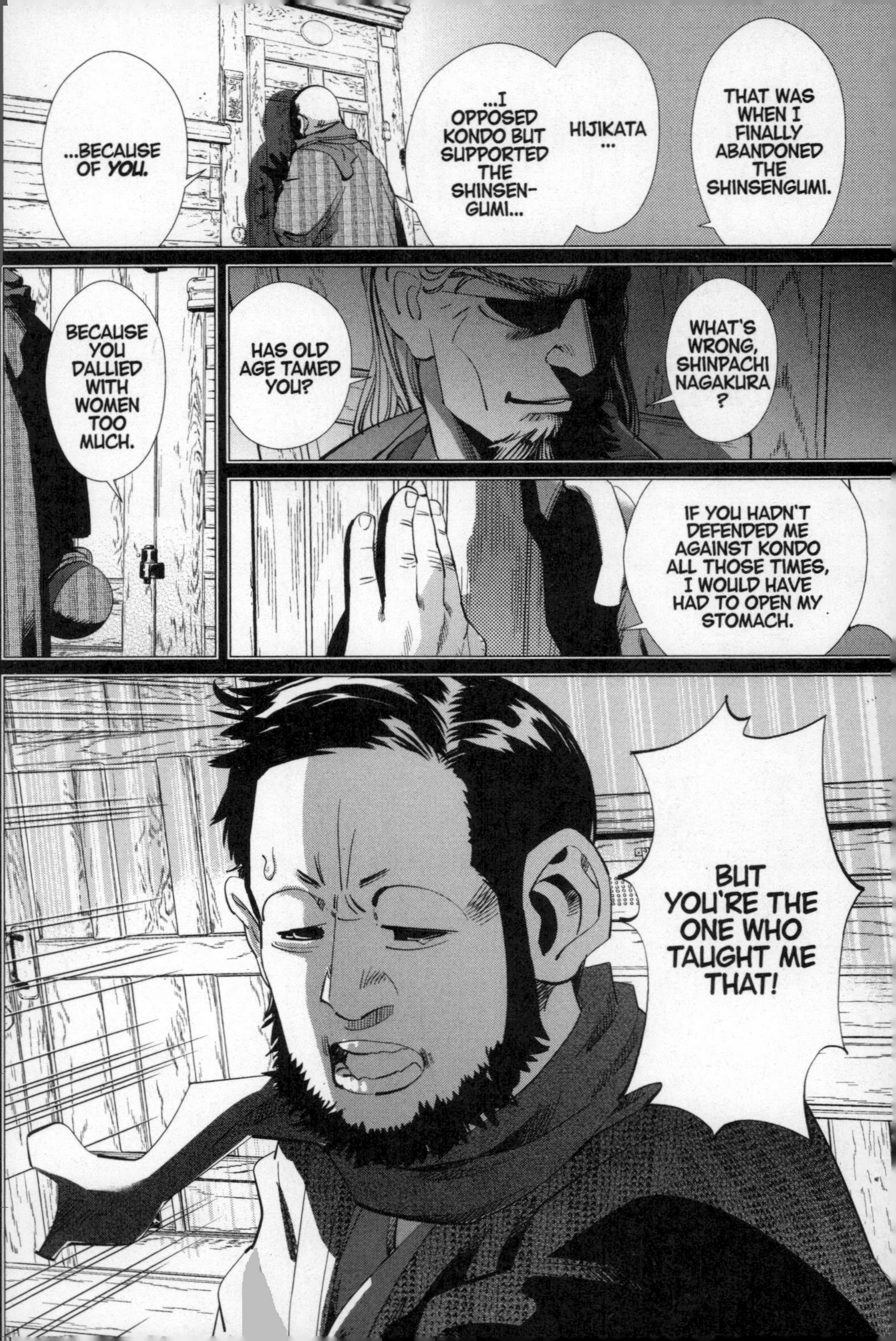
THAT WAS WHEN I FINALLY ABANDONED THE SHINSENGUMI.
HIJIKATA...
...I OPPOSED KONDO BUT SUPPORTED THE SHINSEN-GUMI...
...BECAUSE OF *YOU.*
WHAT'S WRONG, SHINPACHI NAGAKURA?
HAS OLD AGE TAMED YOU?
IF YOU HADN'T DEFENDED ME AGAINST KONDO ALL THOSE TIMES, I WOULD HAVE HAD TO OPEN MY STOMACH.
BECAUSE YOU DALLIED WITH WOMEN TOO MUCH.
BUT YOU'RE THE ONE WHO TAUGHT ME THAT!

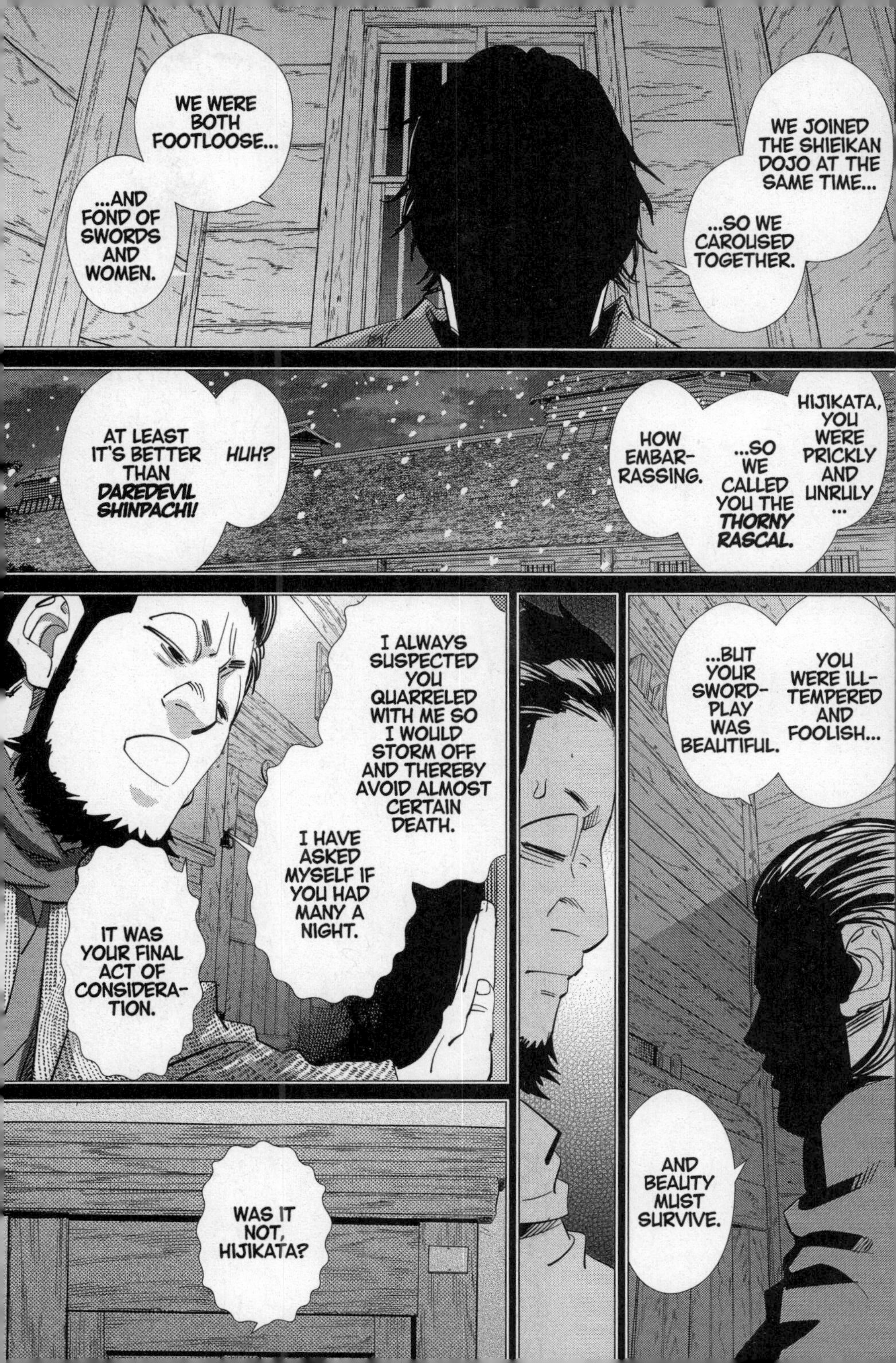
WE JOINED THE SHIEIKAN DOJO AT THE SAME TIME...
...SO WE CAROUSED TOGETHER.
WE WERE BOTH FOOTLOOSE...
...AND FOND OF SWORDS AND WOMEN.
HIJIKATA, YOU WERE PRICKLY AND UNRULY...
...SO WE CALLED YOU THE *THORNY RASCAL.*
HOW EMBARRASSING.
HUH?
AT LEAST IT'S BETTER THAN *DAREDEVIL SHINPACHI!*
YOU WERE ILL-TEMPERED AND FOOLISH...
...BUT YOUR SWORDPLAY WAS BEAUTIFUL.
AND BEAUTY MUST SURVIVE.
I ALWAYS SUSPECTED YOU QUARRELED WITH ME SO I WOULD STORM OFF AND THEREBY AVOID ALMOST CERTAIN DEATH.
I HAVE ASKED MYSELF IF YOU HAD MANY A NIGHT.
IT WAS YOUR FINAL ACT OF CONSIDERATION.
WAS IT NOT, HIJIKATA?

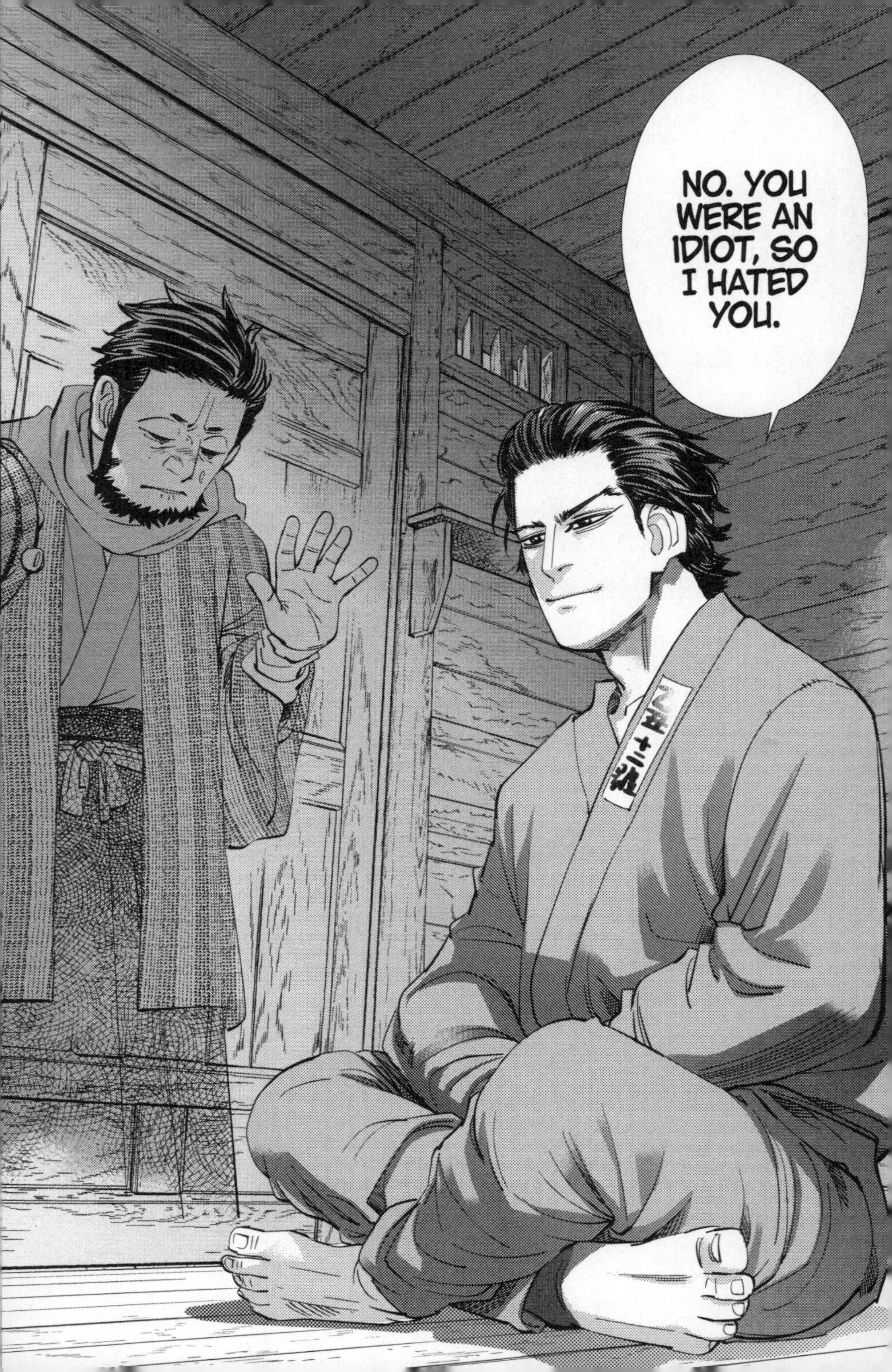
NO. YOU WERE AN IDIOT, SO I HATED YOU.

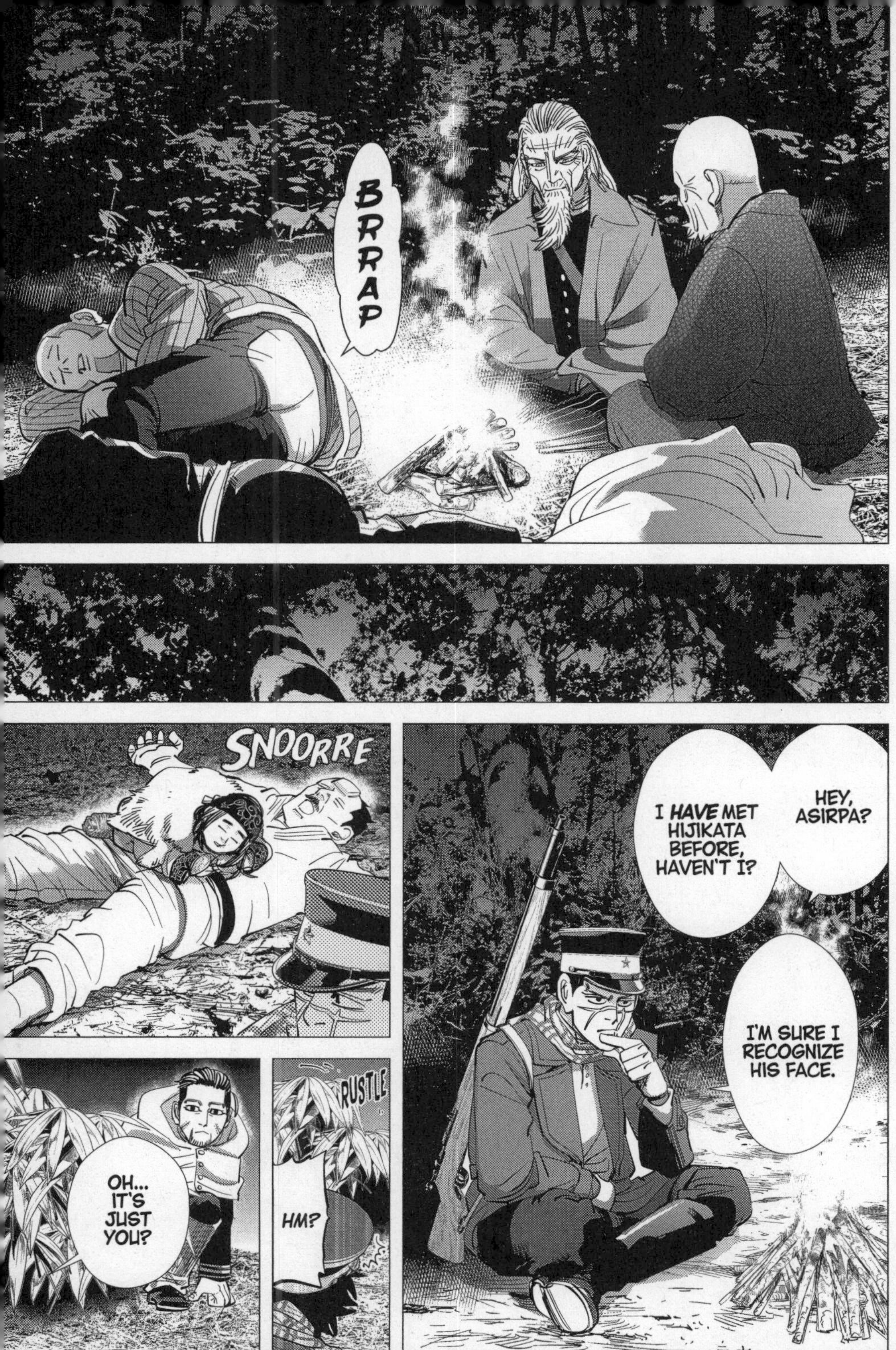
BRRAP
HEY, ASIRPA?
I *HAVE* MET HIJIKATA BEFORE, HAVEN'T I?
I'M SURE I RECOGNIZE HIS FACE.
SNOORRE
RUSTLE
HM?
OH... IT'S JUST YOU?

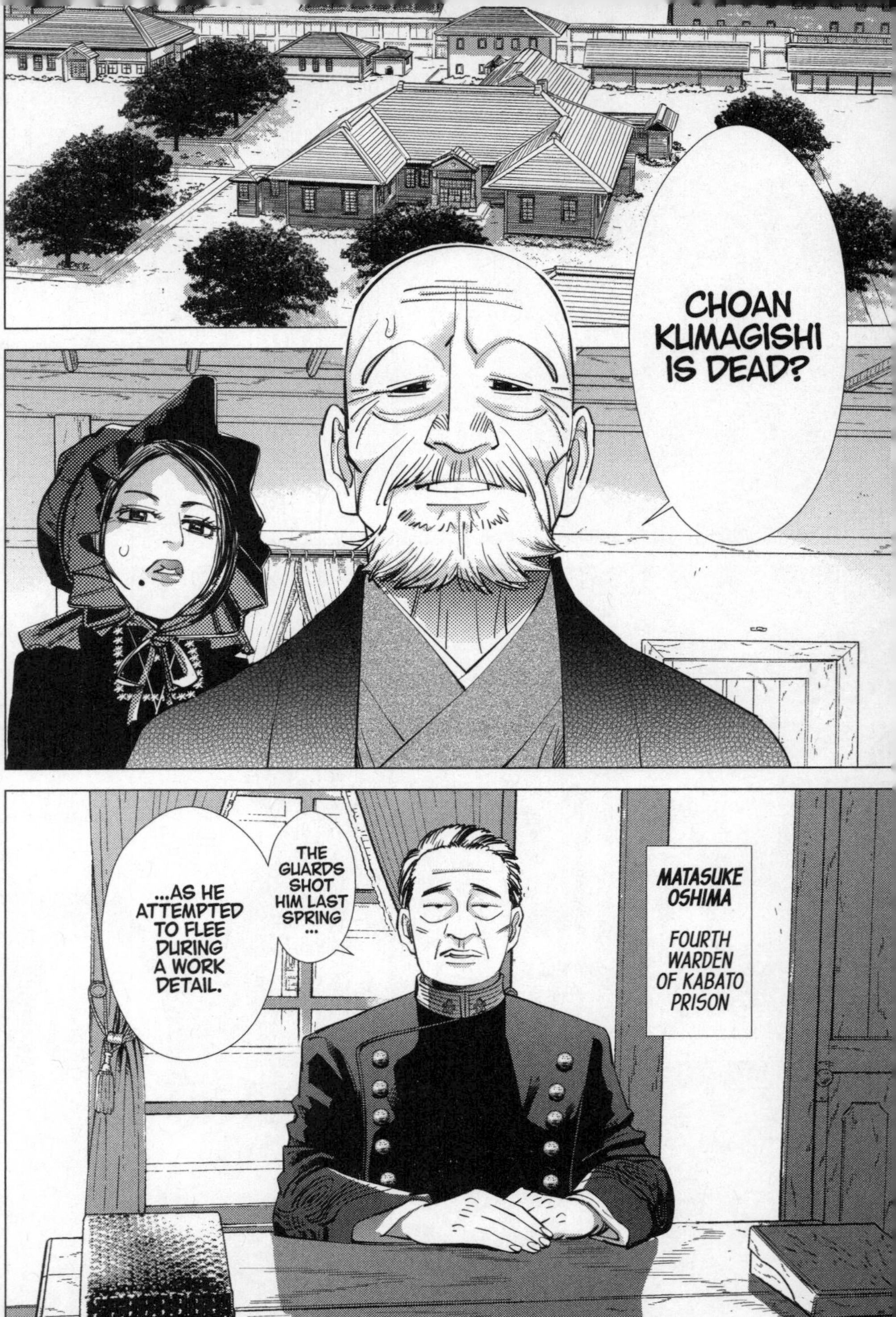
CHOAN KUMAGISHI IS DEAD?
MATASUKE OSHIMA
FOURTH WARDEN OF KABATO PRISON
THE GUARDS SHOT HIM LAST SPRING ...
...AS HE ATTEMPTED TO FLEE DURING A WORK DETAIL.

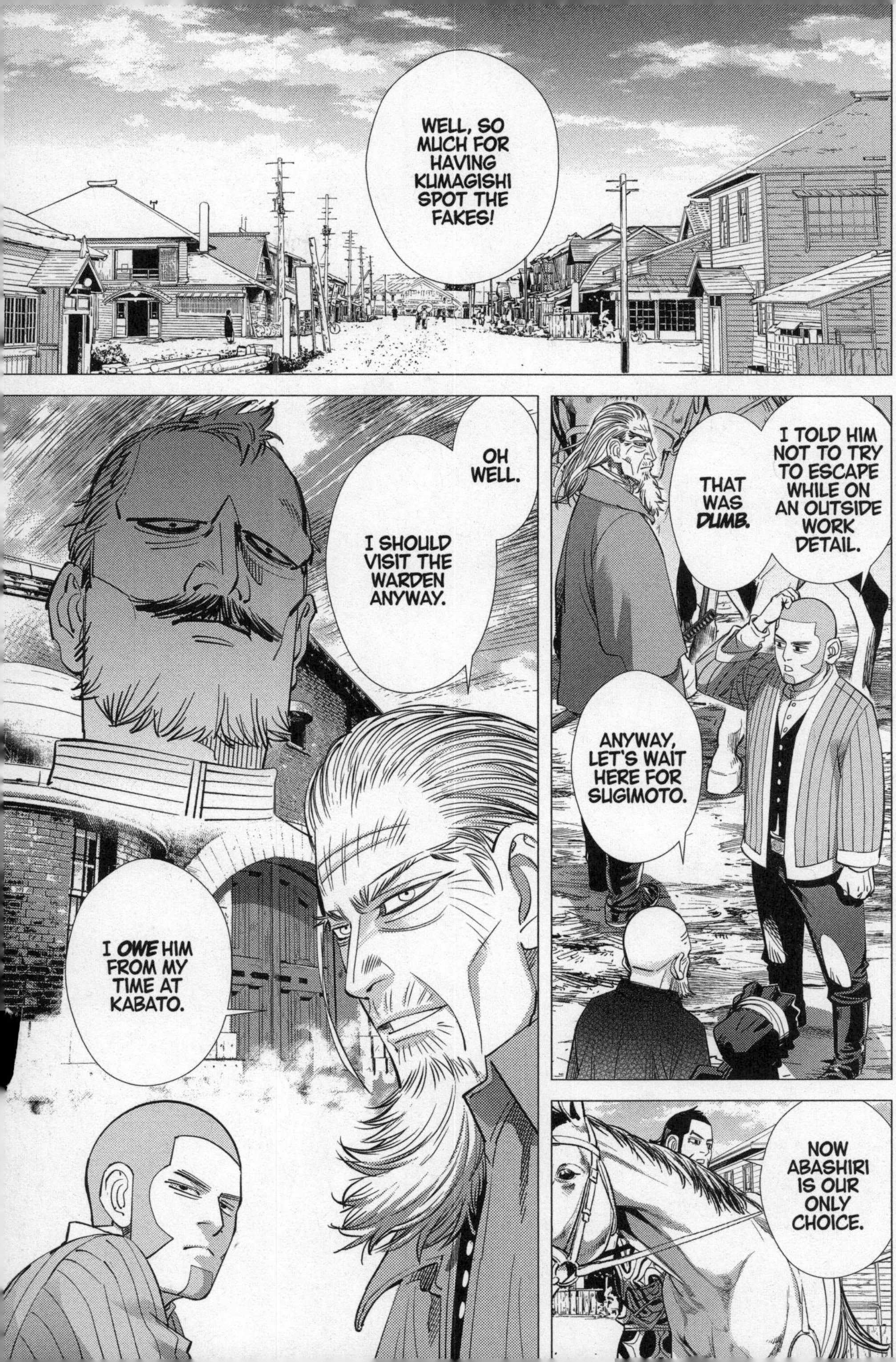
WELL, SO MUCH FOR HAVING KUMAGISHI SPOT THE FAKES!
I TOLD HIM NOT TO TRY TO ESCAPE WHILE ON AN OUTSIDE WORK DETAIL.
THAT WAS DUMB.
ANYWAY, LET'S WAIT HERE FOR SUGIMOTO.
NOW ABASHIRI IS OUR ONLY CHOICE.
OH WELL.
I SHOULD VISIT THE WARDEN ANYWAY.
I OWE HIM FROM MY TIME AT KABATO.

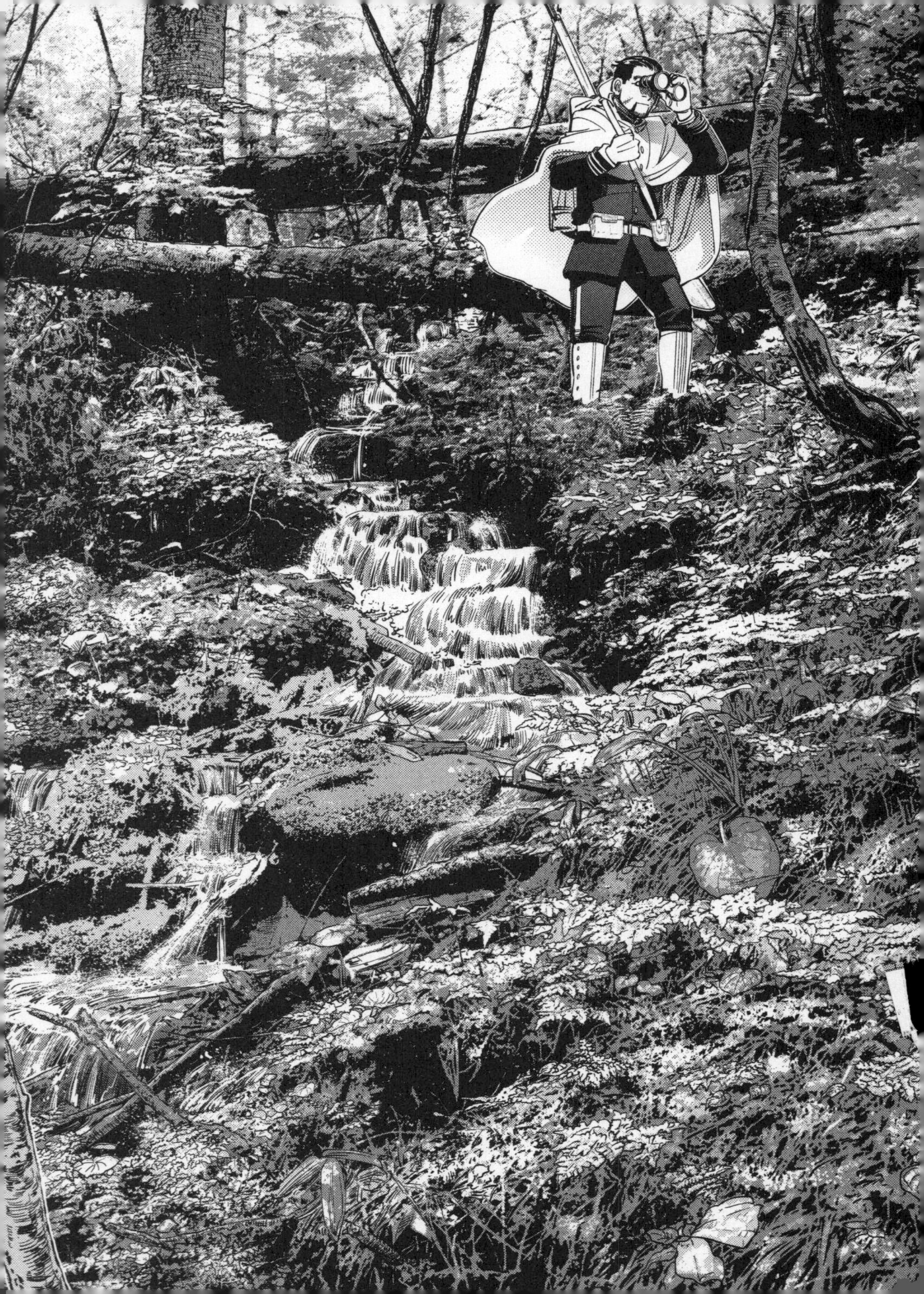

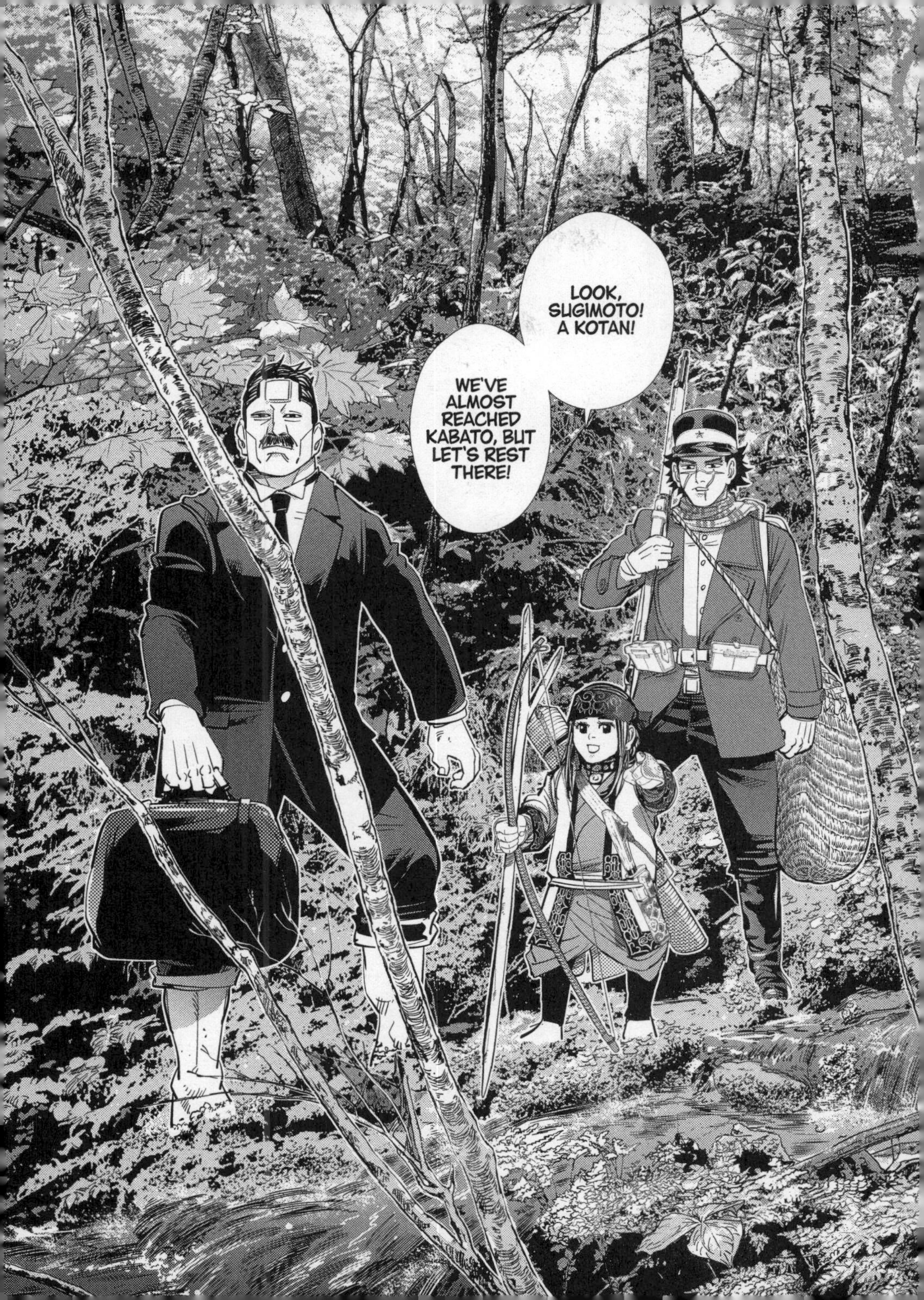
LOOK, SUGIMOTO! A KOTAN!
WE'VE ALMOST REACHED KABATO, BUT LET'S REST THERE!

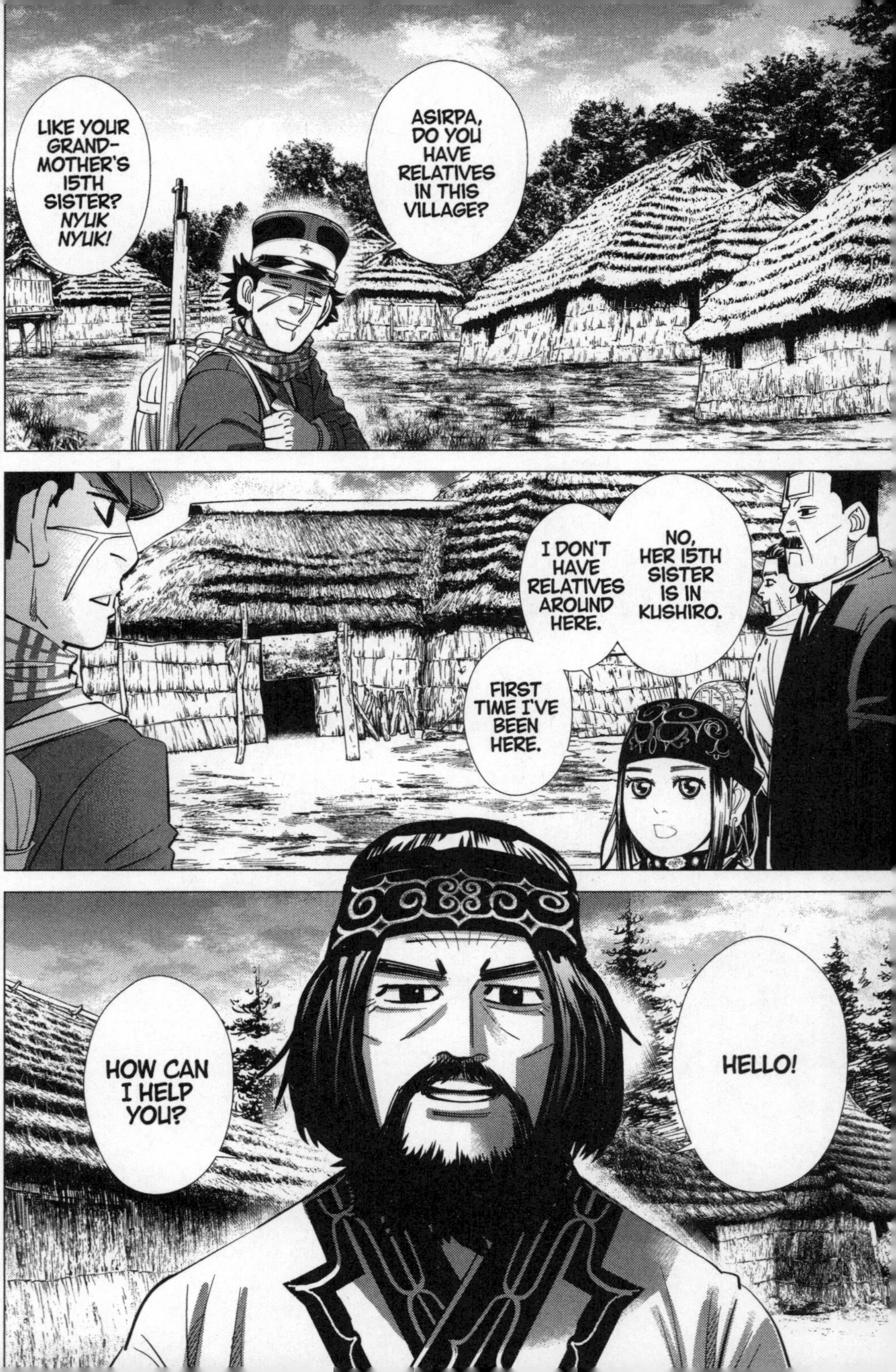
ASIRPA, DO YOU HAVE RELATIVES IN THIS VILLAGE?
LIKE YOUR GRAND-MOTHER'S 15TH SISTER? NYUK NYUK!
NO, HER 15TH SISTER IS IN KUSHIRO.
I DON'T HAVE RELATIVES AROUND HERE.
FIRST TIME I'VE BEEN HERE.
HELLO!
HOW CAN I HELP YOU?

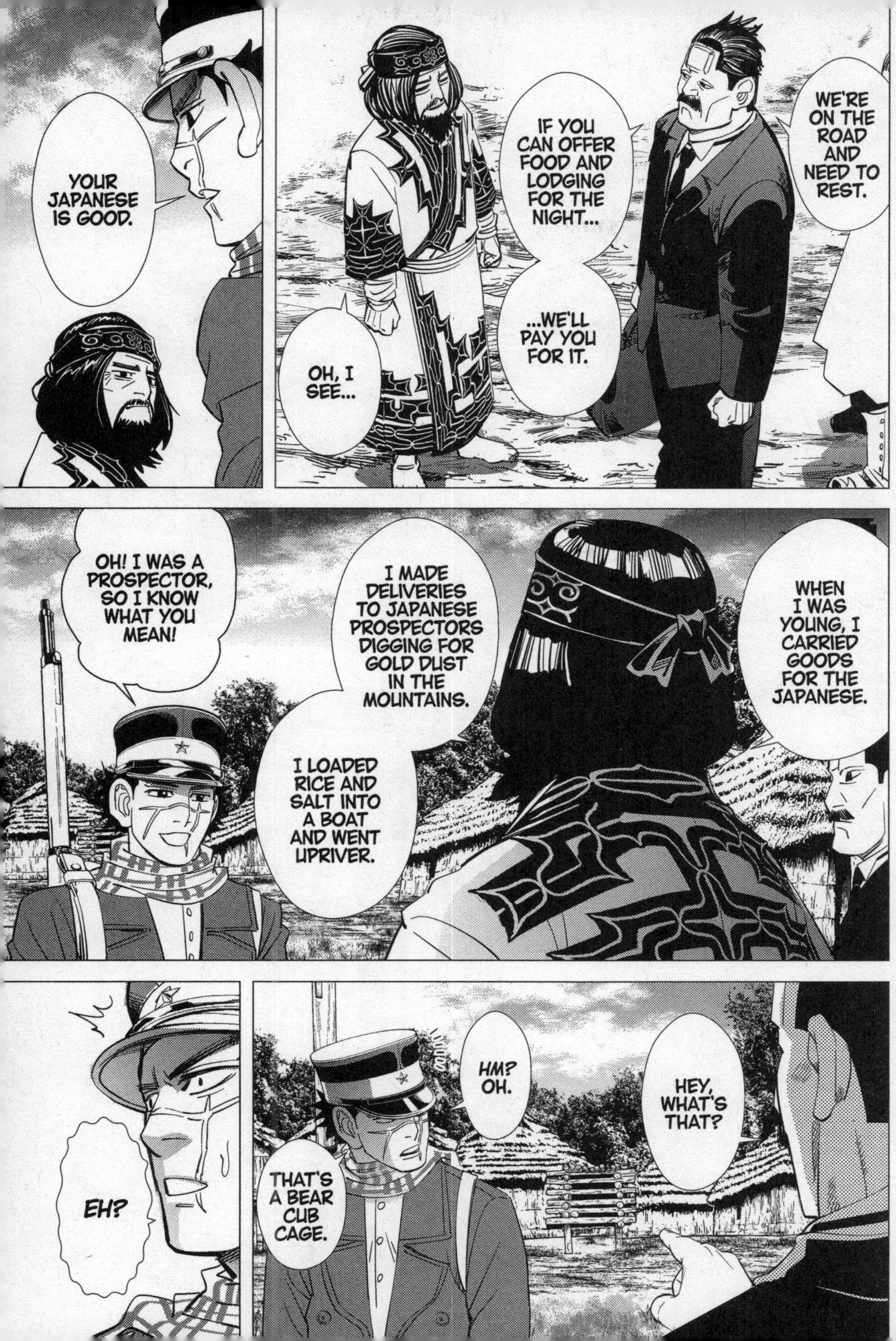
WE'RE ON THE ROAD AND NEED TO REST.
IF YOU CAN OFFER FOOD AND LODGING FOR THE NIGHT...
...WE'LL PAY YOU FOR IT.
OH, I SEE...
YOUR JAPANESE IS GOOD.
WHEN I WAS YOUNG, I CARRIED GOODS FOR THE JAPANESE.
I MADE DELIVERIES TO JAPANESE PROSPECTORS DIGGING FOR GOLD DUST IN THE MOUNTAINS.
I LOADED RICE AND SALT INTO A BOAT AND WENT UPRIVER.
OH! I WAS A PROSPECTOR, SO I KNOW WHAT YOU MEAN!
HEY, WHAT'S THAT?
HM? OH.
THAT'S A BEAR CUB CAGE.
EH?

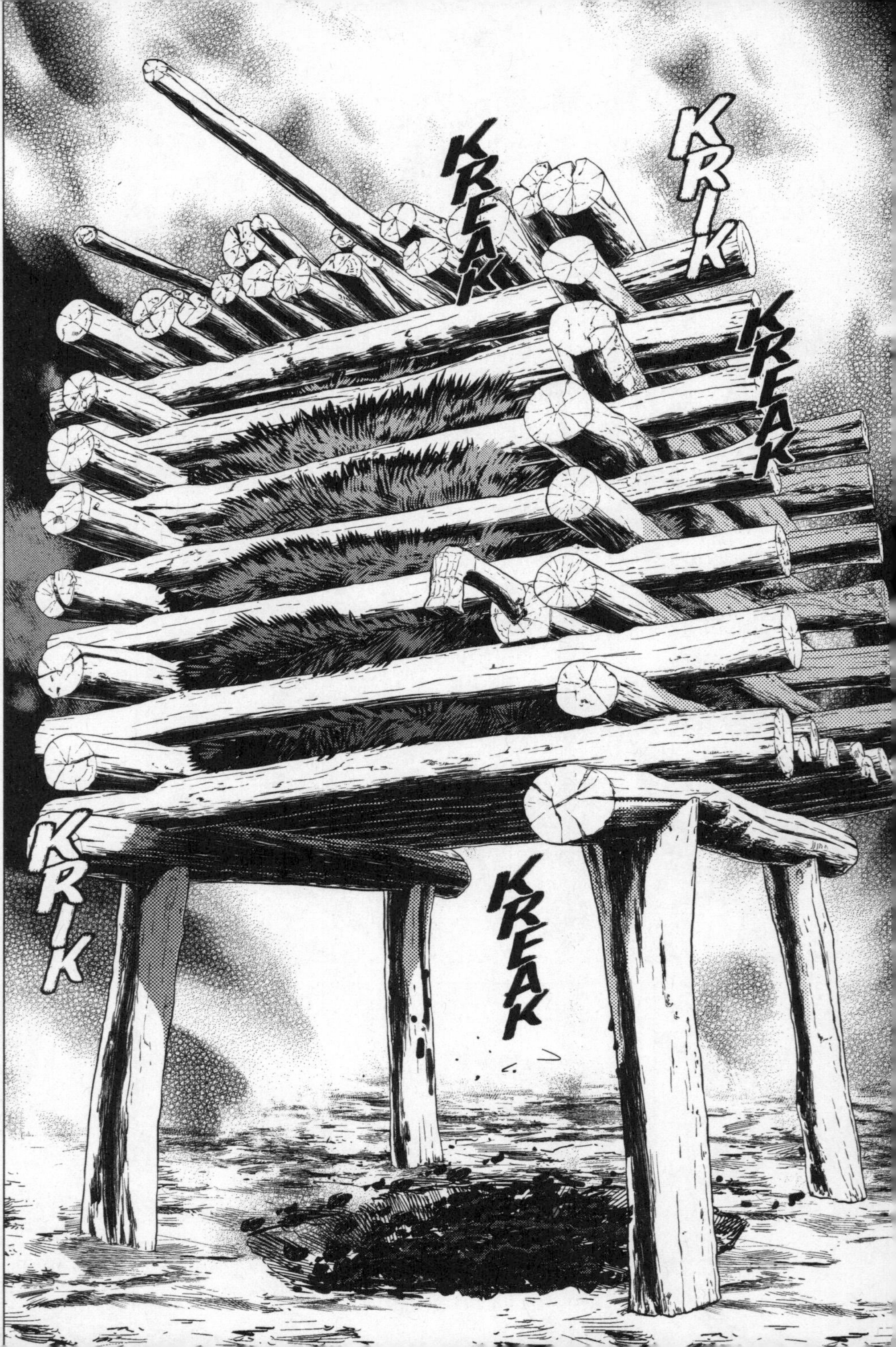
KRIK
KREAK
KREAK
KREAK
KRIK

Chapter 87: Manners

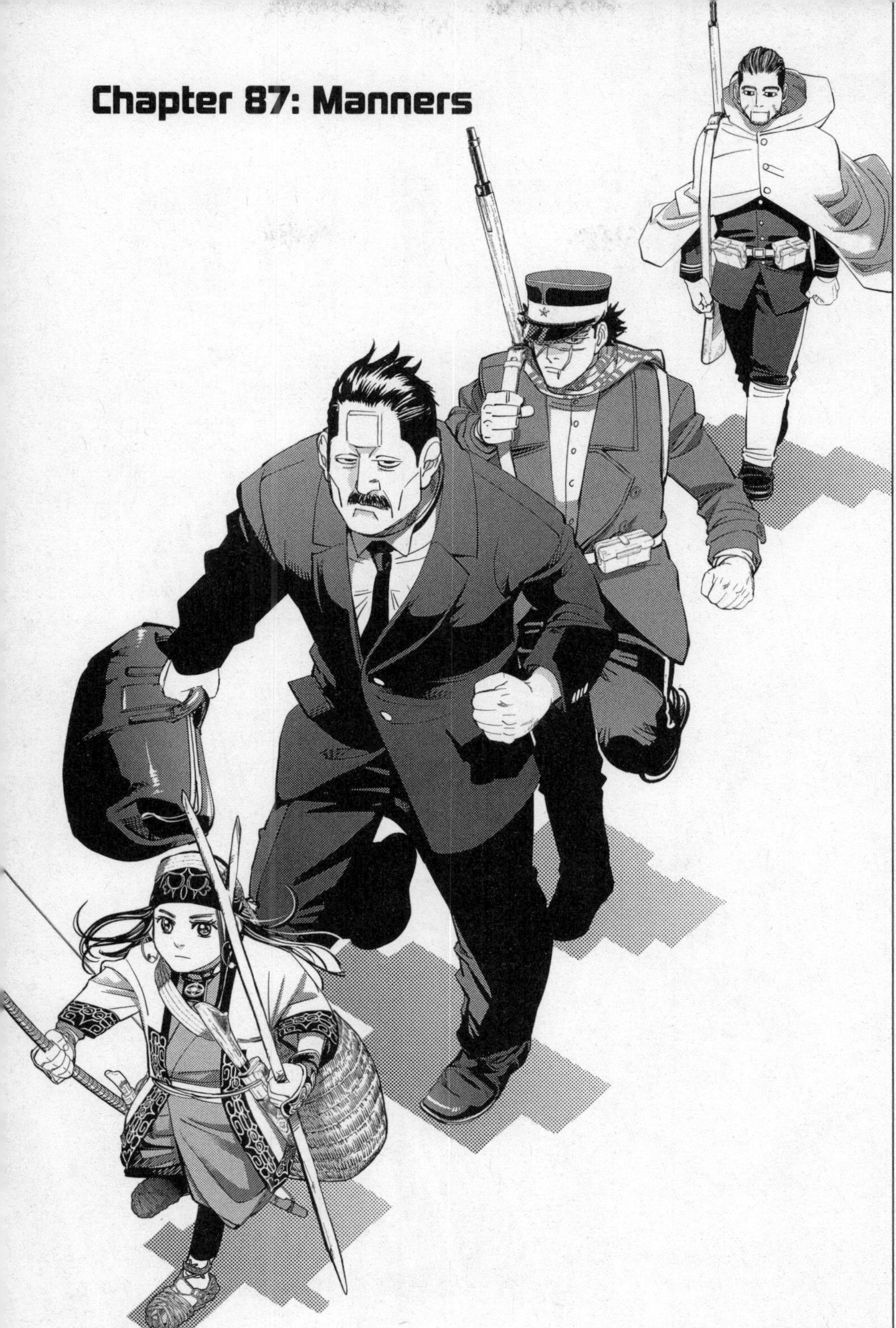

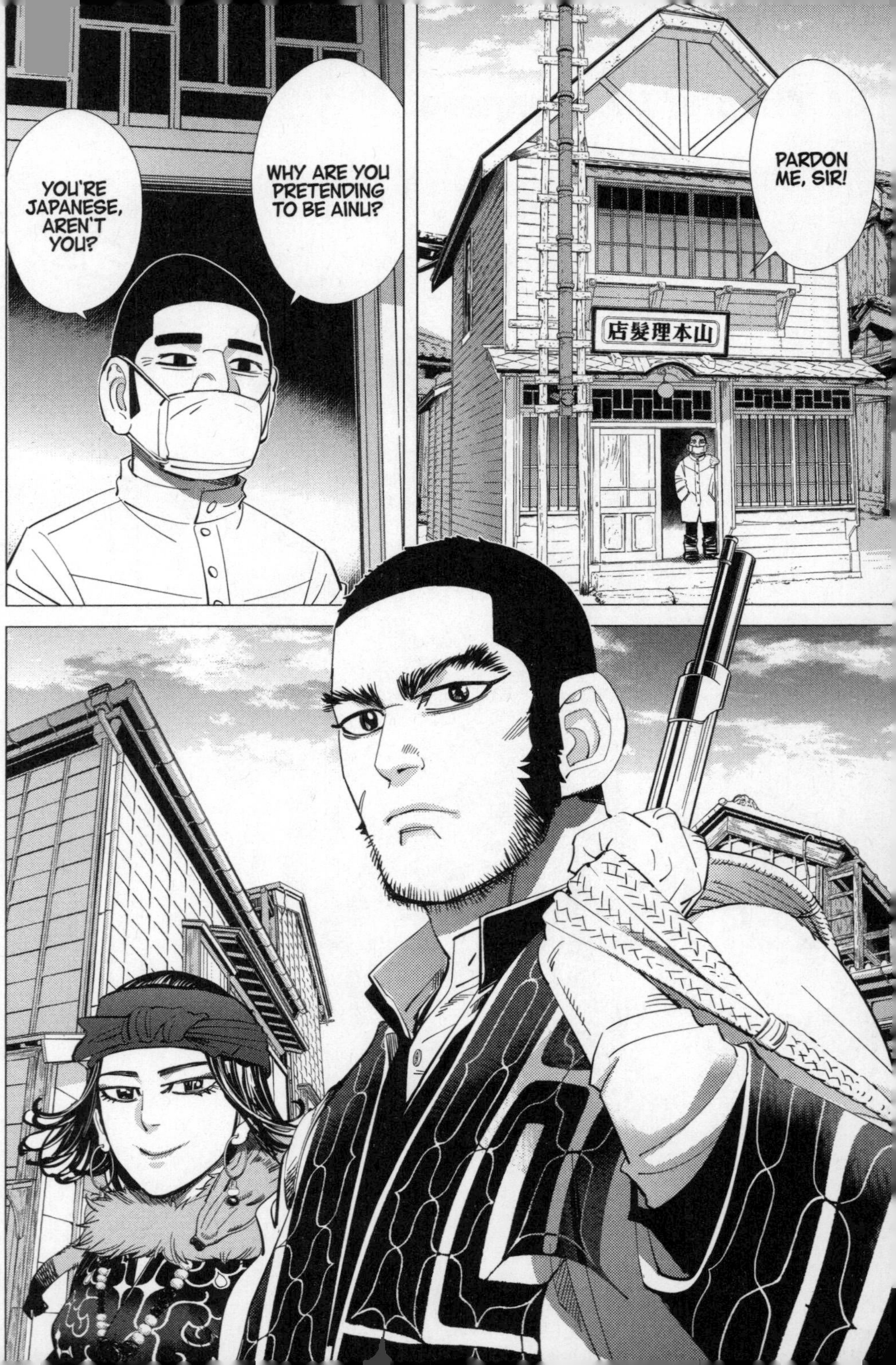
PARDON ME, SIR!
山本理髪店
WHY ARE YOU PRETENDING TO BE AINU?
YOU'RE JAPANESE, AREN'T YOU?

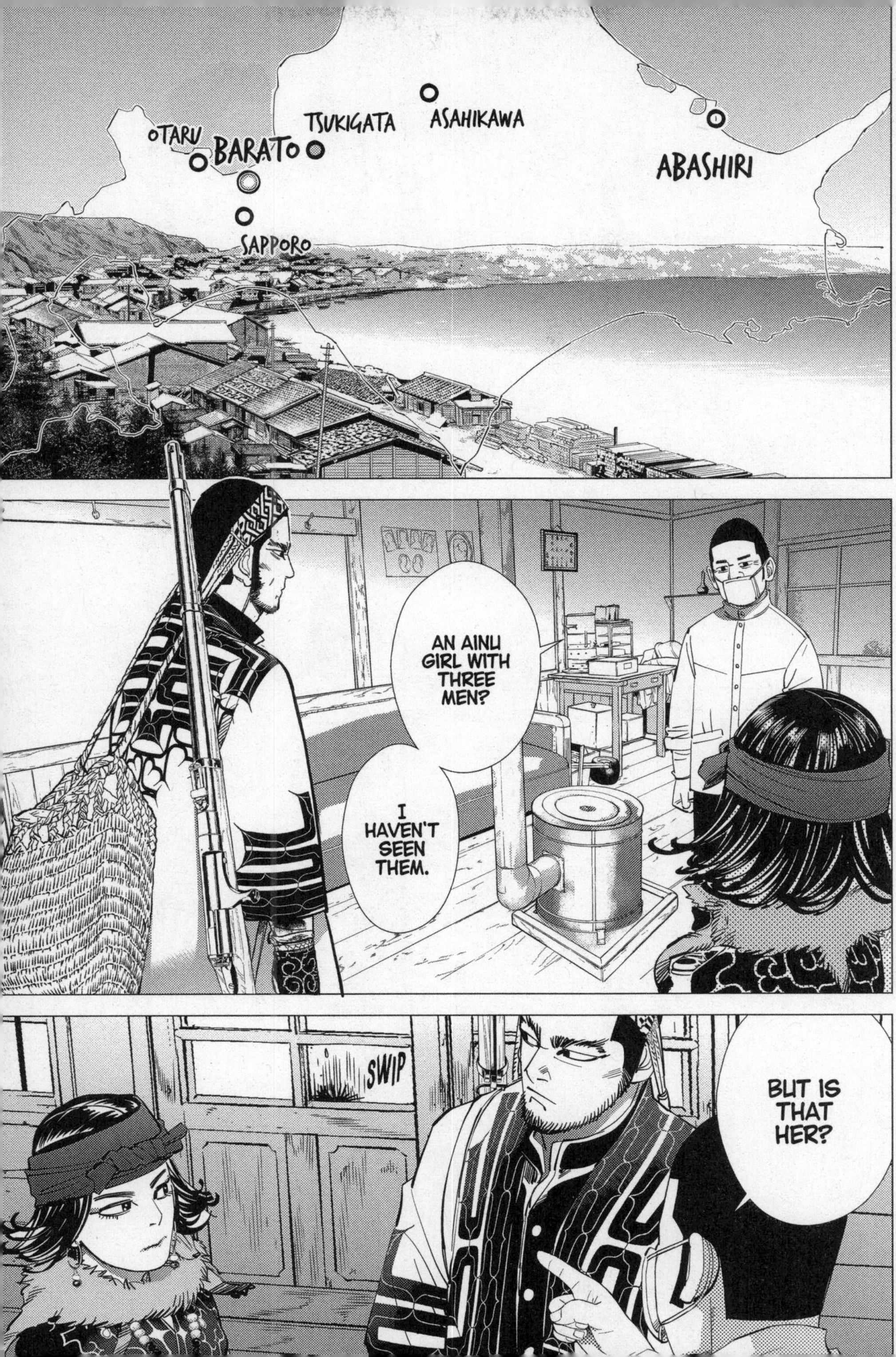
OTARU
BARATO
TSUKIGATA
ASAHIKAWA
ABASHIRI
SAPPORO
AN AINU GIRL WITH THREE MEN?
I HAVEN'T SEEN THEM.
BUT IS THAT HER?
SWIP

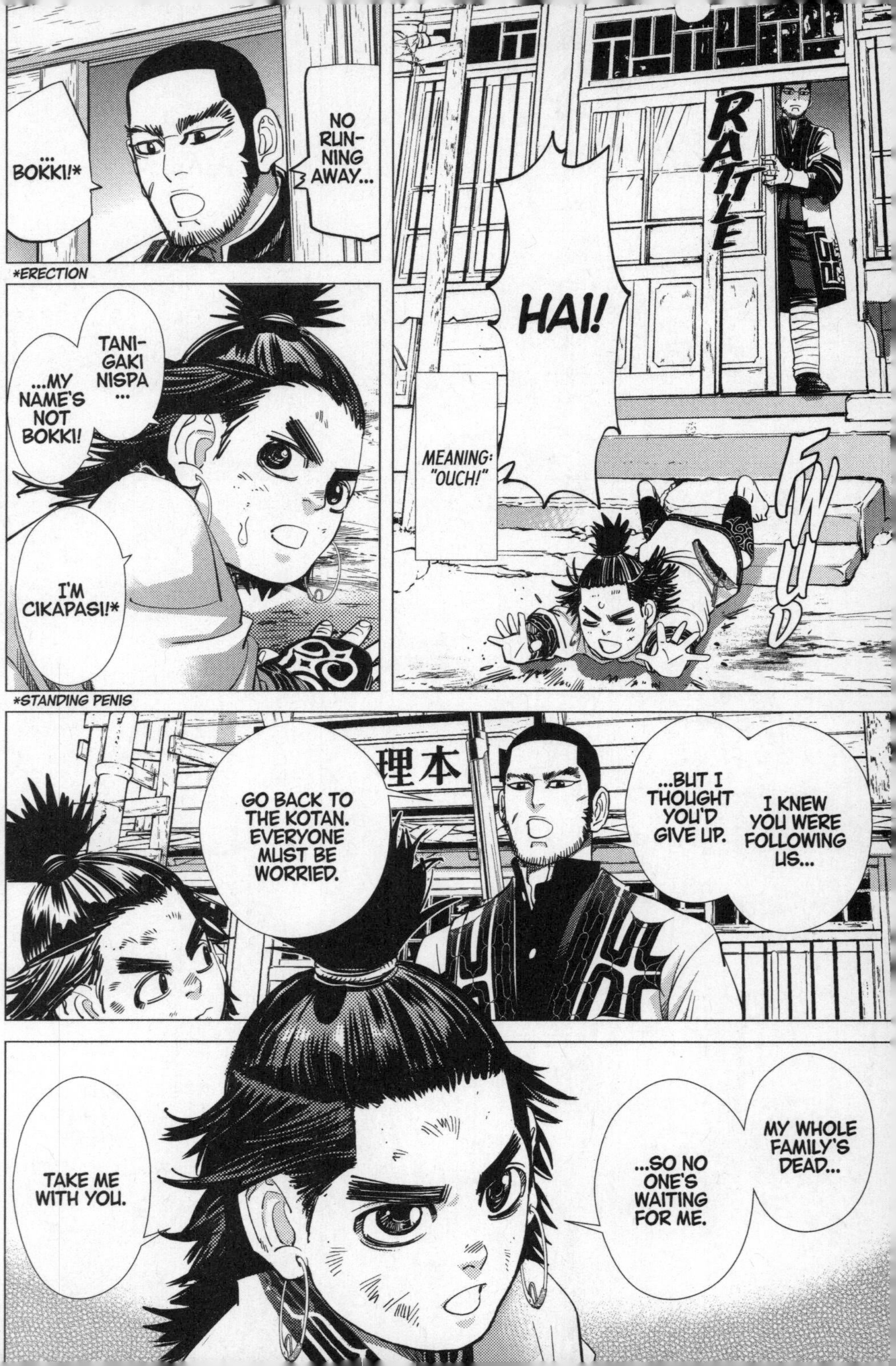
RATTLE
HAI!
MEANING: "OUCH!"
FWUD
NO RUN-NING AWAY...
... BOKKI!*
*ERECTION
TANI-GAKI NISPA ...
...MY NAME'S NOT BOKKI!
I'M CIKAPASI!*
*STANDING PENIS
I KNEW YOU WERE FOLLOWING US...
...BUT I THOUGHT YOU'D GIVE UP.
理本
GO BACK TO THE KOTAN. EVERYONE MUST BE WORRIED.
MY WHOLE FAMILY'S DEAD...
...SO NO ONE'S WAITING FOR ME.
TAKE ME WITH YOU.

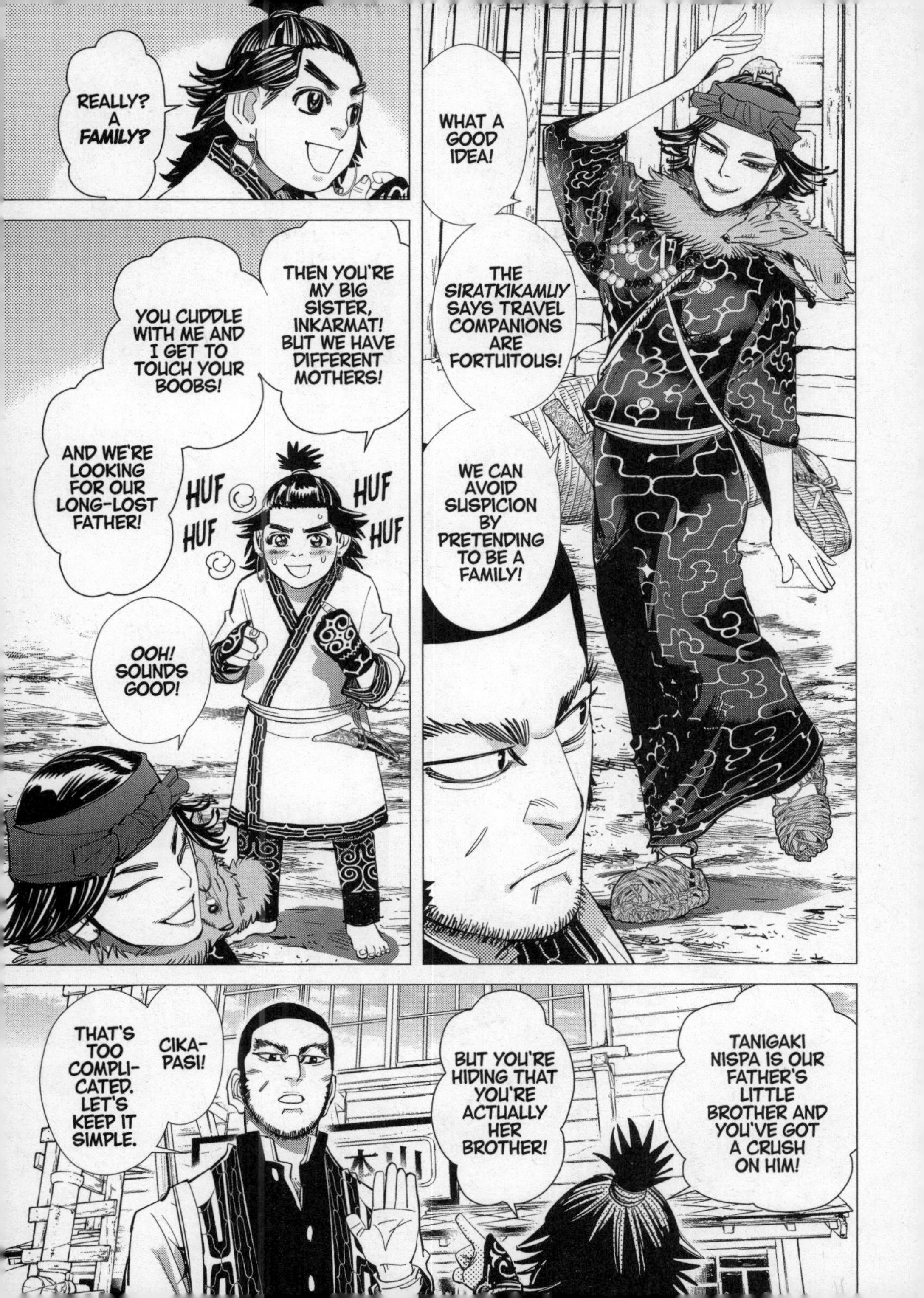
WHAT A GOOD IDEA!
THE SIRATKIKAMUY SAYS TRAVEL COMPANIONS ARE FORTUITOUS!
WE CAN AVOID SUSPICION BY PRETENDING TO BE A FAMILY!
REALLY? A FAMILY?
THEN YOU'RE MY BIG SISTER, INKARMAT! BUT WE HAVE DIFFERENT MOTHERS!
YOU CUDDLE WITH ME AND I GET TO TOUCH YOUR BOOBS!
HUF HUF
HUF HUF
AND WE'RE LOOKING FOR OUR LONG-LOST FATHER!
OOH! SOUNDS GOOD!
TANIGAKI NISPA IS OUR FATHER'S LITTLE BROTHER AND YOU'VE GOT A CRUSH ON HIM!
BUT YOU'RE HIDING THAT YOU'RE ACTUALLY HER BROTHER!
CIKA-PASI!
THAT'S TOO COMPLICATED. LET'S KEEP IT SIMPLE.

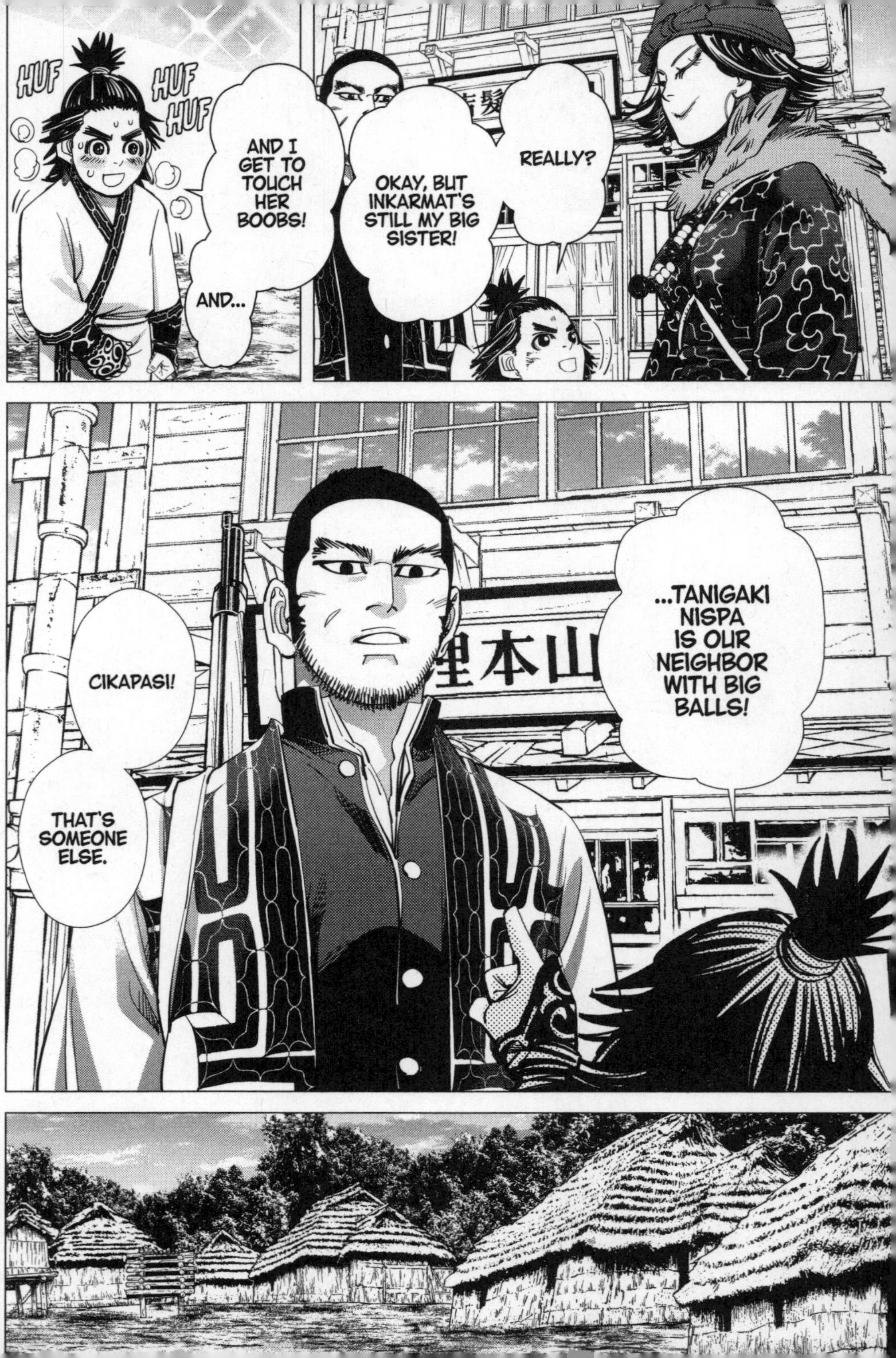
REALLY?
OKAY, BUT INKARMAT'S STILL MY BIG SISTER!
HUF HUF HUF
AND I GET TO TOUCH HER BOOBS!
AND...
...TANIGAKI NISPA IS OUR NEIGHBOR WITH BIG BALLS!
CIKAPASI!
THAT'S SOMEONE ELSE.

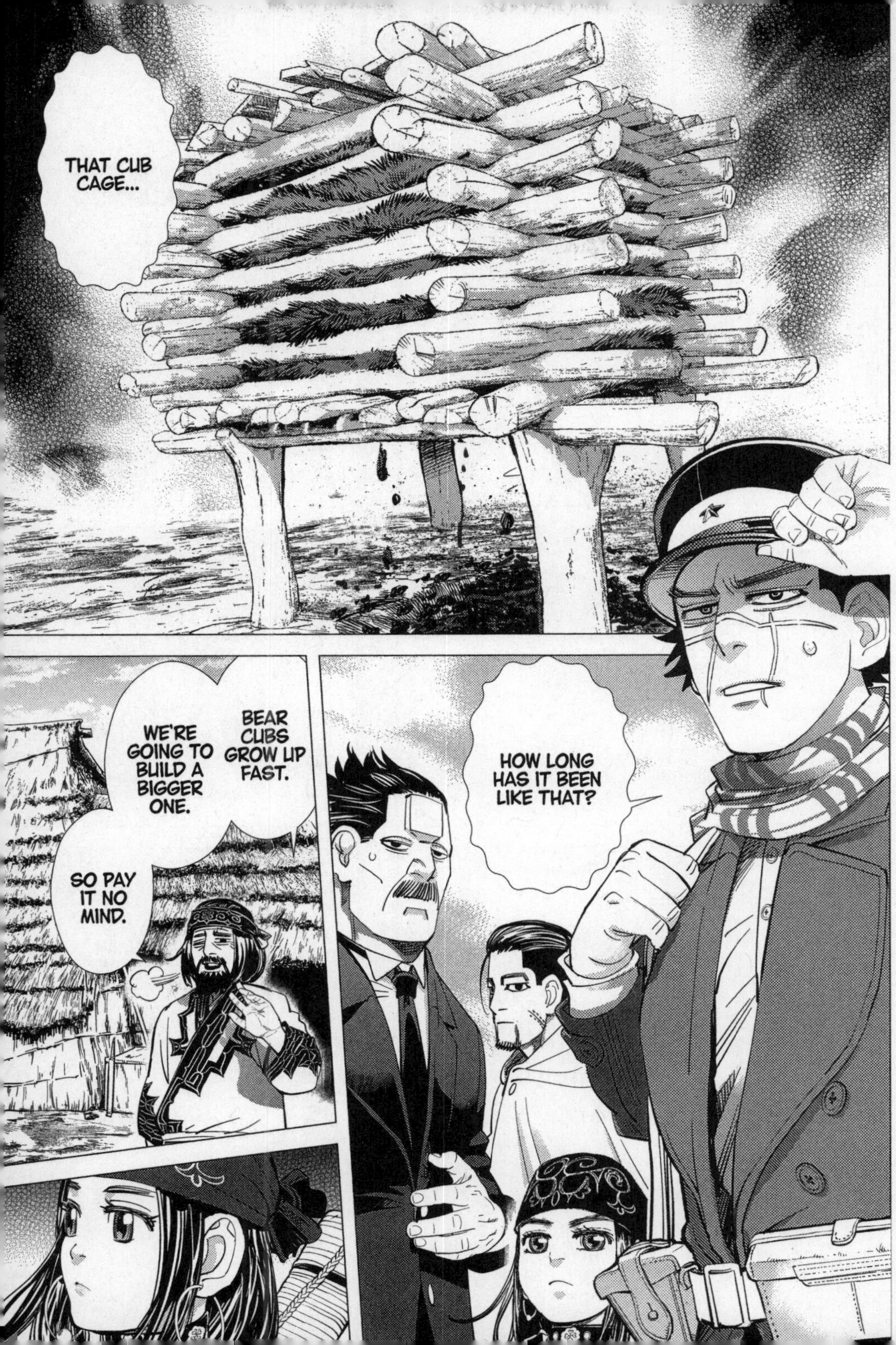
THAT CUB CAGE...
HOW LONG HAS IT BEEN LIKE THAT?
BEAR CUBS GROW UP FAST.
WE'RE GOING TO BUILD A BIGGER ONE.
SO PAY IT NO MIND.

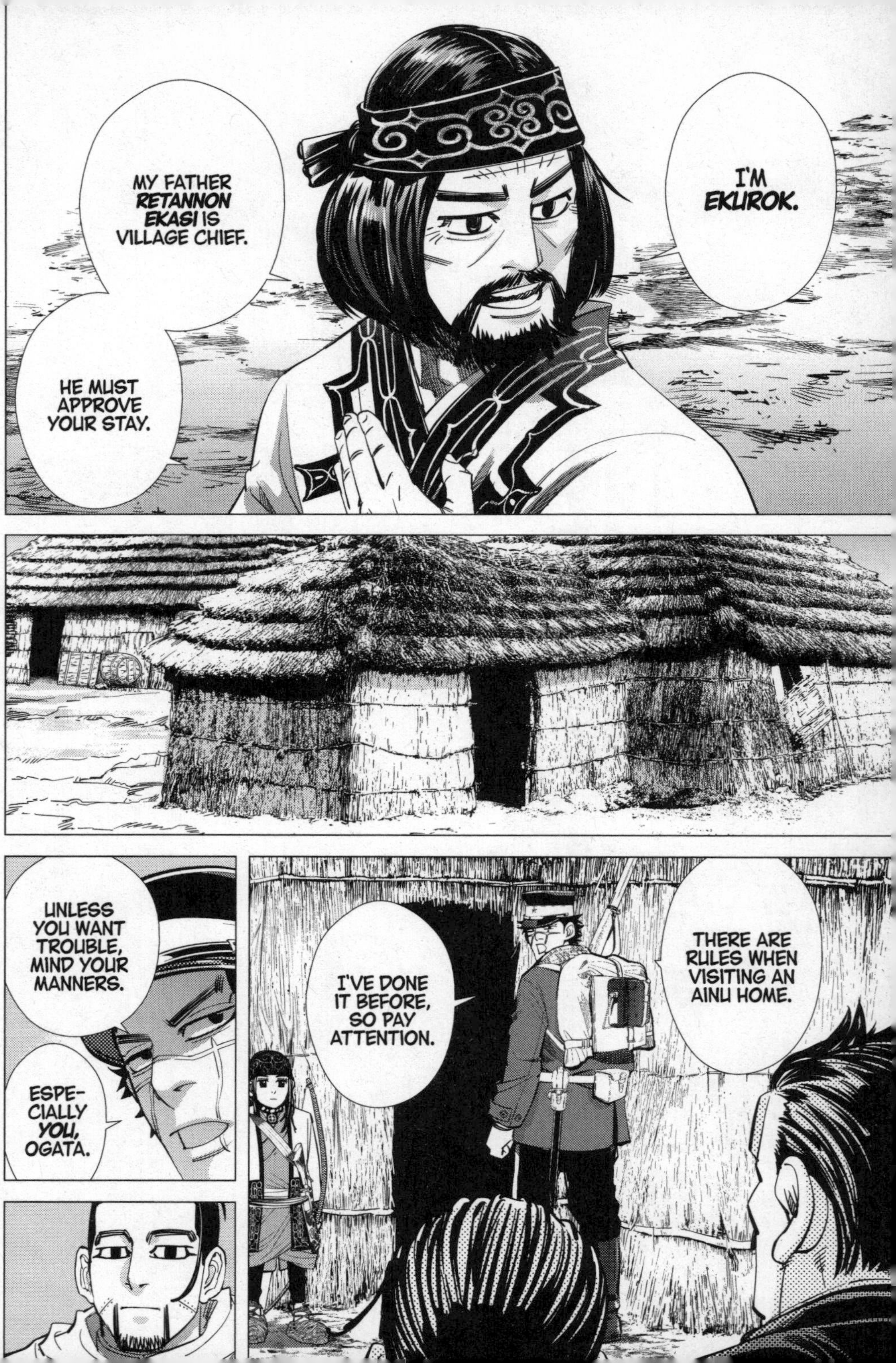
I'M EKUROK.
MY FATHER RETANNON EKASI IS VILLAGE CHIEF.
HE MUST APPROVE YOUR STAY.
THERE ARE RULES WHEN VISITING AN AINU HOME.
I'VE DONE IT BEFORE, SO PAY ATTENTION.
UNLESS YOU WANT TROUBLE, MIND YOUR MANNERS.
ESPE-CIALLY YOU, OGATA.

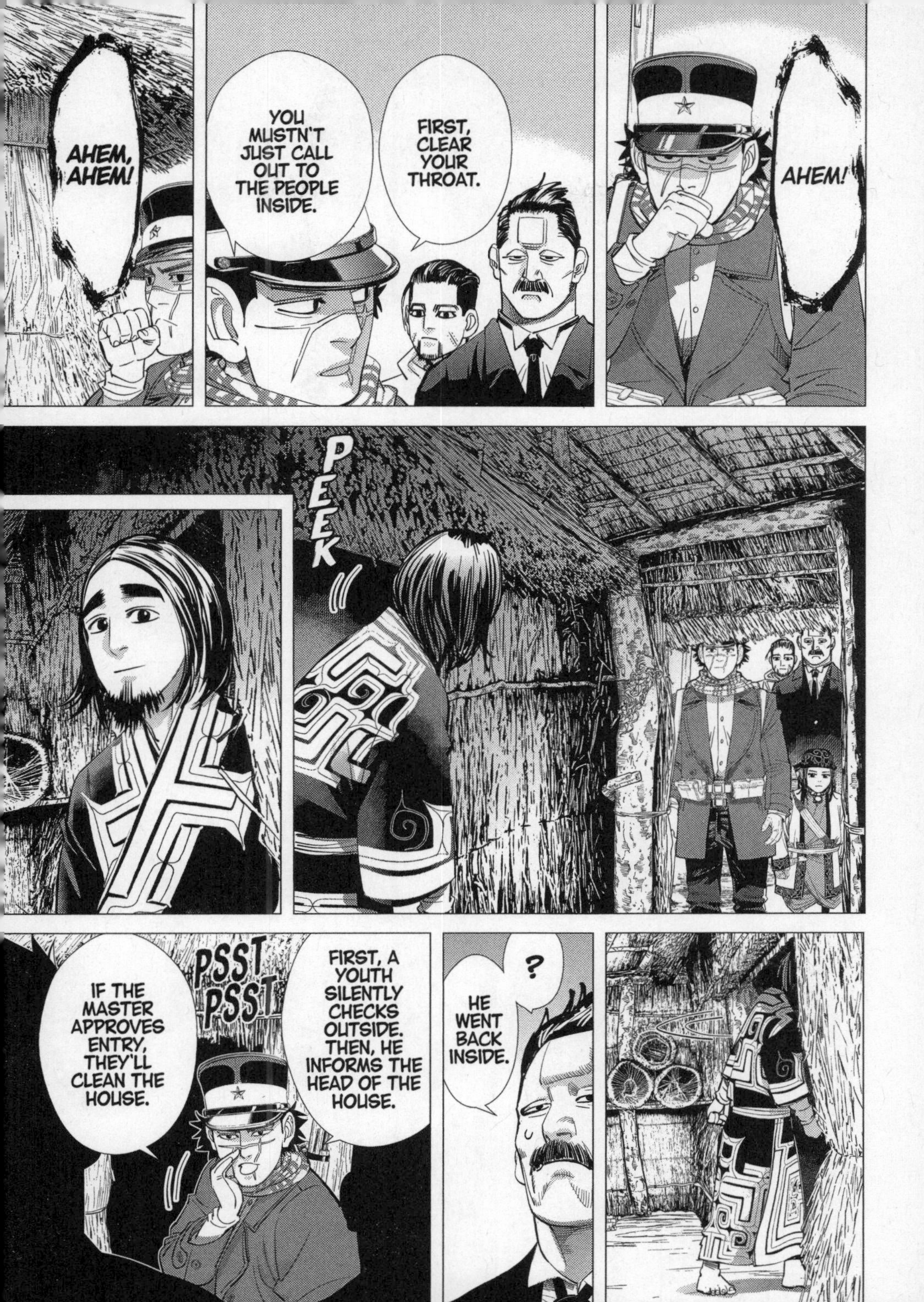
AHEM!
FIRST, CLEAR YOUR THROAT.
YOU MUSTN'T JUST CALL OUT TO THE PEOPLE INSIDE.
AHEM, AHEM!
PEEK
?
HE WENT BACK INSIDE.
FIRST, A YOUTH SILENTLY CHECKS OUTSIDE. THEN, HE INFORMS THE HEAD OF THE HOUSE.
PSST PSST
IF THE MASTER APPROVES ENTRY, THEY'LL CLEAN THE HOUSE.

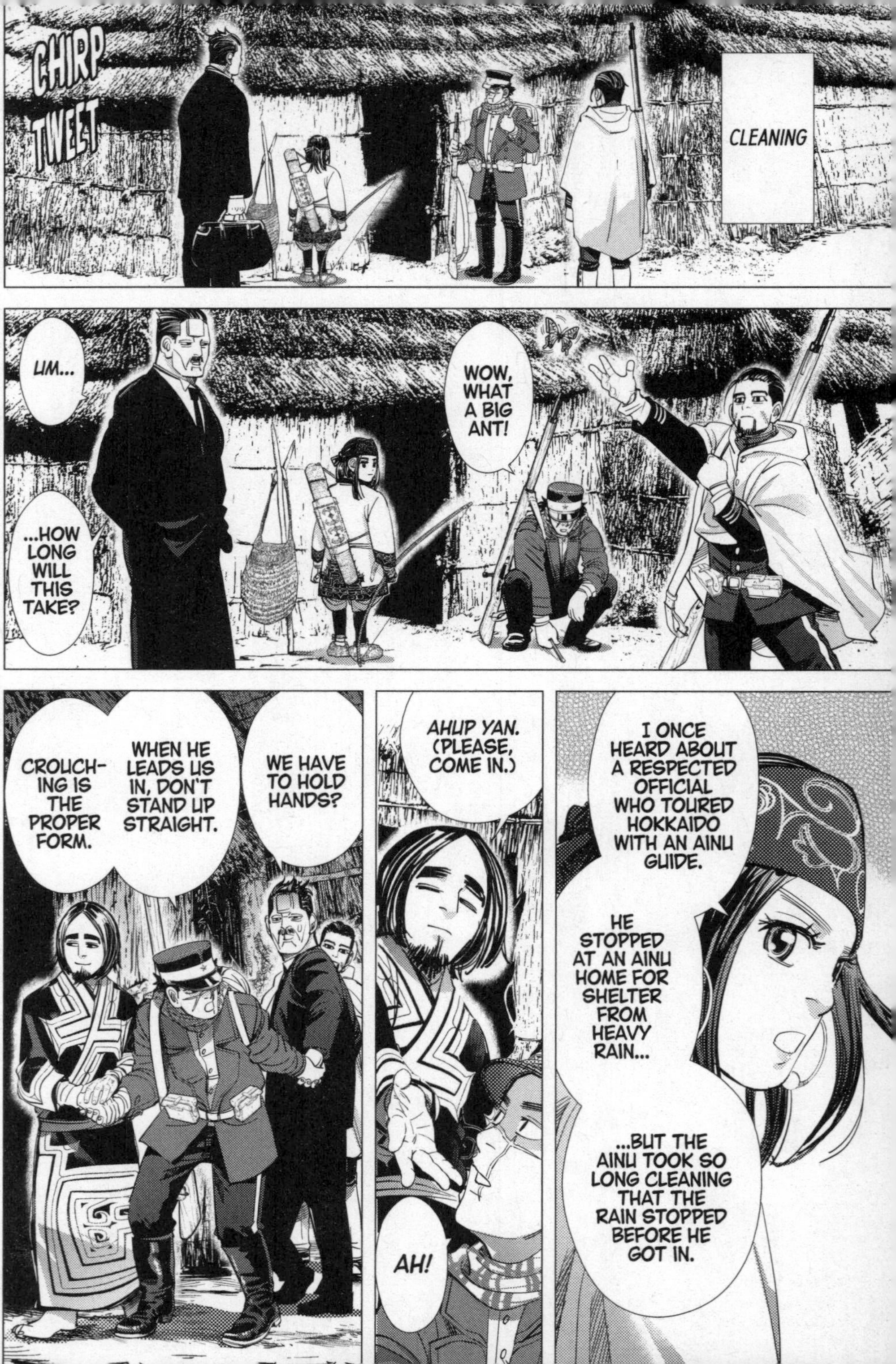
CLEANING
CHIRP
TWEET
WOW, WHAT A BIG ANT!
UM...
...HOW LONG WILL THIS TAKE?
I ONCE HEARD ABOUT A RESPECTED OFFICIAL WHO TOURED HOKKAIDO WITH AN AINU GUIDE.
HE STOPPED AT AN AINU HOME FOR SHELTER FROM HEAVY RAIN...
...BUT THE AINU TOOK SO LONG CLEANING THAT THE RAIN STOPPED BEFORE HE GOT IN.
AHUP YAN. (PLEASE, COME IN.)
AH!
WE HAVE TO HOLD HANDS?
WHEN HE LEADS US IN, DON'T STAND UP STRAIGHT.
CROUCHING IS THE PROPER FORM.

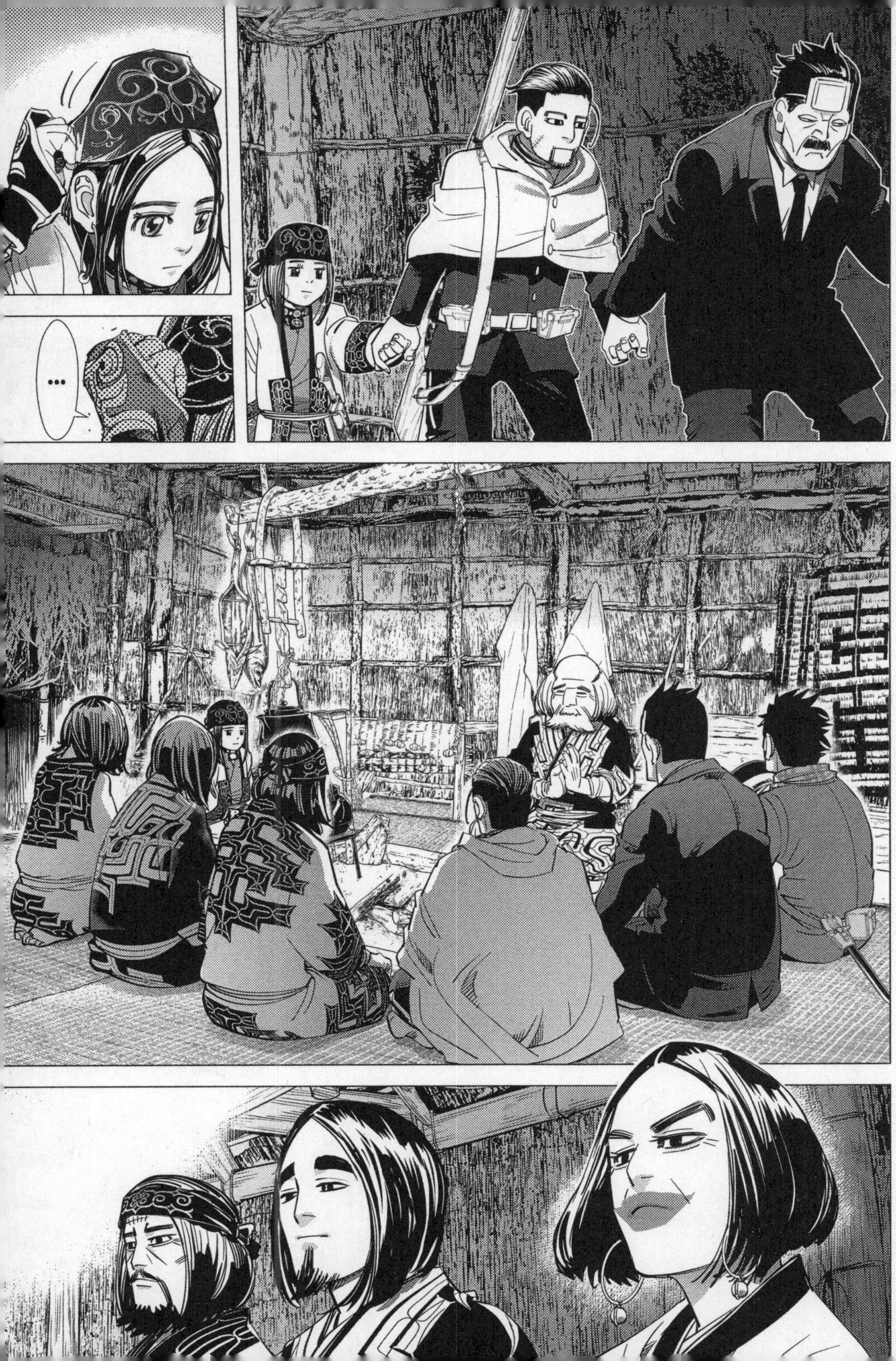
...

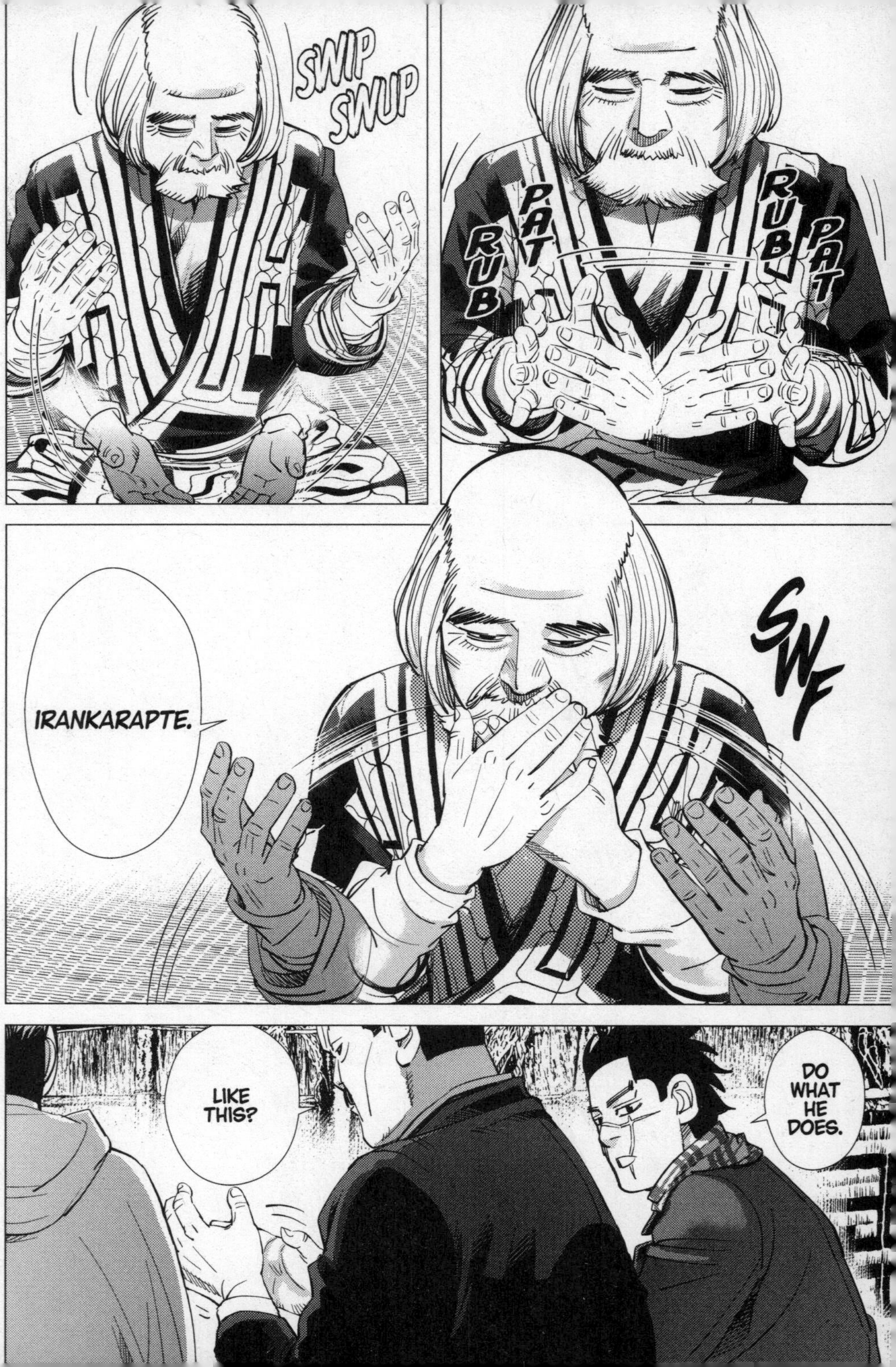
RUB PAT RUB PAT
SWIP SWUP
SNF
IRANKARAPTE.
DO WHAT HE DOES.
LIKE THIS?

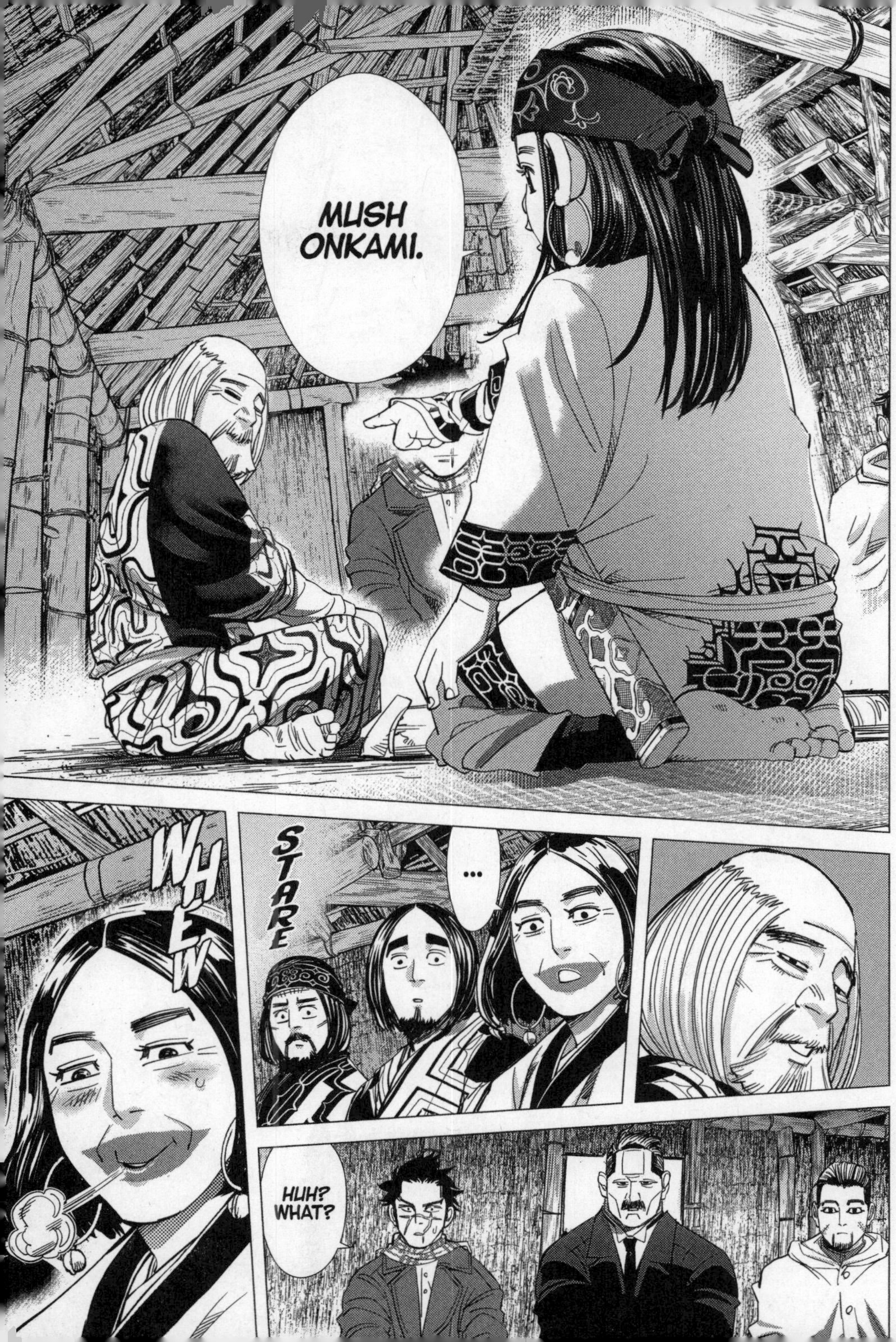
MUSH ONKAMI.
...
STARE
WHEW
HUH? WHAT?

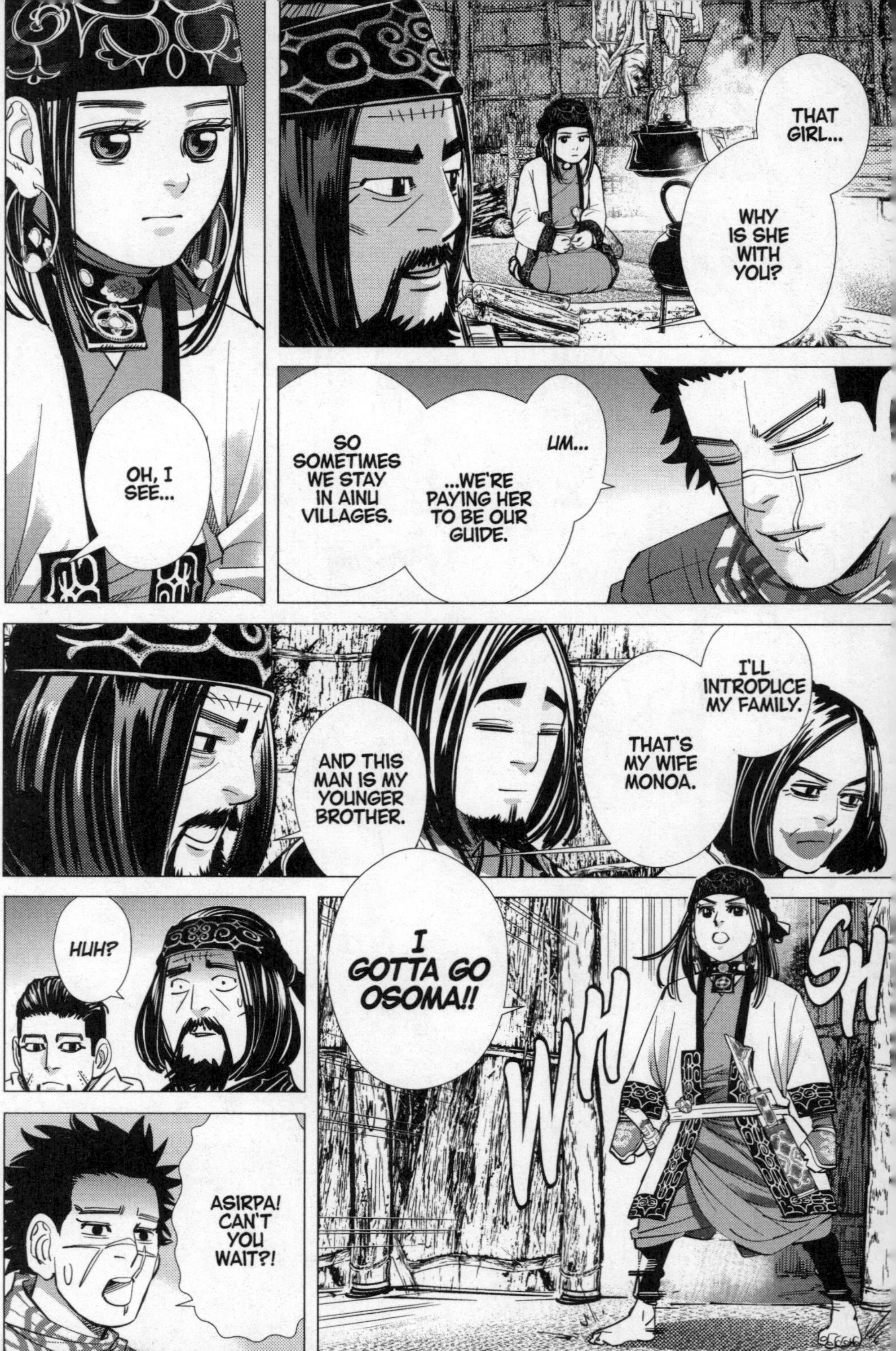
THAT GIRL...
WHY IS SHE WITH YOU?
UM...
...WE'RE PAYING HER TO BE OUR GUIDE.
SO SOMETIMES WE STAY IN AINU VILLAGES.
OH, I SEE...
I'LL INTRODUCE MY FAMILY.
THAT'S MY WIFE MONOA.
AND THIS MAN IS MY YOUNGER BROTHER.
SH
I GOTTA GO OSOMA!!
WH
HUH?
ASIRPA! CAN'T YOU WAIT?!

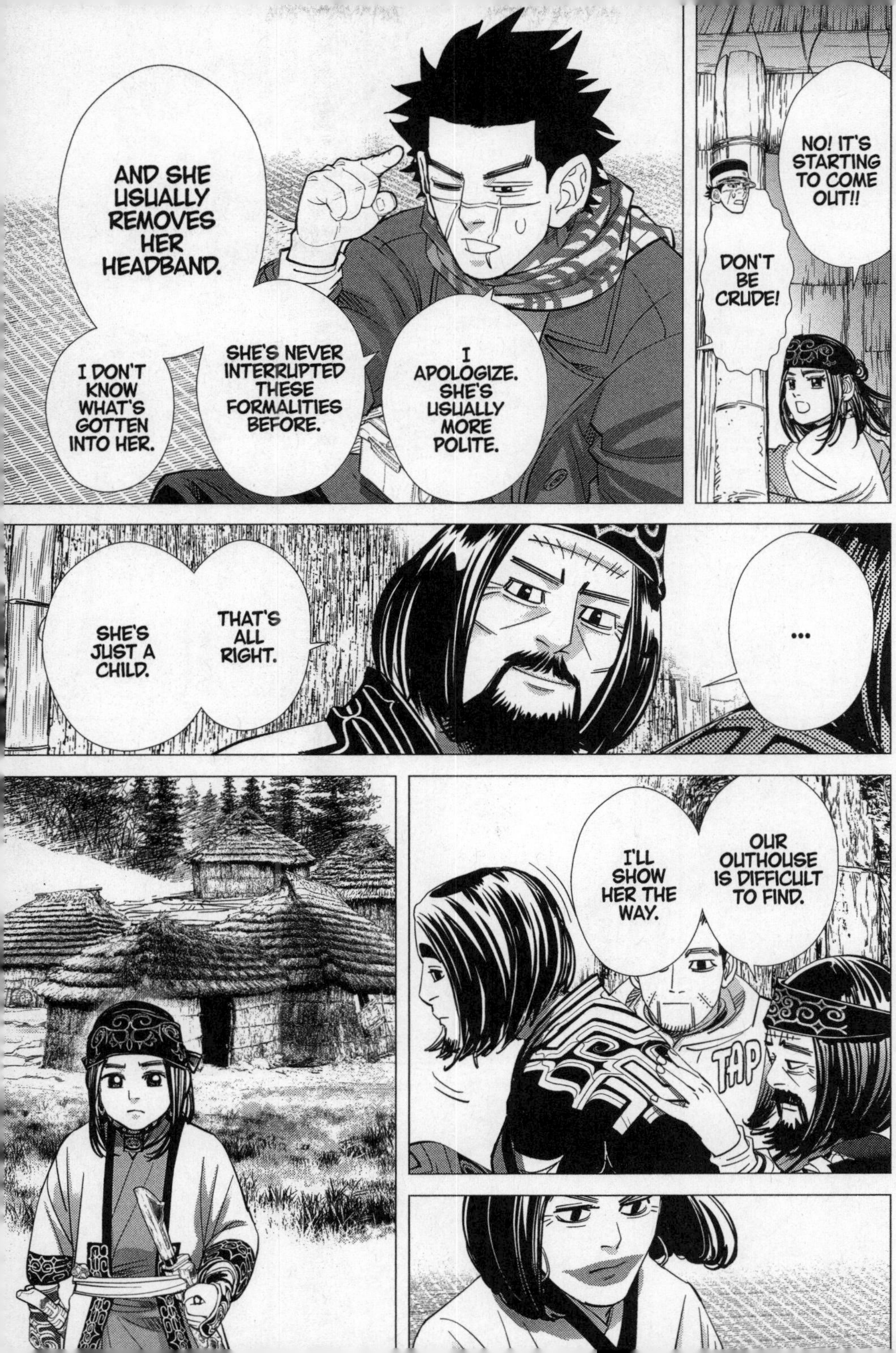
NO! IT'S STARTING TO COME OUT!!
DON'T BE CRUDE!
I APOLOGIZE. SHE'S USUALLY MORE POLITE.
SHE'S NEVER INTERRUPTED THESE FORMALITIES BEFORE.
I DON'T KNOW WHAT'S GOTTEN INTO HER.
AND SHE USUALLY REMOVES HER HEADBAND.
...
THAT'S ALL RIGHT.
SHE'S JUST A CHILD.
OUR OUTHOUSE IS DIFFICULT TO FIND.
I'LL SHOW HER THE WAY.
TAP

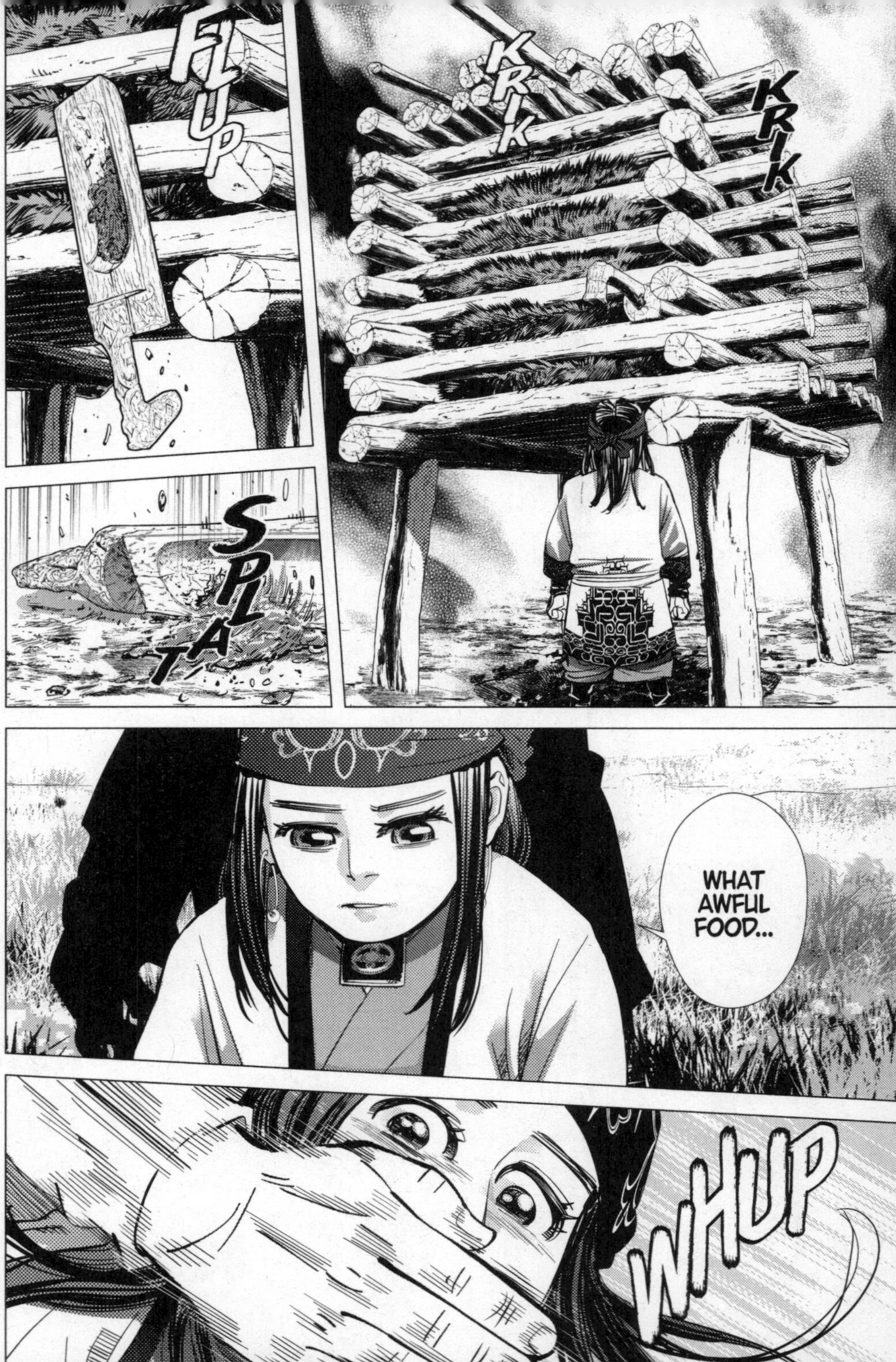
KRIK
KRIK
FLUP
SPLAT
WHAT AWFUL FOOD...
WHUP

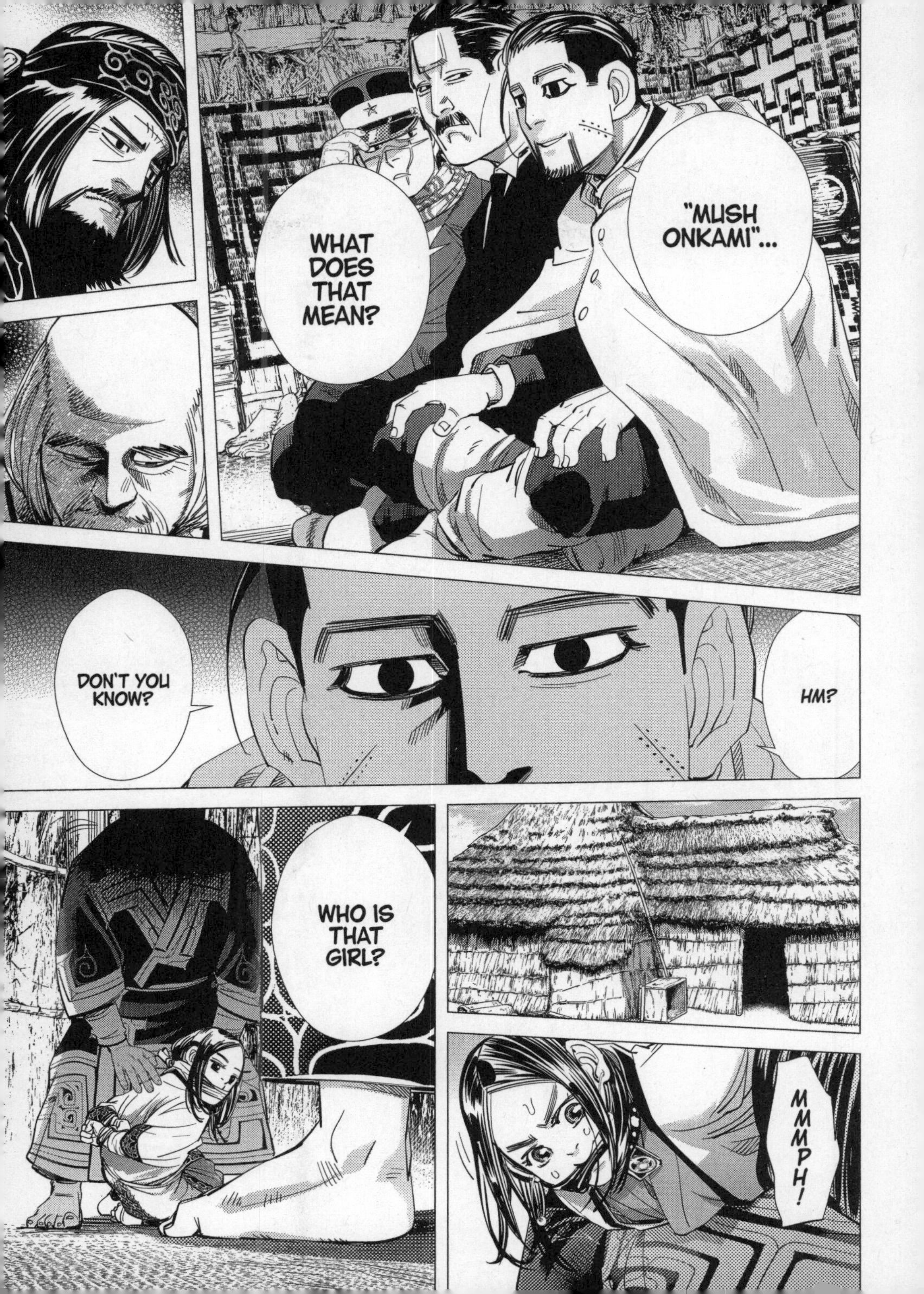
"MUSH ONKAMI"...
WHAT DOES THAT MEAN?
HM?
DON'T YOU KNOW?
MMMPH!
WHO IS THAT GIRL?

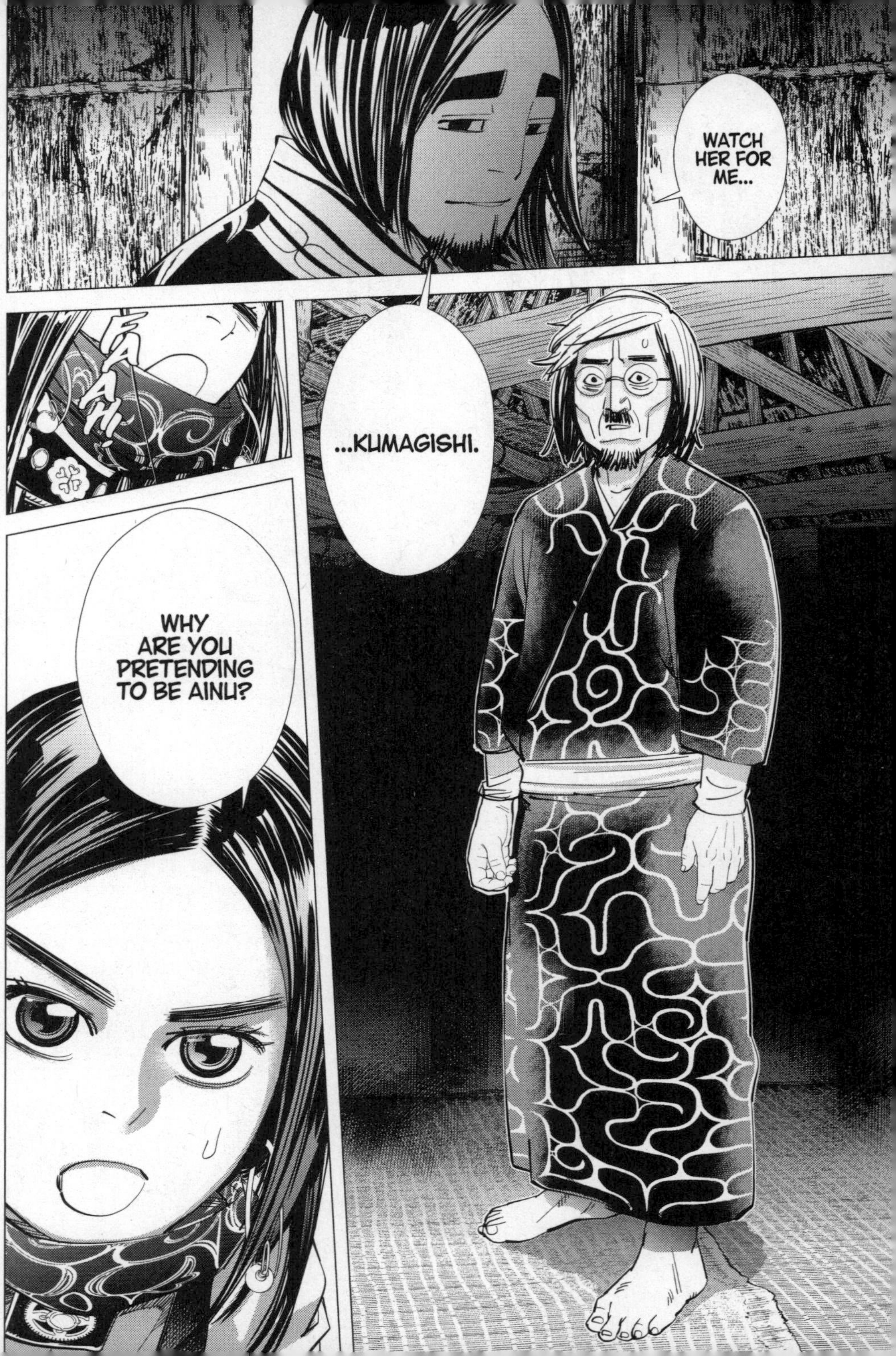
WATCH HER FOR ME...
...KUMAGISHI.
FAAH!
WHY ARE YOU PRETENDING TO BE AINU?

Chapter 88: The Long-Eared Monster Cometh

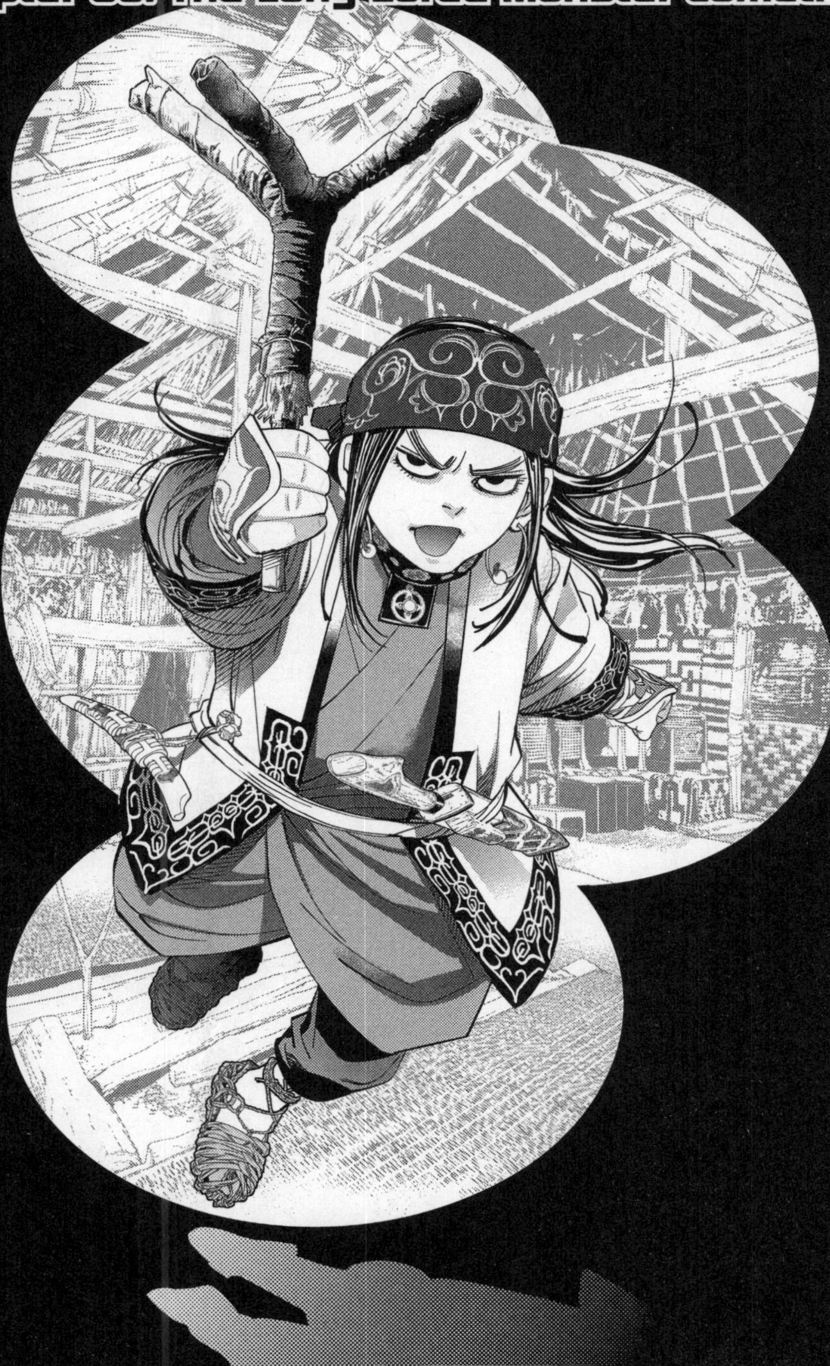

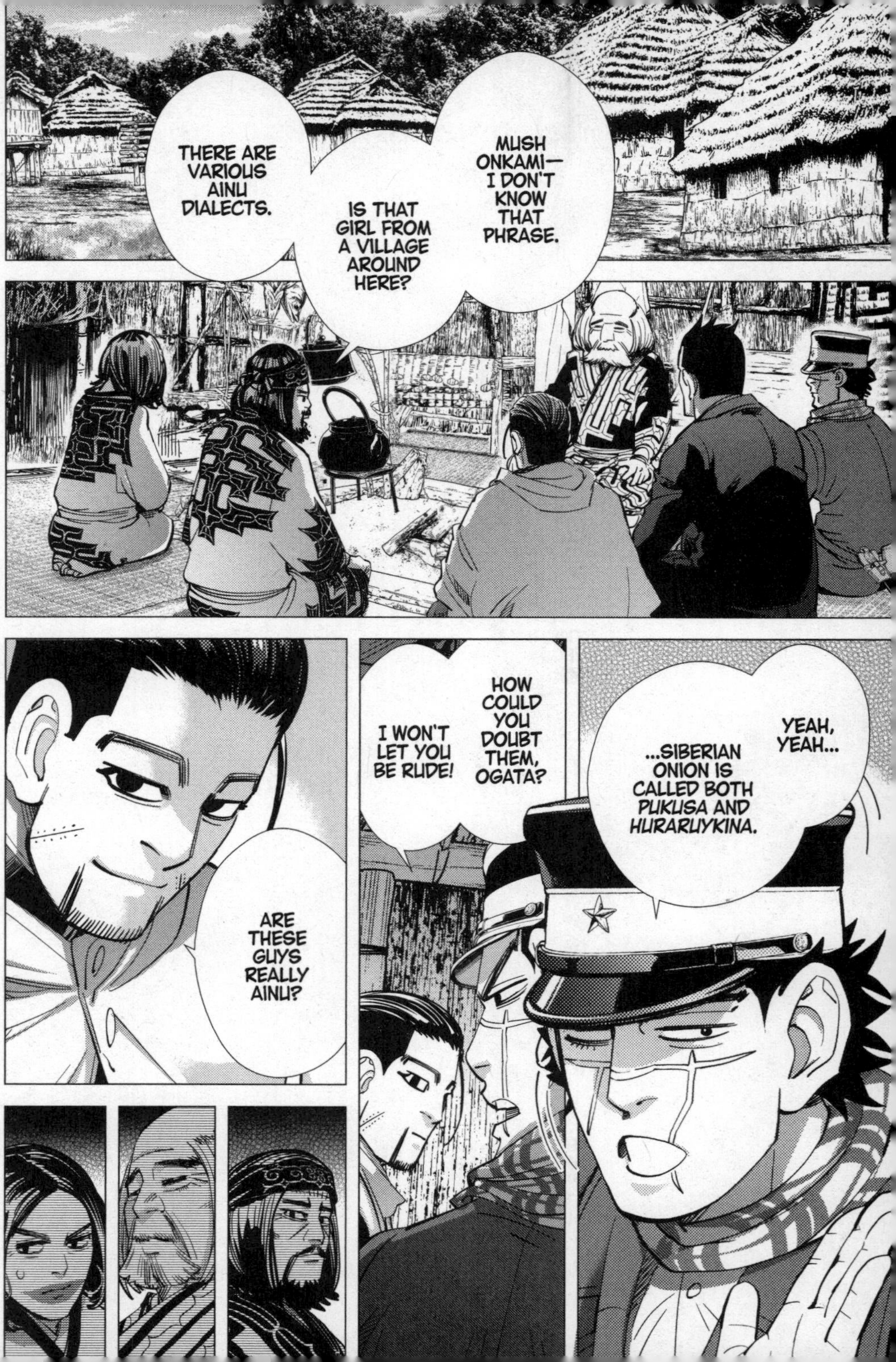
MUSH ONKAMI— I DON'T KNOW THAT PHRASE.
IS THAT GIRL FROM A VILLAGE AROUND HERE?
THERE ARE VARIOUS AINU DIALECTS.
YEAH, YEAH...
...SIBERIAN ONION IS CALLED BOTH PUKUSA AND HURARUYKINA.
HOW COULD YOU DOUBT THEM, OGATA?
I WON'T LET YOU BE RUDE!
ARE THESE GUYS REALLY AINU?

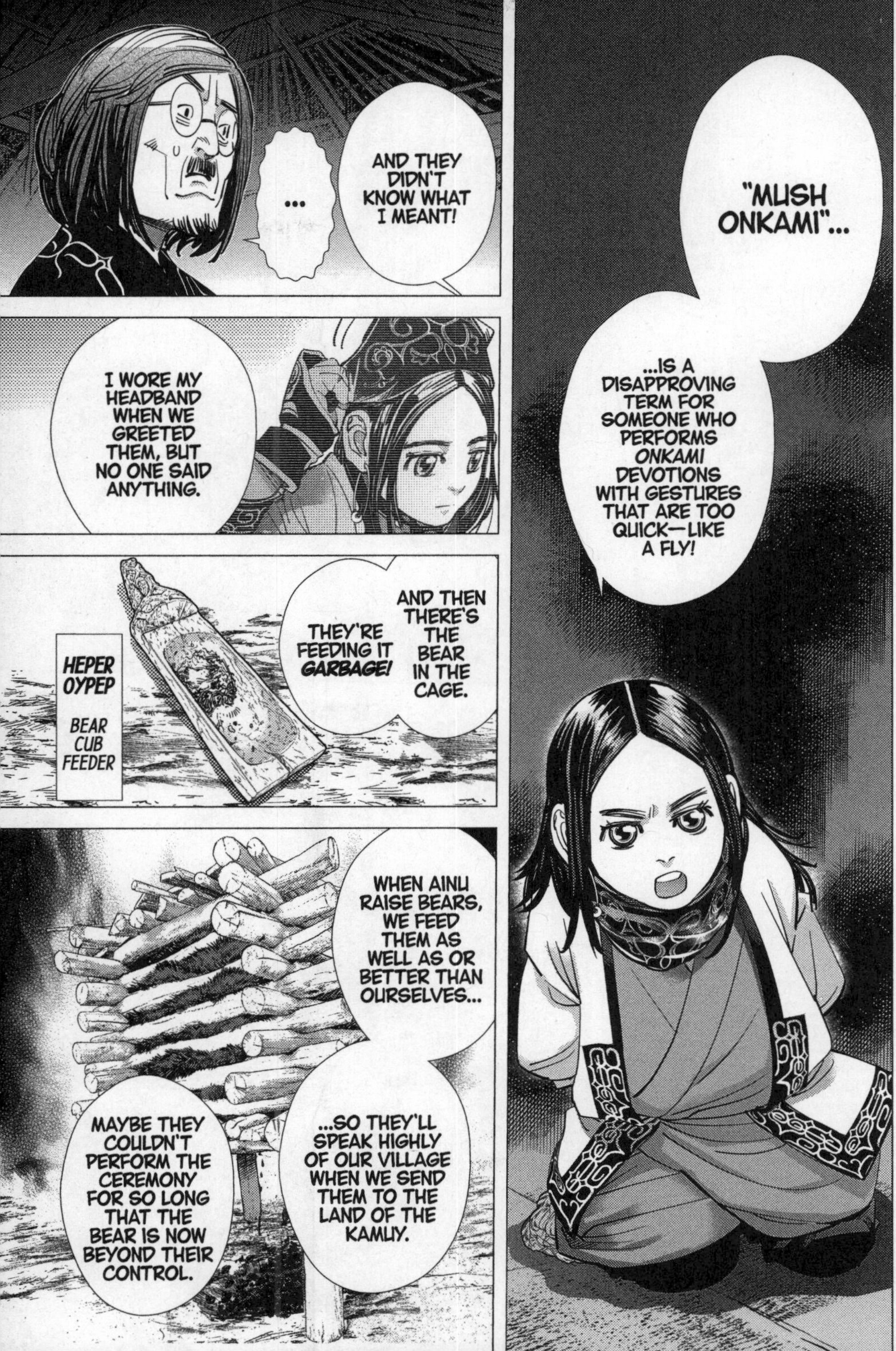
"MUSH ONKAMI"...
...IS A DISAPPROVING TERM FOR SOMEONE WHO PERFORMS ONKAMI DEVOTIONS WITH GESTURES THAT ARE TOO QUICK—LIKE A FLY!
AND THEY DIDN'T KNOW WHAT I MEANT!
...
I WORE MY HEADBAND WHEN WE GREETED THEM, BUT NO ONE SAID ANYTHING.
AND THEN THERE'S THE BEAR IN THE CAGE.
THEY'RE FEEDING IT GARBAGE!
HEPER OYPEP
BEAR CUB FEEDER
WHEN AINU RAISE BEARS, WE FEED THEM AS WELL AS OR BETTER THAN OURSELVES...
...SO THEY'LL SPEAK HIGHLY OF OUR VILLAGE WHEN WE SEND THEM TO THE LAND OF THE KAMUY.
MAYBE THEY COULDN'T PERFORM THE CEREMONY FOR SO LONG THAT THE BEAR IS NOW BEYOND THEIR CONTROL.

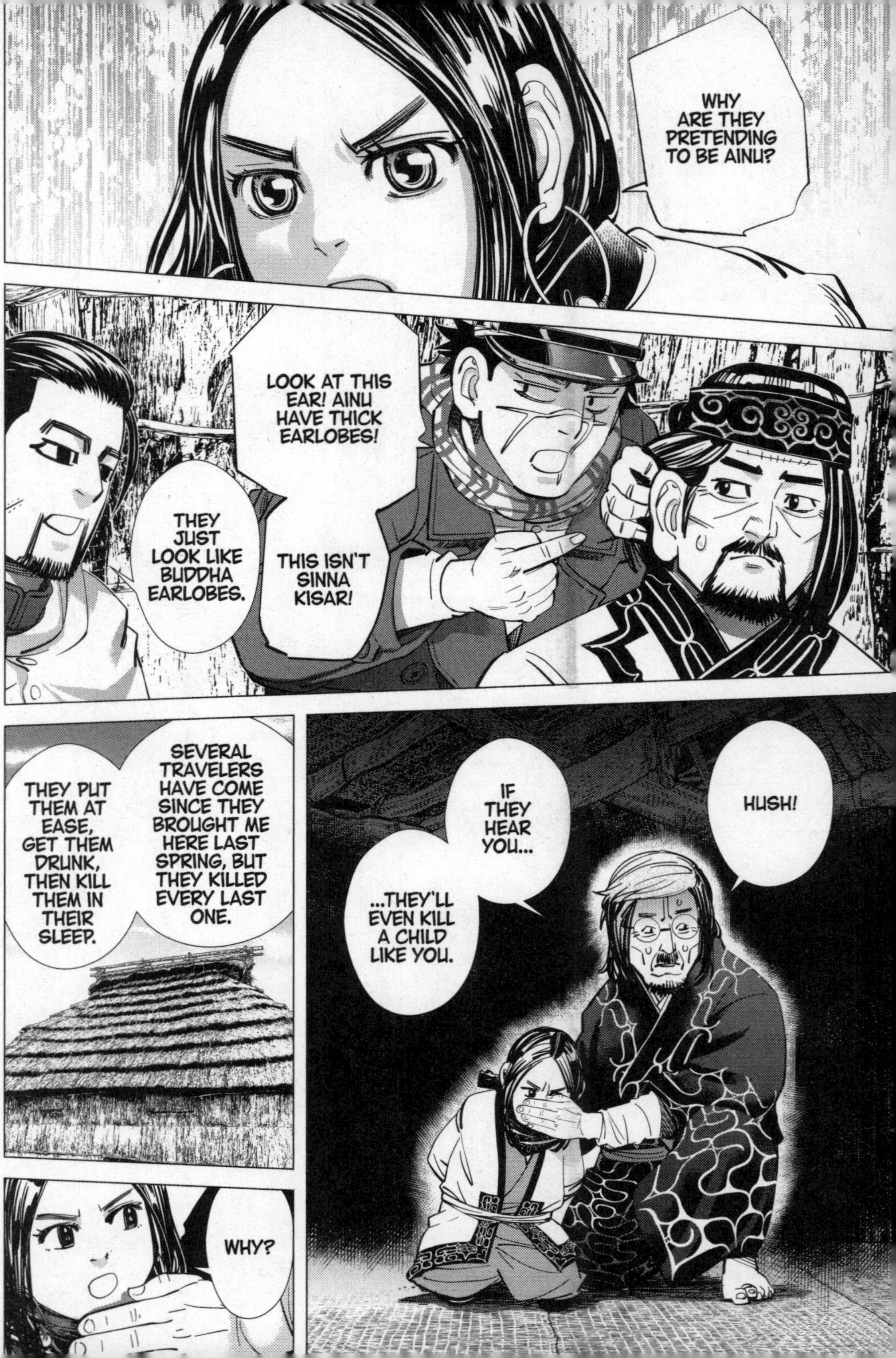
WHY ARE THEY PRETENDING TO BE AINU?
LOOK AT THIS EAR! AINU HAVE THICK EARLOBES!
THIS ISN'T SINNA KISAR!
THEY JUST LOOK LIKE BUDDHA EARLOBES.
HUSH!
IF THEY HEAR YOU...
...THEY'LL EVEN KILL A CHILD LIKE YOU.
SEVERAL TRAVELERS HAVE COME SINCE THEY BROUGHT ME HERE LAST SPRING, BUT THEY KILLED EVERY LAST ONE.
THEY PUT THEM AT EASE, GET THEM DRUNK, THEN KILL THEM IN THEIR SLEEP.
WHY?

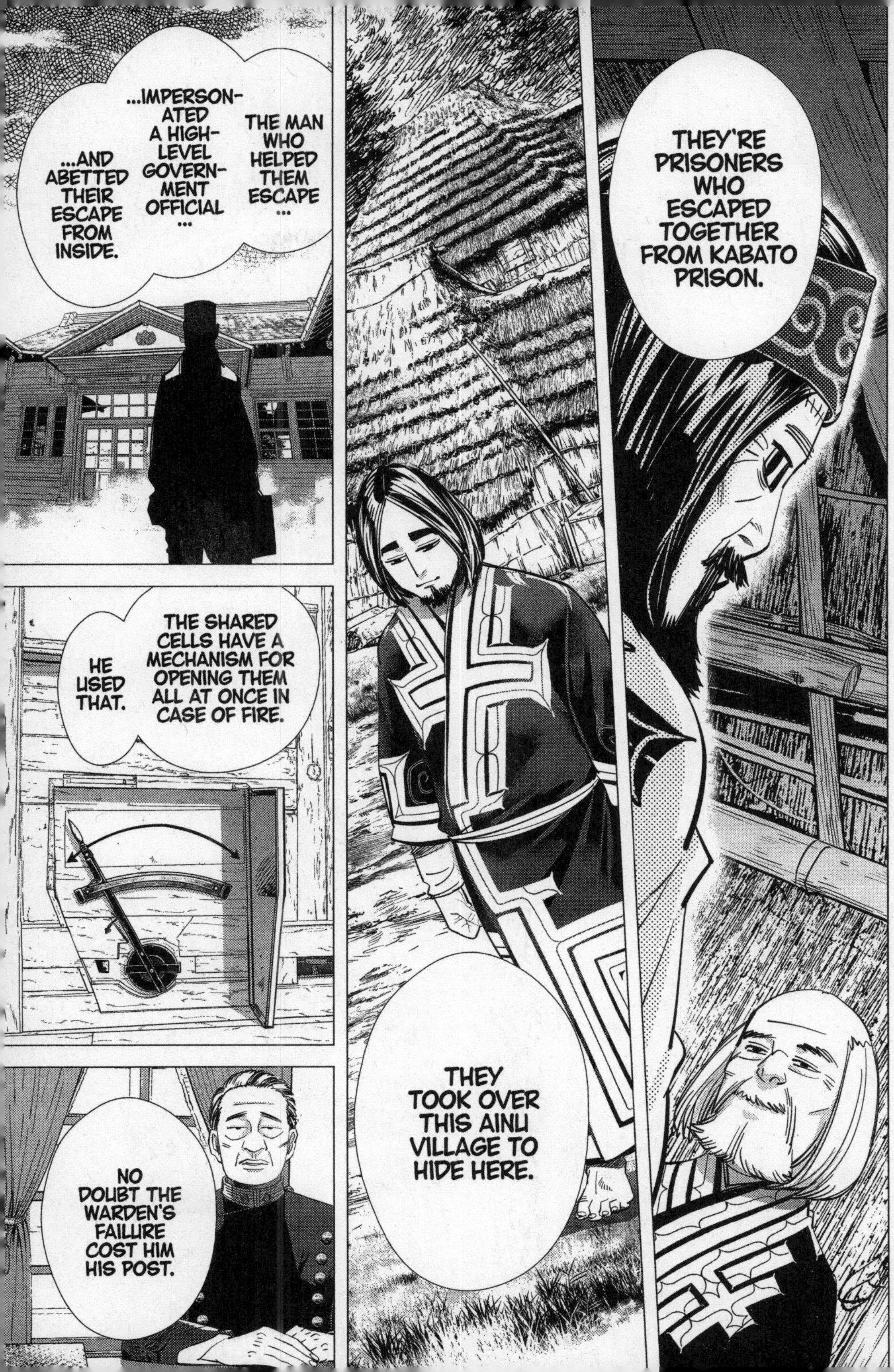
THEY'RE PRISONERS WHO ESCAPED TOGETHER FROM KABATO PRISON.
THEY TOOK OVER THIS AINU VILLAGE TO HIDE HERE.
THE MAN WHO HELPED THEM ESCAPE...
...IMPERSON-ATED A HIGH-LEVEL GOVERN-MENT OFFICIAL...
...AND ABETTED THEIR ESCAPE FROM INSIDE.
THE SHARED CELLS HAVE A MECHANISM FOR OPENING THEM ALL AT ONCE IN CASE OF FIRE.
HE USED THAT.
NO DOUBT THE WARDEN'S FAILURE COST HIM HIS POST.

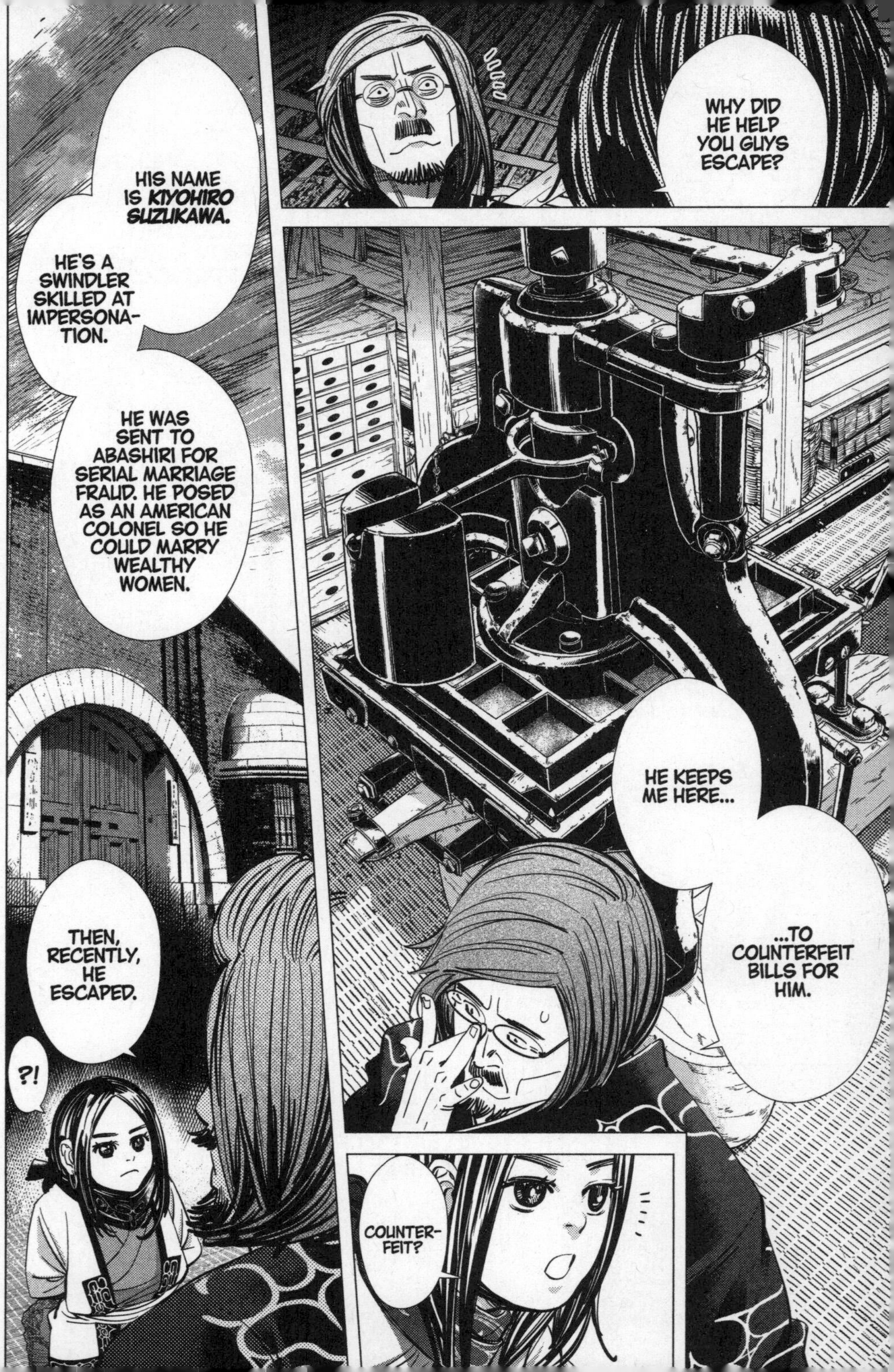
WHY DID HE HELP YOU GUYS ESCAPE?
HE KEEPS ME HERE...
...TO COUNTERFEIT BILLS FOR HIM.
COUNTER-FEIT?
HIS NAME IS KIYOHIRO SUZUKAWA.
HE'S A SWINDLER SKILLED AT IMPERSONA-TION.
HE WAS SENT TO ABASHIRI FOR SERIAL MARRIAGE FRAUD. HE POSED AS AN AMERICAN COLONEL SO HE COULD MARRY WEALTHY WOMEN.
THEN, RECENTLY, HE ESCAPED.
?!

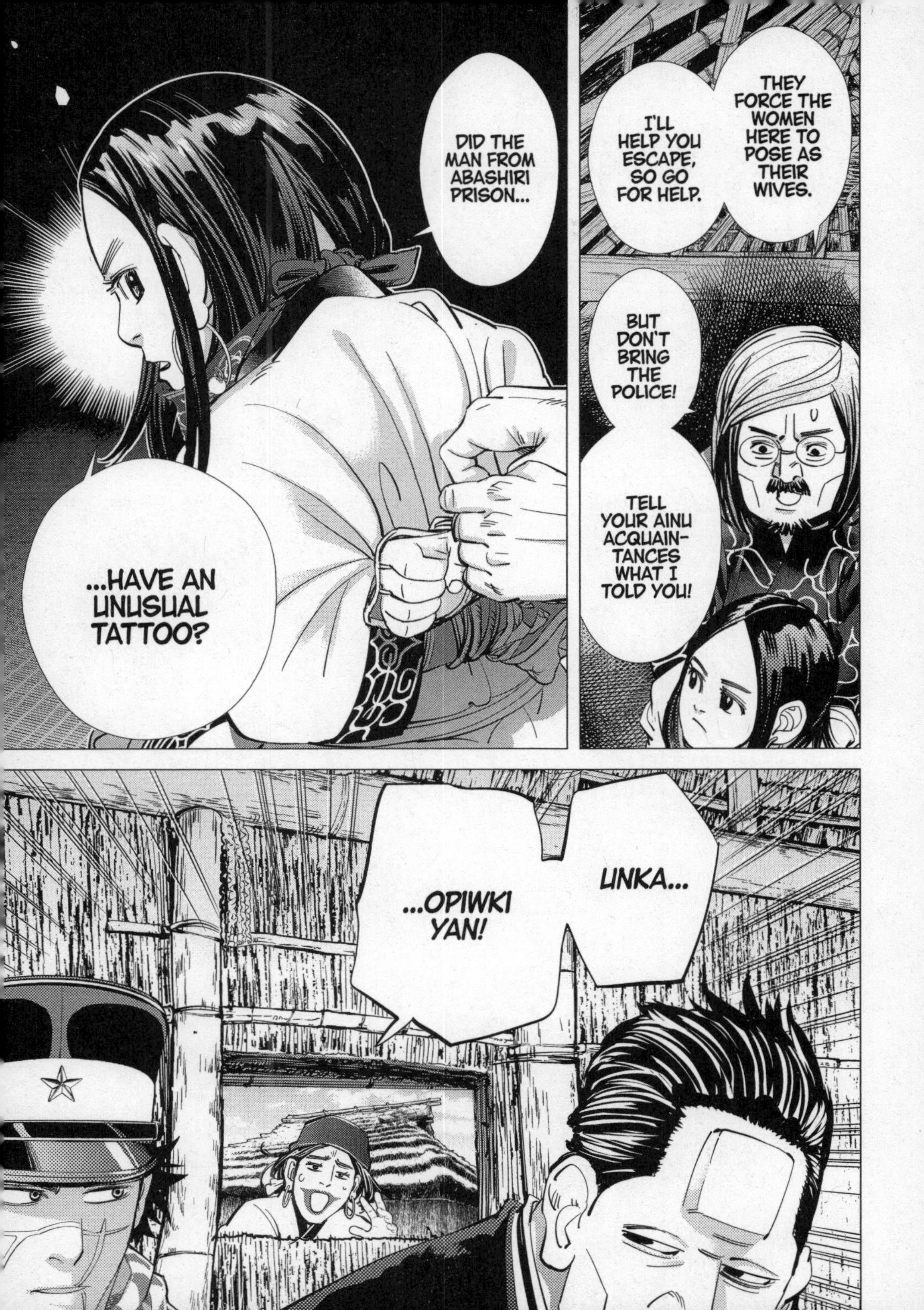
THEY FORCE THE WOMEN HERE TO POSE AS THEIR WIVES.
I'LL HELP YOU ESCAPE, SO GO FOR HELP.
BUT DON'T BRING THE POLICE!
TELL YOUR AINU ACQUAINTANCES WHAT I TOLD YOU!
DID THE MAN FROM ABASHIRI PRISON...
...HAVE AN UNUSUAL TATTOO?
UNKA...
...OPIWKI YAN!

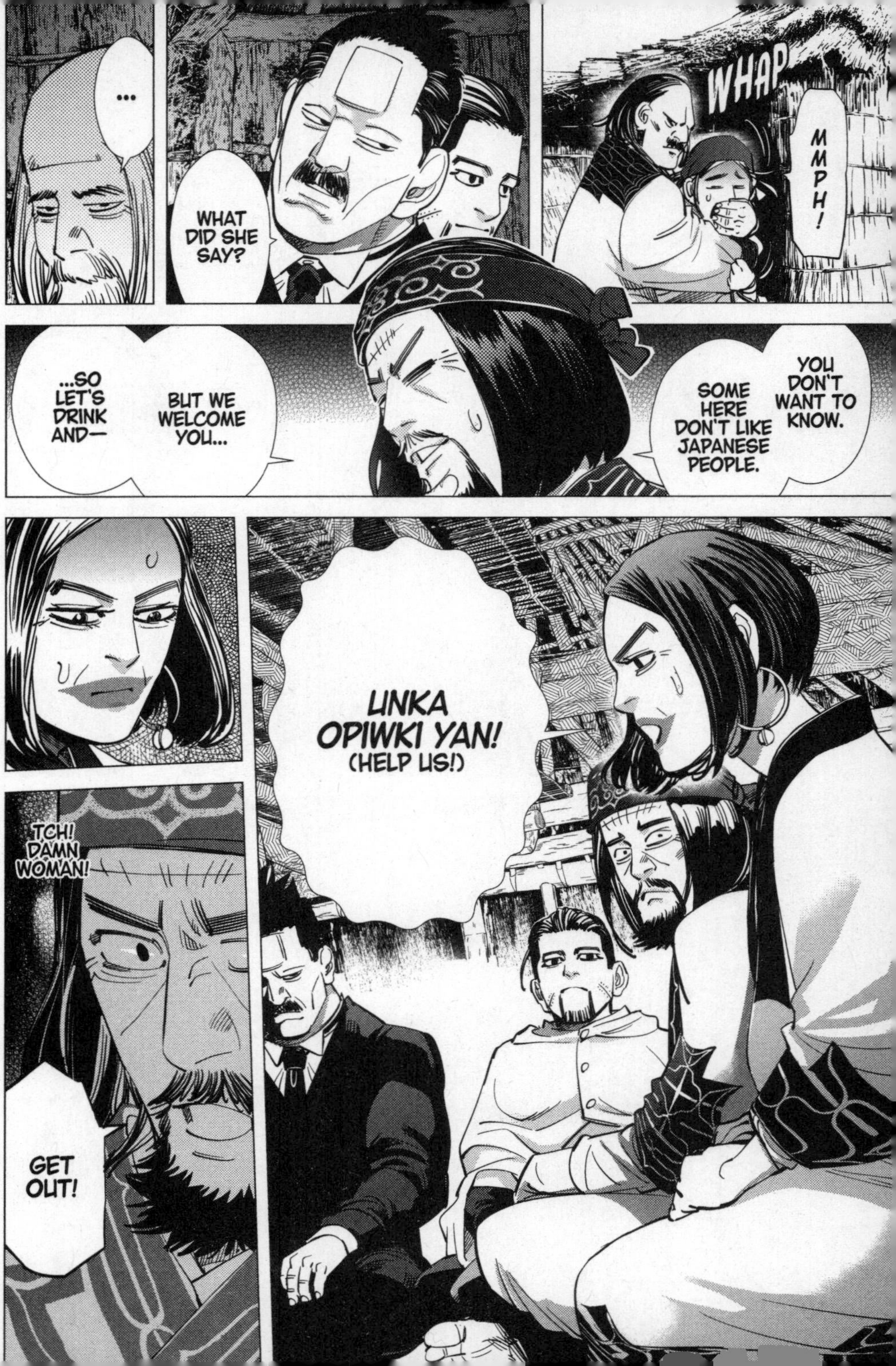
WHAP
MMPH!
WHAT DID SHE SAY?
...
YOU DON'T WANT TO KNOW.
SOME HERE DON'T LIKE JAPANESE PEOPLE.
BUT WE WELCOME YOU...
...SO LET'S DRINK AND—
UNKA OPIWKI YAN! (HELP US!)
TCH! DAMN WOMAN!
GET OUT!

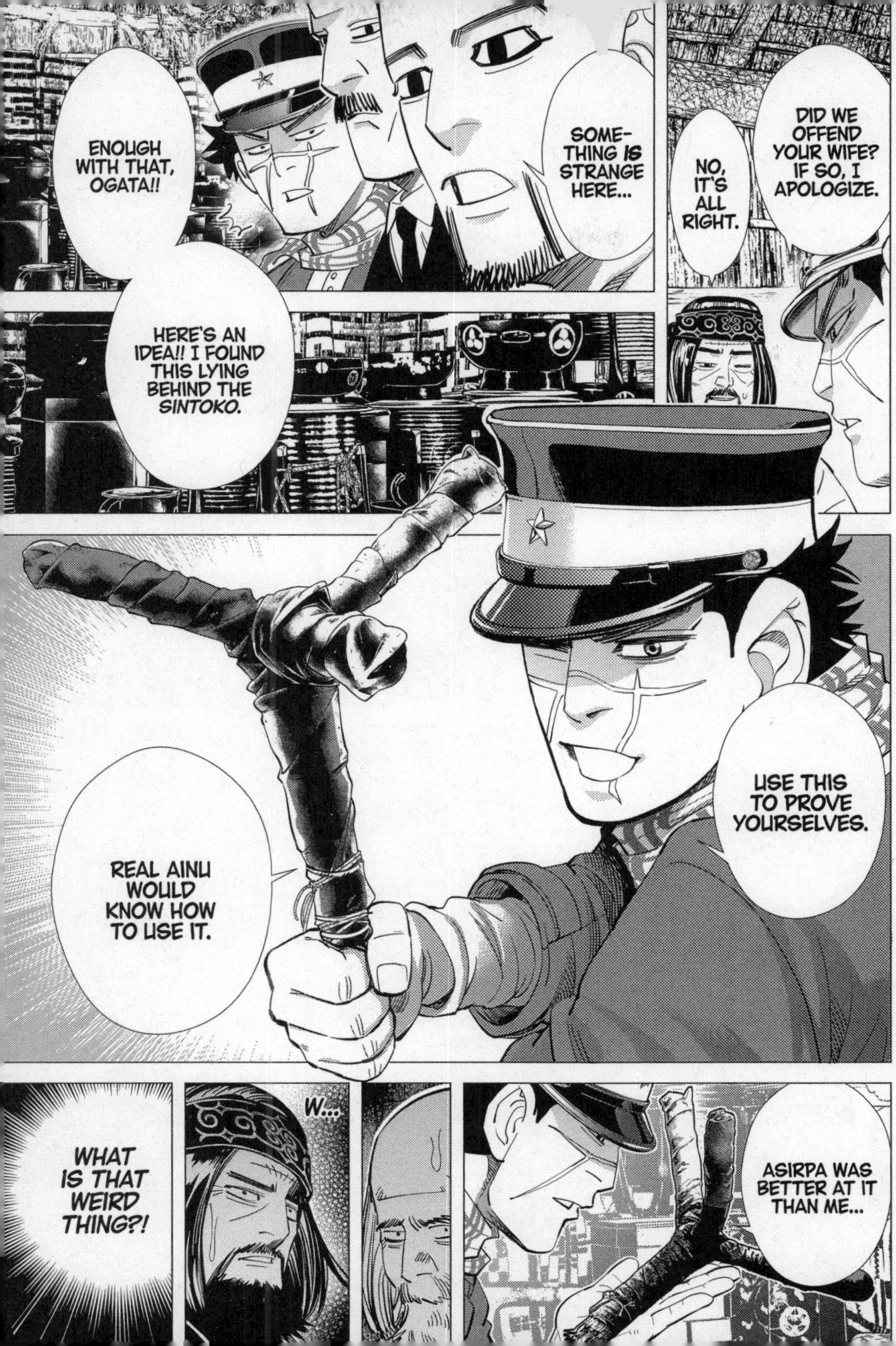
DID WE OFFEND YOUR WIFE? IF SO, I APOLOGIZE.
NO, IT'S ALL RIGHT.
SOME-THING IS STRANGE HERE...
ENOUGH WITH THAT, OGATA!!
HERE'S AN IDEA!! I FOUND THIS LYING BEHIND THE SINTOKO.
USE THIS TO PROVE YOURSELVES.
REAL AINU WOULD KNOW HOW TO USE IT.
ASIRPA WAS BETTER AT IT THAN ME...
W...
WHAT IS THAT WEIRD THING?!

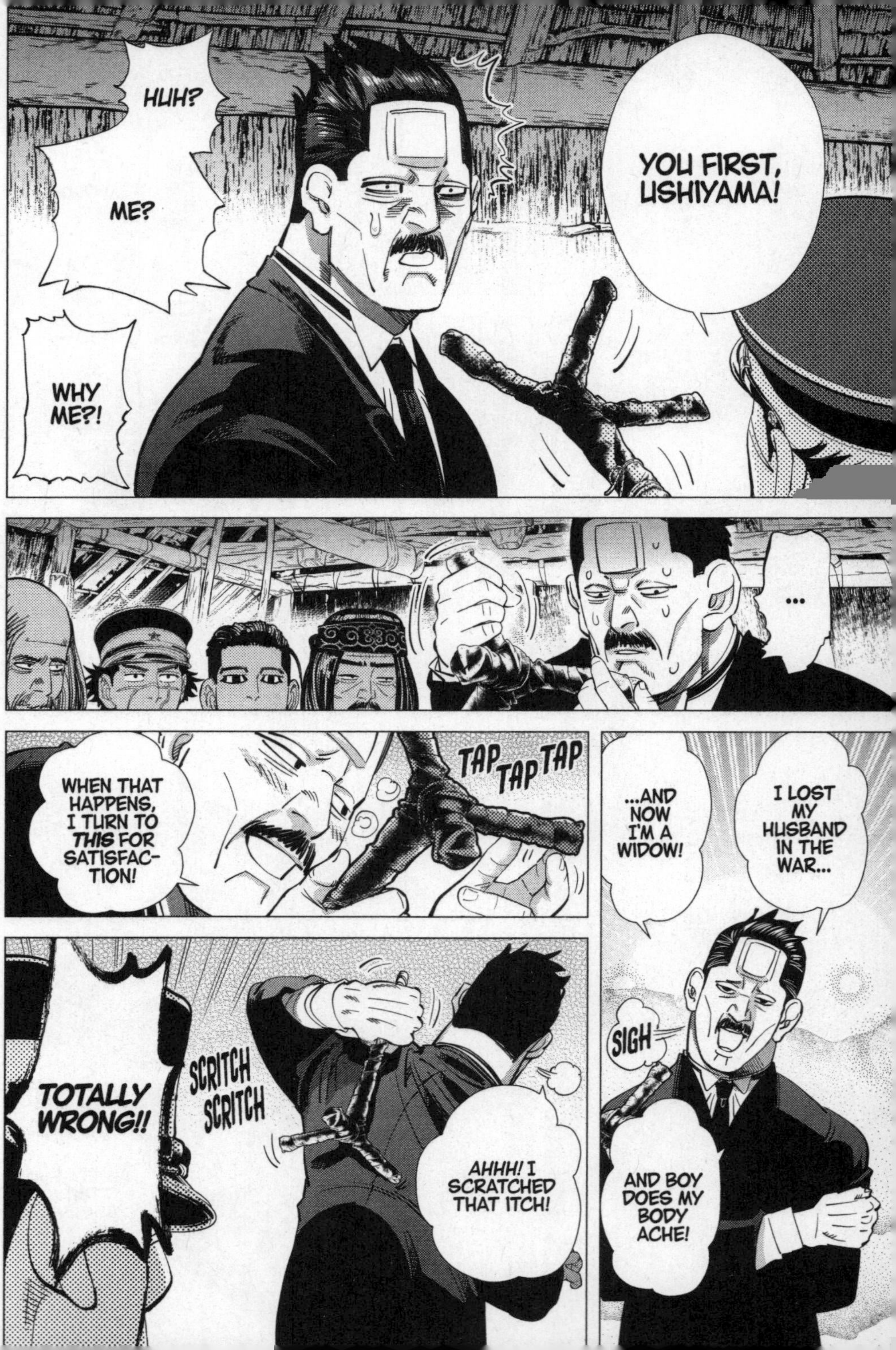
YOU FIRST, USHIYAMA!
HUH?
ME?
WHY ME?!
...
I LOST MY HUSBAND IN THE WAR...
...AND NOW I'M A WIDOW!
SIGH
AND BOY DOES MY BODY ACHE!
TAP TAP TAP
WHEN THAT HAPPENS, I TURN TO *THIS* FOR SATISFACTION!
AHHH! I SCRATCHED THAT ITCH!
SCRITCH SCRITCH
TOTALLY WRONG!!

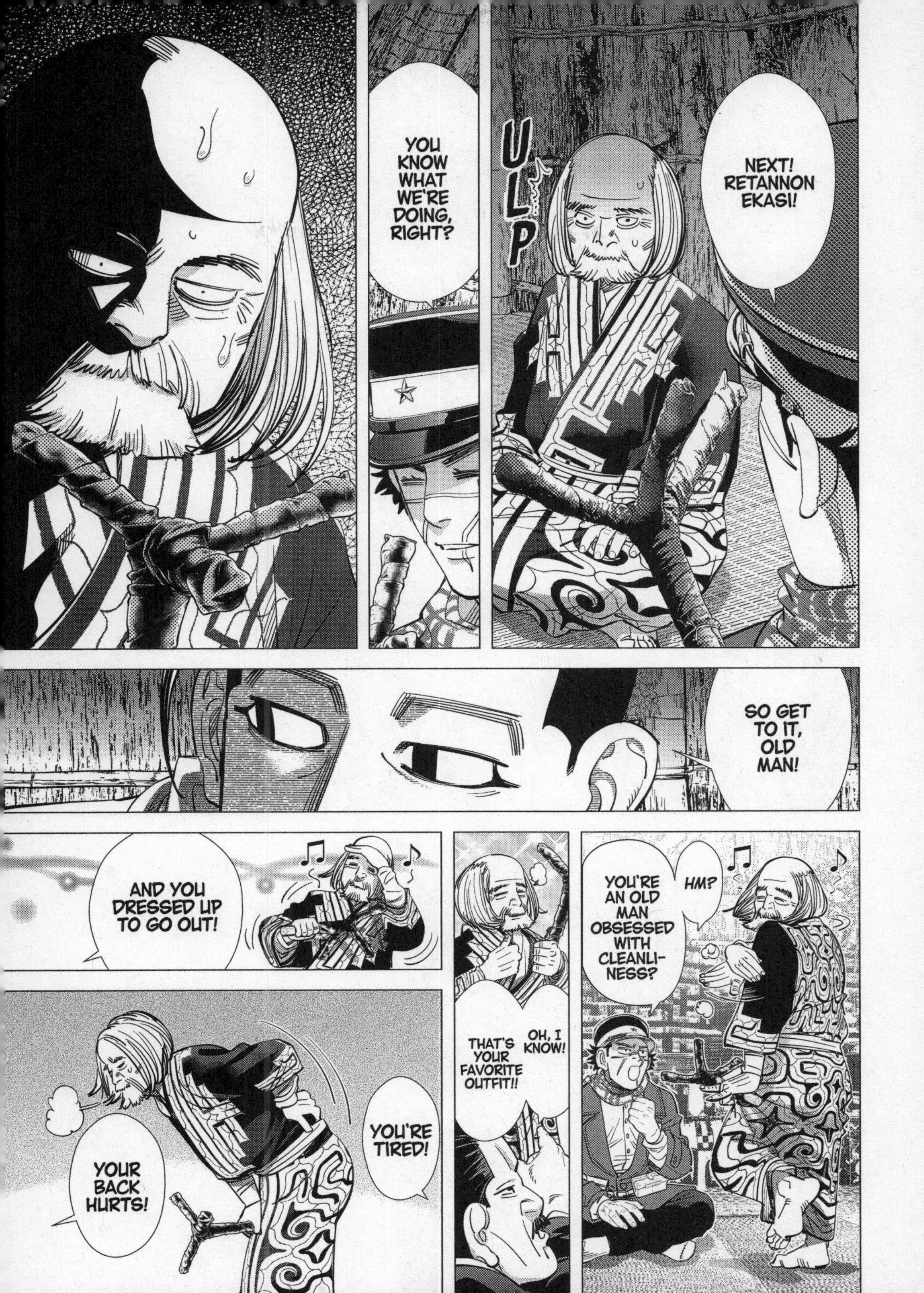
NEXT! RETANNON EKASI!
ULP
YOU KNOW WHAT WE'RE DOING, RIGHT?
SO GET TO IT, OLD MAN!
HM?
YOU'RE AN OLD MAN OBSESSED WITH CLEANLI-NESS?
OH, I KNOW!
THAT'S YOUR FAVORITE OUTFIT!!
AND YOU DRESSED UP TO GO OUT!
YOU'RE TIRED!
YOUR BACK HURTS!

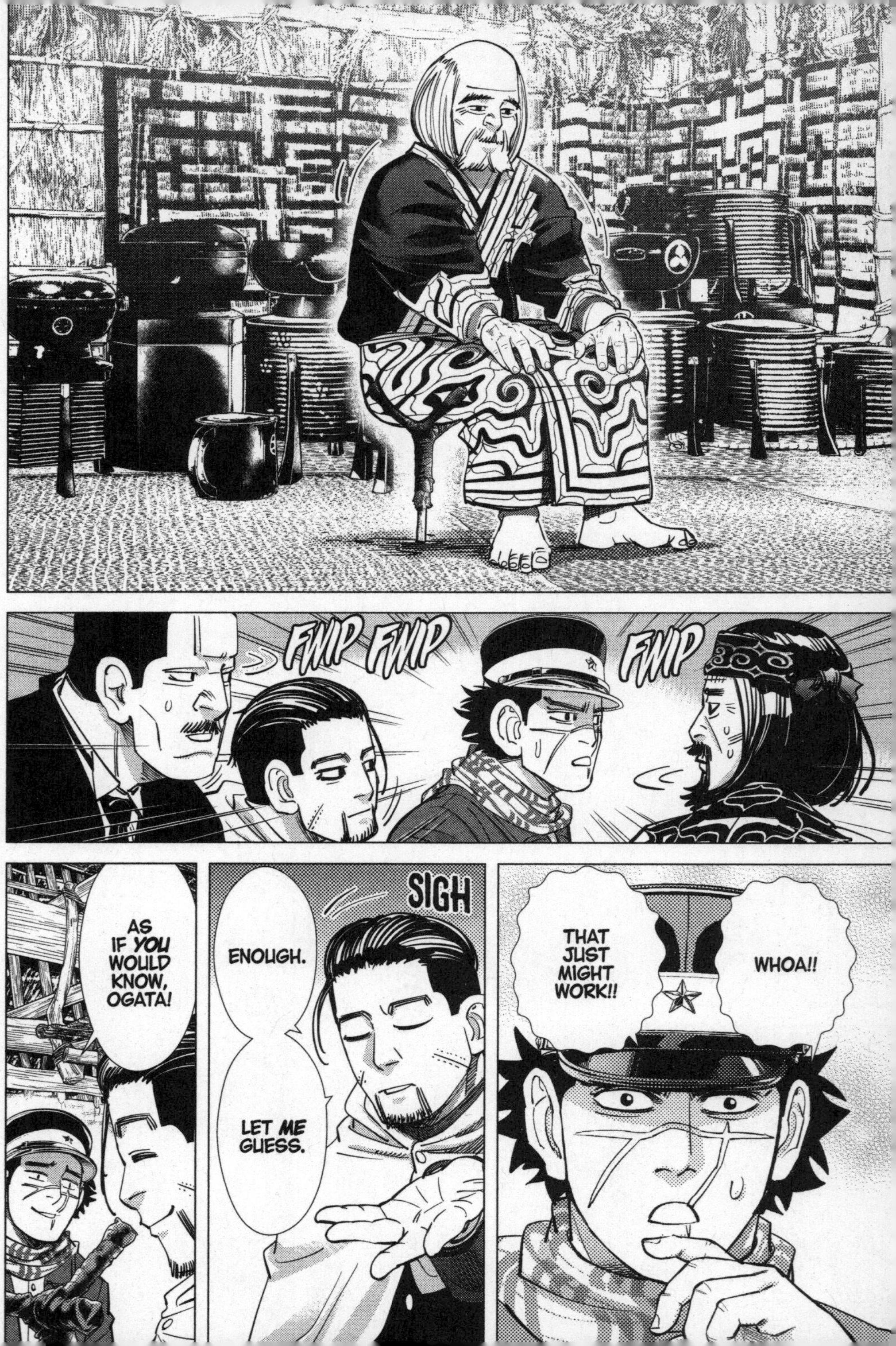
FWIP
FWIP FWIP
WHOA!!
THAT JUST MIGHT WORK!!
SIGH
ENOUGH.
LET ME GUESS.
AS IF YOU WOULD KNOW, OGATA!

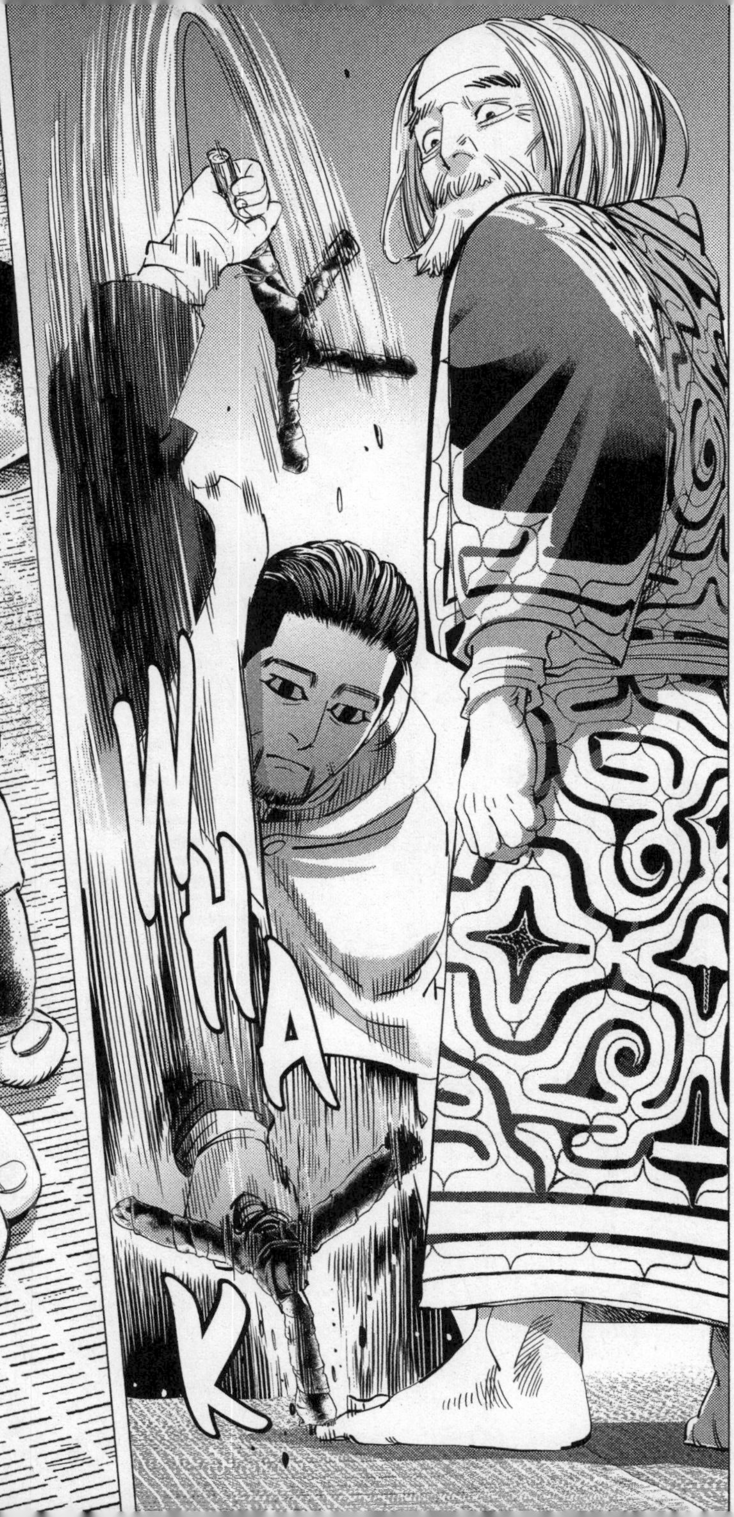
WHAKK
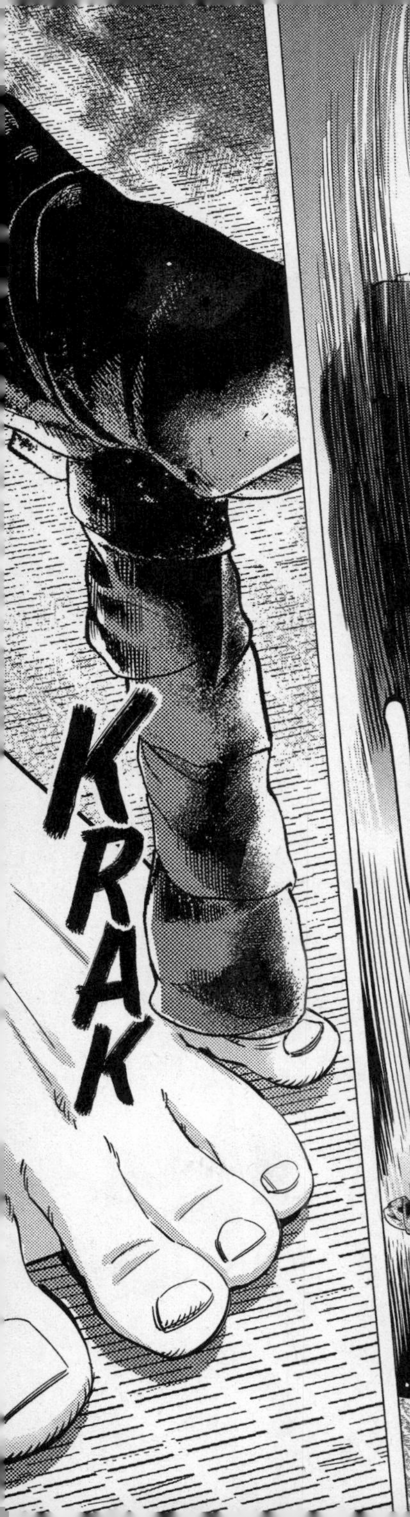
KRAK

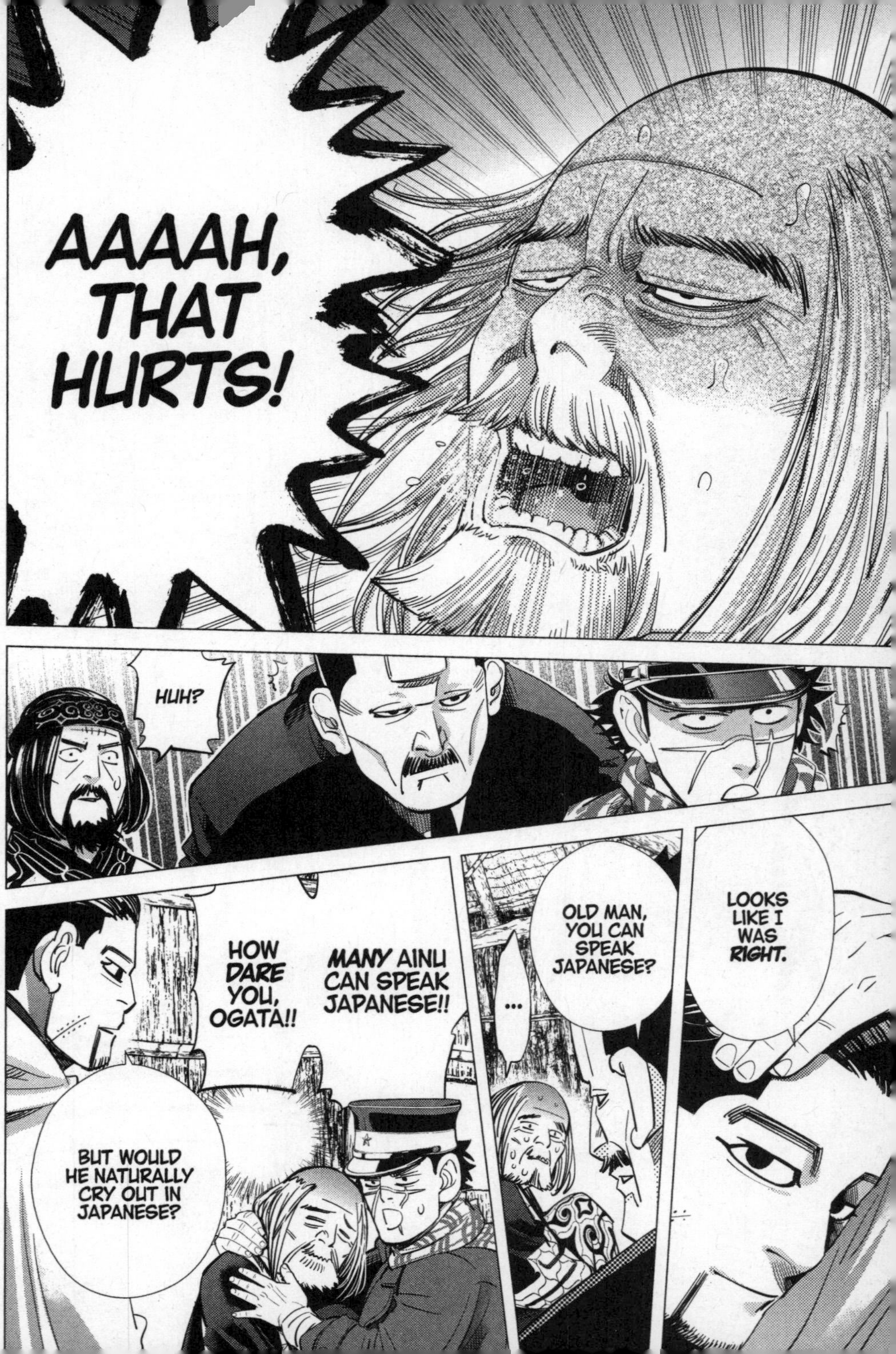
AAAAH, THAT HURTS!
HUH?
LOOKS LIKE I WAS RIGHT.
OLD MAN, YOU CAN SPEAK JAPANESE?
...
MANY AINU CAN SPEAK JAPANESE!!
HOW DARE YOU, OGATA!!
BUT WOULD HE NATURALLY CRY OUT IN JAPANESE?

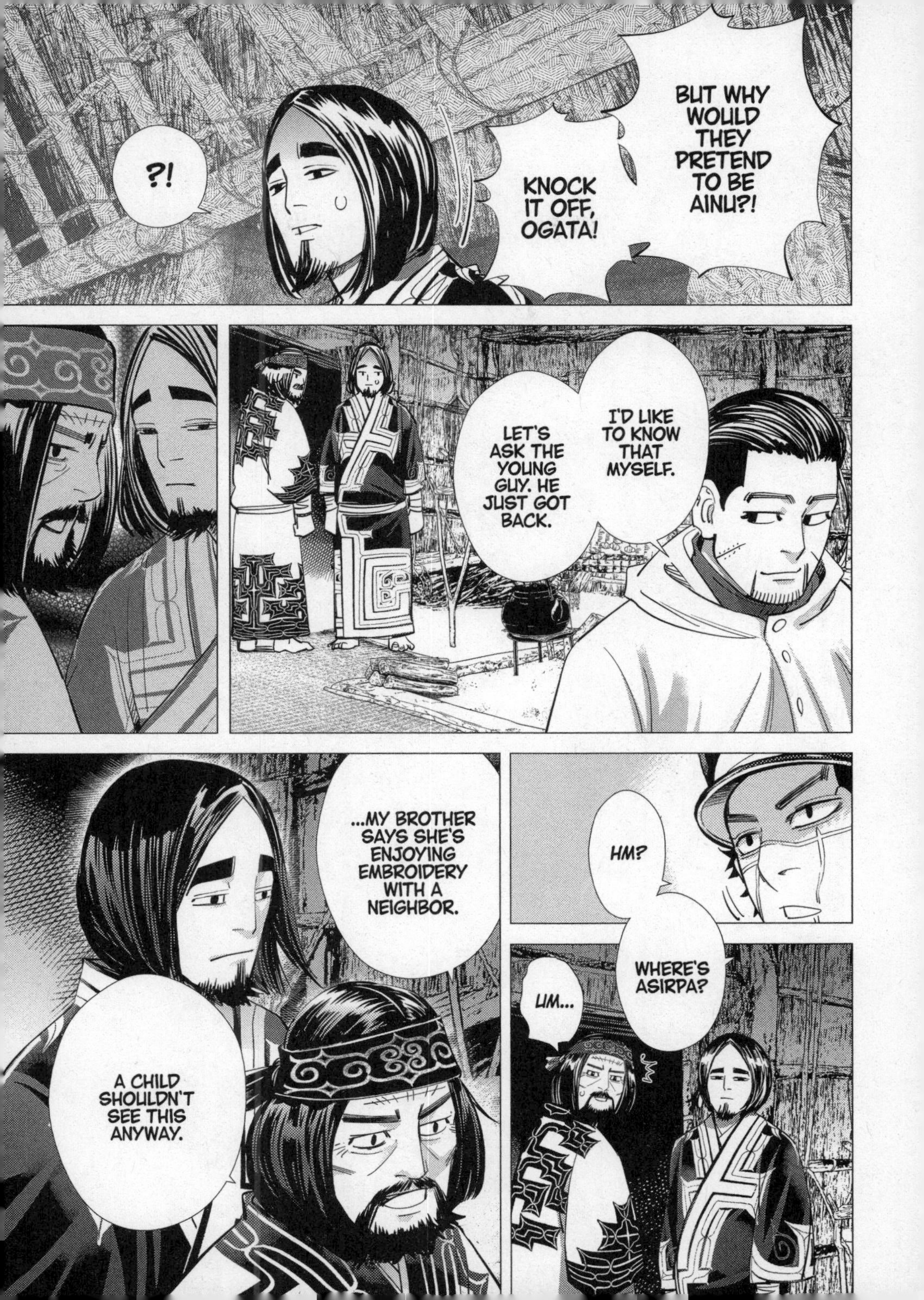
BUT WHY WOULD THEY PRETEND TO BE AINU?!
KNOCK IT OFF, OGATA!
?!
I'D LIKE TO KNOW THAT MYSELF.
LET'S ASK THE YOUNG GUY. HE JUST GOT BACK.
HM?
WHERE'S ASIRPA?
UM...
...MY BROTHER SAYS SHE'S ENJOYING EMBROIDERY WITH A NEIGHBOR.
A CHILD SHOULDN'T SEE THIS ANYWAY.

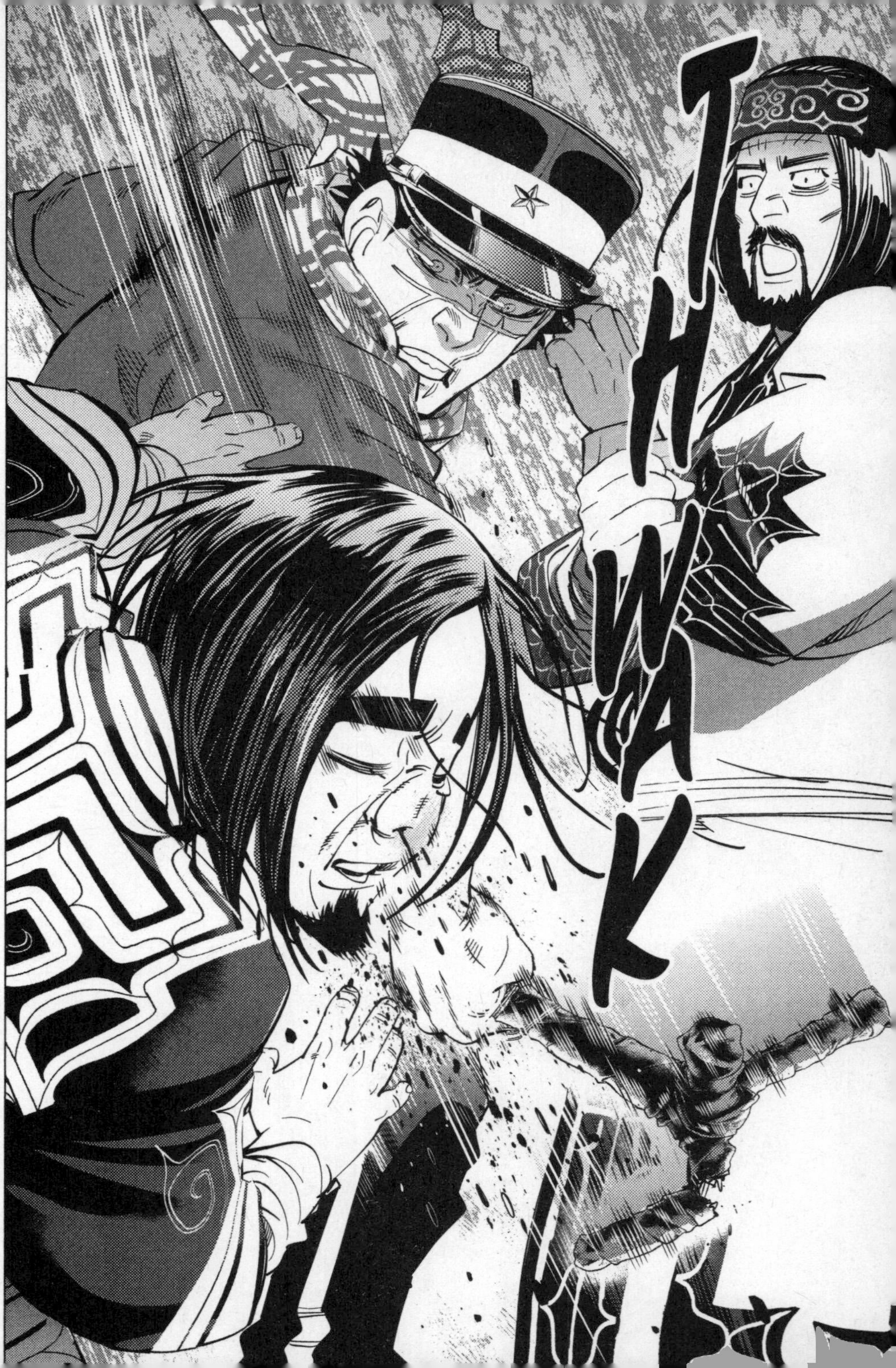
THWACK

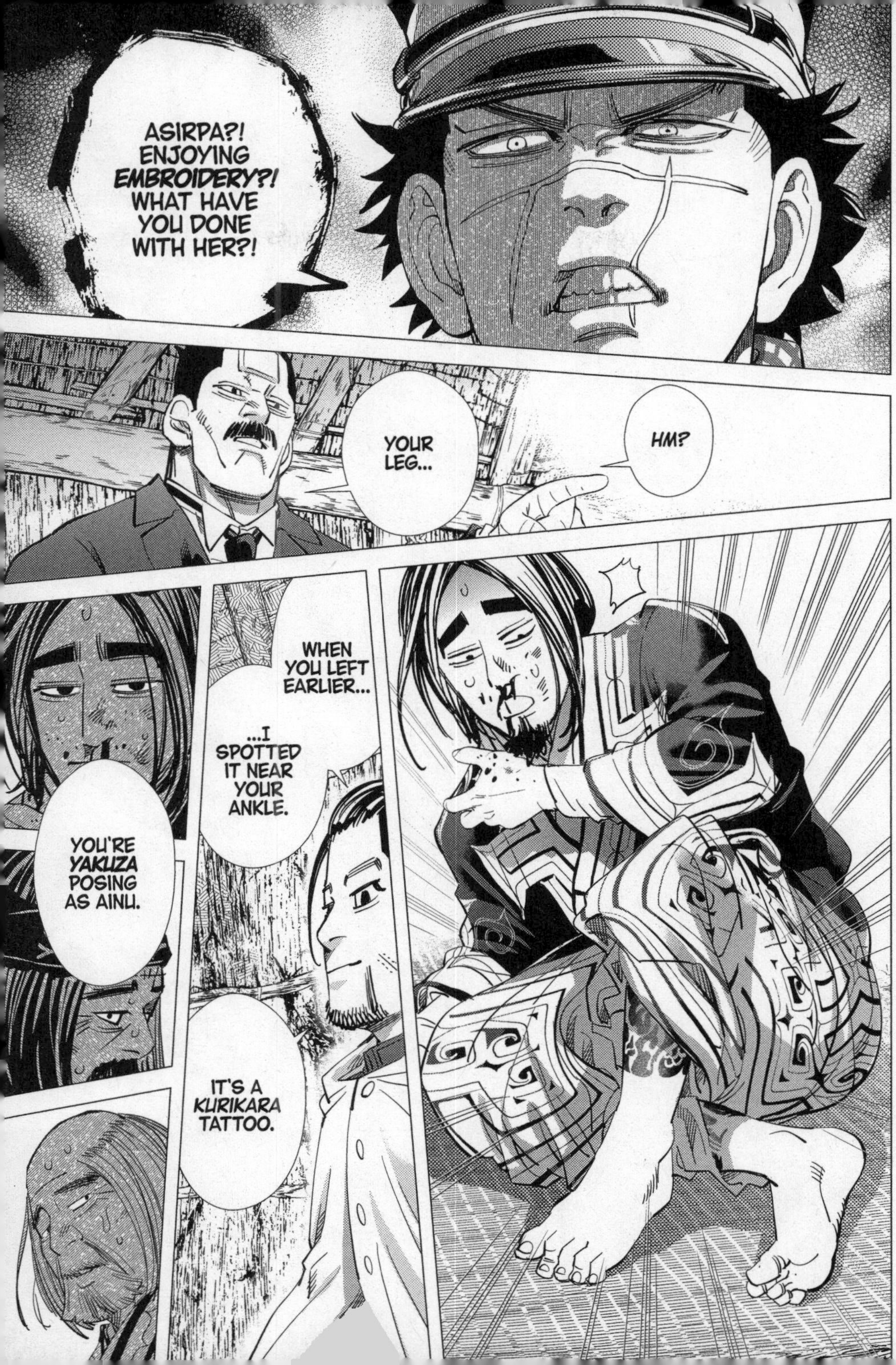
ASIRPA?! ENJOYING EMBROIDERY?! WHAT HAVE YOU DONE WITH HER?!
HM?
YOUR LEG...
WHEN YOU LEFT EARLIER...
...I SPOTTED IT NEAR YOUR ANKLE.
IT'S A KURIKARA TATTOO.
YOU'RE YAKUZA POSING AS AINU.

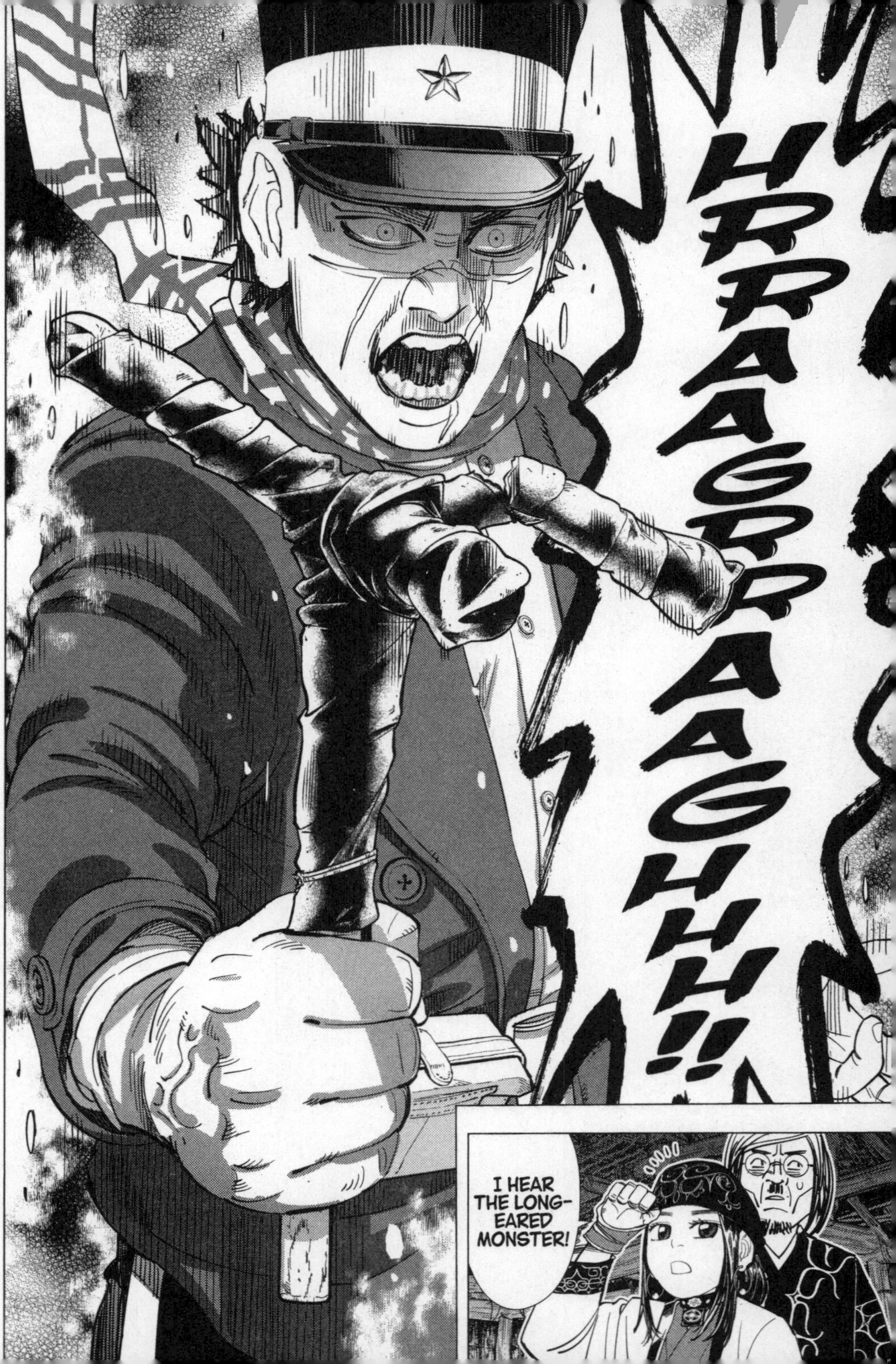
HRRAAGRRAAGHHH!!
I HEAR THE LONG-EARED MONSTER!

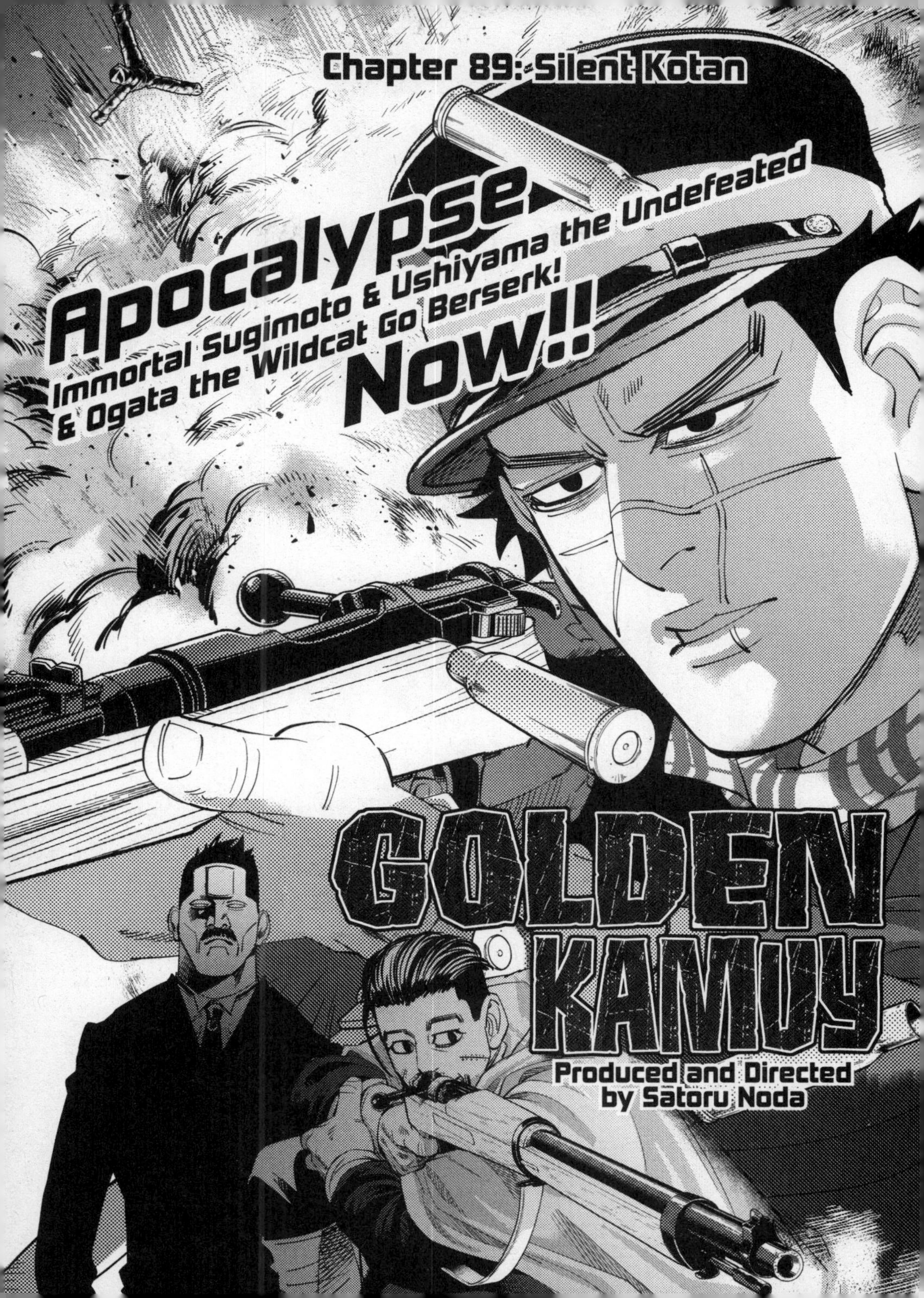
Chapter 89: Silent Kotan
Apocalypse Now!!
Immortal Sugimoto & Ushiyama the Undefeated & Ogata the Wildcat Go Berserk!
GOLDEN KAMUY
Produced and Directed by Satoru Noda

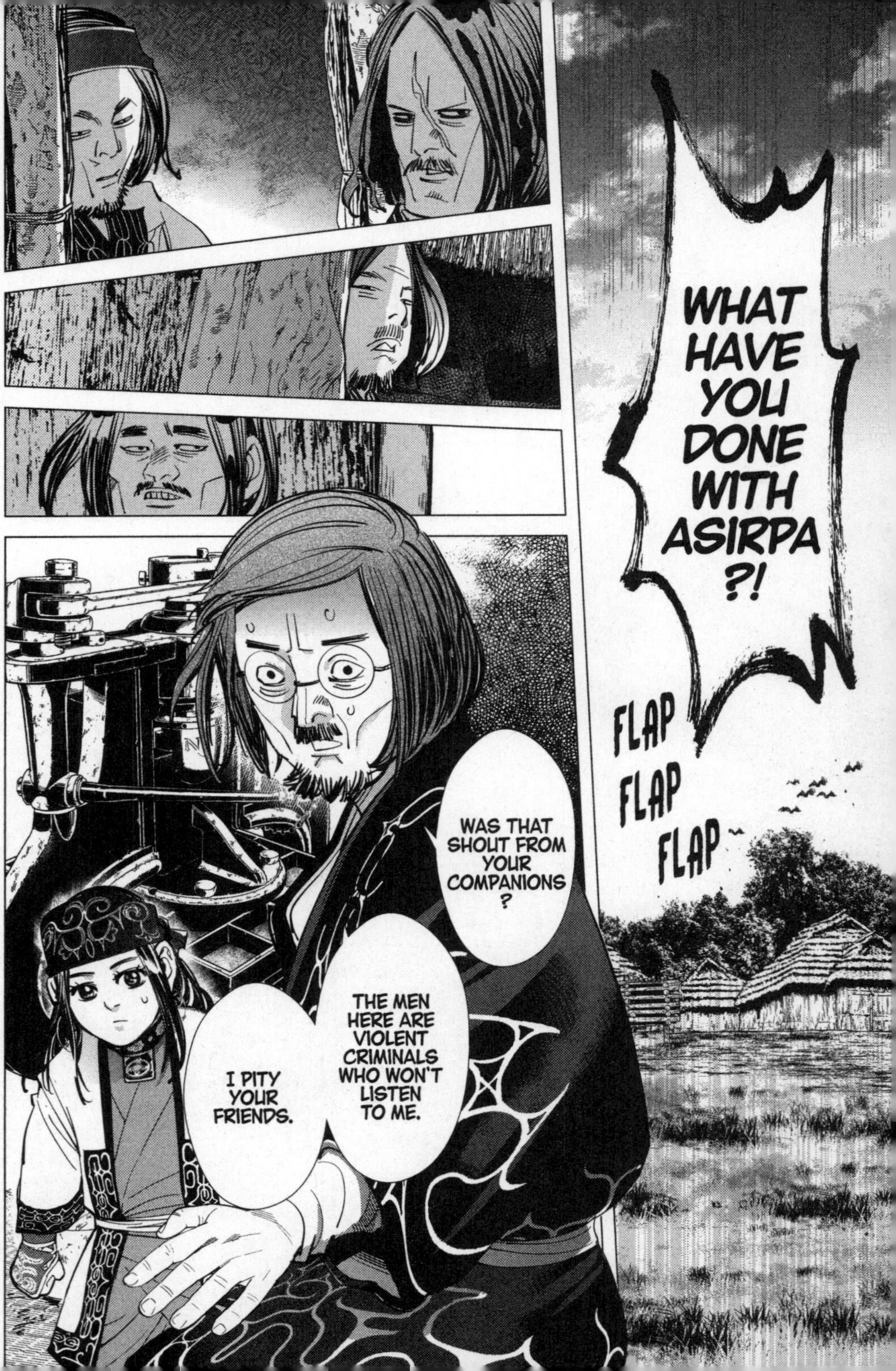
WHAT HAVE YOU DONE WITH ASIRPA?!
FLAP FLAP FLAP
WAS THAT SHOUT FROM YOUR COMPANIONS?
THE MEN HERE ARE VIOLENT CRIMINALS WHO WON'T LISTEN TO ME.
I PITY YOUR FRIENDS.

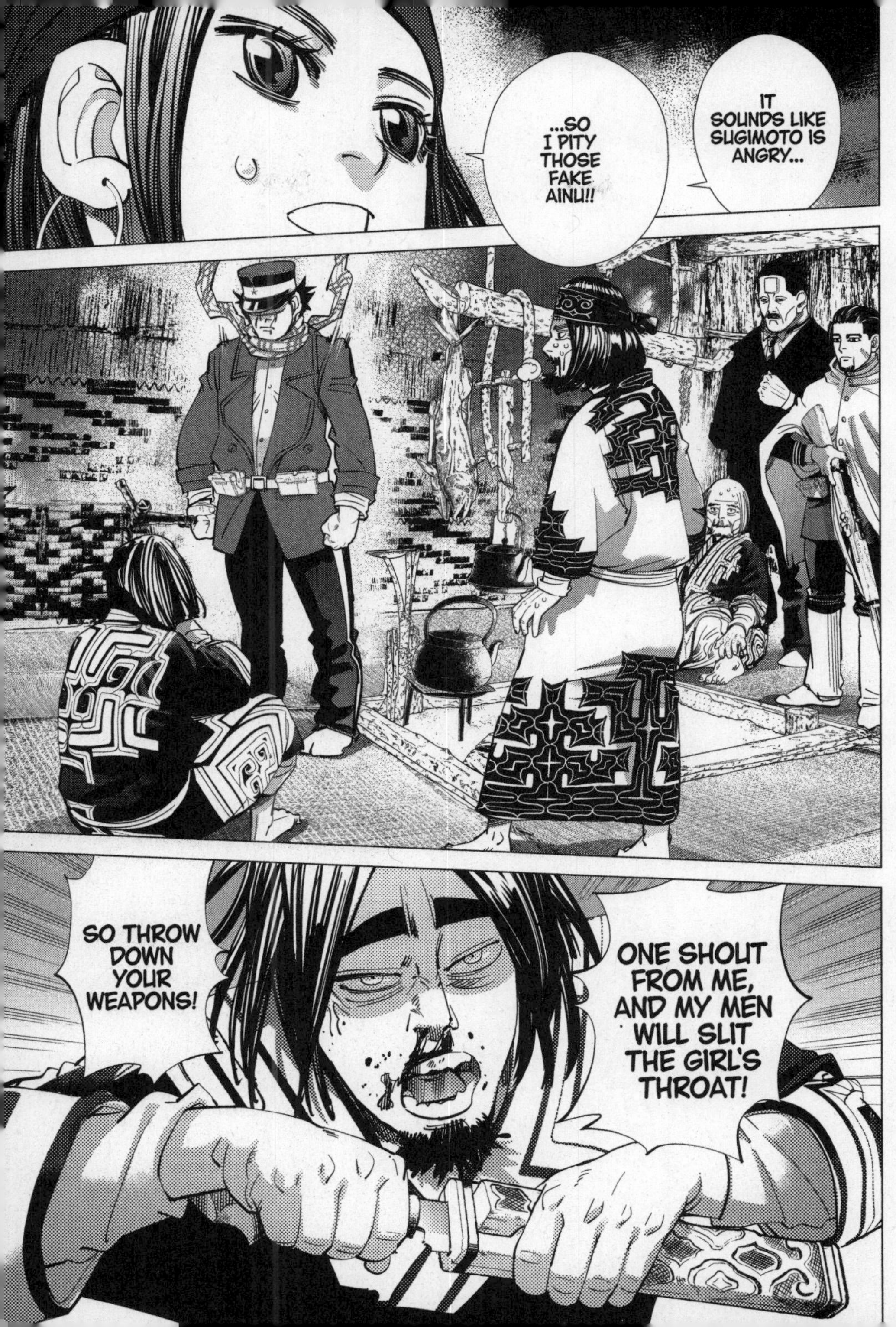
IT SOUNDS LIKE SUGIMOTO IS ANGRY...
...SO I PITY THOSE FAKE AINU!!
ONE SHOUT FROM ME, AND MY MEN WILL SLIT THE GIRL'S THROAT!
SO THROW DOWN YOUR WEAPONS!

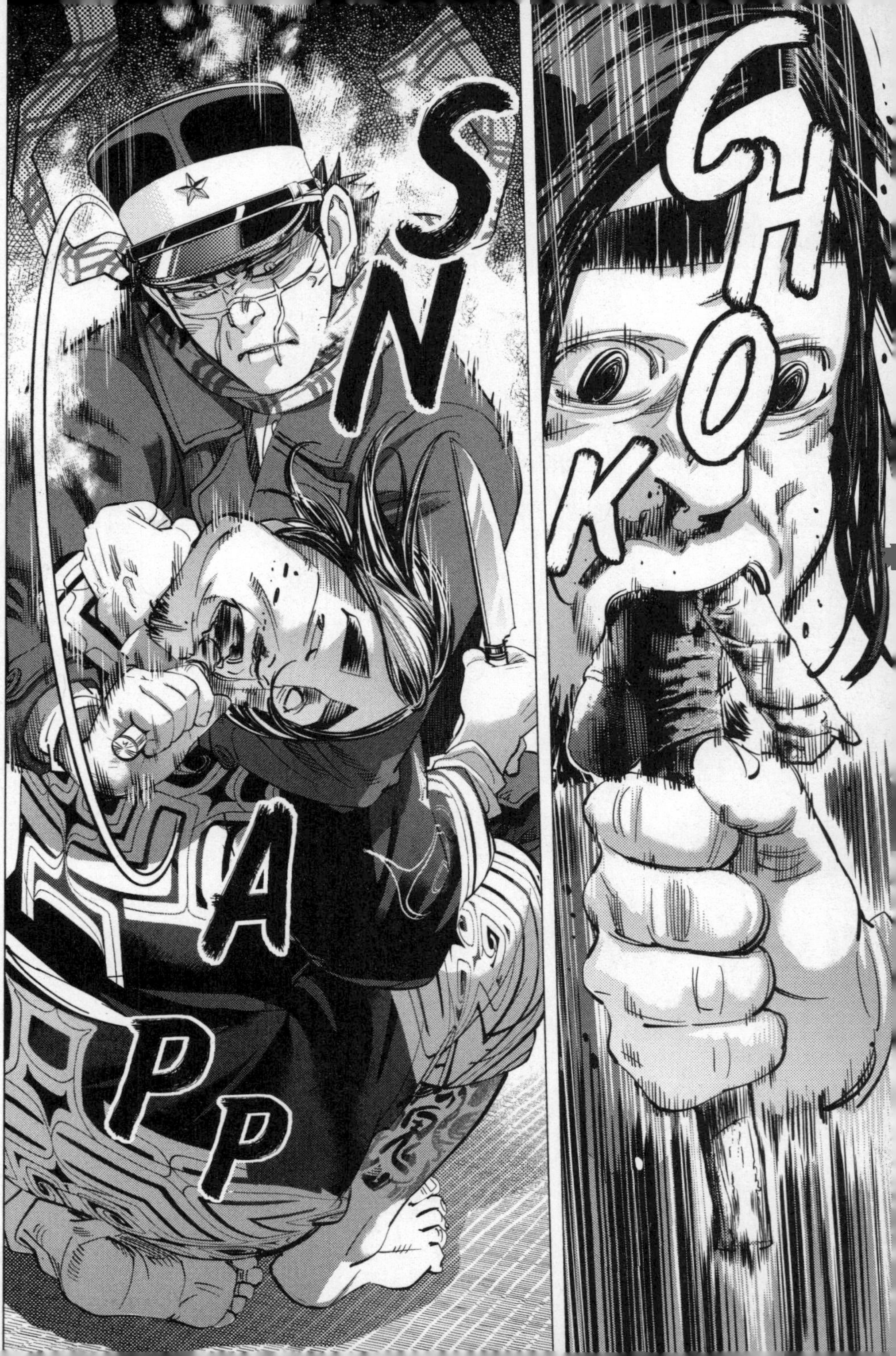
CHOK
SNAPP

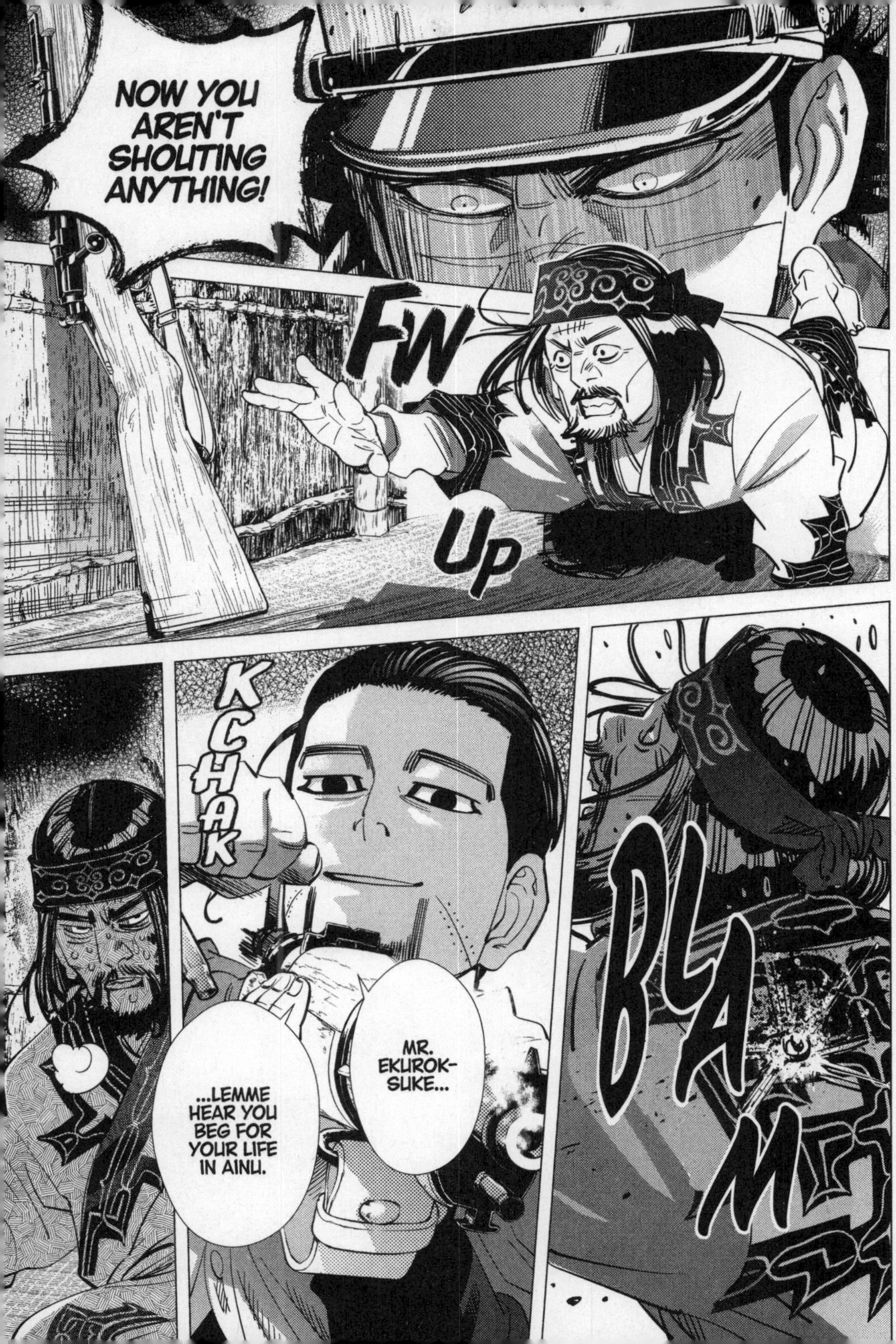
NOW YOU AREN'T SHOUTING ANYTHING!
FW
UP
BLAM
KCHAK
MR. EKUROK-SUKE...
...LEMME HEAR YOU BEG FOR YOUR LIFE IN AINU.

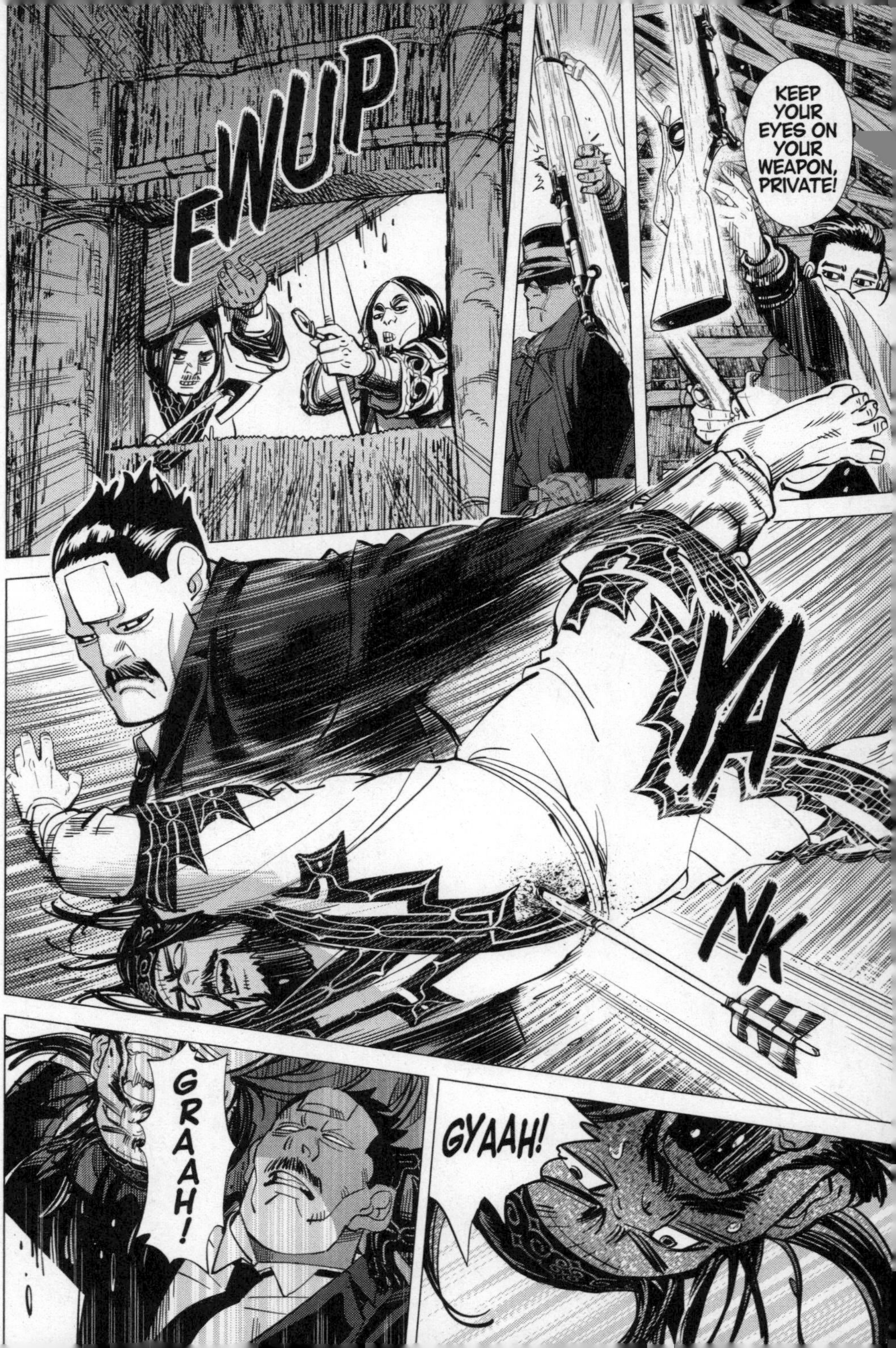
KEEP YOUR EYES ON YOUR WEAPON, PRIVATE!
FWUP
YANK
GYAAH!
GRAAH!

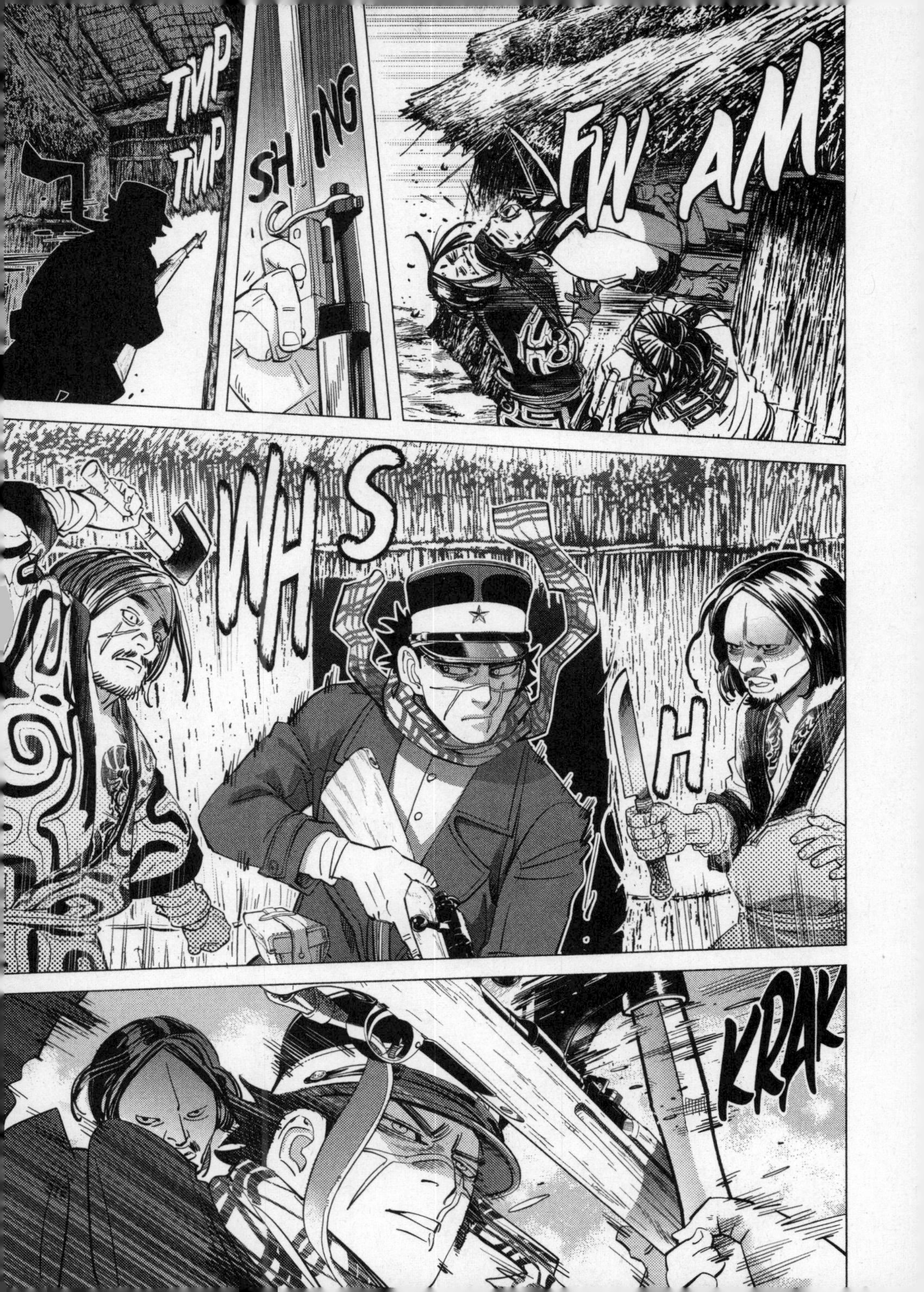
FWAM
SHING
TMP
TMP
WHS
H
KRAK

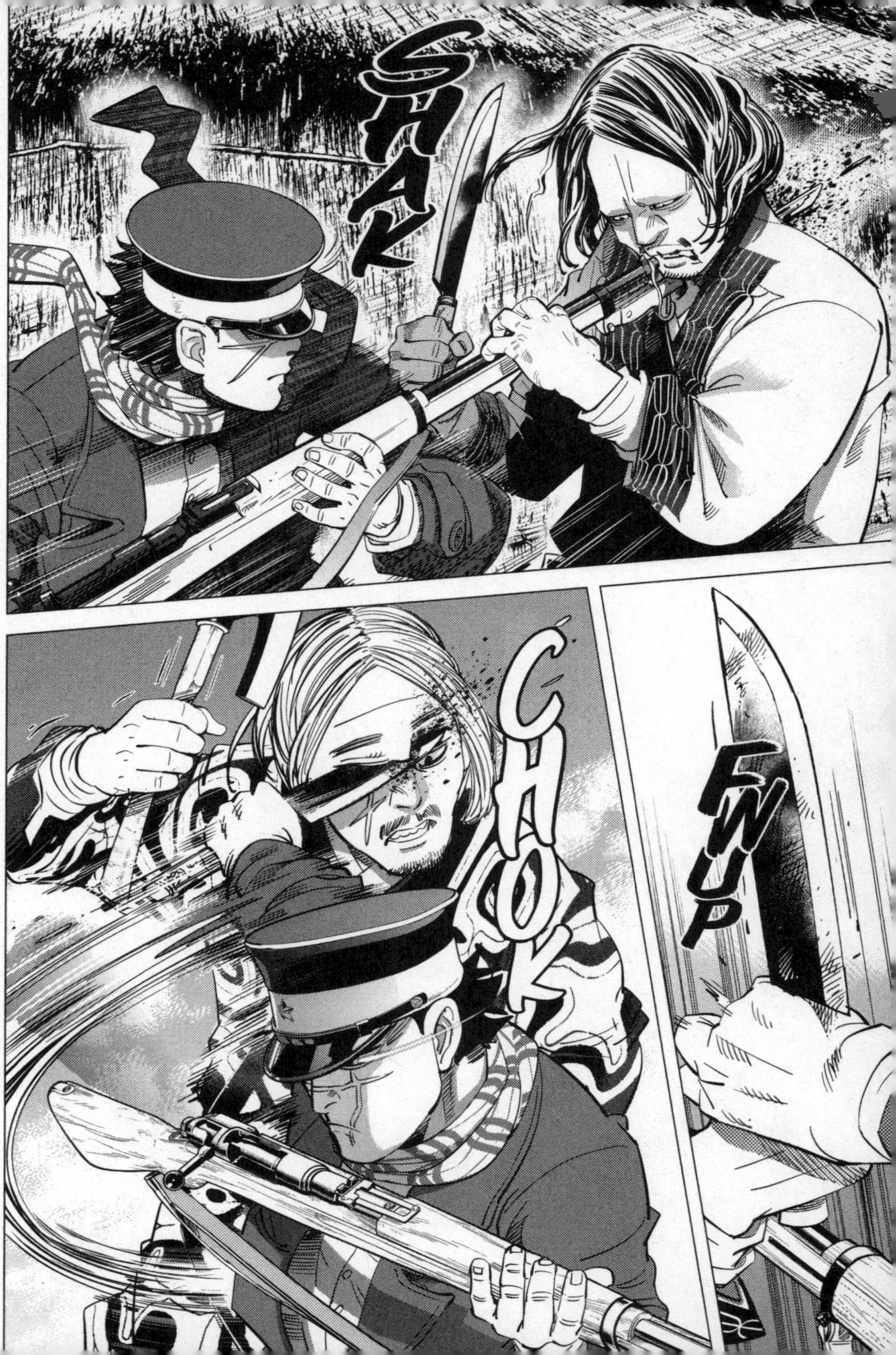
SHAK
FWUP
CHOK

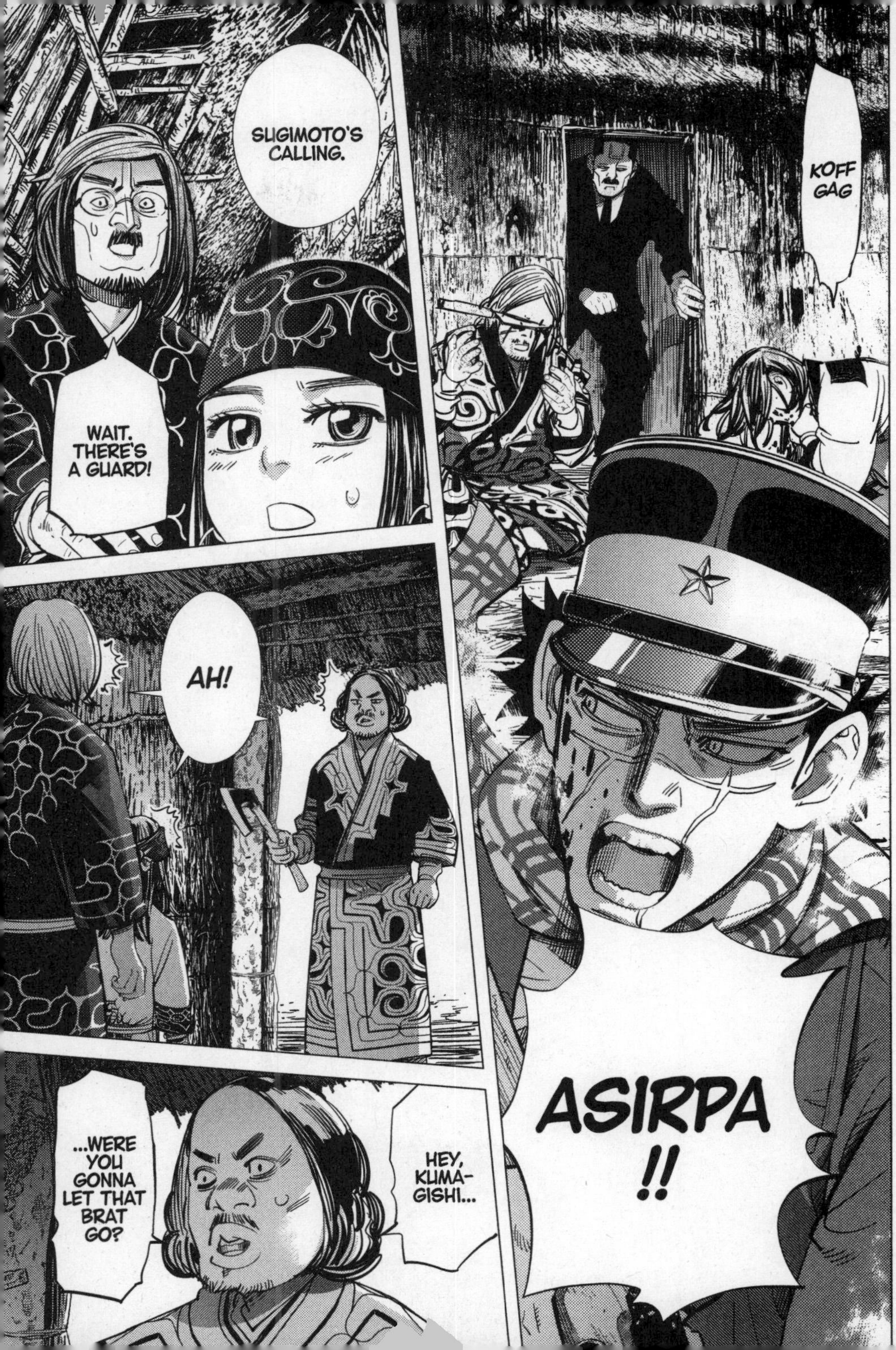
KOFF GAG
ASIRPA !!
SUGIMOTO'S CALLING.
WAIT. THERE'S A GUARD!
AH!
HEY, KUMAGISHI...
...WERE YOU GONNA LET THAT BRAT GO?

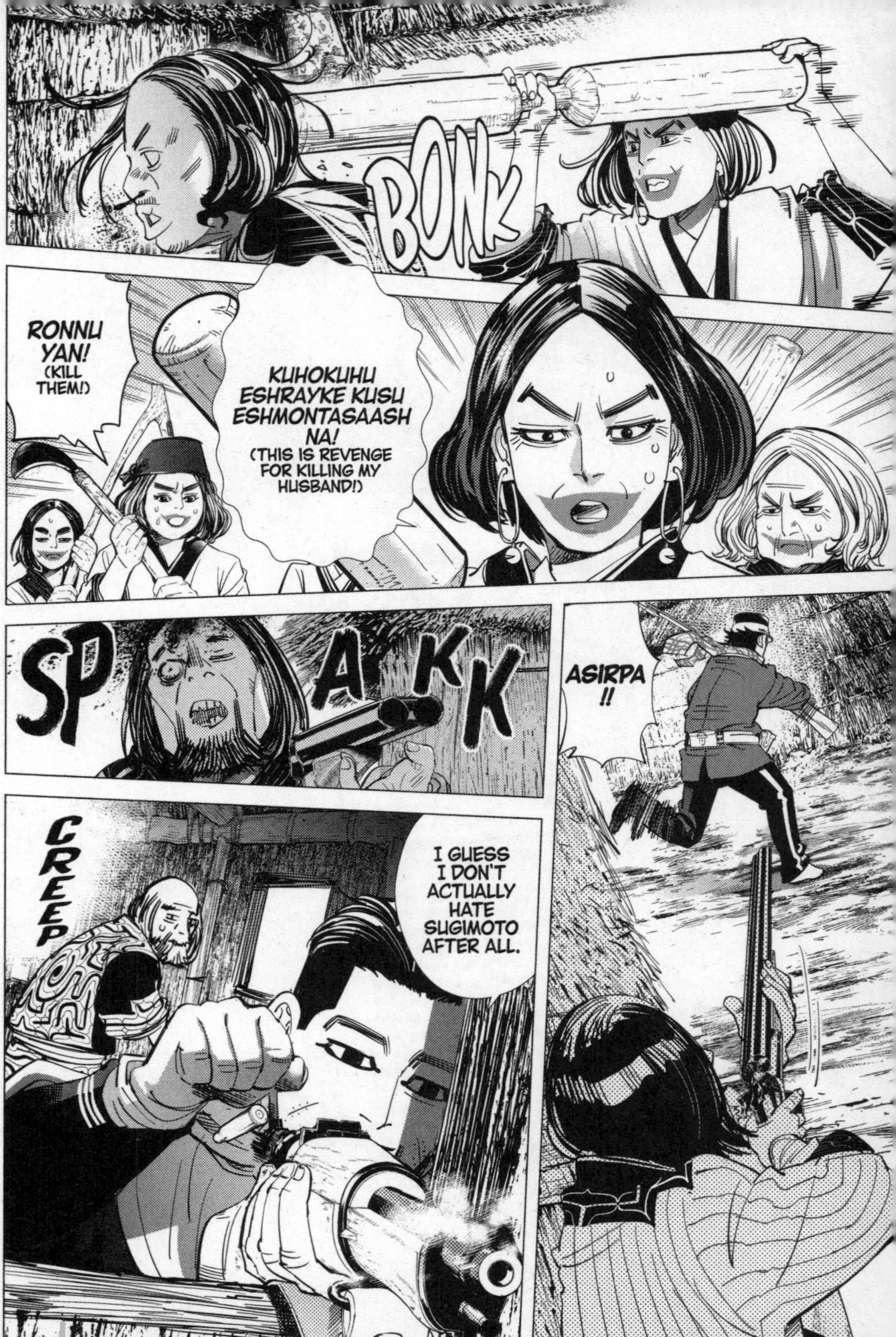
BONK
KUHOKUHU ESHRAYKE KUSU ESHMONTASAASH NA! (THIS IS REVENGE FOR KILLING MY HUSBAND!)
RONNU YAN! (KILL THEM!)
ASIRPA !!
SPAKK
I GUESS I DON'T ACTUALLY HATE SUGIMOTO AFTER ALL.
CREEP

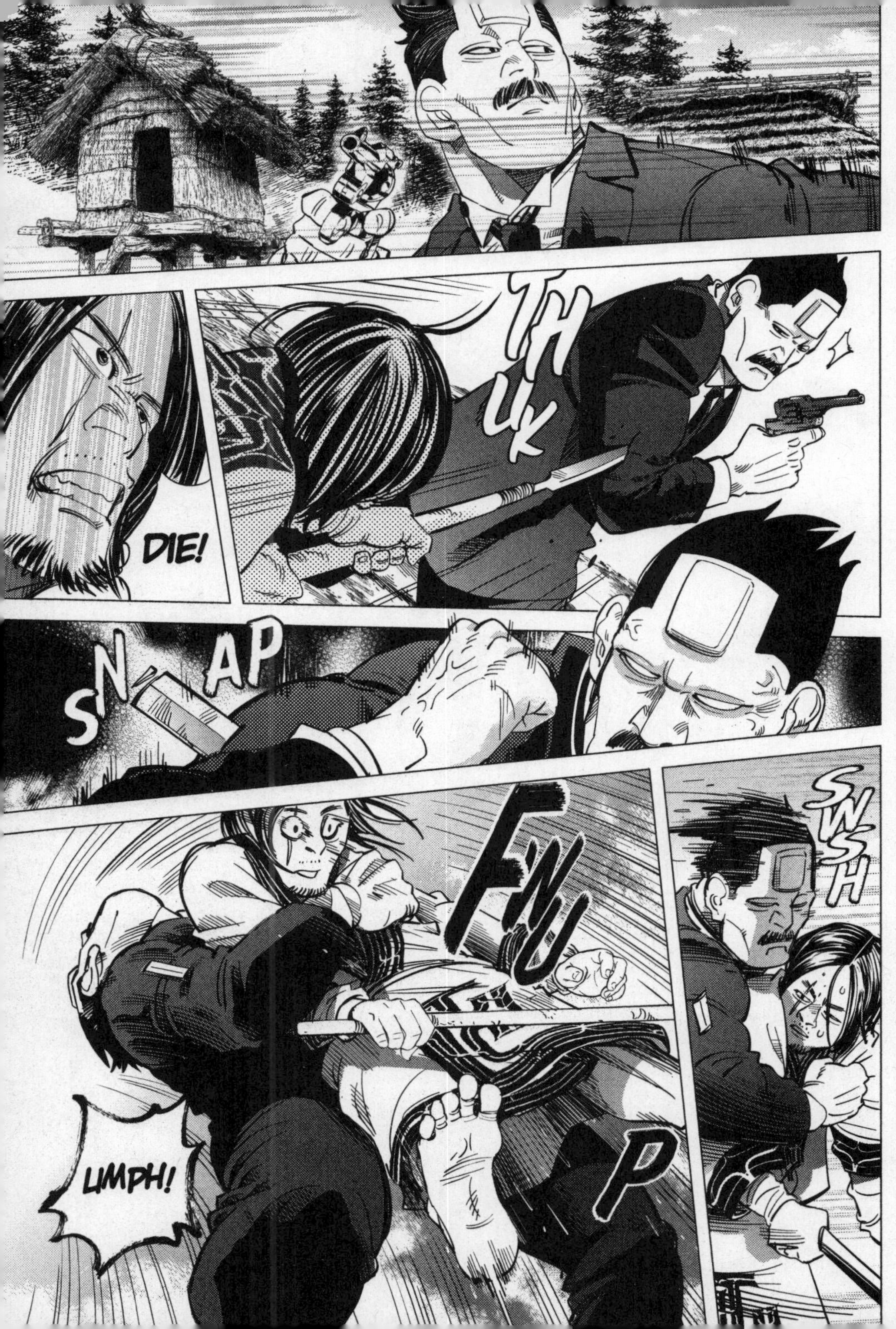
THUK
DIE!
SNAP
SWSH
FWUP
UMPH!

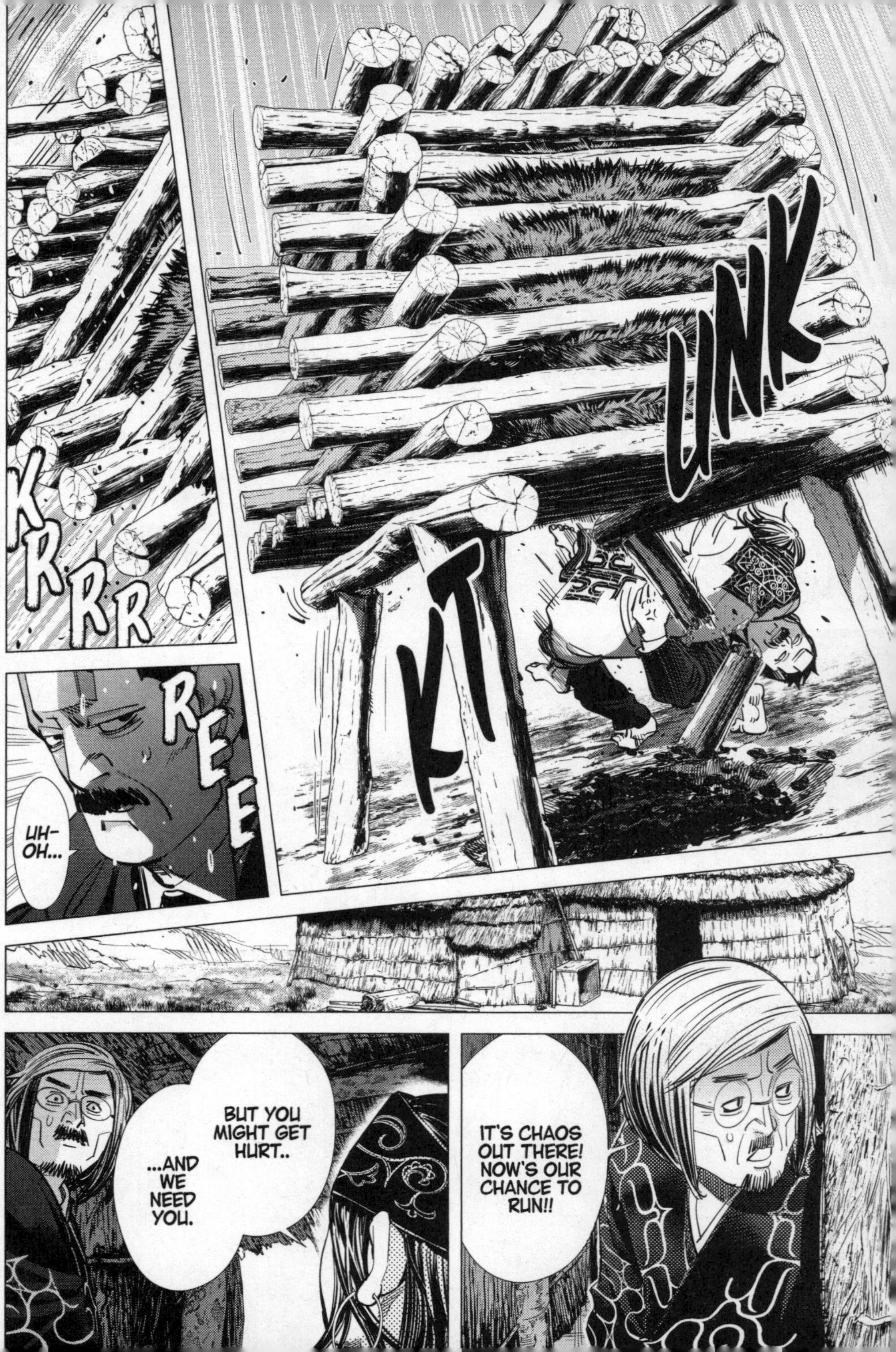

UNK
KT
KRRR
REEE
UH-OH...
IT'S CHAOS OUT THERE! NOW'S OUR CHANCE TO RUN!!
BUT YOU MIGHT GET HURT..
...AND WE NEED YOU.

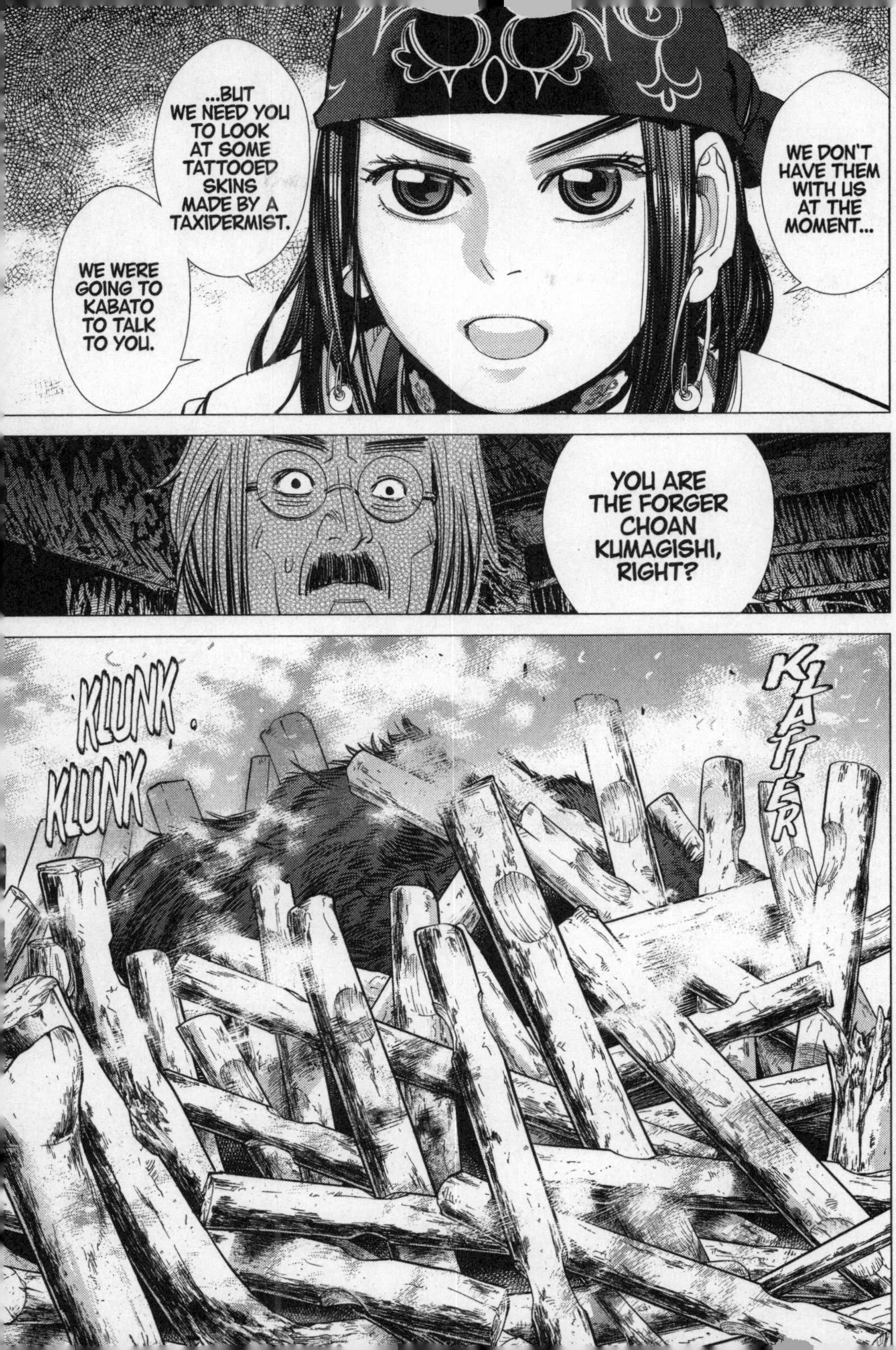
WE DON'T HAVE THEM WITH US AT THE MOMENT...
...BUT WE NEED YOU TO LOOK AT SOME TATTOOED SKINS MADE BY A TAXIDERMIST.
WE WERE GOING TO KABATO TO TALK TO YOU.
YOU ARE THE FORGER CHOAN KUMAGISHI, RIGHT?
KLATTER
KLUNK
KLUNK

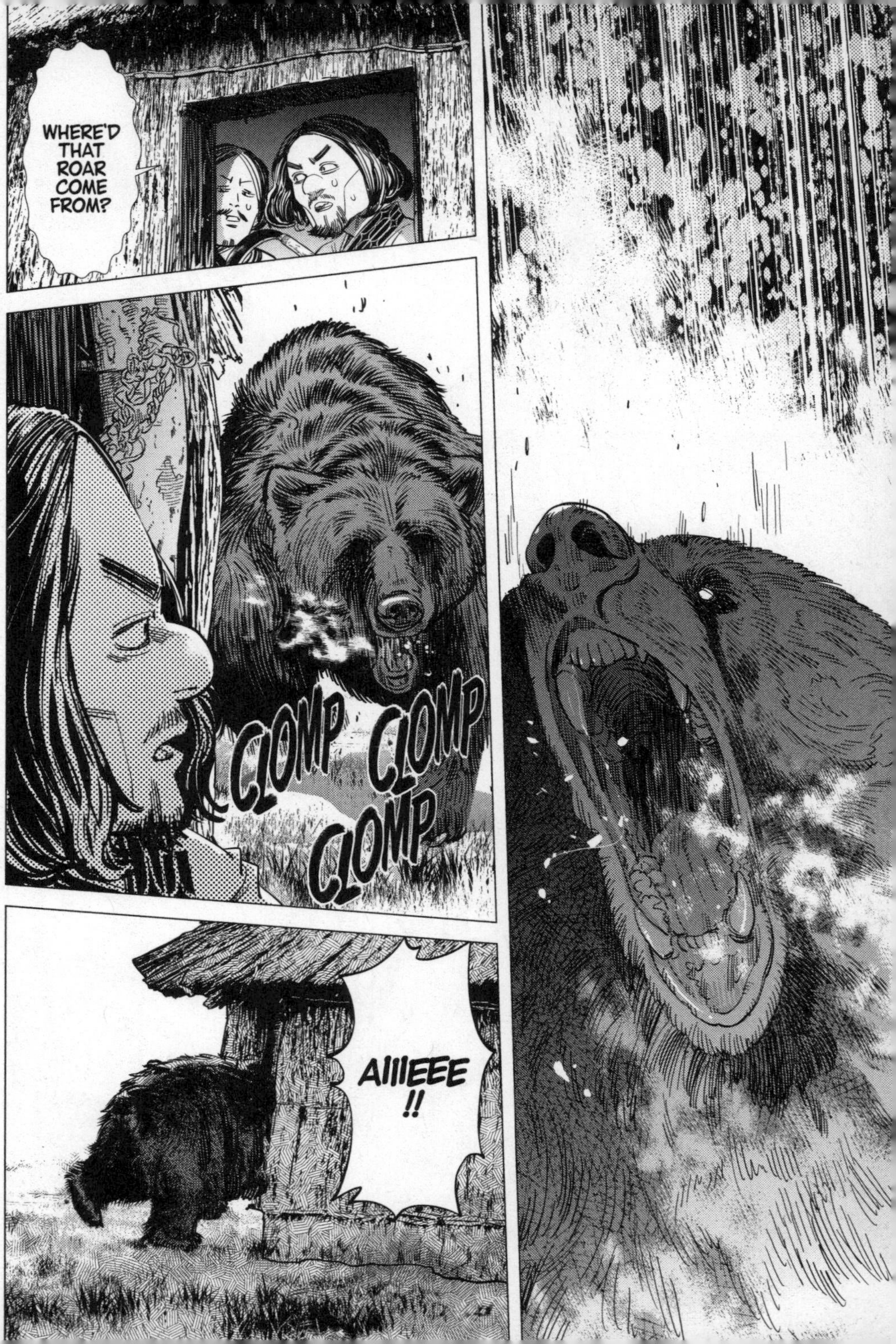
WHERE'D THAT ROAR COME FROM?
CLOMP CLOMP CLOMP CLOMP
AIIIEEE !!

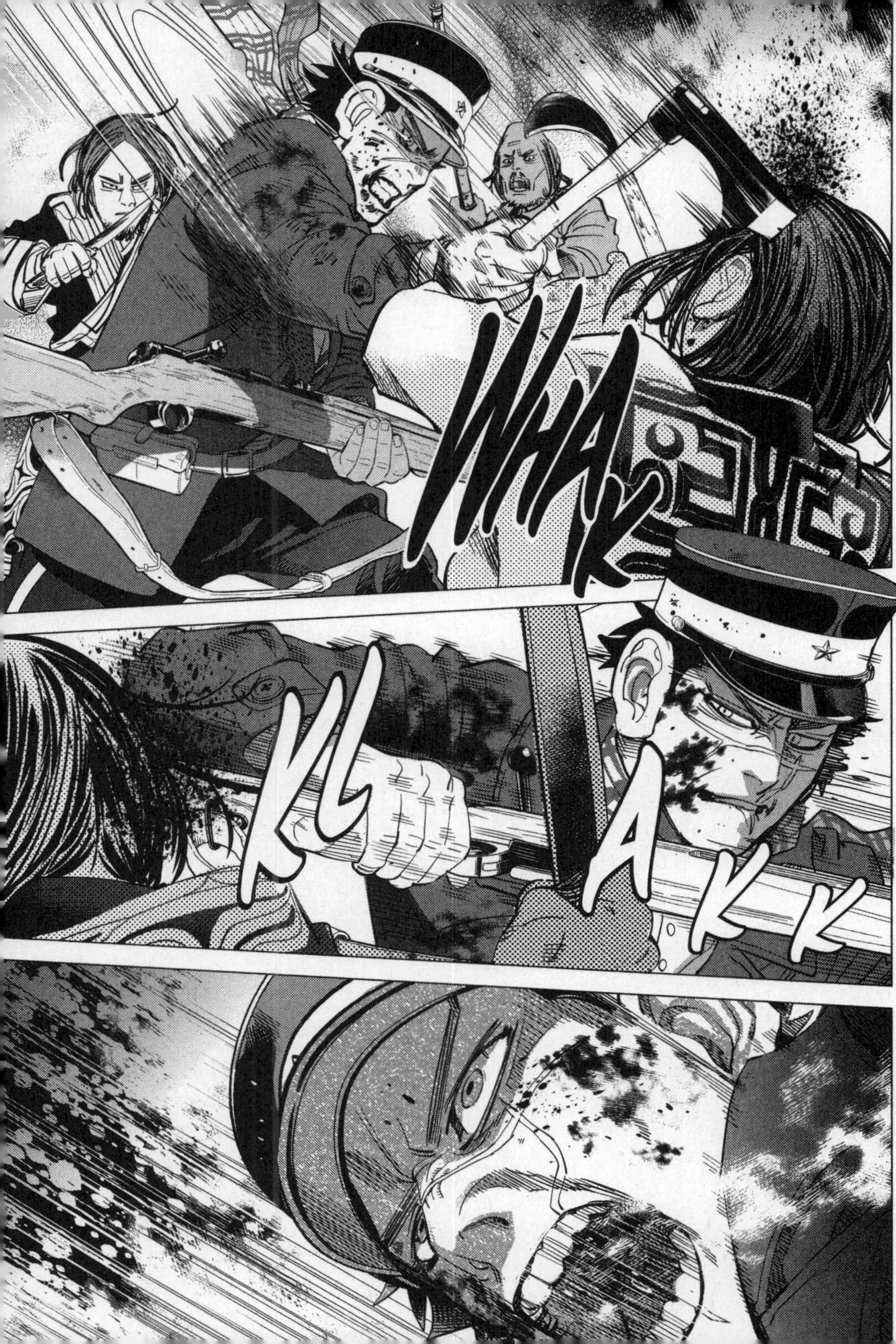
WHAK
KLAKK

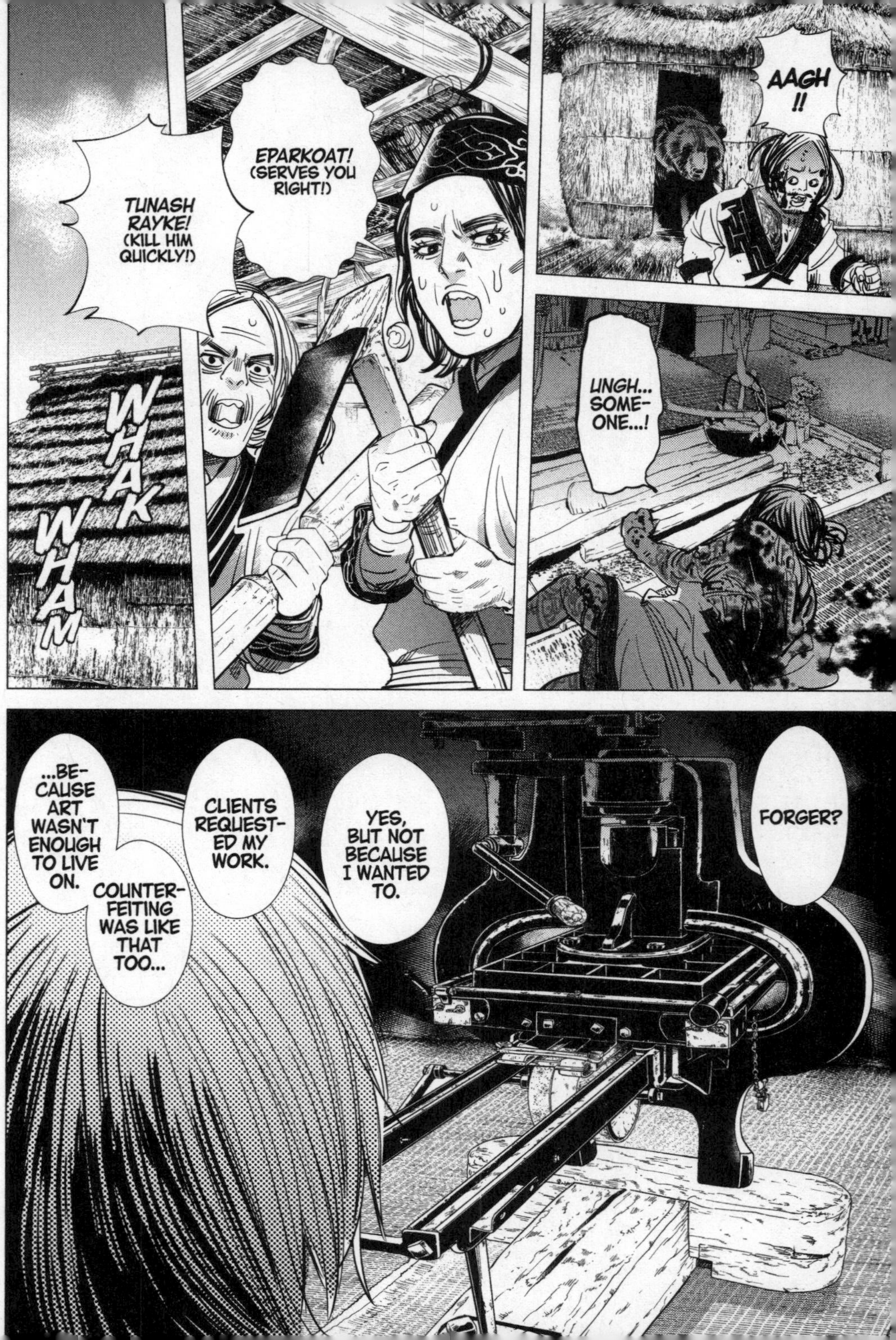
AAGH !!
UNGH... SOME-ONE...!
EPARKOAT! (SERVES YOU RIGHT!)
TUNASH RAYKE! (KILL HIM QUICKLY!)
WHAK
WHAM
FORGER?
YES, BUT NOT BECAUSE I WANTED TO.
CLIENTS REQUEST-ED MY WORK.
...BE-CAUSE ART WASN'T ENOUGH TO LIVE ON.
COUNTER-FEITING WAS LIKE THAT TOO...

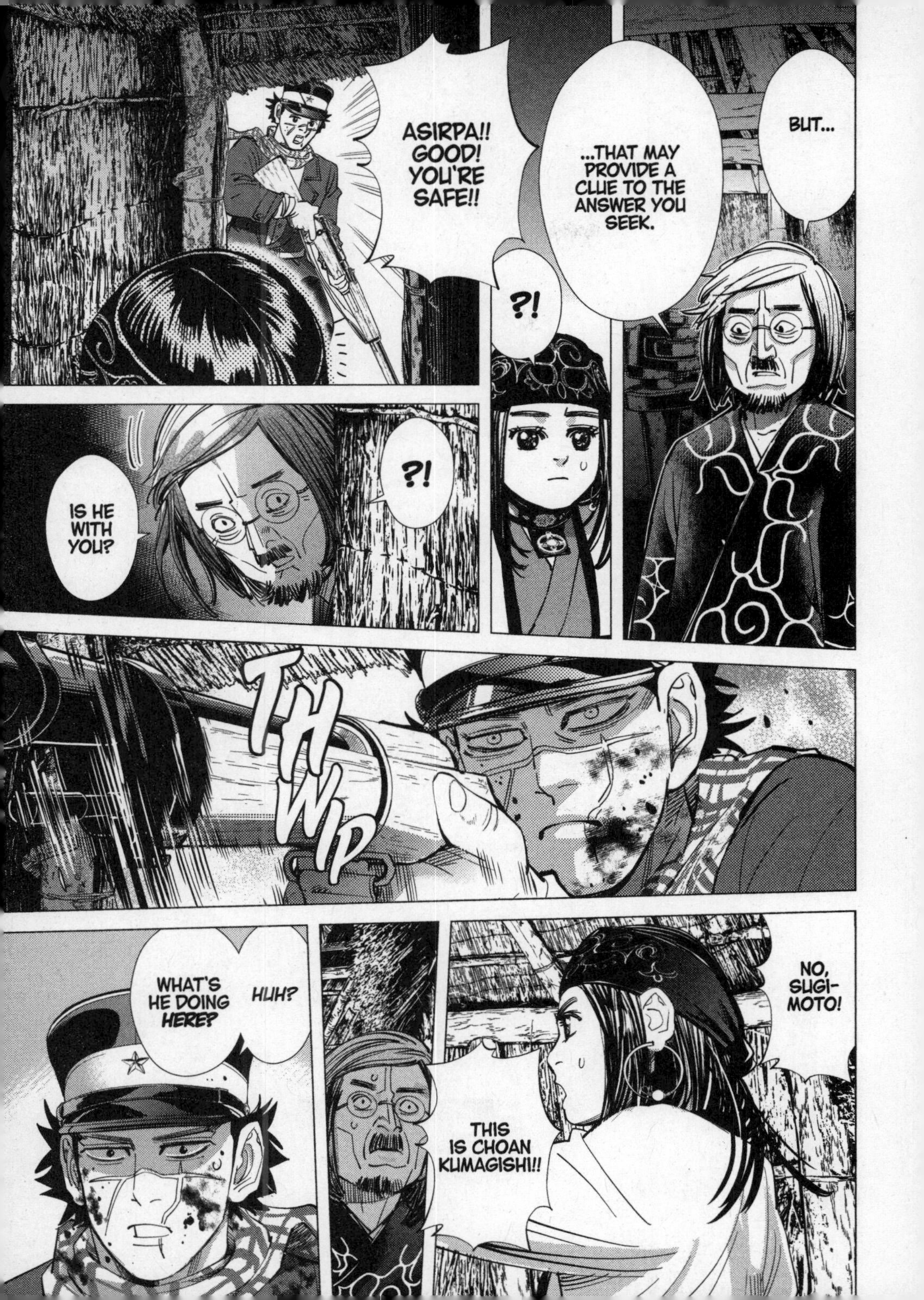
BUT...
...THAT MAY PROVIDE A CLUE TO THE ANSWER YOU SEEK.
?!
ASIRPA!! GOOD! YOU'RE SAFE!!
?!
IS HE WITH YOU?
THWIP
NO, SUGI-MOTO!
THIS IS CHOAN KUMAGISHI!!
HUH?
WHAT'S HE DOING HERE?

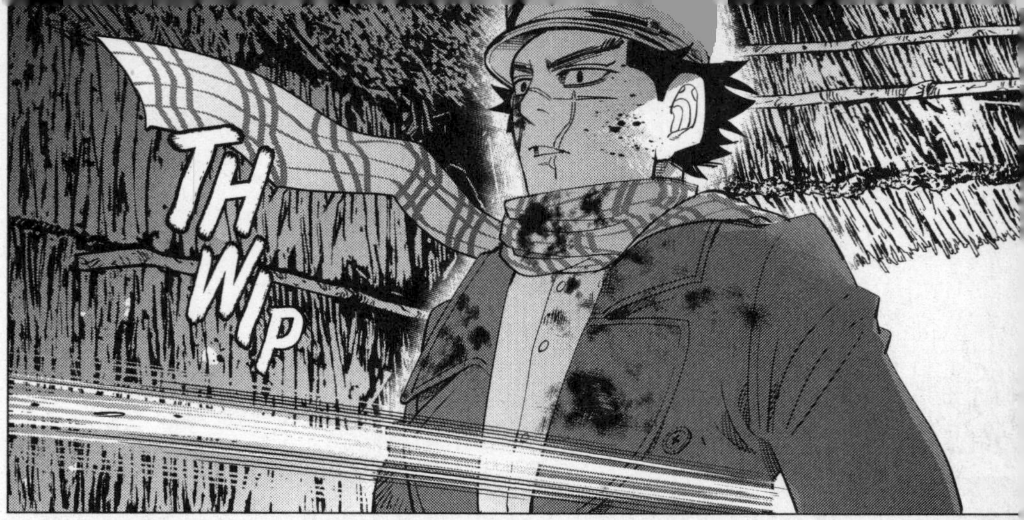
THWIP
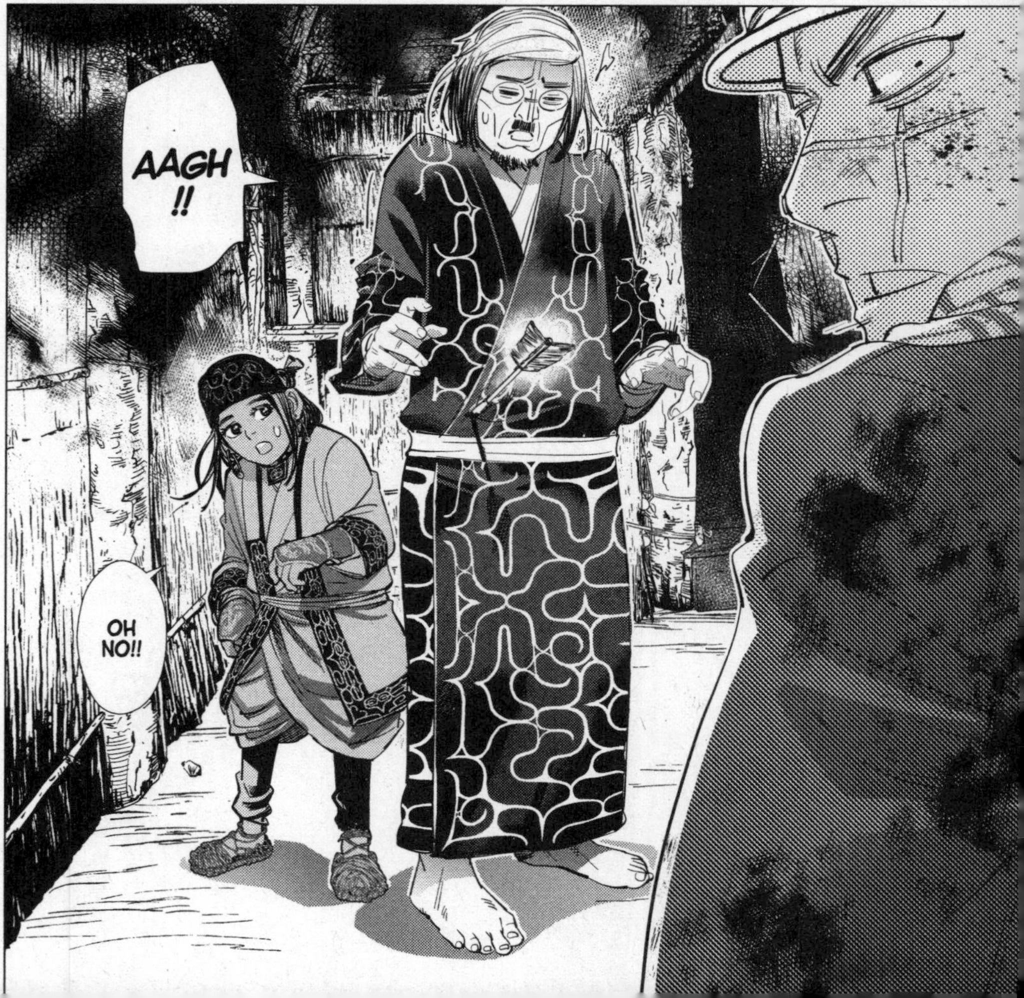
AAGH!!
OH NO!!

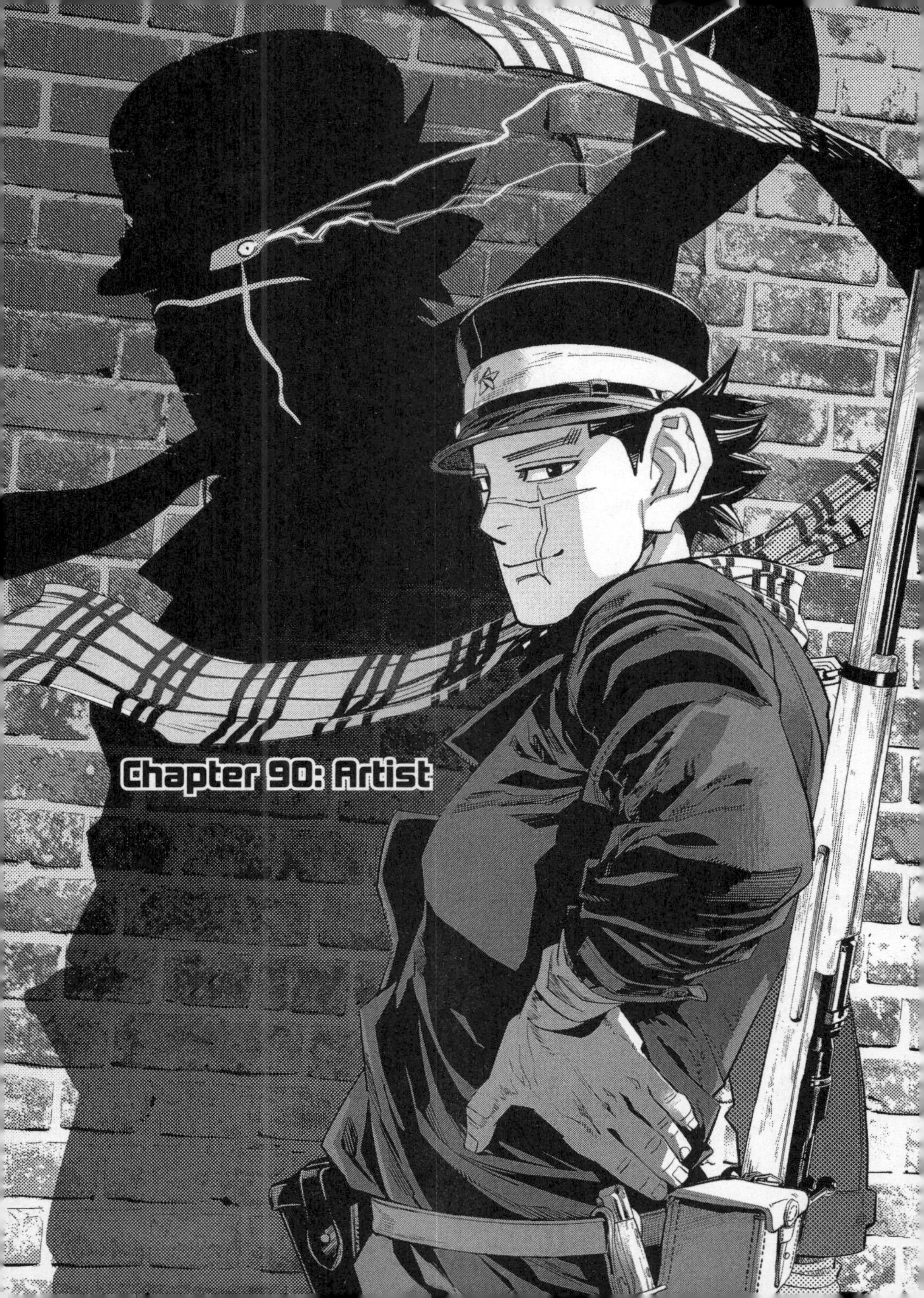
Chapter 90: Artist

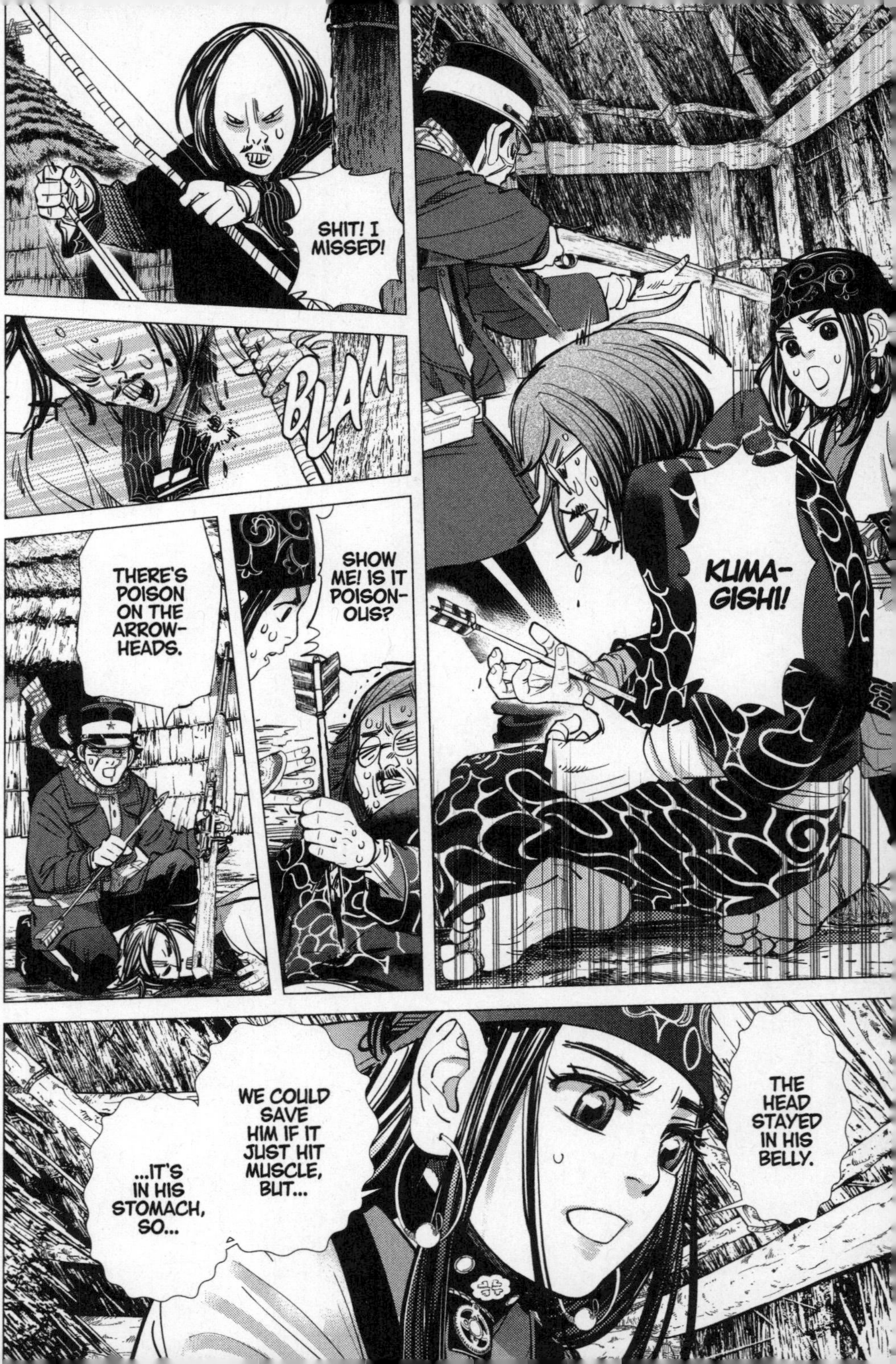
KUMA-GISHI!
SHIT! I MISSED!
BLAM
SHOW ME! IS IT POISONOUS?
THERE'S POISON ON THE ARROWHEADS.
THE HEAD STAYED IN HIS BELLY.
WE COULD SAVE HIM IF IT JUST HIT MUSCLE, BUT...
...IT'S IN HIS STOMACH, SO...

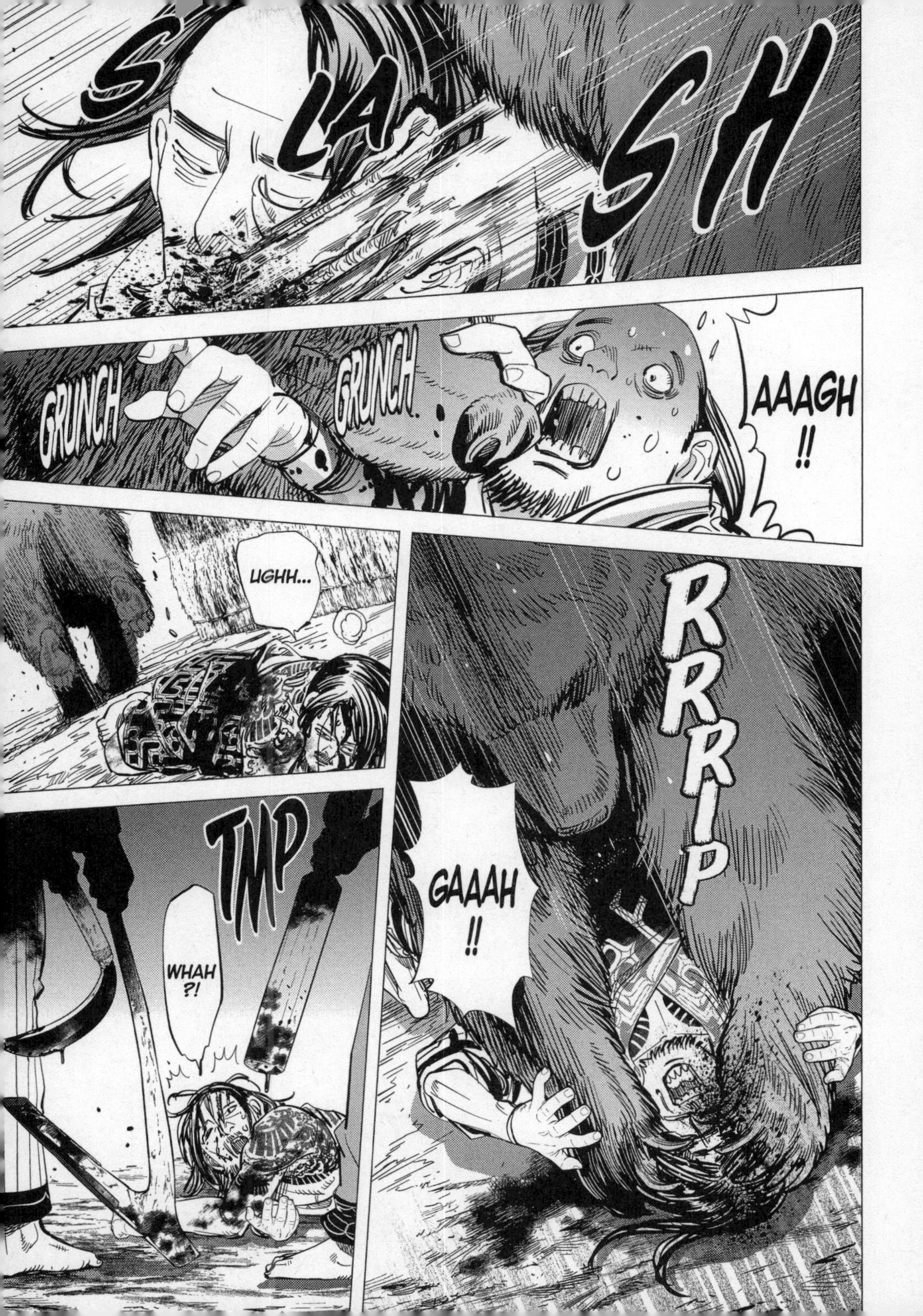
SLASH
AAAGH!!
GRUNCH
GRUNCH
RRRIP
GAAAH!!
UGHH...
TMP
WHAH ?!

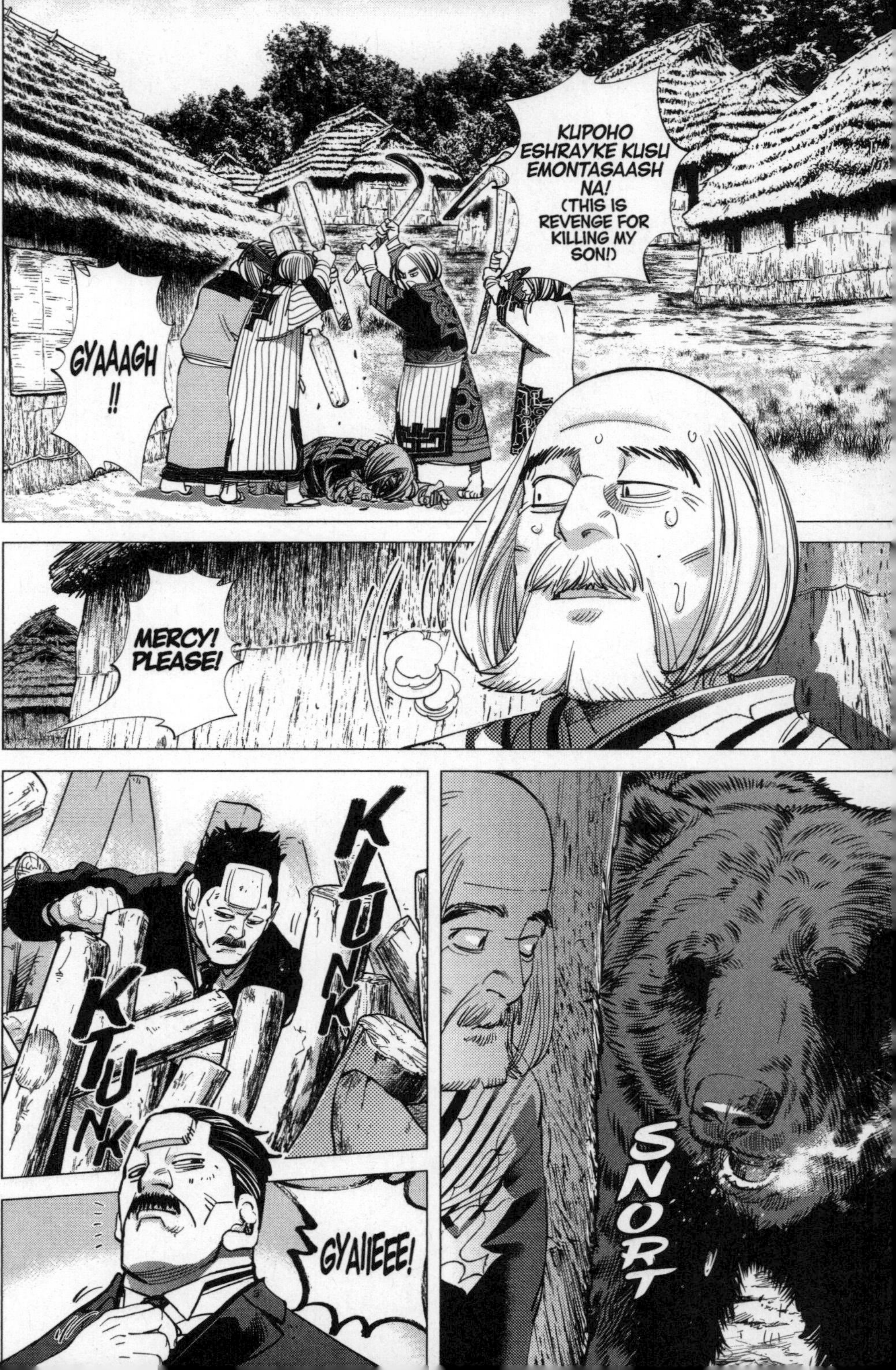
KUPOHO ESHRAYKE KUSU EMONTASAASH NA! (THIS IS REVENGE FOR KILLING MY SON!)
GYAAAGH!!
MERCY! PLEASE!
SNORT
KLUNK
KLUNK
GYAIIEEE!

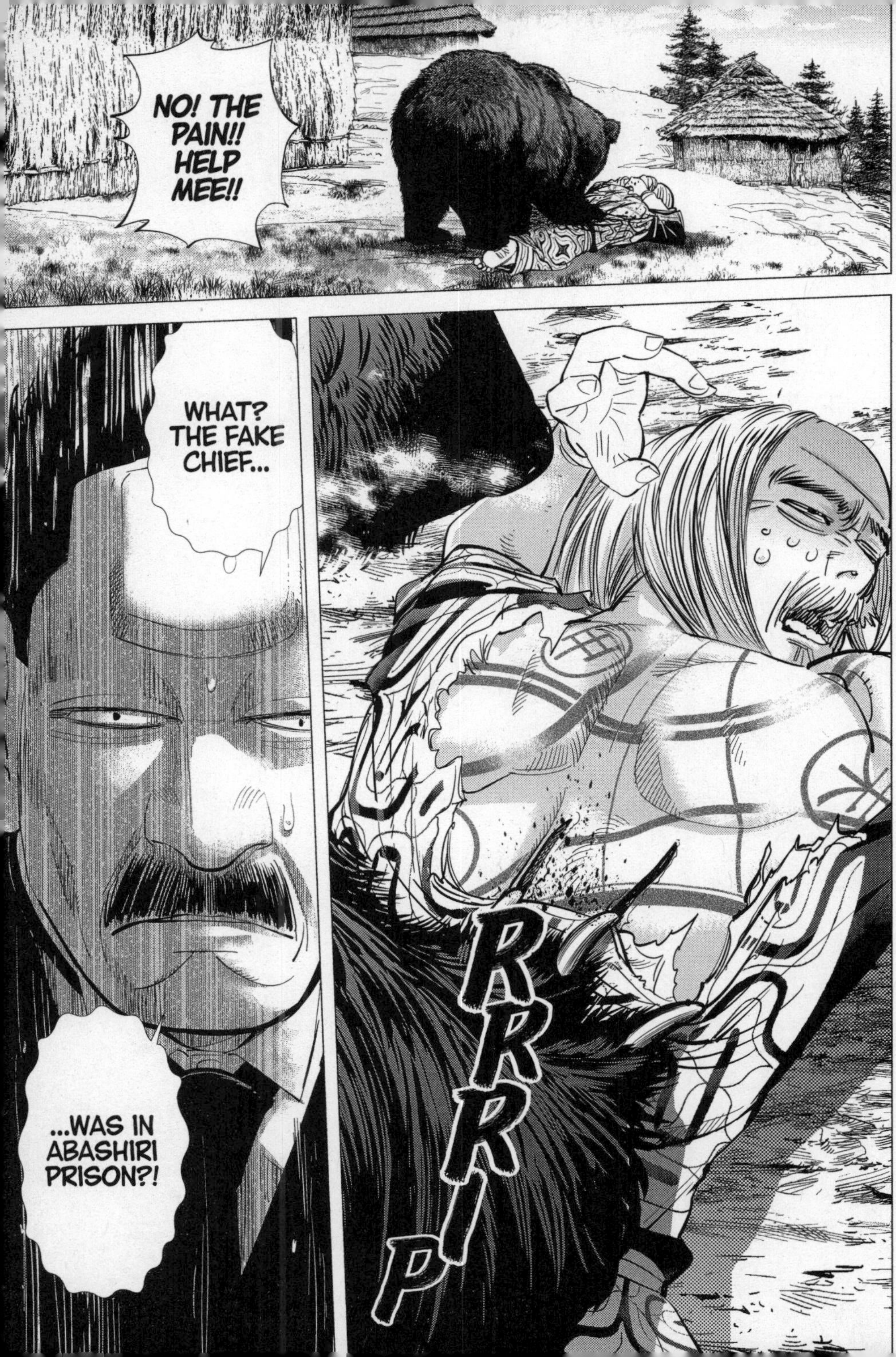
NO! THE PAIN!! HELP MEE!!
RRRIP
WHAT? THE FAKE CHIEF...
...WAS IN ABASHIRI PRISON?!

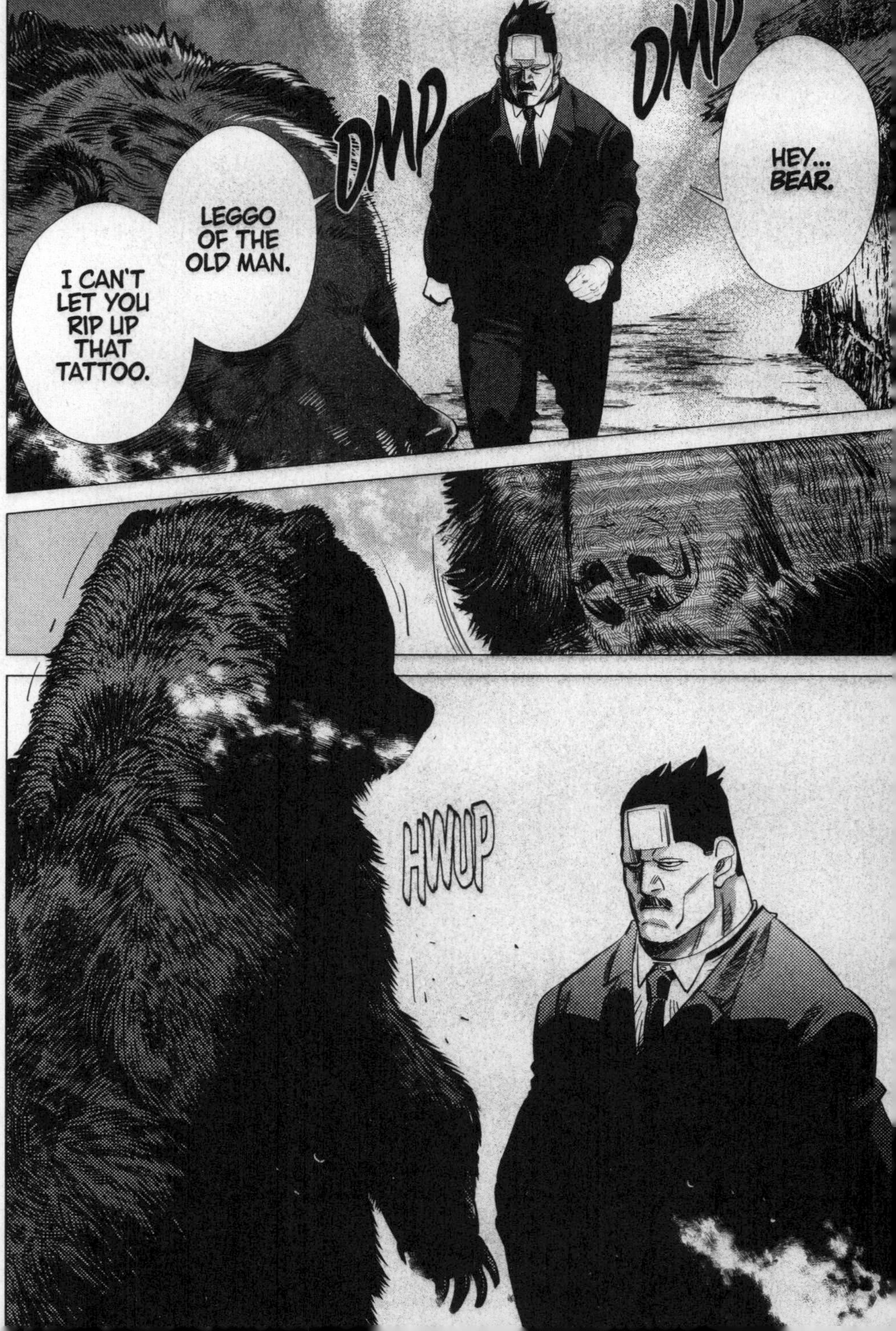
HEY... BEAR.
DMP
DMP
LEGGO OF THE OLD MAN.
I CAN'T LET YOU RIP UP THAT TATTOO.
HWUP

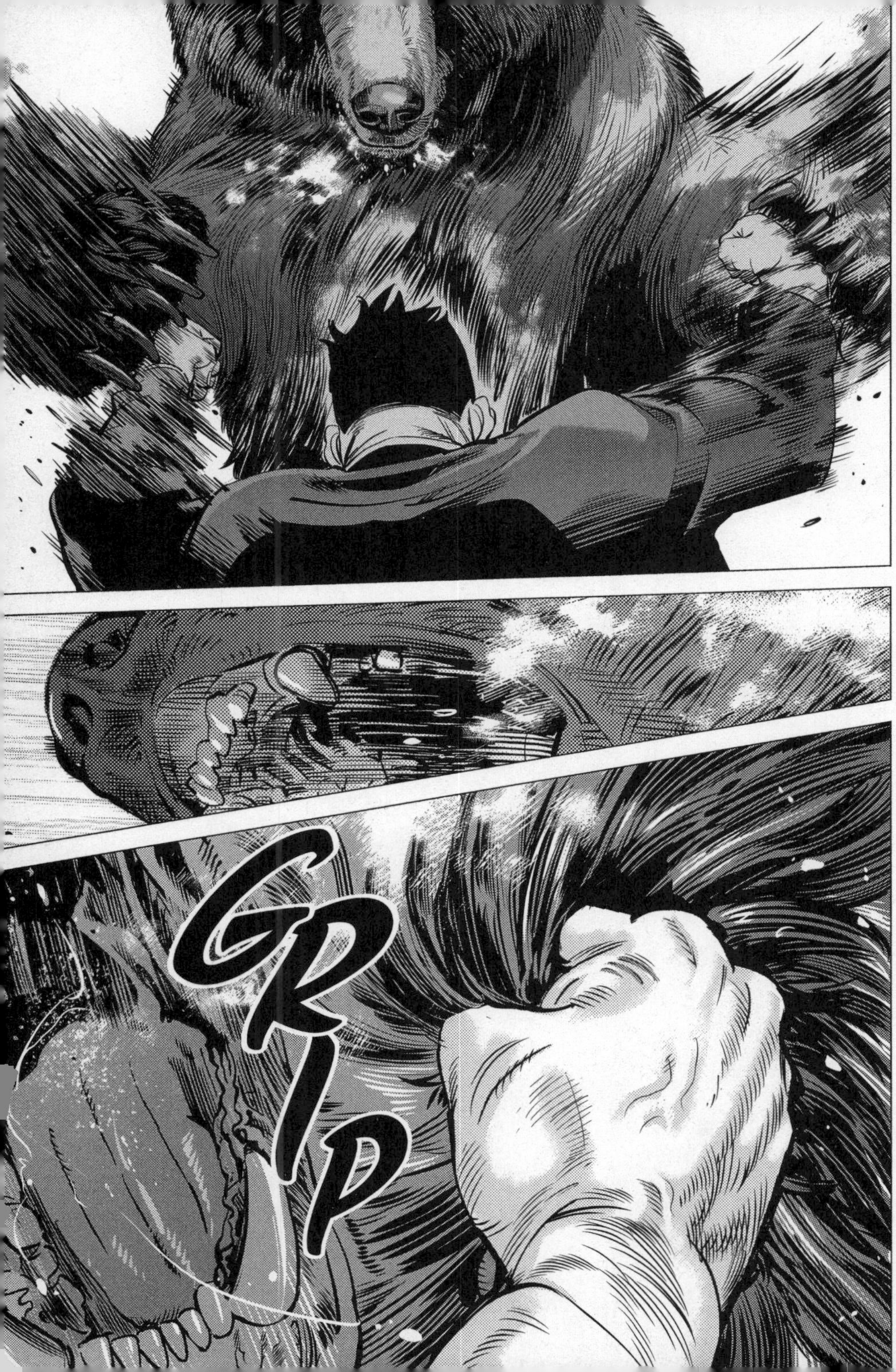
GRIP

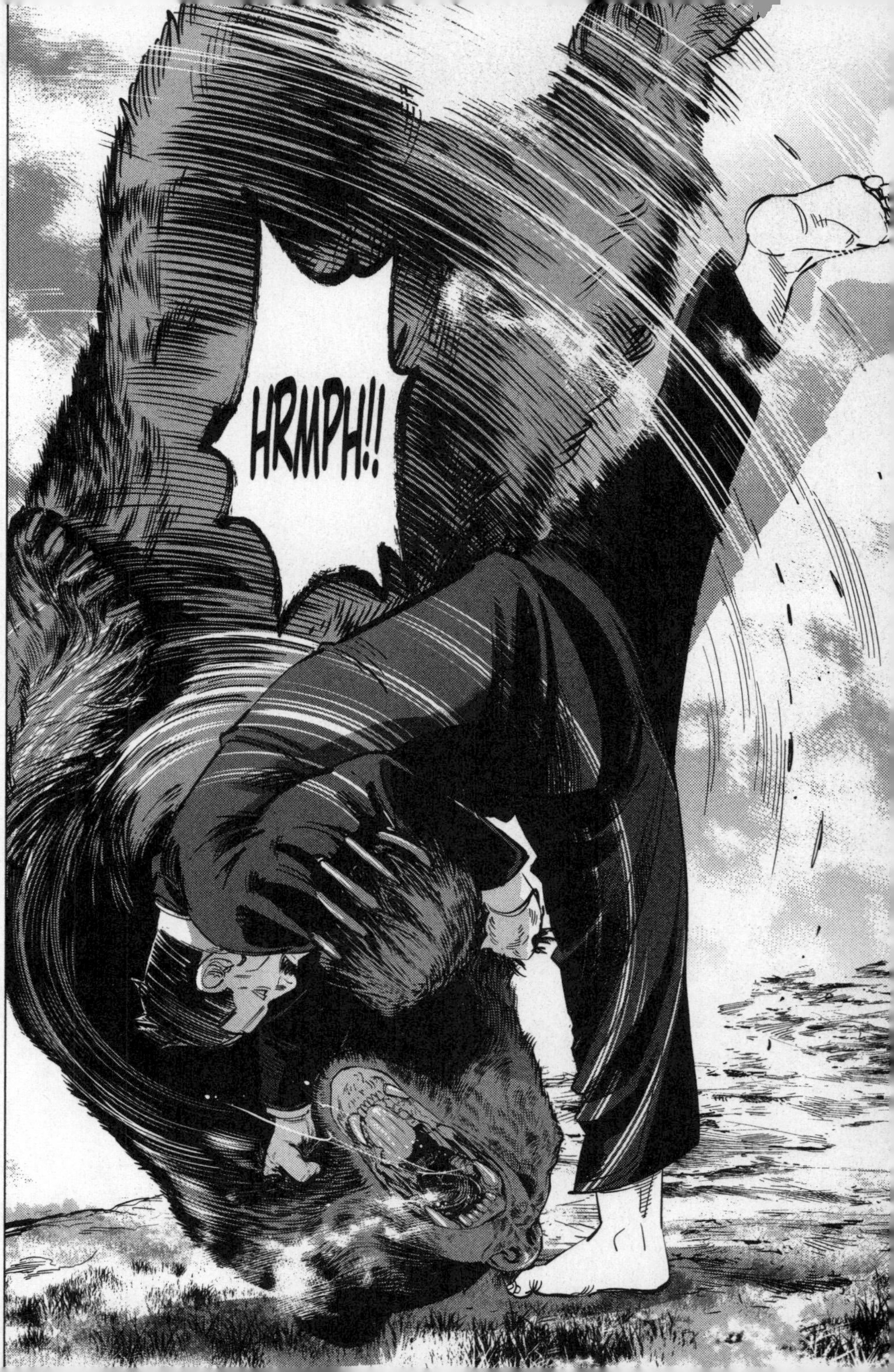
HRMPH!!

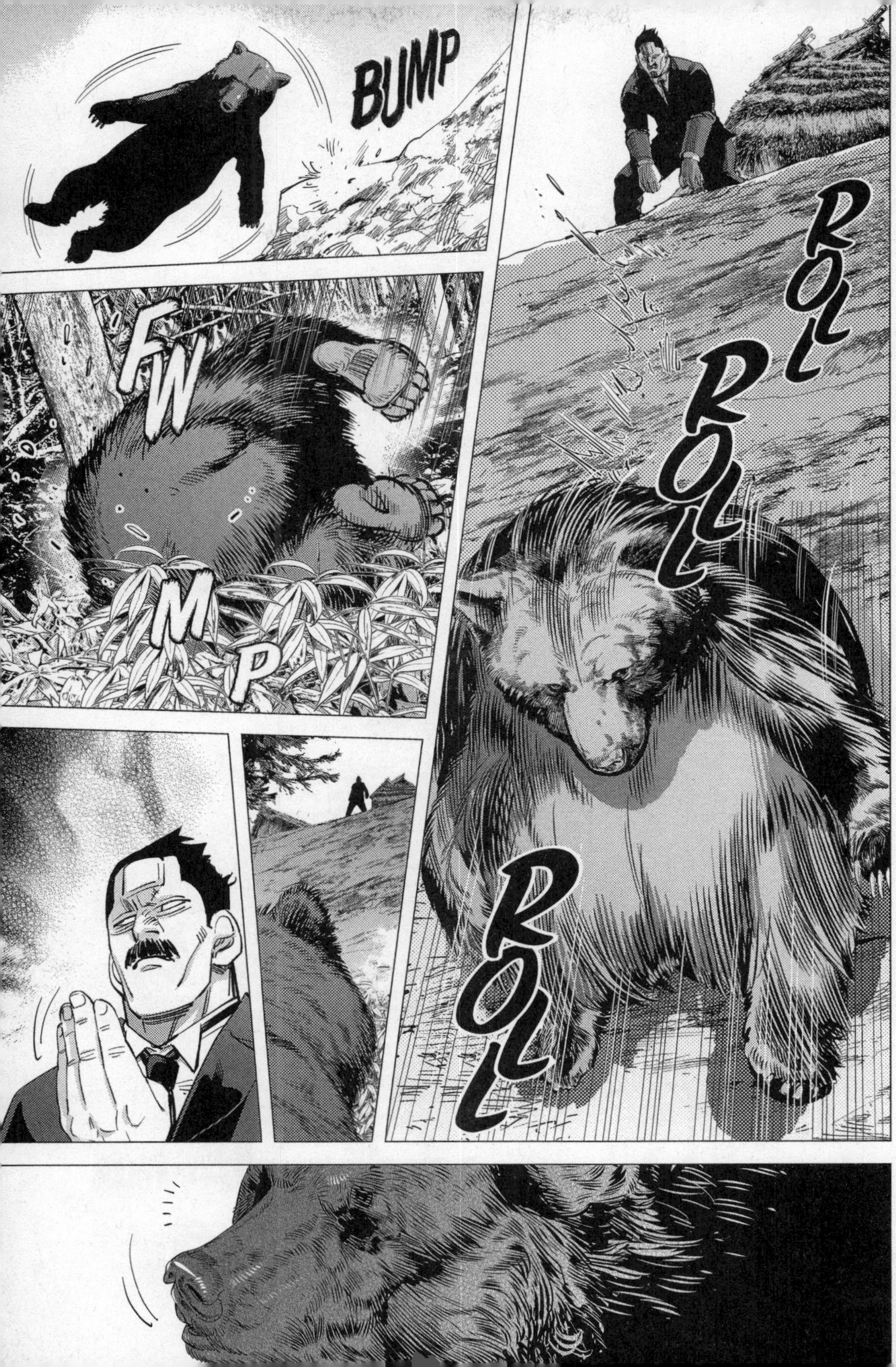
ROLL
ROLL
ROLL
BUMP
FWMP

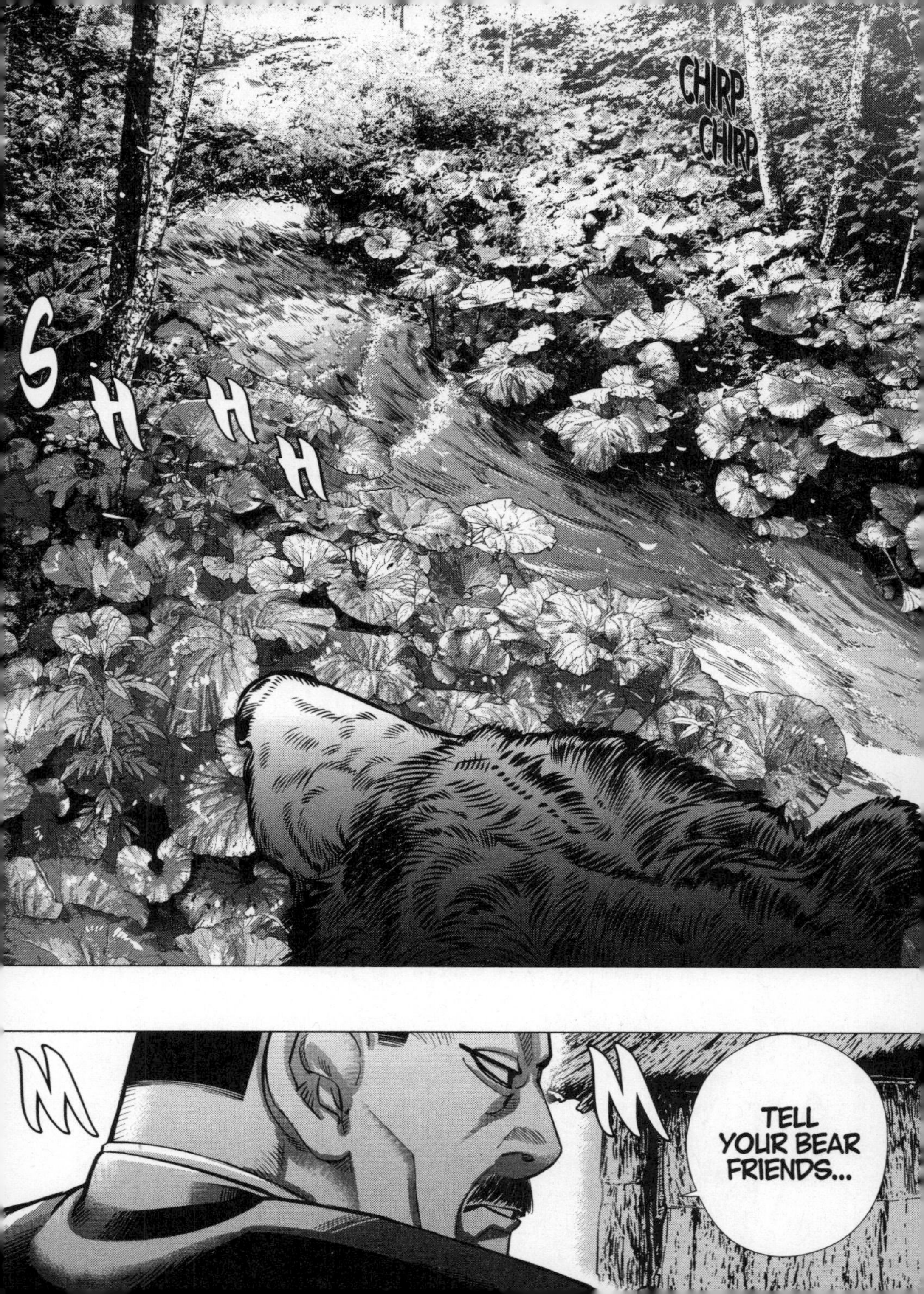
CHIRP CHIRP
SHHHH
TELL YOUR BEAR FRIENDS...
M
M

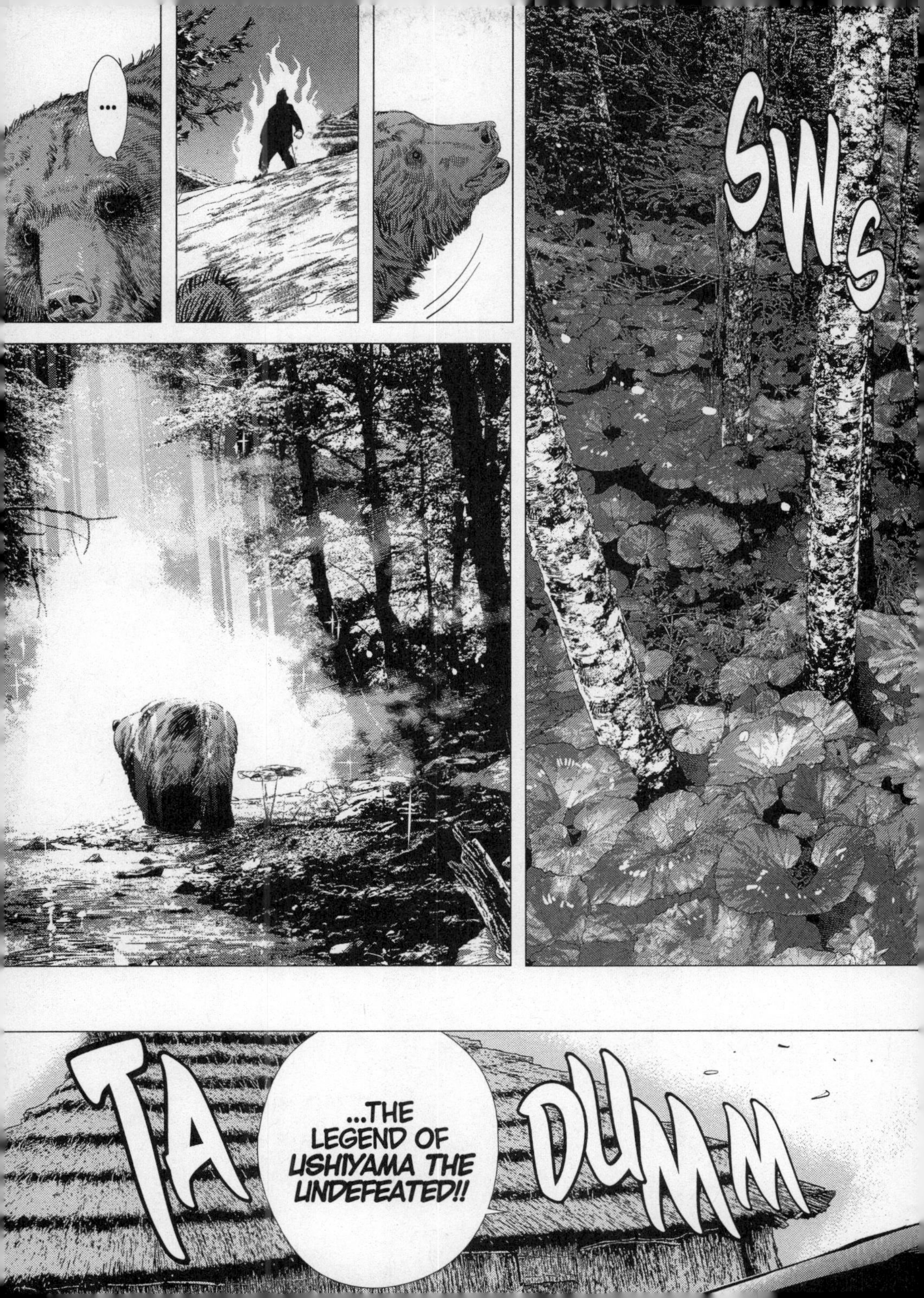
SWS
...
...THE LEGEND OF USHIYAMA THE UNDEFEATED!!
TA DUMM

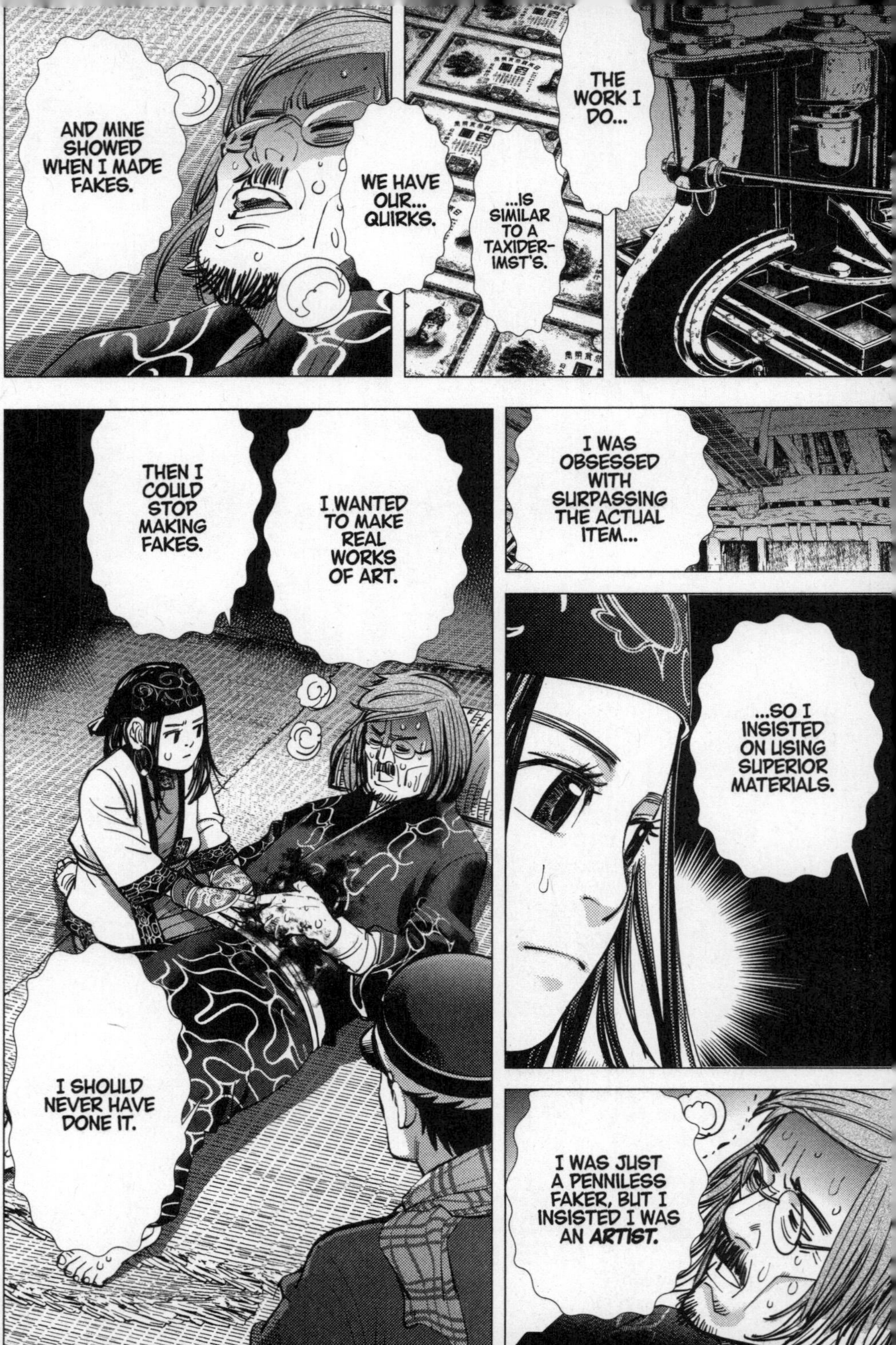
THE WORK I DO...
...IS SIMILAR TO A TAXIDER-IMST'S.
WE HAVE OUR... QUIRKS.
AND MINE SHOWED WHEN I MADE FAKES.
I WAS OBSESSED WITH SURPASSING THE ACTUAL ITEM...
...SO I INSISTED ON USING SUPERIOR MATERIALS.
I WAS JUST A PENNILESS FAKER, BUT I INSISTED I WAS AN *ARTIST*.
I WANTED TO MAKE REAL WORKS OF ART.
THEN I COULD STOP MAKING FAKES.
I SHOULD NEVER HAVE DONE IT.

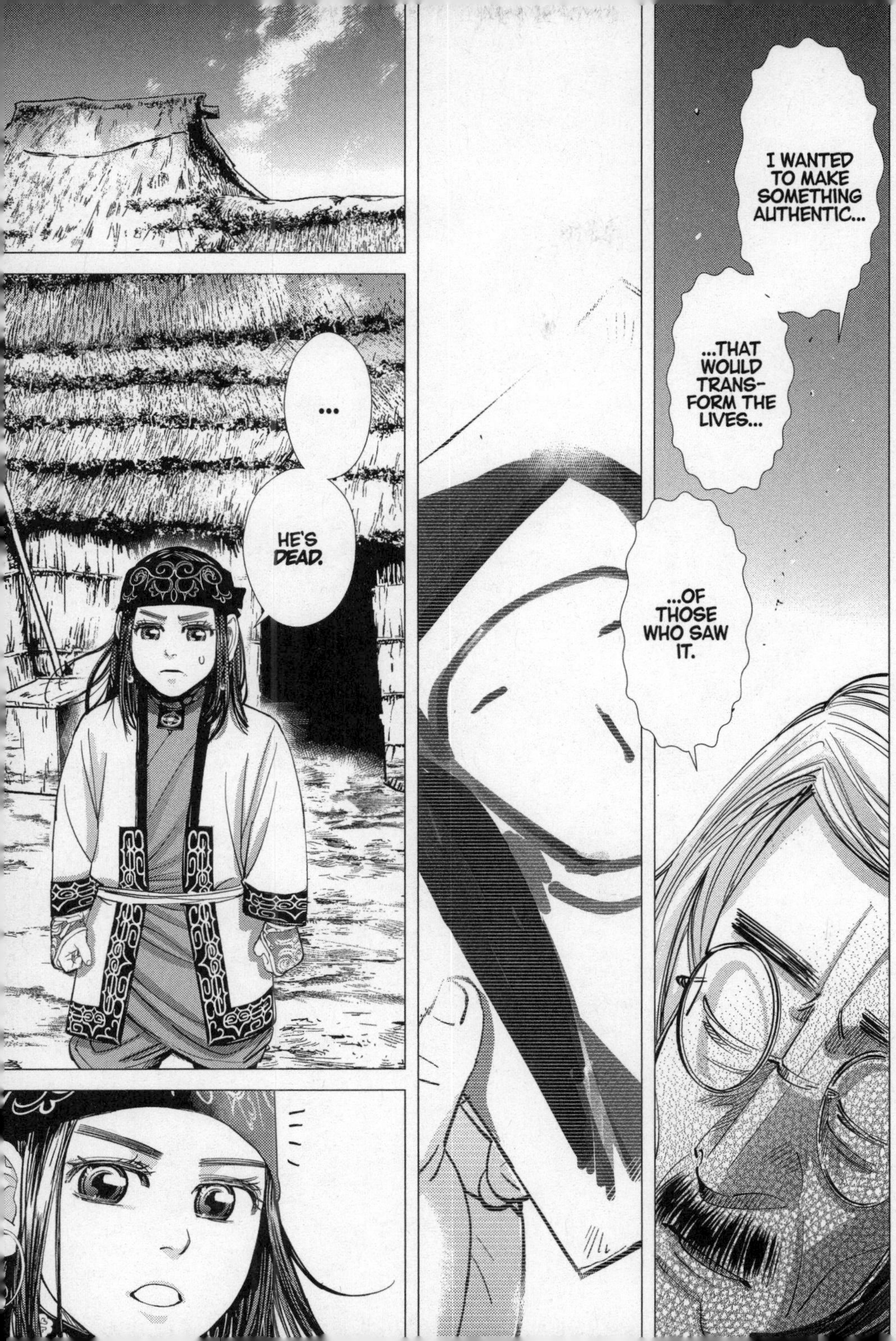
I WANTED TO MAKE SOMETHING AUTHENTIC...
...THAT WOULD TRANS-FORM THE LIVES...
...OF THOSE WHO SAW IT.
...
HE'S DEAD.

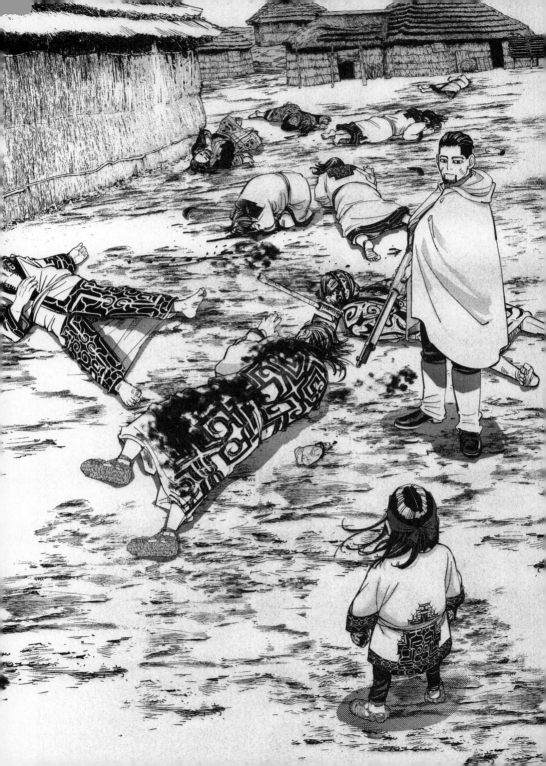

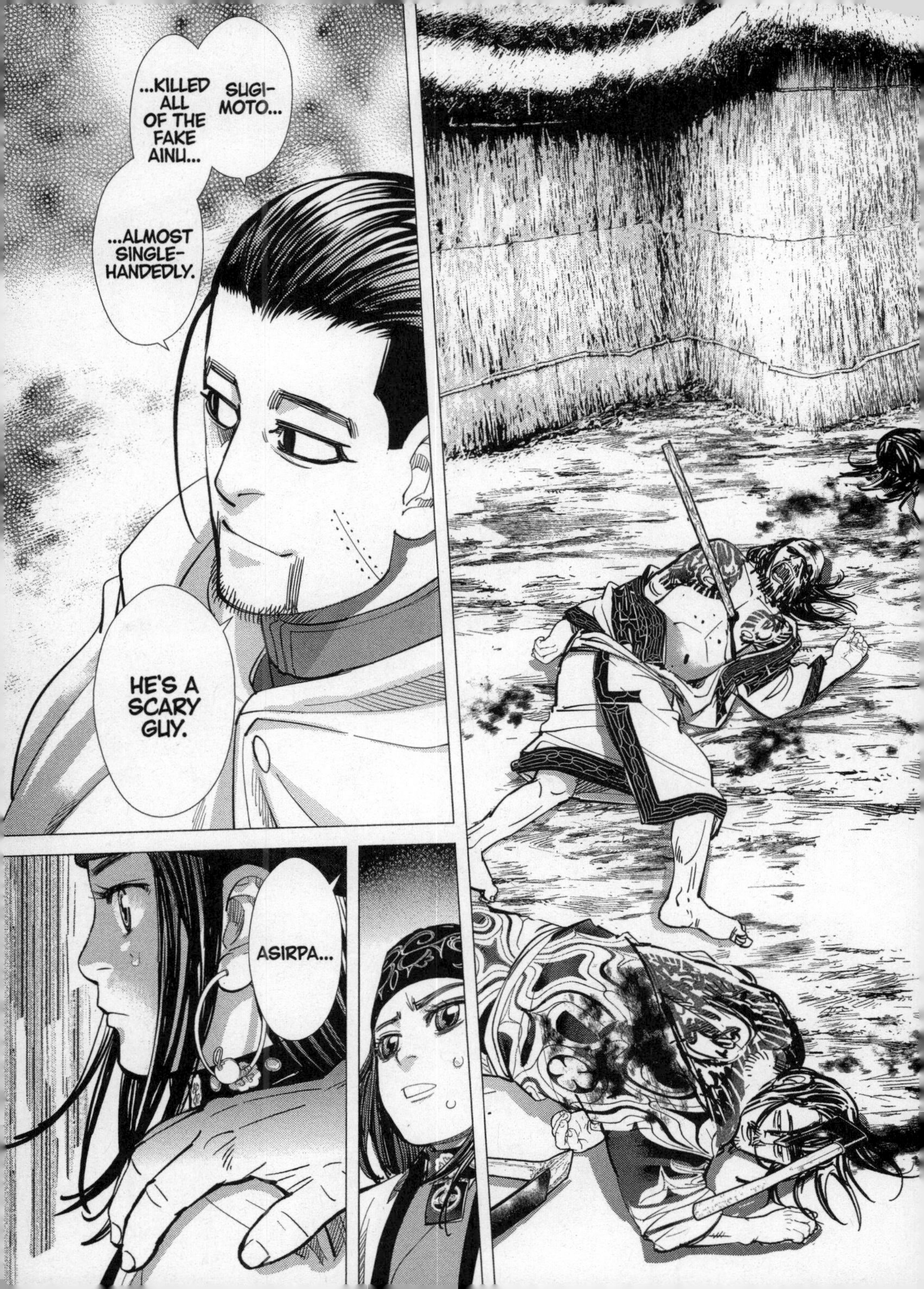
SUGI-MOTO...
...KILLED ALL OF THE FAKE AINU...
...ALMOST SINGLE-HANDEDLY.
HE'S A SCARY GUY.
ASIRPA...

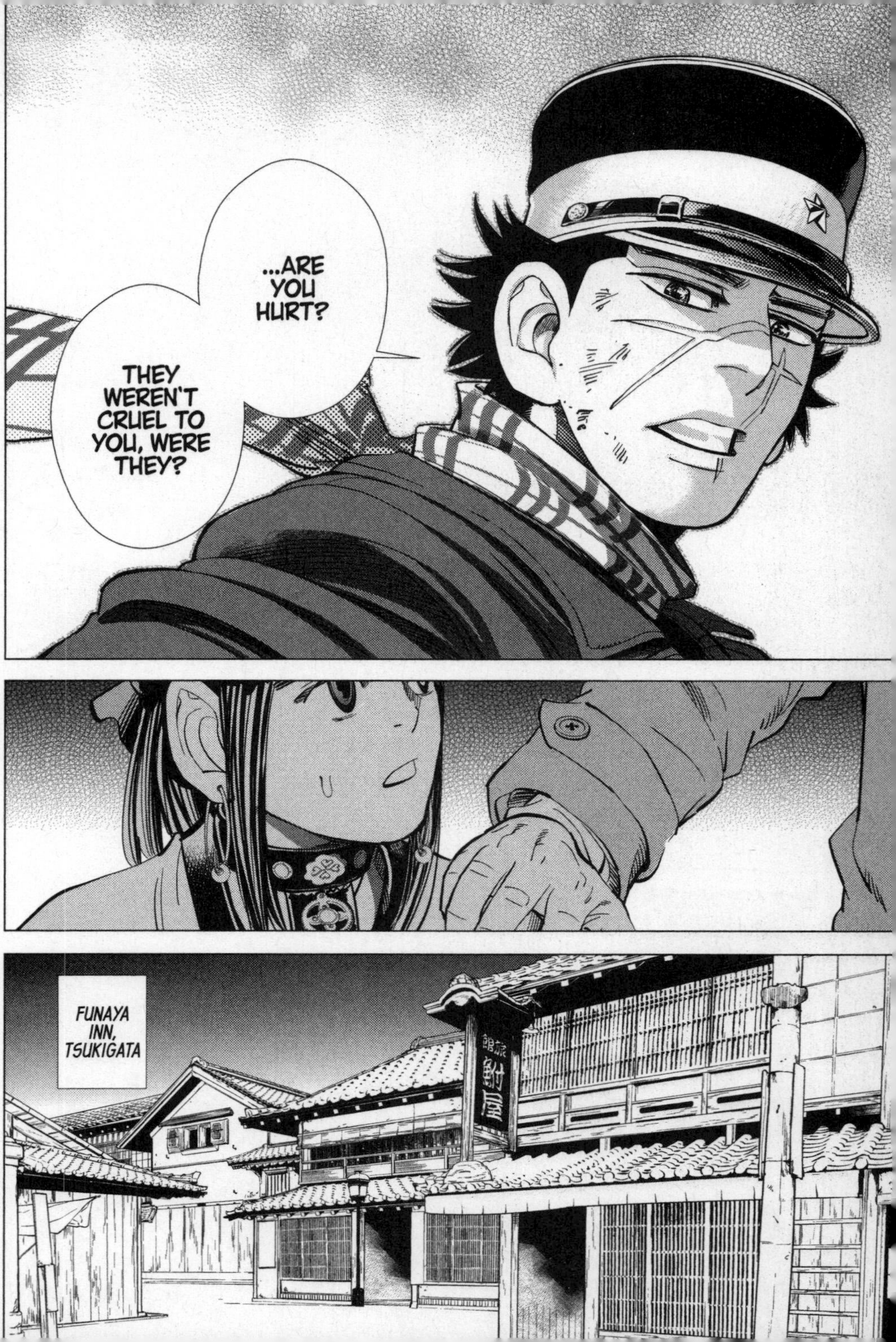
...ARE YOU HURT?
THEY WEREN'T CRUEL TO YOU, WERE THEY?
FUNAYA INN, TSUKIGATA

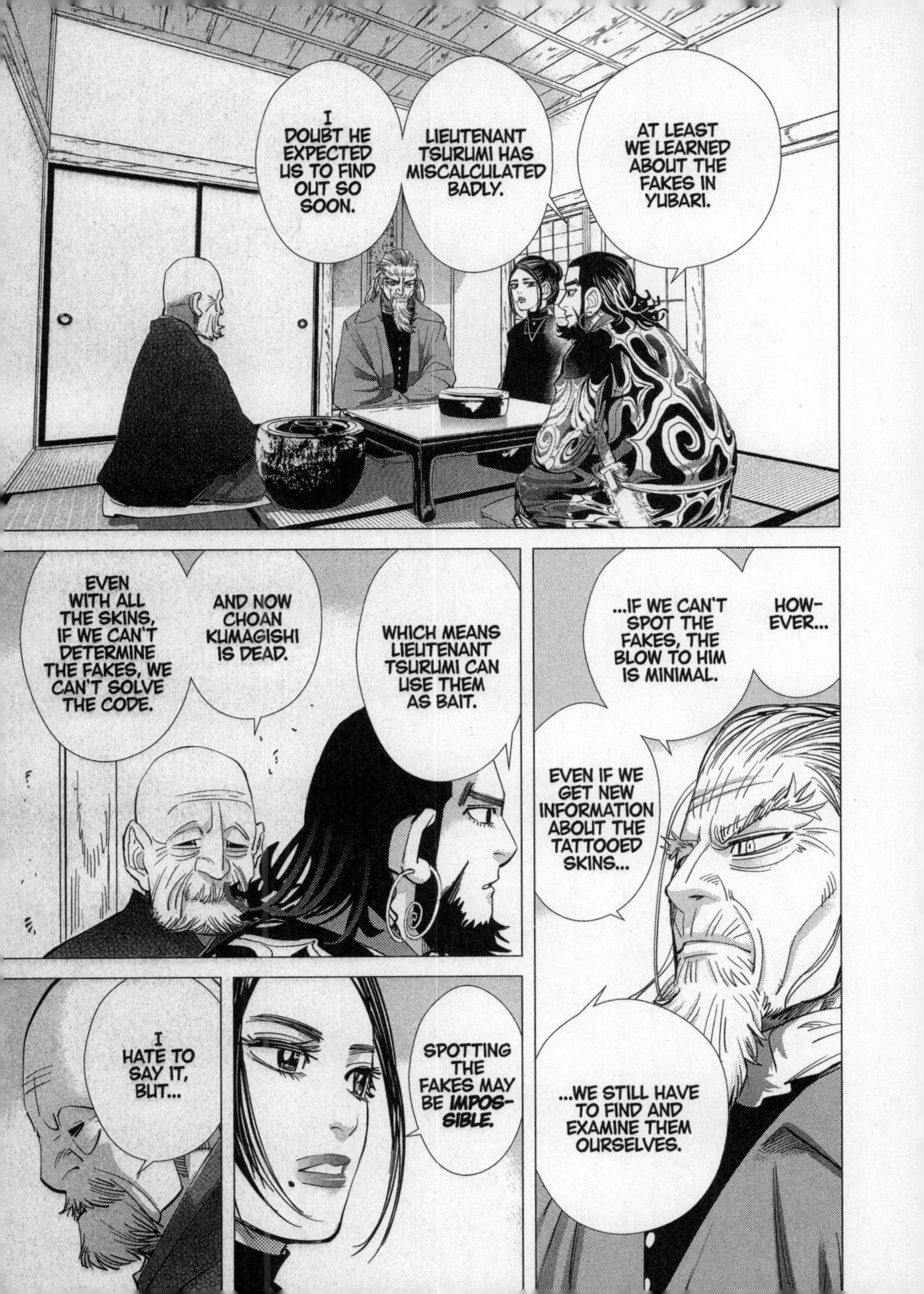
AT LEAST WE LEARNED ABOUT THE FAKES IN YUBARI.
LIEUTENANT TSURUMI HAS MISCALCULATED BADLY.
I DOUBT HE EXPECTED US TO FIND OUT SO SOON.
HOW-EVER...
...IF WE CAN'T SPOT THE FAKES, THE BLOW TO HIM IS MINIMAL.
EVEN IF WE GET NEW INFORMATION ABOUT THE TATTOOED SKINS...
...WE STILL HAVE TO FIND AND EXAMINE THEM OURSELVES.
WHICH MEANS LIEUTENANT TSURUMI CAN USE THEM AS BAIT.
AND NOW CHOAN KUMAGISHI IS DEAD.
EVEN WITH ALL THE SKINS, IF WE CAN'T DETERMINE THE FAKES, WE CAN'T SOLVE THE CODE.
SPOTTING THE FAKES MAY BE *IMPOSSIBLE.*
I HATE TO SAY IT, BUT...

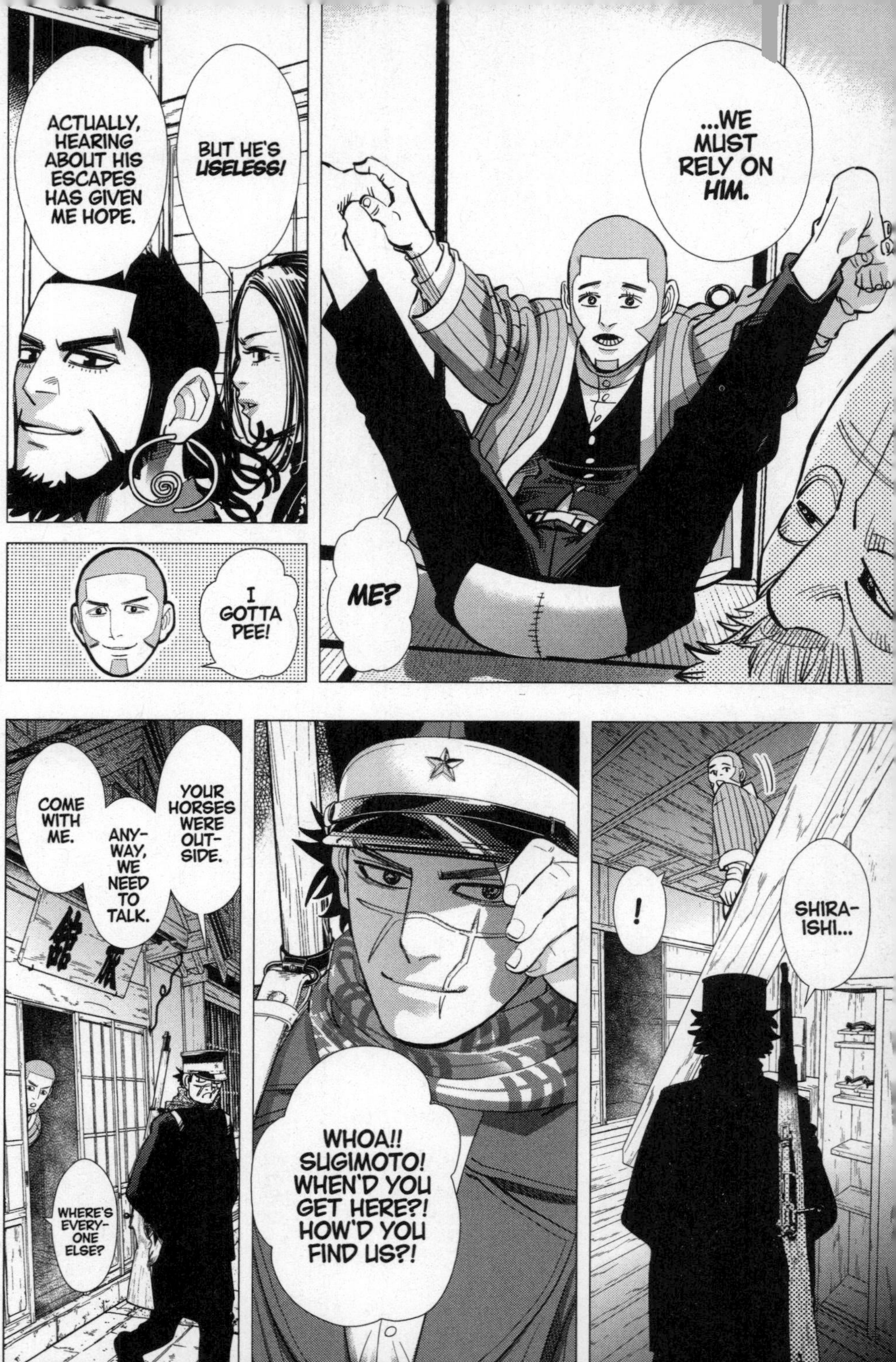
...WE MUST RELY ON HIM.
ME?
BUT HE'S USELESS!
ACTUALLY, HEARING ABOUT HIS ESCAPES HAS GIVEN ME HOPE.
I GOTTA PEE!
SHIRA-ISHI...
!
WHOA!! SUGIMOTO! WHEN'D YOU GET HERE?! HOW'D YOU FIND US?!
YOUR HORSES WERE OUT-SIDE.
ANY-WAY, WE NEED TO TALK.
COME WITH ME.
WHERE'S EVERY-ONE ELSE?

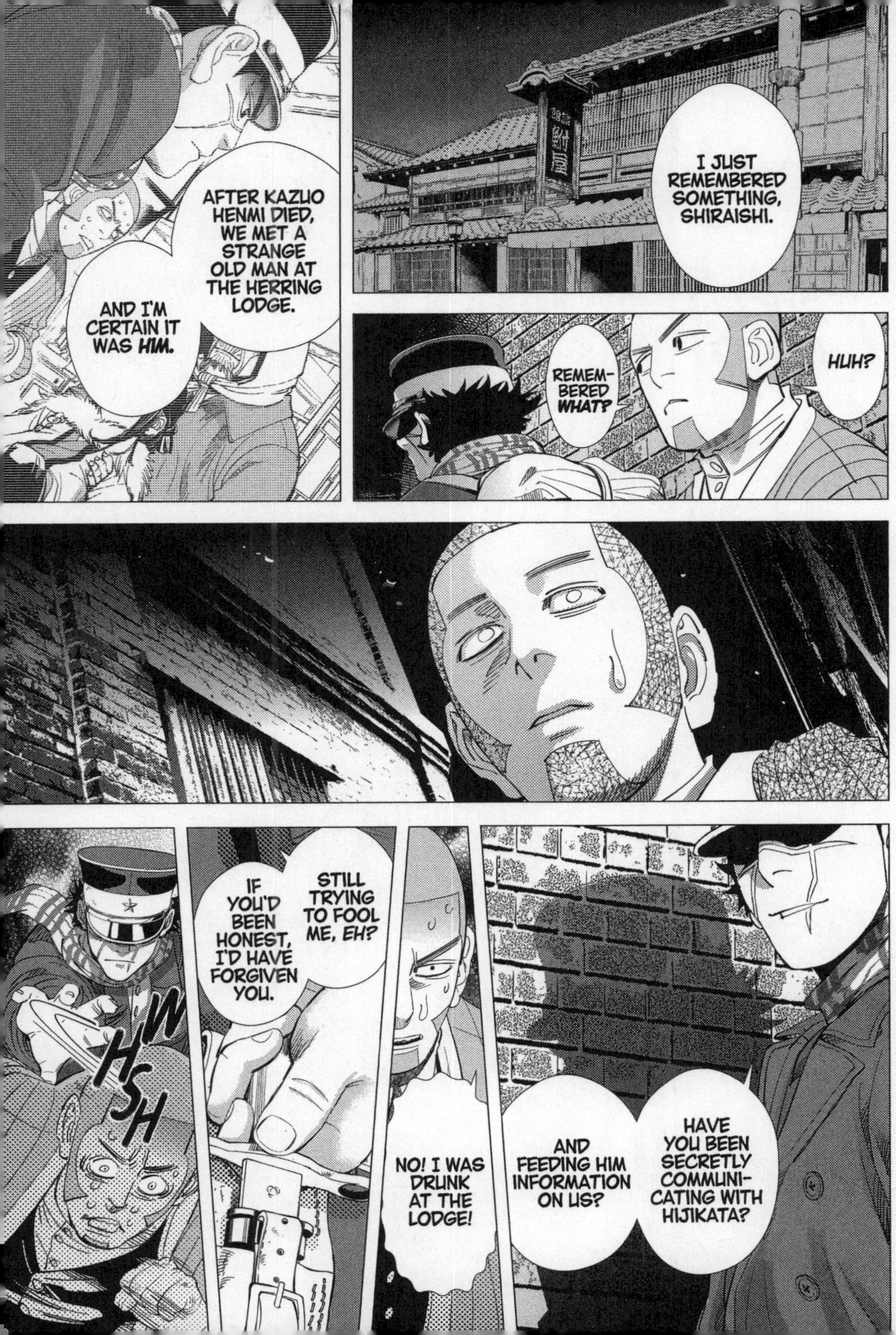
I JUST REMEMBERED SOMETHING, SHIRAISHI.
HUH?
REMEMBERED WHAT?
AFTER KAZUO HENMI DIED, WE MET A STRANGE OLD MAN AT THE HERRING LODGE.
AND I'M CERTAIN IT WAS **HIM.**
HAVE YOU BEEN SECRETLY COMMUNICATING WITH HIJIKATA?
AND FEEDING HIM INFORMATION ON US?
NO! I WAS DRUNK AT THE LODGE!
STILL TRYING TO FOOL ME, EH?
IF YOU'D BEEN HONEST, I'D HAVE FORGIVEN YOU.
WHSH

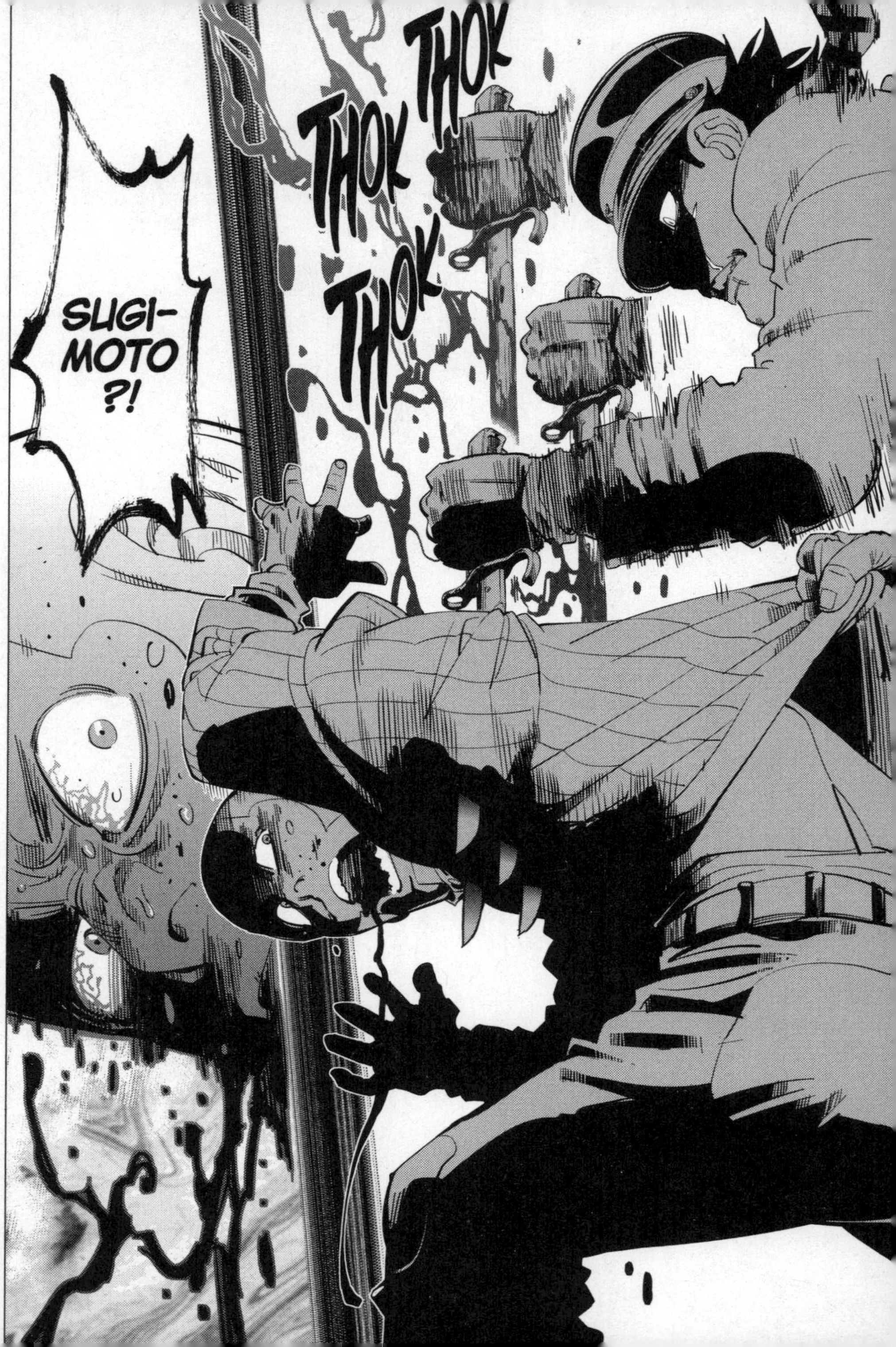
THOK THOK
THOK THOK
SUGI-MOTO ?!

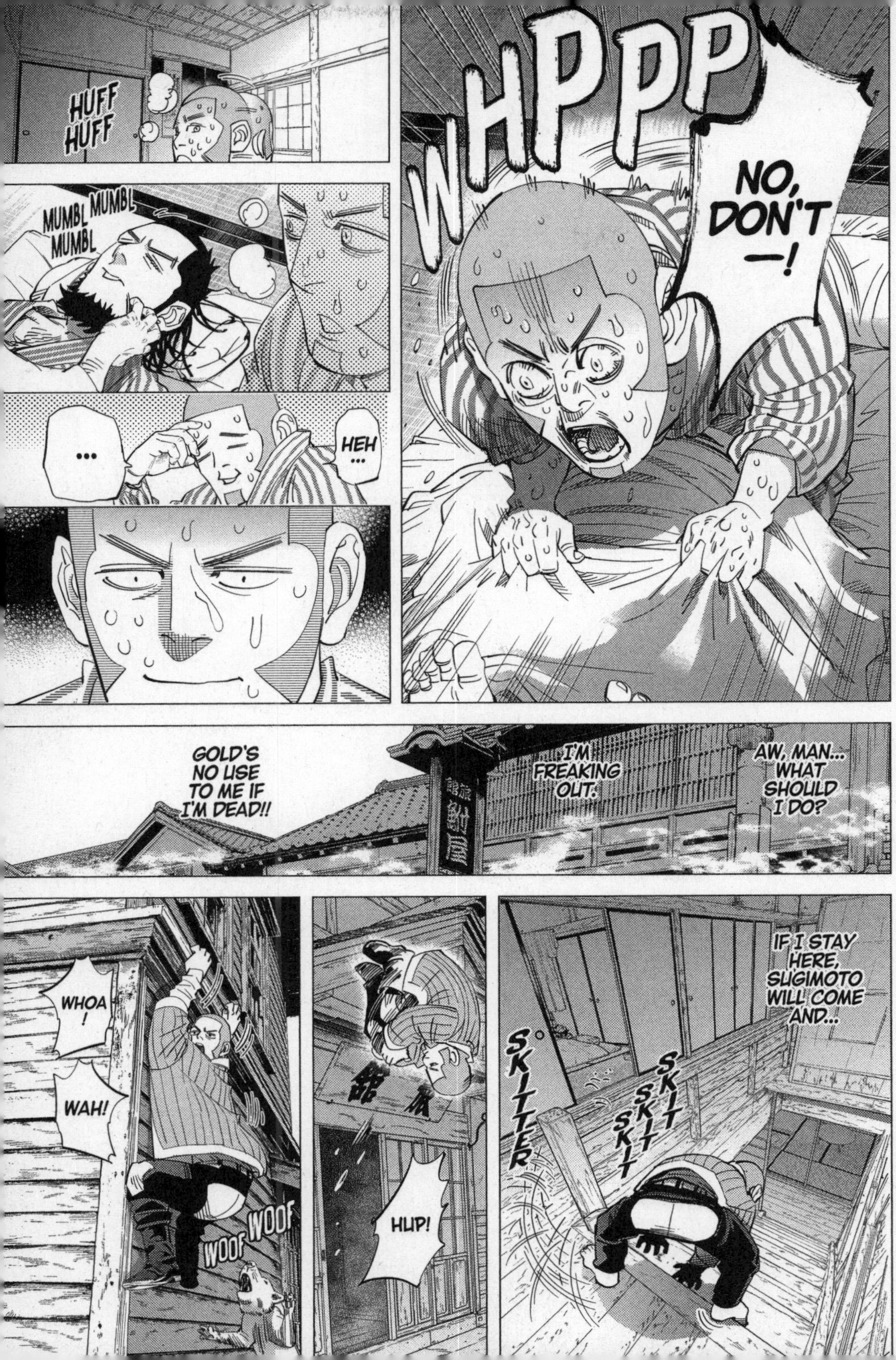
WHPPP
NO, DON'T—!
HUFF HUFF
MUMBL MUMBL MUMBL
HEH...
...
AW, MAN... WHAT SHOULD I DO?
I'M FREAKING OUT.
GOLD'S NO USE TO ME IF I'M DEAD!!
IF I STAY HERE, SUGIMOTO WILL COME AND...
SKIT SKIT SKIT
SKITTER
HUP!
WHOA!
WAH!
WOOF WOOF

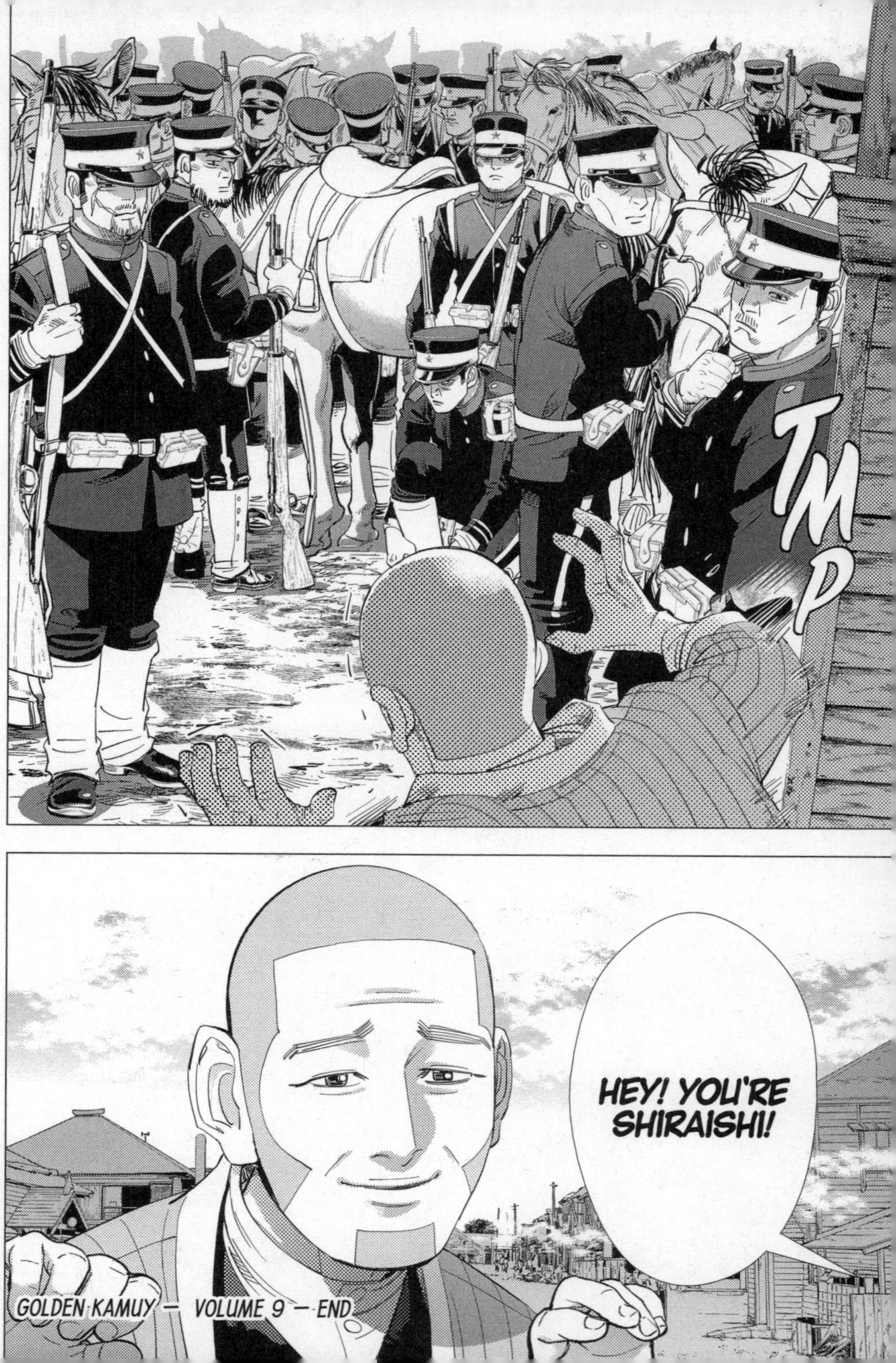
TMP
HEY! YOU'RE SHIRAISHI!
GOLDEN KAMUY — VOLUME 9 — END

Ainu Language Supervision • Hiroshi Nakagawa

Cooperation from • Hokkaido Ainu Association and the Abashiri Prison Museum
Otaru City General Museum • Waseda University Aizu Museum • Goto, Kazunobu •
Botanic Garden and Museum, Hokkaido University • National Museum of Ethnology
Nibutani Ainu Culture Museum • The Ainu Museum • Moon Kabato Museum

Photo Credits • Takayuki Monma Takanori Matsuda Kozo Ishikawa

Ainu Culture References

Chiri, Takanaka and Yokoyama, Takao. *Ainugo Eiri Jiten* (Ainu Language Illustrated Dictionary).
Tokyo: Kagyusha, 1994

Kayano, Shigeru. *Ainu no Mingu* (Ainu Folkcrafts). Kawagoe: Suzusawa Book Store, 1978

Kayano, Shigeru. *Kayano Shigeru no Ainugo Jiten* (Kayano Shigeru's Ainu Language Dictionary).
Tokyo: Sanseido, 1996

Musashino Art University – The Research Institute for Culture and Cultural History. *Ainu no Mingu Jissoku Zushu*
(Ainu Folkcrafts – Collection of Drawing and Figures). Biratori: Biratori-cho Council for Promoting Ainu Culture, 2014

Satouchi, Ai. *Ainu-shiki ekoroji-seikatsu: Haruzo Ekashi ni manabu shizen no chie* (Ainu Style Ecological Living:
Haruzo Ekashi Teaches the Wisdom of Nature). Tokyo: Kabushiki gaisha Shogakukan, 2008

Chiri, Yukie. *Ainu Shin'yoshu* (Chiri Yukie's Ainu Epic Tales). Tokyo: Iwanami Shoten, 1978

Namikawa, Kenji. *Ainu Minzoku no Kiseki* (The Path of the Ainu People).
Tokyo: Yamakawa Publishing, 2004

Mook. *Senjuumin Ainu Minzoku* (Bessatsu Taiyo) (The Ainu People (Extra Issue Taiyo).Tokyo: Heibonsha, 2004

Kinoshita, Seizo. *Shiraoikotan Kinoshita Seizo Isaku Shashin Shu* (Shiraoikotan: Kinoshita Seizo's Posthumous
Photography Collection). Hokkaido Shiraoi-gun Shiraoi-cho: Shiraoi Heritage Conservation Foundation, 1988

The Ainu Museum. *Ainu no Ifuku Bunka* (The Culture of Ainu Clothing). Hokkaido Shiraoi-gun Shiraoi-cho:
Shiraoi Ainu Museum, 1991.

Keira, Tomoko and Kaji, Sayaka. *Ainu no Shiki* (Ainu's Four Seasons). Tokyo: Akashi Shoten, 1995

Fukuoka, Itoko and Sato, Kazuko. *Ainu Shokubutsushi* (Ainu Botanical Journal). Chiba Urayasu-Shi: Sofukan, 1995

Hayakawa, Noboru. *Ainu no Minzoku* (Ainu Folklore). Iwasaki Bijutsusha, 1983

Sunazawa, Kura. *Ku Sukuppu Orushibe* (The Memories of My Generation). Hokkaido, Sapporo-shi:
Miyama Shobo, 1983

Haginaka, Miki et al., *Kikigaki Ainu no Shokuji* (Oral History of Ainu Diet).
Tokyo: Rural Culture Association Japan, 1992

Nakagawa, Hiroshi. *New Express Ainu Go*. Tokyo: Hakusuisha, 2013

Nakagawa, Hiroshi. *Ainugo Chitose Hogen Jiten* (The Ainu-Japanese dictionary). Chiba Urayasu-Shi: Sofukan, 1995

Nakagawa, Hiroshi and Nakamoto, Mutsuko. *Kamuy Yukara de Ainu Go wo Manabu*
Learning Ainu with Kamuy Yukar). Tokyo: Hakusuisha, 2007

Nakagawa, Hiroshi. *Katari au Kotoba no Chikara – Kamuy tachi to Ikiru Sekai*
(The Power of Spoken Words – Living in a World with Kamuy). Tokyo: Iwanami Shoten, 2010

Sarashina, Genzo and Sarashina, Hikari. Kotan Seibutsu Ki <1 Juki / Zassou hen>
(Kotan Wildlife Vol. 1 – Trees and Weeds). Hosei University Publishing, 1992/2007

Sarashina, Genzo and Sarashina, Hikari. *Kotan Seibutsu Ki <2 Yacho / Kaijuu / Gyozoku hen>*
(Kotan Wildlife Vol. 2 – Birds, Sea Creatures, and Fish). Hosei University Publishing, 1992/2007

Sarashina, Genzo and Sarashina, Hikari. *Kotan Seibutsu Ki <3 Yachou / Mizudori / Konchu hen>*
(Kotan Wildlife Vol. 3 – Shorebirds, Seabirds, and Insects). Hosei University Publishing, 1992/2007

Kawakami Yuji. *Sarunkur Ainu Monogatari* (The Tale of Sarunkur Ainu). Kawagoe: Suzusawa Book Store, 2003/2005

Kawakami, Yuji. *Ekashi to Fuchi wo Tazunete* (Visiting Ekashi and Fuchi). Kawagoe: Suzusawa Book Store, 1991

Council for the Conservation of Ainu Culture, Ainu Minzokushi (Ainu People Magazine). Dai-ichi Hoki, 1970

Hokkaido Cultural Property Protection Association. *Ainu Ifuku Chousa Houkokusho <1 Ainu Josei ga Denshou Suru
Ibunka>* (The Ainu Clothing Research Report Vol. 1 – Traditional Clothing Passed Down Through Generations of Ainu
Women). 1986

Okamura, Kichiemon and Clancy, Judith A. *Ainu no Ishou* (The Clothes of the Ainu People). Kyoto Shoin, 1993

Yotsuji, Ichiro. Photos by Mizutani, Morio. *Ainu no Monyo* (Decorative Arts of the Ainu). Kasakura Publishing, 1981

Yoshida, Iwao. *Ainushi Shiryoshu* (Collection of Ainu Historical Documents).
Hokkaido Publication Project Center, 1983.

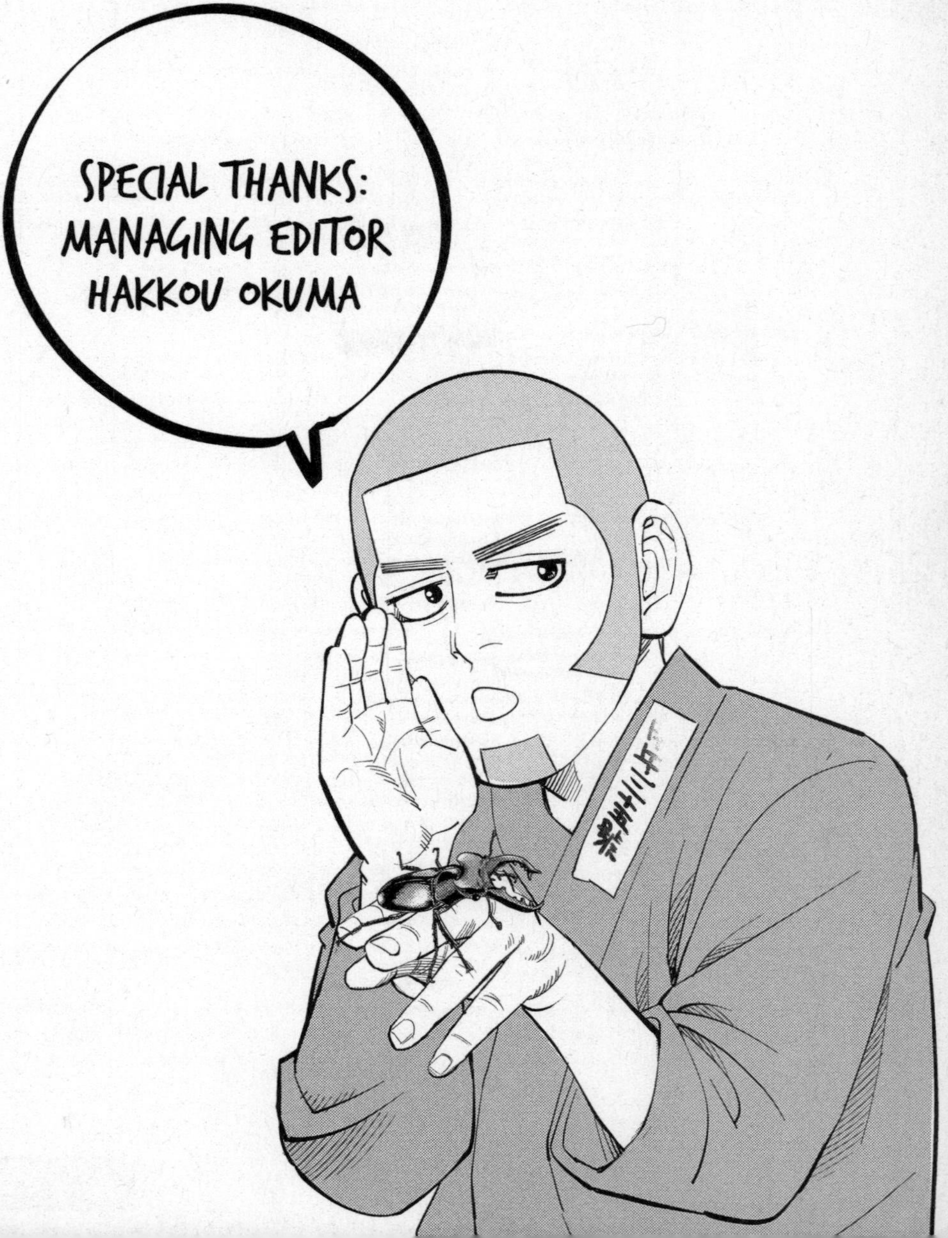
SPECIAL THANKS: MANAGING EDITOR HAKKOU OKUMA

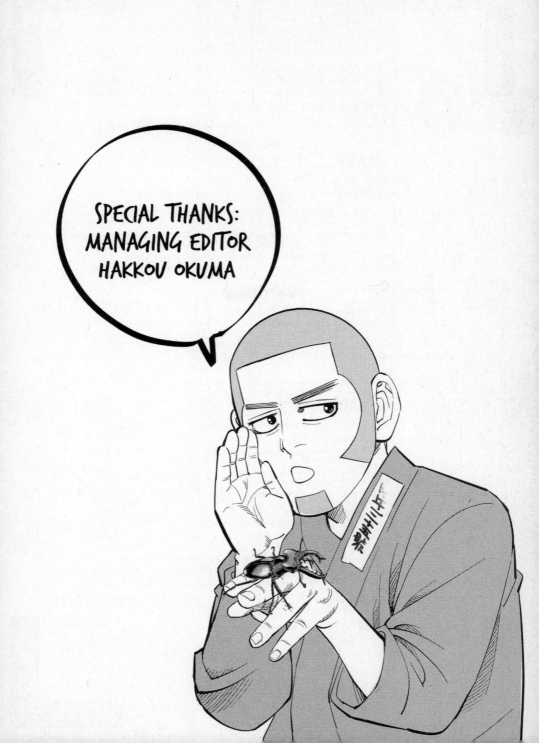

Kanto or wa yaku sak no arankep sinep ka isam.

Nothing comes from heaven without purpose.　—Ainu proverb

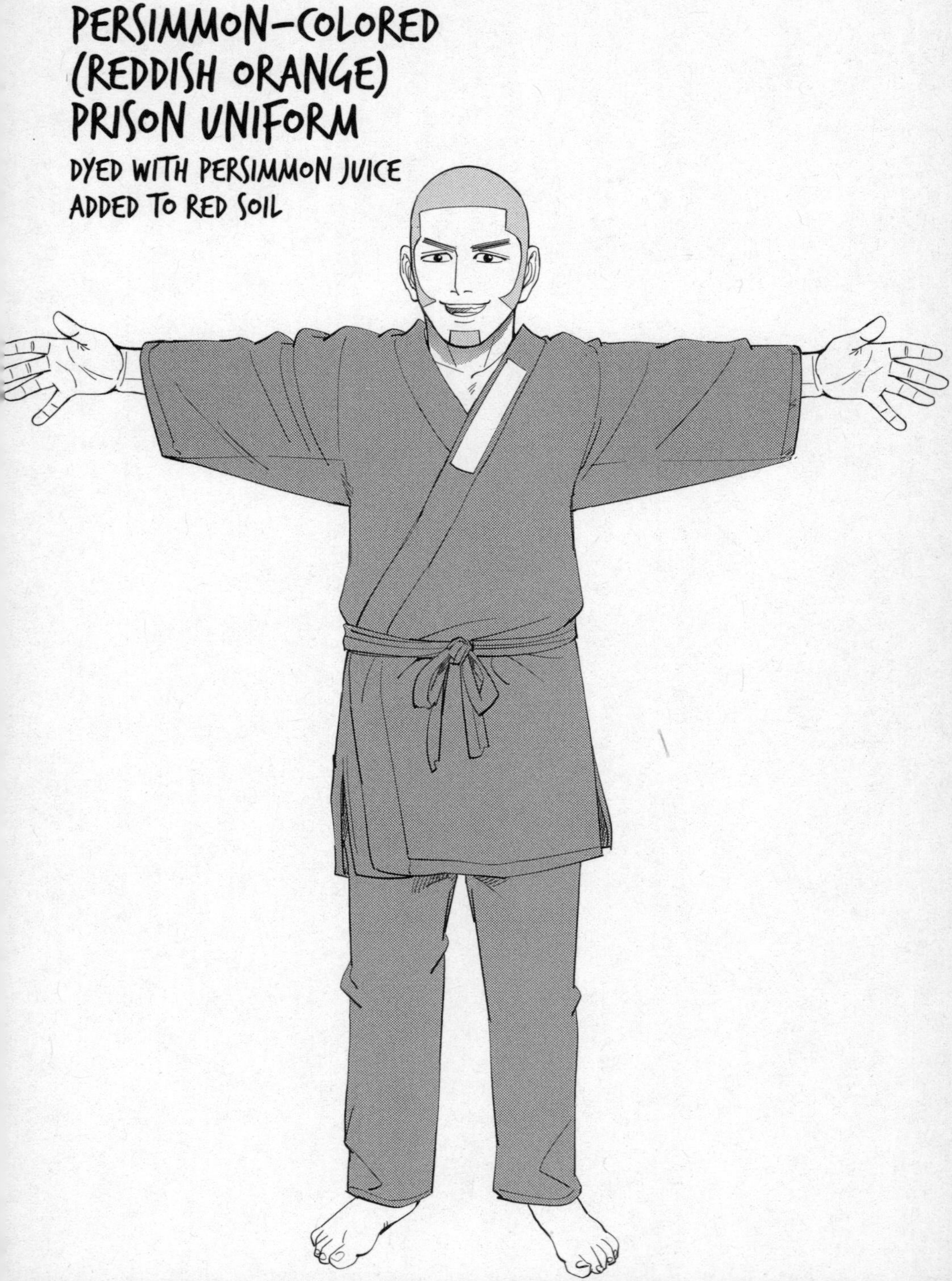
PERSIMMON-COLORED (REDDISH ORANGE) PRISON UNIFORM
DYED WITH PERSIMMON JUICE ADDED TO RED SOIL

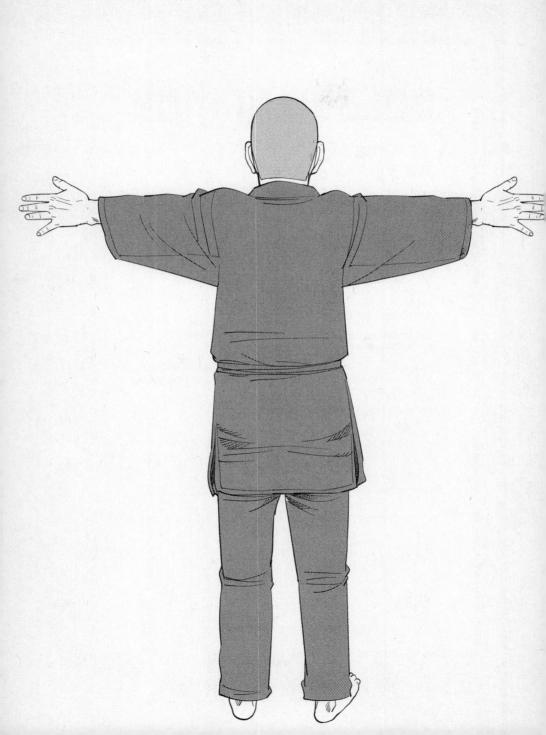

GOLDEN KAMUY

Volume 9
VIZ Signature Edition

Story/Art by Satoru Noda

GOLDEN KAMUY © 2014 by Satoru Noda
All rights reserved.
First published in Japan in 2014 by SHUEISHA Inc., Tokyo.
English translation rights arranged by SHUEISHA Inc.

Translation/John Werry
Touch-Up Art & Lettering/Steve Dutro
Design/Shawn Carrico
Editor/Mike Montesa

The stories, characters and incidents mentioned in this
publication are entirely fictional.

No portion of this book may be reproduced or transmitted in
any form or by any means without written permission from the
copyright holders.

Printed in the U.S.A.

Published by VIZ Media, LLC
P.O. Box 77010
San Francisco, CA 94107

10 9 8 7 6 5 4 3 2 1
First printing, April 2019

viz.com

PARENTAL ADVISORY
GOLDEN KAMUY is rated M for Mature and
recommended for mature readers. This
volume contains graphic violence, nudity,
strong language and adult themes.